Dancing to the State

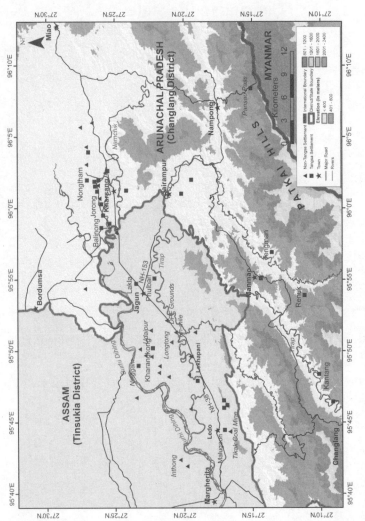

Map Detailed Map of the Field Area in Northeast India

Source: Sukanya Lehnhardt.

Note: Map not to scale and does not represent authentic international boundaries.

Dancing to the State

*Ethnic Compulsions of the
Tangsa in Assam*

MEENAXI BARKATAKI-RUSCHEWEYH

OXFORD
UNIVERSITY PRESS

OXFORD
UNIVERSITY PRESS

Oxford University Press is a department of the University of Oxford.
It furthers the University's objective of excellence in research, scholarship,
and education by publishing worldwide. Oxford is a registered trademark of
Oxford University Press in the UK and in certain other countries

Published in India by
Oxford University Press
YMCA Library Building, 1 Jai Singh Road, New Delhi 110 001, India

ISBN-13: 978-0-19-947259-8
ISBN-10: 0-19-947259-9

Typeset in ITC Giovanni Std 9.5/13
by The Graphics Solution, New Delhi 110 092
Printed in India by Replika Press Pvt. Ltd

Contents

Maps, Figures, Photographs, Sketches, and Tables

Maps

Figures

Photographs

Sketches

Tables

Preface

The handful of Tangsa in Assam live at the fringes, both in terms of their location and their situation. They want to be taken seriously but have come to understand that they really do not matter a great deal in the larger scheme of things. This is the story of how they, or at least some of them, try to remain in the reckoning, despite their marginality. Whether they succeed or not in this endeavour, and the reasons thereof, will be examined in the chapters that follow. But this story about the Tangsa cannot be told without bringing in some others around them who are part of the larger picture and who contribute in various ways to their predicament. That is where the 'mainstream' Assamese community living in the state, communities such as the Nepali and the Singpho who live close by, some insurgent groups who are active in the region, as well as the Tangsa living elsewhere, come in. That is also where the state comes in.

More generally, this is a story about hills and plains, and about the interactions and antagonisms of some people who inhabit those lands. This is a story about power—about those who have power, those who try to wrest power for themselves, and those who are at the receiving end of these struggles. Hence, this is also a story about colonialism, in forms that live on even today in formerly colonized lands. Viewed through another prism, it is a story about centres and peripheries, and about the everyday concerns of those who live in the fuzzy borderlands that separate them. Simply stated, it is a story of a 'they' and an 'us' and all those 'others', along with the manifold hidden implications of such hurtful divisions.

My work with the Tangsa started in 2008 and has progressed over several phases, each of which has contributed in some measure to the final account contained in this book. My first contact with the Tangsa was through a project that was aimed chiefly at documenting endangered languages. Soon after joining the project, I registered as a PhD student in anthropology at Göttingen, Germany. The four years of working as part of the project team, and the four years since working on my own with my Tangsa consultants, and with my academic colleagues and mentors in Europe and elsewhere, have been years, not just of exploration and discovery of the Tangsa life-worlds but also of self-discovery. Hence, this book is not just about the Tangsa, but also about me and the Assamese community I was born into.

There comes a time when one feels that a certain phase in one's life has come a full circle. For my engagement with the Tangsa, it happened not just with the completion of my PhD but also with the realization that the ground situation in the field had changed. For me, it was a clear signal to move on. But, I needed to write this book before I did so because I wanted to describe and capture the moment that had just given way. That would be my way of saying thank you to all those who had so unreservedly believed in me and had so generously shared their homes, their stories, and their knowledge with me. I write this book in all humility, knowing that no matter how much I think I know about the Tangsa, there is much more out there that I do not know. I also know that this exercise of mine, of putting the Tangsa centre stage and reporting faithfully on what I saw and experienced in the field, can be read differently by some. I would be very sorry if that were to happen because the one wish I have had, above all else, while writing this book, is that it will be a bridge between these different worlds, and help to clear the haze of unfamiliarity and mistrust that keeps them apart.

Acknowledgements

This book is based on my doctoral dissertation which I eventually submitted to the Vrije Universiteit (VU), Amsterdam. My doctoral journey has seen many delays and disruptions and would have perhaps not reached its destination if it were not for the last minute intervention of Dr Ellen Bal and Professor Willem van Schendel. Thank you for your friendship and patience, Ellen, and for your calm and reassuring support, Willem. It is good to know that people like you still exist. A special word of gratitude to everyone at the Department of Social and Cultural Anthropology at the VU for adopting me and for lavishing so much care and attention on me.

My heartfelt thanks and gratitude go to the Documentation of Endangered Languages (DOBES)-project leader, Dr Stephen Morey, who has also been my friend, teacher, and guide, both in the field and away from it. He introduced me to my first Tangsa interlocutors and generously shared all his knowledge and contacts with me. He also read and commented on various drafts of this work. Thanks also to my DOBES-project guru, Professor Barend Terwiel (Baas) and project colleague Dr Jürgen Schöpf. Baas and his wife also gave me a home in Göttingen.

I also thank my teachers at Göttingen, especially Professors Andrea Lauser and Elfriede Hermann (and Professor Elisabeth Schömbucher at Würzburg) for helping me take the first steps in anthropology. Four committed anthropologists, three of them experts on northeast India, have read and given me detailed feedback on earlier versions of this text; they are Philippe Ramirez, Bengt Karlsson, Ellen Bal, and Sondra Wentzel—my sincere gratitude to all of them. Many accomplished social scientists, notably, Sanjib Baruah, A.C. Bhagabati, Erik de Maaker, and Roman Loiermeier, have goaded me on, at different stages of my journey, even when the going was tough. Over the years— I have also benefited from interactions with Professors Sarah Turner, Hans Harder, Martin Gaenzsle, Martin Fuchs, William Sax, Toni Huber, Roland Mischung, and Sarit Kumar Chaudhuri. To each one of them I say a sincere thank you.

Special word of thanks to my graduate student friends in Göttingen, especially Jelka and Jasmin who read and commented on draft versions. Professors Jyoti and Anita Tamuli (and their students, especially Palash Nath and Iftikar Ahmed) gave me an academic home in Guwahati; thanks also to Mélanie Vandenhelsken, Jelle Wouters, Kerstin Grothmann, and well as to Hema, Chandan, Kaustubh, Upasana, Anna, Cornelia, Lea, and many others for friendship and intellectual support.

Moving to the field, my work would have been much more difficult, if not impossible, but for the help and support of two Assamese gentlemen—first Rajen Mech for solid logistical support in the field and for allowing me to use his home as my base camp, where I was so lovingly taken care of by Didi, and next Bhaskar Phukan who I first met when he was sub-divisional officer (SDO) at Margherita but who has since then helped me in many different ways to understand the technicalities of official rules and administrative structure. Thanks, Bhaskar, also for allowing me to use your personal library and for generously sharing your vast knowledge of the region and its people.

As for my Tangsa interlocutors, they are really too many to name exhaustively, but my grateful respects to my Tangsa father in Assam— Lukam Tonglum—and the ones in Arunachal Pradesh, GB Phanglim Kimching and GB Laoko Langching, and my Tangsa mother, Renya Tonglum; respects also to the Tangsa elders—the late Shimo babu and Chachi, Mohen, Wamjung, Phulim, to my Man Friday in the field, Chanwang Nocte, and to my many Tangsa friends in Assam: Molu bhai, Kamthoi, late Moirang Ronrang and his family, Simon, GB Tehon Hakhun, Khithong, Kamchat and Rennan Lungri, Yenim and Ko Mossang, Lumjung and Daw Nyalek, Tongtong, Chonja, Mebang, Dongkin, Nongtang, Kaman, Jerina, and many others at Kharangkong, and in Arunachal Pradesh: Abu Kimsing and Baideo, Setong Sena and

Mrs Sena, Latsam Khimhun Saheb, Sentum Ronrang, Satum, Sujong Hakhun, Lemjong Latam, Lemkhum Mossang, the Mungrey brothers, Renu Baideo, John Jugli and Mrs Jugli, Komoli Mossang Baideo, Tangkam and Datho Langching, Sunumi, Noimila, and many others.

Besides the Tangsa, I also met and benefited from my association with many others in the field—foremost the Singpho leaders Manjela, Rajesh, and Rajib Ningkhi (and Panlong) besides the Bisa Roja, the Ningda family, and Sadhan Gogoi. Writer Dibyalata Dutta gave me a home in Margherita while my school friend Gayatri and her husband, Kaushik Bora, gave me a home in Digboi, as did Abu Kimching and his wife in Nampong; the blessings of Suren Barua accompanied me in the field.

Ministers Pradyut Bordoloi in Assam and Setong Sena in Arunachal Pradesh have been very encouraging and supportive of my work. A special word of thanks to the recently deceased Sena Saheb for helping me in so many different ways. My visit to Nagaland was facilitated by my dear friend Upasana, Professor S. Ao at Mokukchung, and Dr Kuolie in Kohima. Sena Saheb's mother in Jairampur, Dibya's mother in Margherita, and my own mother in Guwahati provided me the conditions under which I could unwind, relax, and allow myself to be pampered, after a hard stint in the field. Many thanks to all of them.

I thank Sukanya Lehnhardt and Jayanta Laskar for drawing those beautiful maps, and Inez Ruscheweyh for all the lovely sketches and very accurate sketch maps. Thanks also to the Assam State Archives for giving permission to include some material in the Appendix. Thanks also to the Volkswagen Foundation for supporting me financially for four years through its DOBES programme. I thank the entire Oxford University Press, New Delhi, editorial team for helping me to convert my dissertation into a book. I also thank the three anonymous referees who gave me such detailed comments and suggestions for the improvement of the book.

Before I end, I wish to thank my husband Stephan, for patiently bearing with my long absences from home and with my absent mindedness and total preoccupation with work even while at home, in the last years. Not only did he forgive me for that, but he also helped me to get on with it. These last years have not always been easy as I have had to battle with many ghosts but Stephan has solidly stood by me, and helped me get over my periods of darkness and indecision.

This work is dedicated to Professor Peter Claus, who gave me my first lessons in anthropology and ethnography, and to Dr Пeter M. Neumann, who was my (mathematics) D. Phil. supervisor at Oxford a long time ago. These two individuals, and what they stand for, have had the maximum impact on my life. Were it not for their continued support and faith in me, I would not have got to where I have. Thank you very much, both of you. I hope I haven't let you down.

Meenaxi Barkataki-Ruscheweyh
Volkach, Germany
January 2017

Abbreviations

AR&T Co.	Assam Railways and Trading Company
CRC	Christian Revival Church
DFT	Dibrugarh Frontier Tract
DPF	Dihing-Patkai Festival
HQ	Headquarters
ILP	Inner Line Permit
MLA	Member of the Legislative Assembly
NEFA	North East Frontier Agency
NH	national highway
NSCN	National Socialist Council of Nagaland
NSCN (I-M)	NSCN (Issac-Muivah)
NSCN (K)	NSCN (Khaplang)
PPWF	Pangsau Pass Winter Festival
SDO	Sub-Divisional Officer
ST	Scheduled Tribe
TBCA	Tangsa Baptist Church Association
THDWA	Tangshang Hakhun (Naga) Development and Welfare Association
ULFA	United Liberation Front of Assam

1 Setting the Scene

'What is so special about the Tangsa that we should want to know about them at all?', a young Assamese researcher had asked me once after my presentation at a conference. It has taken me a while to work it out but here is the long answer to his question.

This is a study about marginality and its consequences, about performance of ethnicity at festivals as sites for both resistance and capitulation, and about the compulsions, imposed by the state and dominant neighbours, that can force small ethnic groups to contribute to their own marginalization. In other words, I seek to answer the question: Can small ethnic groups survive, as distinct cultural entities, in areas with great ethnic and cultural diversity? What are the choices such groups have, and what are some of the strategies such groups employ to ensure their cultural survival? And how successful are such communities in resisting the efforts of the state (or the majority) to erase cultural difference? I study these questions in the case of the Tangsa living in the northeast Indian state of Assam.

The Tangsa in Assam are a tiny 'tribal' community of less than 5,000 people, living together with people of other communities, in mixed villages scattered over a relatively large area.[1] Assam has more than a hundred such tribal groups, some of whom, such as the Bodo, have more than a million members. Hence, the Tangsa living in Assam are marginal even amongst the minority communities in Assam. Although there are people of the Tangsa community also living in the neighbouring

Indian state of Arunachal Pradesh (often referred to hereafter simply as Arunachal), the situation for the tiny Tangsa population in Assam is much more complicated. This is because while Arunachal is a tribal-majority state, Assam is not; hence the Tangsa in Assam cannot avail of the special privileges reserved for tribal communities in Arunachal. At the same time, the states of Assam and Arunachal Pradesh as well as the region of India now commonly known as Northeast India (see Map 1.1, which shows all the states of northeast India except Sikkim) to which they belong is also locationally peripheral and politically 'marginalized' in relation to the other regions of 'mainland' India.[2] Thus, the Tangsa are, in some sense, at the very *margins of the margins*, and hence are beginning to feel an existential threat of being completely ignored and forgotten.

However, it is not easy for the Tangsa to assert their existence, first because there is no consensus even within the community about what it means to be Tangsa. The term itself is of a recent origin, coined in the 1950s in post-Independent India as an umbrella term for a loose collection of disparate tribal groups, speaking different languages (some of them mutually unintelligible), and having differing cultural and

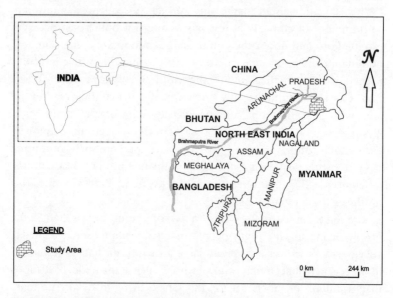

Map 1.1   Location Map of the Study Area in Northeast India

Source: Jayanta Laskar.
Note: Map not to scale and does not represent authentic international boundaries.

'traditional' practices.[3] Although the Tangsa were earlier clubbed under the larger Naga umbrella, the Tangsa are deeply divided on this issue today; this question has become even more problematic due to the ongoing insurgency led by some Naga groups in the region.[4]

Therefore, the project of creating a common pan-Tangsa identity is highly complicated. But it is deemed necessary, for although some of the older Tangsa groups have been assimilated into the greater Assamese fold, that is not what the rest wish for themselves.[5] However, changes in livelihood patterns after moving down from the Patkai hills to the plains and their acceptance of a 'modern' way of life, coupled with increased efforts by Christian missionaries to induce them to convert to Christianity, have resulted in a situation where many Tangsa people have given up their older traditions and customs.[6] In the words of one Tangsa writer, 'Truthfully, people have no tradition left to practise' (Simai 2008: 121).

Moreover, once the initial fascination had worn off, neither their new religions nor their new 'modernity' have been able to compensate for a sense of 'loss' of their old world amongst some of the older Tangsa people (Simai 2008: 33). All these factors have contributed to a sense of insecurity and uncertainty amongst a section of the Tangsa population in Assam regarding their common Tangsa cultural identity as an ethnic group and their social identity within the broader framework of the Assamese society around them.[7]

On the other hand, with greater contact with the local administration has come increased awareness among certain sections of the Tangsa about the need to be visible and to be in a position to compete for economic resources and political power within the state of Assam to ensure their survival.[8] Given this scenario, I explore the steps some Tangsa living in Assam have taken in order to negotiate a place for themselves in the world around them. While doing so, I take a closer look at some of their attempts to reformulate and rearticulate their 'past' traditions in forms more amenable to present times, and such that they can then be more easily used to construct a new pan-Tangsa identity.[9]

Interactions with outsiders (including foreign academics) and with other neighbouring communities have influenced identity considerations of the Tangsa. The impact of state policies on minority tribal groups also need to be factored in to understand the options such small communities have, and the strategies they employ, to ensure their survival in the midst of other competing groups around them. One such strategy has been to relocate to the neighbouring tribal-majority state of Arunachal, demonstrating the crucial role played by political boundaries, however invisible (such as those between two states of the Indian union), in determining the future of the communities living near them.

More generally, this study is about relations between hill people and people living in the plains as well as those between tribals and non-tribals, in particular between the predominantly non-Hindu tribal population, such as the Tangsa and the Singpho, and the caste-Hindu non-tribal people, such as the Assamese and the Nepali.[10] I will highlight the growing inter-tribal solidarity to be seen amongst the older tribal groups living in the area as a reaction to their gradual loss of land and priority to the settler communities—both tribal and non-tribal—who have recently arrived in the area and continue to come. I explore and expose the role that significant 'others', notably the state and the larger dominant communities, have in forcing small minority groups into precarious positions of vulnerability and insecurity, from where, no matter how hard they try, there is very little room to manoeuvre.

The Frame Project

The fact that the Tangsa spoke a mind-boggling variety of languages, many of which had very few speakers left, was the principal reason why the Tangsa were of great interest to linguists. The principal aim of the multidisciplinary project that employed me for four years was to document endangered languages.[11] We also wanted to find an answer to the corresponding question about the Tangsa to the one E.R. Leach asked more than half a century ago with respect to the ethnic groups living in Highland Burma: 'Here are populations of nearly identical culture seemingly maintaining differences of language at great inconvenience to themselves. Why?' (1954: 46).[12] My brief in the project (as a non-linguist) was to figure out what it meant for the people to be Tangsa, despite their deep linguistic divisions. And I was encouraged to use the data collected and experience gained to write a doctoral thesis in anthropology.

But that quickly led to methodological contradictions, for although anthropologists do not see any value in just documentation per se, in terms of our project aims, language documentation with rich contextual metadata had the highest priority, as the numbers of language speakers of some of the languages we were working with were decreasing very fast.[13] Hence, while linguists have no trouble at all in categorizing such languages as highly endangered, it is more problematic for anthropologists to use such categories (see Eriksen 2010: 159).

Projecting down to my Tangsa reality, however, it was hard for me to tell myself that there was no need to panic when the only man in the village who could sing their epic Wihu song, or who knew how to do augury, died. In terms of our documentation aims, these were clear examples of ritual and traditional practices which were rapidly 'disappearing' and hence needed to be recorded and documented before they were 'lost' forever. Moreover, when my Tangsa interlocutors themselves were using phrases like 'our culture is disappearing fast' and talking about 'deterioration of our culture' due to its 'voluntary abandonment' (Simai 2008: 33), it was clear that evading these issues would not help me in understanding what they were really concerned about, if not make me miss the point altogether.

While in the field, I postponed worrying about the intellectual contradictions inherent in what I was doing and tried to concentrate on the immediate job at hand. Back at my desk, I could see that most of those contradictions had to do with differing perceptions about the meaning of the term 'culture' as well as with different approaches to scholarship, one requiring scholarship to be entirely an end in itself while the other demanding that scholarship also engage with the community, more so given that there is a growing sense that academics should be doing something for the communities they study (see Lassiter 2005; Hale 2006). The specific aims and nature of our project as well as my special position as not quite an insider (since I was not Tangsa) but also not quite an outsider to the community (as I was from the region) not only made it possible for me, but also demanded of me, to think more inclusively and be able to make and maintain the distinction between the analytically tempered demands of my discipline and that of a clearly normative documentation project such as ours.

The presence of researchers (such as those in our project team) who were interested in knowing more about and recording their 'traditional' practices triggered off some sort of interest (and perhaps even pride) amongst certain community members to make a greater effort to discover more about and to give more value to their past.[14] A community elder told us, 'You have taught us to value our past which we had earlier thought to not be worth talking about. We were even ashamed of how we lived during "ajanti" times,' referring back to a time when they were untouched by 'civilization'. While it could be the case that our Tangsa interlocutors were saying those things simply because they felt we wanted to hear them, and while it can be debated whether such sort of interventionist action is desirable or not, in terms of the project aims, it was gratifying to reach a stage when some young community members have volunteered to carry on the work of documentation started by the project. In that sense, we had succeeded in setting in motion the process of 'salvaging', at least partially, their past traditions.[15]

But I needed to find my own position in all of this. In terms of my ethnographic data, while I could never be certain whether events in the Tangsa villages would have evolved along similar lines if the project had not happened, since the project did happen, I would have to factor that into my conclusions.[16] I could even go one step further and turn that uncertainty into a strength and investigate how my Tangsa interlocutors instrumentalized the presence of outsiders (especially foreign academics) for their own ends.

There were other problems too; As most of our data was elicited and since we were mostly dealing with village and community elders who could tell us more about the time before they had moved down to the plains and before they had converted to Christianity, it was not easy to find a topic on which to base my ethnographic work. We had documented many Tangsa festivals—both big and small—some at the village level and others at the community level. While it is a fact that our very presence certainly did impact on what we got to see at those festivals, since they were not elicited (in the sense that they would have taken place even if we were not there), I decided to base my study on them.

However, although I could choose which aspects of the festivals to study, the choices as well as the methodology were limited to what was possible while remaining within the larger project aims. As a result, there were considerable differences in the approach and methods I used from those say, of a lone ethnographer staying for an extended period of time at one field location. For instance, as our project team wished to make contact with as many different Tangsa groups as possible, *multisitedness* was inbuilt into our project frame. Furthermore, since there were linguists in our team who were specifically 'doing' languages, I did not make any real effort to learn any of the Tangsa languages. My unique position in the project team as the only woman—the sole aspiring anthropologist and (very often) the only Assamese (Indian) person—also gave me a particular vantage point, both within the group and with respect to our field hosts and informants. This book is based on the experiences and data gathered during my years in the field, both as a member of the project team as well as an ethnographer seeking an understanding of the Tangsa world view.

Aims and Claims

This work is first and foremost an introduction to the Tangsa people living in Assam. It describes not only the internal divisions amongst the various Tangsa groups in terms of language and cultural practices, and their past and present ways of life, but also the changes that hill communities have come to accept after moving down to the plains and after beginning to participate as equal citizens of a democratic state. It is also an attempt to place the Tangsa in their geographical and historical context by looking at their migration histories and their linkages with other groups.

As a piece of ethnography, this book explores the Tangsa trail in three distinct but related directions in the main ethnographic chapters. The first is to give a description of life in three Tangsa villages in Assam, chosen simply because they are interesting for different reasons, not just in terms of religious affiliations or location but also in their livelihood patterns, linkages with others, and attitudes towards change and resistance. While drawing out these different aspects, I seek to understand the internal logic of the differences between them and the mechanism of how they function as units. My explorations reveal how these village communities negotiate amongst themselves and with other groups around them for economic as well as political space, in an effort to secure their lives and existence. The situation of the Tangsa in Assam will also be put in perspective by comparing and contrasting it with that of the Tangsa living in neighbouring Arunachal Pradesh. This is the first story, the aim being to give the reader a general introduction to the Tangsa people and also a sense of what it is like to be a Tangsa living in one of those villages.

The second goal is to do a detailed documentation of a few Tangsa festivals in order to record and understand their attempts at preservation, revival, and revitalization of some of their past cultural traditions and as well as their deliberate attempts at creating new ones. In doing so, I wish to establish how village festivals 'reflect' as well as 'cause' cultural change in a community. By analysing the factors that determine the form of the festival itself, and also the impact of this representation on the self-image and cultural identity of the Tangsa themselves, I explore the basic question of what it means to be Tangsa, at least for my interlocutors, and to those around them, in the present-day context.[17]

A section of the Tangsa are actively involved in the process of 'constructing, deconstructing, and reconstructing' (Handler 1994: 27) their cultural identity by selecting and modifying elements from their past as well as incorporating new elements. It is productive, therefore, to explore what terms such as 'culture' and 'ethnicity' mean for my Tangsa interlocutors, and how they use their perceived notions of these concepts to construct their new pan-Tangsa identity. These perceived notions depend on a host of factors including external ones such as state policy and the views of outsiders (such as our project team) and those of other communities around them. They seek to project a new pan-Tangsa identity which draws not only from their past but also from their modern present reality—they wish to assert their ethnicity and their uniqueness, but in modern terms, in the language of citizens of a secular democratic state.

This study of the Tangsa in Assam explores not only the relationships between some members of the Tangsa community living in Assam but also those between them and at least three other groups—the dominant Assamese community that has administrative control and wields political power in Assam (as a result of which most of the representatives of the state the Tangsa come into contact with, such as the police and administrative officials, are Assamese), other minority groups, such as the Singpho, living in the same geographical area, and finally the Tangsa living elsewhere in India, and to a lesser extent, those living in Myanmar. Intertwined in this net of group relationships is another network of individual relationships that I, as a researcher, as a member of my research team, and also as an individual belonging to the dominant

Assamese community, already had with the Assamese community and those that I developed with my Tangsa and non-Tangsa interlocutors during the course of my fieldwork.

The third and final aim is, therefore, to follow my own personal journey in the field in order to reflect at every stage the relations between the Tangsa and the others around them in general, and between me and my Tangsa interlocutors in particular. Moreover, my somewhat unusual position as an almost native researcher and as an intermediary between my Tangsa interlocutors and my foreign project colleagues have revealed many insights into the nature of doing ethnography, and the tensions and affinities in the fieldwork situation.

I have deliberately chosen to tell this (third) story as it unfolds at the end of each chapter rather than compress it into a chapter at the beginning because I believe that the ways and attitudes of the Tangsa 'others' have a huge role to play in the determination of the Tangsa 'self', as with the Mapuche in Chile in the quote below.

> The effective categorization of a group of people by a more powerful 'other' is not … 'just' a matter of classification (if, indeed, there is any such thing). It is necessarily an intervention in that group's social world which will, to an extent and in ways that are a function of the specifics of the situation, alter that world and the experience of living in it. [Hence] the Chileans have the capacity to constitute, in part, the experience of 'being' a Mapuche. (Jenkins 1994: 217–18)

In the same vein, my Tangsa interlocutors in Assam are what they are today also because the Assamese (and the other significant 'others') around them are who they are. Therefore, neither my description of the Tangsa world nor my analysis of Tangsa festivals would be complete without this mainly reflexive but also self-critical component.

Furthermore, while doing so, I believe it is important to lay *all* the cards on the table. While it is a fact that identity considerations have become a very important issue in the discussions and deliberations of the Tangsa elite in recent years, it is not clear whether festivals and their performance would have assumed such a significant role in this process of identity-construction and projection for the Tangsa if our team of researchers had not landed on the scene and expressed great interest in documenting and recording their Wihu song and dances (see Barkataki-Ruscheweyh 2013). Hence, I also wish to place on record 'our own role in the creation of the phenomenon we study' (Moerman 1993: 90).

Flagging the Conclusions

The recurring theme that binds together the various locations and the different perspectives in this study is my claim that the performance of ethnic identity as evidenced at festivals, for marginal groups like the Tangsa, is a strategy for survival, and for negotiating a place for themselves in the world around them. In that sense, my Tangsa interlocutors instrumentalize their ethnicity, and their identity is suitably adjusted and articulated, case by case, in forms which are amenable for achieving other larger ends.

However, rather than considering these actions as calculated or manipulative, it is more productive to consider them as acts of self-preservation and of self-definition, stemming from their fear of being overlooked and forgotten in the world they inhabit and call their own. Many Tangsa people that I met have a strong inherent sense of belonging—a perception of Tangsa-ness—even if they cannot really define what it means, but which none of them are willing to give up. It is this sense that forces them to do something, even play the game according to the new rules if required, with the hope that if not everything then at least something about them and their Tangsa-ness will remain in the end.

And this is important because although many of my older interlocutors know and live their Tangsa-ness they can see that, given the increasing impact of external influences on their world, it would be harder for their children to hold on to just vague notions. Their continued survival in the world around them requires more concrete definitions, which in the Tangsa case, fraught with divergent religious affiliations, varied cultural traditions, and diverse linguistic repertoires, is asking for something extremely difficult, if not impossible. This study seeks to place on record some of those attempts at self-definition in order to resist marginalization and possible erasure.

In summary, this book is first and foremost about describing and understanding some of the strategies my Tangsa interlocutors use to gain agency and to resist marginalization.[18] Next it is about how the Tangsa leaders go about constructing a new pan-Tangsa ethnic identity which is both modern as well as traditional, by analysing how they (re)present themselves at festivals; it is also about discovering how their 'culture' is sought to be preserved, by reinventing it first, if required, to fit the new requirements and then articulated. Finally, I also seek to explore and expose the role the significant 'others' of the Tangsa, notably the state and the bigger communities around them, have had in influencing the above processes as well as in forcing the Tangsa into the precarious position of vulnerability and insecurity where they find themselves at present and from where they have been forced to speak up for themselves. In that sense, the Tangsa performing their ethnicity at festivals is not so much a sign of their newly acquired agency as it is of their continued marginalization.

Positioning the Text

In terms of monographs, this book comes closest to the work of Karlsson (2000), Bal (2007a), Pachuau (2014), and Ramirez (2014). All these authors look at questions of identity, ethnicity, culture, and marginalization, amongst the Rabha, Garo, Mizo, and Karbi communities respectively. Like the Tangsa, Karlsson's Rabhas too dance 'to communicate their distinctiveness or difference to the audience and importantly, to themselves' (2000: xvi), but the Rabha are a forest people and they face a tangible threat—that of having their forests taken away from them not only by the dominant Bengali 'Other' but by the forests and wildlife conservation officials. Bal's work on the Garos focuses on the processes of ethnic identity formation while Ramirez demonstrates the fluidity of ethnic categorizations and the process of ethnic transformation across boundaries. Pachuau's work (2014) shows how the Mizos use their cultural practices, as do the Tangsa, to define their identity. However, the Mizo are a much larger group, almost all professing Christianity, and have a territory to call their own. The Tangsa in Assam are very few and widely scattered and present a much more fragmented picture. Moreover, if the Mizos, as people from the northeast, feel ignored by mainland India, the Tangsa feel forgotten even in Assam, where they live. Thus, their marginalization goes one step deeper.

Most of these studies also reveal the hierarchical relationships that exist between the majority so-called mainstream populations and the minority ethnic groups. In Bal's work, one learns how the majority Bengali Muslim population in Bangladesh view the supposedly 'frog-eating' Achiks (or Garos). My work also reveals the asymmetry in the relations between the dominant power-wielding Assamese and the numerically weak and culturally different Tangsa.

Two more books that also deal with similar issues are Mandy Sadan's (2013) monograph on the transborder Kachins and Louisa Schein's (2000) ethnography of a Chinese minority people known as the Miao.[19] Sadan's work based in the Kachin state in Burma, northeast India, and the Yunnan province of China shows parallels with this ethnography in that the Singpho living in India try to trace and assert their transborder affinities in ways perhaps not very different from what some Tangsa seek to do.[20] Schein's Miao (who speak many distinct and mutually unintelligible dialects, just as the Tangsa) are a group long seen as remote and backward by other Chinese people. Schein shows, in ways clearly relevant to the Tangsa, how Miao ethnicity is constructed and appropriated by the state and non-state elites, but also by the Miao themselves, all in the context of an expansionist development state. This ethnography, then, is a contribution not only to the understanding of small ethnic minorities in northeast India but also to the wider field of 'Zomia studies' (see Van Schendel 2002; Michaud 2010).

However, none of the above authors, except for Ramirez, have looked at issues related to minority groups through the lens of 'festivals'. For that aspect, I have gained from the recent work of Alban von Stockhausen (2008), Mélanie Vandenhelsken (2011), Erik de Maaker (2013), and Sara Shneiderman (2015), to name just a few. Von Stockhausen's work on the Naga expressions of identity at festivals has given me a point of reference, while de Maaker's study (2013) on the Garo Wangala festival and Vandenhelsken's description of the festivities in Sikkim around the Panglhabsol dance have lent comparative dimensions to my work. Shneiderman's recent work also focuses on the expressive dimensions of ethnicity, as mine does. However, she shows how ethnic identities can be produced through ritual practice; that is not quite how my Tangsa interlocutors define their ethnicity.

Another important difference is the fact that my work is a micro-study—a look from below—in the classical anthropological sense, and hence I refrain from making any claims about the whole Tangsa community as such. However, I believe that such a detailed ethnography of the lives and concerns of a few people living in only three Tangsa villages in Assam can be instructive in understanding bigger questions affecting the world in which such small marginal communities live and function as well as in understanding the internal dynamics of the group as a whole.[21] More so because, as already mentioned, the Tangsa happen to be a heterogeneous collection of trans-Patkai tribes, professing different religions, speaking different languages, whose antecedents (as well as links to the better-known Naga groups) are not clearly known and who live in areas with differential access to power and resources.

The available literature on the Tangsa is very meagre, among them Dutta (1969), Rao (2006), and Simai (2008). While Dutta's work (1969) is outdated, Simai focuses only on his own Tangsa group—the Tikhak—in a descriptive manner. Rao's work, on the other hand, is outright misleading at places, as it attempts to link the older Tangsa practices to ancient Hindu traditions, while omitting to mention the fact that many Tangsa today are Christian. In fact, most recent literature on the Tangsa, as well as on the Naga, such as Saul (2005), almost completely ignore the impact of the Tangsa moving down to the plains and adopting a 'modern' way of life as well as of their conversion to Christianity. This book wishes to correct these misrepresentations and present a plausible portrait of the everyday life of the Tangsa. In that sense, this book is the first detailed ethnographic study of the Tangsa living in Assam. Furthermore, it is perhaps also the first ethnography that seeks to link the question of the survival of small marginalized groups in multi-ethnic milieus to the performance of their ethnicity at the village, community, and trans-community level festivals.

The Analytical Frame

Festivals, Rituals, and Performance

From Geertz's (1973) classic description of the Balinese cock-fight to more recent contributions such as Jonsson (2001), Harnish (2005), and nearer to my field area, the study of the Khiksaba festival of the Sherdukpen community in Arunachal by Dollfus and Jacquesson (2013), and the Wangala of the Garos by De Maaker (2013), festivals have been studied by many anthropologists.[22] However, a brief justification of why anthropologists study festivals is in place here. One basic reason is because 'the contemporary festival becomes a potential site for representing, encountering, incorporating, and researching aspects of cultural difference' (Bennet, Taylor, and Woodward 2014: 1).

Moreover, public events such as festivals 'are privileged points of penetration into other social and cultural universes' (Handelman 1990: 9). In India there is another reason for looking at festivals. What Singer observed a very long time ago about 'cultural events' such as weddings, temple festivals, plays, and dances is relevant even today: 'Indians, and perhaps all peoples, think of their culture as encapsulated in such discrete performances, which they can exhibit to outsiders as well as to themselves' (Singer 1959: ix, xii). So in India, most people believe that there is a link between a community's 'culture' and its 'performance' in festivals and other such events.[23]

Moreover, 'festivals' organized by one or a group of communities to showcase their 'culture' are taking place more and more often in northeast India.[24] The reasons for the growing importance of such festivals are to be found in the increasing awareness of ethnic groups of the need to project their identity as 'tribals' in order to be entitled for special privileges as Scheduled Tribes (STs). Thus, festival grounds today have become the sites not only for the performance of a community's culture, but also where the political project of the community's ethnic identity form(ul)ation and (re)presentation take place. While 'traditional' festivals usually comprised a fixed set of rituals, present-day festivals also include a component of entertainment often through the staging of 'cultural shows'.[25]

There is a difference between 'traditional' rituals and the newer ones on the basis of who the ritual is addressed to or is meant for (see Shneiderman 2015). While traditional rituals are usually addressed to some spirit or deity, the newer rituals are addressed primarily to the audience. Hence they are 'performed', as are songs and dances, and will be assumed to be a part of the cultural performance or show. Given this distinction, it becomes possible even for older traditional rituals to be 'performed' and hence transformed into newer ones, where the actions remain more or less the same, but the intentions might have changed.

This is in line with De Maaker's (2013) view that rather than carrying a single message, rituals usually have multiple meanings. What matters is the overall agreement among participants that a particular ritual is important, and charged with a certain intentionality. Consequently, the performance is about something, although people need not be explicit about it or agree on what that something is. It is the attribution of intentionality that counts.

I take the fact that 'performances are done to be seen' as the difference between ritual and performance, regardless of questions about the intentionality of the performer and the efficacy of the performance. Following this rule, whatever is enacted in public spaces during festivals will be considered to be *performance* and ritual actions performed in the private space of people's homes will be considered to be *rituals*. Hence, secular ritualized actions like a flag-hoisting ceremony, a public meeting, or a cultural procession will also be considered to be performances as they are enacted in the public space.

Culture, Identity, and Ethnicity

Culture, identity, and ethnicity are the most important concepts that inform my work since my ethnography seeks to demonstrate how communities such as the Tangsa use their culture to give a tangible form to their ethnic identity.[26] Following Eriksen, I consider ethnicity to be an 'emic category of ascription' (2010 [1994]: 16). Festivals, therefore, are a stage for the 'cultural expressions' and 'the symbolic formulations of ethnic identity' of a community. By focusing on festivals, I stress on the expressive dimension of ethnicity.[27]

I take Chit Hlaing's definition of culture as 'what any set of people attributes to itself as their way-of-life without regard to any objective uniformity of custom and practice, variation being taken to be "mere" variation on a common core' as my working definition of culture (2012: 245). While essentialist definitions no longer hold ground in academia, they cannot be written off completely as they still convey deep symbolic meanings for the people themselves.[28] The Tangsa understanding of their culture—or their Tangsa-ness—is, as predicted by Baumann (1999: 91), essentialist in rhetoric, but processual in activity. In this sense, Tangsa-ness is multilayered, and is constantly changing as it is being renegotiated and redefined.

As for the identity of a group, it is best described in terms of processes which express 'shared difference from others' (Sökefeld 2001: 536). In that sense, social identities are mostly defined relationally and are based on difference from other groups while cultural identity is defined on perceived sameness and commonality of certain cultural traits among members of the same group. The ethnic identity of a group is a more political construct and is based on what the members of the group claim they are, which is not always the same as what they actually believe they are or perceive themselves to be. All these constructs are fluid and dynamically change over time and with context.

Although religion is usually considered to be a part of culture, that inclusion is not so automatic amongst communities, such as the Tangsa, who have converted recently and whose present differences in religious affiliations make it difficult for them to forge a common ethnic identity. So for this study, although a person's religion is definitely part of his individual identity, it need not necessarily be a part of his cultural identity.[29] Conversely, culture will be understood to be secular, to transcend religion in the Tangsa case. Moreover, religion, in this study, will not automatically be supposed to have underlying political connotations.

Rather than going into the 'constructedness' of terms like 'ethnicity', 'identity', and so forth (Linnekin 1992: 251), it is more productive to consider them to be strategic, positional (Hall 1996b), and also context-dependent. 'Construction' or 'invention' also seem to imply that people lend meaning to their identity in strictly intentional ways (Van Ginkel 1995). This is not how I understand the situation in the Tangsa case. Furthermore, like Ramirez, I believe that these terms have some 'real' meaning for the people themselves: 'It is not cultural homogeneity that makes an "ethnic group" but a perception. It is through such representations that people feel they belong to a coherent and perennial entity. In this sense, the Assamese ethnic groups, or "tribes" as they are called and call themselves, are real' (2007: 92).

In the Tangsa case, these 'perceptions' have something of value in themselves. They go deeper, and also have to do, not only with belonging together, but also with a nostalgia for as well as a sense of continuity with an imagined or perceived past. The term 'articulation' of identity conveys this sense. Moreover, Hall's use of the term 'articulation' carries the double meaning of 'being' as well as of 'becoming', of 'expressing' as well as of 'linking'.[30] It is exactly this notion that allows selection of certain elements and rejection of others, not forever but for the present moment, while building up identity; hence making the study of the process of identity-construction very interesting.

I hesitate to use 'invention of tradition' (Hobsbawm and Ranger 1983) because the Tangsa practices that I saw being (re)articulated in the field are strictly more 'custom' than 'tradition' (Hobsbawm 1983).

Perhaps Tangsa 'traditions' are in the process of being 'invented' out of their 'customs' but the situation is too fluid and still in the making for saying anything definite. Furthermore, it is not whether traditions are invented or not that is the crucial question in my study, but rather what use they are put to, by whom, for what ends, and what they reveal about agency or the marginalization of the community in question.

The (re)presentation and articulation of culture evident during festivals involves not only the processes of politicization of performance (Cohen 1969, 1981, also see Parkin, Caplan, and Fischer 1996) but also that of politicization of ethnic identity. That is not surprising as the need to have an ethnic identity is itself prompted by state policies as discussed in the next section. This brings in the role of the state and the gradual emergence of elites (Brass 1991) from within the community to mediate between the state and the community. Moreover, the actions of neighbouring communities have a mimetic influence on the processes of ethnicity articulation and identity formulation of a community (see Jonsson 2010). As a subtext, the still persisting colonial attitudes of plains people belonging to the dominant communities towards minority hill groups as well as the attempts at instrumentalization of minority communities by political leaders from dominant communities to further their own agendas will become evident.

Tribals, State Policy, and the Rise of Ethnic Consciousness

Although the term 'tribe', with its racial connotations, is no longer used as an analytical category in the social sciences, in the Indian state (where much of its colonial legacy still persists till date) the word tribe—Scheduled Tribe (ST), to be precise—is an officially defined category (Xaxa 2010), and is still in common use. Curiously, there are different ST lists for different states in India.[31] The 23 notified STs in Assam account for around 13 per cent of the total population of Assam.[32] Even more curiously, there are two ST lists for different parts of Assam and many tribal groups living in Assam still do not have an official ST status, hence the actual proportion of tribal people living in Assam will certainly be much greater than the official figures.[33]

Replacing the word 'tribal' with other terms like 'indigenous people' or 'adivasi' or 'janajati' has also not found favour in India, even within the tribal communities themselves, since as Van Schendel points out:

'Many groups have a stake in self-identification as "tribal"' (2011: 27). In the Indian state, a policy of 'reservation' or protective/positive discrimination exists in favour of the communities listed as Scheduled Tribes which entitle them to special privileges and concessions (cf. Neog 1999). This system of 'compensatory discrimination' (Galanter 1991) is paradoxical in the sense that it identifies groups along cultural criteria to compensate socio-economic disadvantages (see also Shneiderman and Middleton 2008). Karlsson calls them 'inconsistencies and uncertainties', and observes that 'the process of scheduling is heavily politicised', since political grounds often determine whether the ST status is given to a community or not (2001: 11).

> The state intends to protect 'tribals' against mainstream society, strengthening "tribal" cultural institutions, while at the same time furthering their integration with mainstream society. However well-intended these measures are, their goals are contradictory, resulting in policies that in one way or another fail to deliver. (De Maaker and Schleiter 2010)

Given this scenario, Baumann's prediction that 'if ethnic belonging becomes a resource in economic competition, then ethnic radicalization is an all but inevitable consequence' (1999: 33) has come true for many ethnic communities in India.

This is the relation between state policies and ethnicization of tribal minorities in borderland regions of northeast India (cf. Bal 2007b). Therefore, in this sense, as stated eloquently by Pachuau, 'it is the nation state that creates ethnicities' (2014: 21). In other words, ethnicization in northeast India is largely a reaction to state policy, since ethnic considerations are intricately linked with the campaigns to acquire and maintain ST status, which in turn is related to essentialized cultural traits.

Furthermore, ethnic communities can sometimes subvert these imposed categories so that they can then be used as a tool by them in their fight for fair representation.

> These civilizing programs also have the unintended side effect of empowering the very groups that they are seeking to assimilate .... Another frequently mentioned by-product of these state development programs and policies is the creation of a heightened sense of ethnic identity among target populations. The government sponsored stereotypes of groups as primitives and backward can often lead to the creation of ethnic pride in response to this disdain, or to a wider recognition of ethnic similarities. (Duncan 2004: 17)

Wimmer's (1993) prediction of minorities being transformed, through a strategy of normative inversion, into 'nations' has proved correct many times over in northeast India.[34] Ramirez sums up the situation neatly as follows: 'Affirmative action aimed at smoothing out inequalities among communities has, by creating new resources, created elites who base their legitimacy on reviving identities and in reinforcing reservations' (2014: 30).

While it is clear that state policies and the actions of the dominant communities are largely responsible for the rise of ethnic conscious- ness, it is also true that '[t]he ethnopolitics of the "tribals" in the region represent to a large extent, an attempt to resist the majority's efforts to eradicate the distinctiveness or otherness' (Pachuau 1997: 766). I demonstrate many of these processes in the Tangsa case in the chapters that follow.

In this book, I ask the question that naturally follows: How suc- cessful are minority communities in resisting the efforts of the state (or the majority) to erase cultural difference? In other words, do they manage to maintain or preserve their cultural or ethnic distinctiveness? While the answer varies depending on the community in question, it shows how this question is linked to the larger question of the survival of ethnic minorities and that of their marginalization by the state and dominant majorities.

Taking the Tangsa example, I show that in the case of the numeri- cally weak minority communities in Assam, their efforts cannot be considered to be real effective resistance. If anything, by participating in state-sponsored projects such as festivals where they perform the role of the exotic tribal expected of them, rather than gaining agency to escape their marginalization, these small groups fall further into the trap of being and remaining marginalized—in fact, they contribute to their own marginalization by confirming the stereotype. The state, on the other hand, gets away without having to concede much, even while putting on the semblance of having done something. Furthermore, in many situations where some action could be taken, it is the dominant community and the establishment that still calls the shots. The grim reality is that the hands of the many small minority groups living in Assam are tied, no matter how vigorously they might sing and dance at festivals.

The Outline

Structure

There are eight chapters in this book; in this introductory chapter I lay the general outline, the second chapter is a general introduction to the 'Tirap' area where the story is located, and the third is an introduction to the Tangsa.[35] Chapters 4, 5, 6, and 7 are the main ethnographic chapters, with the first three focused on three Tangsa villages in Assam—Kharangkong, Malugaon, and Phulbari (located as in Map 2.2)—and the last describing the Tangsa situation in Arunachal. The final chapter, Chapter 8, will draw all the different threads together.

Besides specific Tangsa festivals that are described in detail in each of the Chapters 4 to 7, the multi-ethnic Dihing-Patkai Festival is discussed in Chapter 2 and some older Tangsa festivals are described in Chapter 3. The public meeting described in the prelude of the final chapter is a public event and hence also a kind of festival. Therefore, each chapter (except this one) includes description of some festival or the other.

Chapters 4 to 8 will be structured as follows—each chapter begins with a narrative section (in italics) as a kind of prelude, followed by the main text comprising a descriptive part and an analytic part. The descriptive part is contained in the sections about certain aspects of life in the villages, the living conditions and the aspirations of the villagers. The sections on festivals in each chapter will contain the analytic part. The final section, which I call the 'Postscript', will discuss other aspects relevant to the understanding of the village. These final sections are thematically different from the preceding sections in which the Tangsa are centre stage, and are devoted to discussing certain aspects of doing fieldwork with the Tangsa, my own field experiences, and the relations of my Tangsa interlocutors vis-à-vis the Assamese and the other communities.[36] The first three chapters do not have preludes.

Since the three villages selected for study in Chapters 4, 5, and 6 are very different from each other, they are described using different perspectives of narration: personal biography in the first, landscape and livelihood in the next, and religion as a way of life in the third. The focus of Chapter 7 dealing with Arunachal is meant to only bring out the differences, in the festivals as well as in the ways of life, between the Tangsa living there and those living in Assam, besides giving a glimpse of the much greater ethnic, linguistic, and religious diversity amongst the Tangsa population in Arunachal Pradesh.

The descriptive style of writing I have chosen has made this text longer, but hopefully, also more accessible to non-specialists. At times, I have moved definitions of certain terms and relevant theoretical observations to chapter endnotes in order to not break the narrative flow of the text. Consequently, there are many chapter endnotes in this work. Non-English words will be italicized and translations given the first time they appear in the text and also in the glossary. Some non-English words, such as *basti* (Hindi for settlement) or *chang-ghar* (Assamese for house on a raised platform), will occur frequently and are worth remembering. When using Tangsa terms, I will not mention the language if I am quoting some Tangsa elder—I will give the form in his/her Tangsa language. Assamese and Hindi words will be marked Ass. and Hin. respectively. Non-English words are reproduced here in a standardized way but without using diacritics and tone-markers.

Summary

Besides giving a general introduction, setting up the theoretical frame, and providing a summary of this work, this first chapter also contains, in a section that follows, a description of the DOBES project under which most of the fieldwork was done. I also discuss the methodological problems involved with doing fieldwork as a team and in 'Tangsaland'—the hypothetical area in India where the Tangsa live today;[37] it also contains my personal background as well as the genesis of the central questions I investigate in the chapters that follow.

The second chapter is a general introduction, both geographical as well as historical, to the 'Tirap' area where the Tangsa live in Assam. It also contains a description of the ethnic diversity of the area, where tribal groups such as the Tangsa, the Singpho, the Sema Naga, and the Tai Phake live together with other communities such as the Nepali, the Ahoms, and the Tea-tribes. Also discussed are the problems that the older tribal groups face as a result of the large number of new settlers coming to the area, the consequent gradual polarization that is taking place there, and the state's reaction to the prevailing situation, which finds expression in two events—first, in the organization of the annual state-sponsored multi-ethnic Dihing-Patkai Festival in that area and secondly in the recent formation of a Development Council for eight ethnic groups (including the Tangsa). A description of the coming of Baptist Christianity amongst the Tangsa and a brief summary of militant activities of the two insurgent organizations, the NSCN (National Socialist Council of Nagaland) and the ULFA (United Liberation Front of Assam), active in the region, are also given. The final section introduces the problem of the Assamese hegemonic attitudes towards the smaller ethnic groups living in Assam.

Chapter 3 focuses on the Tangsa, and discusses their linguistic classification as well as their division into subgroups such as the Pangwa; also discussed are their relations to the Naga and the Singpho, as well as some of their 'traditional' practices, their festivals, their lifestyle, and their social and cultural traditions. Starting with the past, I end in the present by describing the changes that have come to their lives with their move down the hills, their conversion to Christianity, and their gradually adopting a 'modern' style of living. The last section of the chapter describes my own introduction to the Tangsa and my first reactions to the differences I noted in their lifestyles with mine.

Chapters 4 to 7 are based on my own fieldwork experiences and records, and form the ethnographic core of this work; while the first three deal with one Tangsa basti in Assam each in turn, the last deals with the differences in the general situation for the Tangsa in Arunachal Pradesh. Chapter 4 unfolds in the Cholim basti of Kharangkong in the home of Aphu Tyanglam, one of the most respected Tangsa elders in Assam. I use Aphu's biography to describe the Tangsa situation in the basti, and also his personal efforts to revive the Wihu festival for the Tangsa in Assam, and some of the problems involved in the process. I end with a discussion of the advantages as well as the problems of having one dominant leader in the village and also of doing fieldwork with such a person.

Chapter 5 moves closer to the urban centres of Margherita and Ledo to the little Baptist Hakhun Tangsa basti of Malugaon perched on top of a hill right next to a coal mine. By focusing on the landscape and livelihood of the Tangsa living there, and by describing the problems caused by insurgent activities as well as the opportunities offered by the informal trade of coal and opium, I try to understand the efforts made by the Hakhun to survive as well as to gain visibility by organizing festivals.

The Ronrang Tangsa basti of Phulbari described in Chapter 6 is also Baptist, but because of its location in the plains close to the Arunachal Pradesh border and because of the strong influence of the Baptist Ronrang Tangsa living in the neighbouring bastis in Arunachal Pradesh, the picture in Phulbari is very different from that in Malugaon. Baptist Christianity plays a defining role in determining the daily routines of many Tangsa people in Phulbari. Efforts of the village leaders towards Tangsa consolidation by organizing a pan-Tangsa festival in Phulbari in 2010 will also be described.

The final sections of Chapters 5 and 6 will deal with various aspects of relations and networks my Tangsa interlocutors have with the wider world around them and of my fieldwork experiences in relation to these villages as well as with respect to the Assamese I came into contact with during the course of my work.

Chapter 7 takes us to Arunachal Pradesh, where I focus only on aspects of Tangsa life there which bring out the difference between the situation there and in Assam, both in terms of the greater diversity of religion and ethnic grouping as well as the differences in the political and administrative set-up. Besides describing a few Tangsa festivals that I attended there, I also describe, in the final section, some critical stages of my stay in the field and the culmination of my fieldwork.

In the concluding chapter, I discuss the various strategies that the Tangsa use in Assam to survive as a small ethnic minority group and how performing identity and ethnicity at festivals can be considered to be yet one more such strategy. This leads to a discussion of Tangsa identity, ethnicity, and culture as well as the role of the state and the Assamese 'other' in defining what it means to be Tangsa. In a 'taking stock' section, I list the shortcomings of this work, and discuss what still remains to be done before some clarity can be achieved in understanding the complex Tangsa picture. The concluding section summarizes my findings to make clear the underlying and undeniable connection between performing ethnicity and negotiating marginalization.

Postscript: Defining My Position in the Project and in the Field

Working in a Multidisciplinary Documentation Project

The fact that I was an Assamese woman based in Germany with an MA in culture studies had got me my job in the Volkswagen-Foundation funded DOBES project.[38] The project was titled 'The Traditional Songs and Poetry of Upper Assam—A Multifaceted Linguistic and Ethnographic Documentation of the Tangsa, Tai, and Singpho Communities in Margherita, Northeast India'.[39] But it was not without trepidation that I, by then already more than 40 years old, joined the international and multidisciplinary project team.[40]

Since I joined the project more than a year after it had already started, there was not much else for me to do but to quickly fall in place and find my stride. The positive side of joining midway was that I could start working right from the first day, as I did not have to do any of the time-consuming initial spadework a researcher would normally have to do when one visits a field site for the first time; that had already been done by my project colleagues.[41] But it did restrict my choice of place and field interlocutors. Also, since our project had to do with 'documenting' the 'traditional' culture of the Tangsa, most of our interlocutors were older men.[42]

I joined the project in December 2008 and in the 4-year period made five trips to the Tangsa area amounting to a total time of 16 months, and another trip for more than 2 months early in 2013.[43] Documentation implied that we did multisited fieldwork, all the more since the Tangsa are subdivided into a number of groups, separated mainly by language, spread over several villages in Assam and Arunachal Pradesh. This implied a considerable amount of travelling to collect field data from different field locations; more so for me, since I wanted to document as many Tangsa festivals as possible.[44]

We always stayed with Tangsa families in their homes. This, however, also implied that after the first introductory trip, I decided to travel alone, because our arriving in groups always put additional pressure on our hosts, as they had to find not just one but two separate spaces for us to sleep—one for me and another for my male colleagues, since it was not considered proper for me to share a room with them. There was another good reason for working alone which had to do with the efficient use of time—since all the team members had mostly to do with the same few (most often only one) interlocutors, it was really quite a waste of resources for us to arrive together as only one of us could really work with him while the others just waited for their turn. However, being alone also creates a large set of technical problems. It is almost impossible to single-handedly video record an interview while trying to conduct it. It is even more difficult to record a whole festival alone.

Our methods comprised basically of conversations and interviews which we recorded using only audio recorders for plain conversations and discussions, and video recorders when singing or dancing was involved. Photographs were mainly used to keep records of places, people, and artefacts, and Global Positioning System (GPS) recordings were made of all the places visited. Sketch maps, field notes, and metadata files were routinely made. Even though not all our Tangsa interlocutors were fluent in Assamese, almost everyone spoke it to some extent. I spoke to most of my interlocutors in Assamese (and sometimes also in Hindi and English), recording conversations and interviews, whenever possible, and later made free translations into English.[45] These translations form the base of my empirical data.[46]

In terms of fieldwork practice, there were some excellent norms, such as the practice of making and giving back copies (often on DVDs) of every recording to at least a few of those who figure in the recordings; we informed our interlocutors that all the data we collected in the field would be archived at the central DOBES archive (for details see Note 40) and would be freely available for use in the future, even by the community. We also routinely asked permission from our interlocutors before making recordings and explained what we would do with the recordings before uploading any data into the archive, and restricted access to particular recordings, if so wished by the interlocutor.

Unconventional Fieldwork Methods and Problems

In order to get the best possible quality of documentation, the technical equipment used by our project was very sophisticated, and there were strict quality standard levels that we were required to maintain.

I was acutely aware that my very presence had an impact on how my interlocutors behaved and what they said, more so when I turned up all wired up with cables and earphones and carrying a professional-looking camera in my hands. I did try to minimize the technical interference by restricting the use of the video cameras much as I could, but still it could not be avoided at times since recording visual data was also part of my job.[47]

As an aspiring anthropologist, I could see that my colleagues, who came from other disciplines, had somewhat other methods of doing fieldwork than what I would have preferred. The main problem was that by the time I joined the team, our interlocutors had got so used to being asked questions (to elicit information) that I really could not get them to understand that I was just happy to hang around and observe what was going on. They expected me to ask questions. And when I did ask questions they were often surprised if I did not ask them to sing me a song or tell me a story.

Given the incredible linguistic diversity of the Tangsa, my knowledge of any one of the Tangsa language would have not got me very far. Therefore, I did not try to learn any of the Tangsa languages. Since the Tangsa, especially those living in Assam, used Asamiya—my mother tongue—as a sort of lingua franca, I never had problems in communication or comprehension.[48] I did not need any assistants/interpreters. While this made communication more direct, it had the disadvantage that my data was not vetted by a second person. It also meant that they could easily switch to their own languages if they did not want to share something with me.

Problems to Do with the Field Area

With time, one gets used to the bad to non-existent roads, rudimentary toilets, basic living conditions, and so on. More annoying were the frequent power cuts in the evenings, poor telephone and internet connectivity, and the subsequent logistical problems of arranging travel and accommodation.[49] There was also the problem of having to carry substantial amounts of cash, since there were hardly any cash machines (automated teller machine [ATMs]) beyond Margherita. Crossing the inter-state borders was also not easy as Indians need to obtain Inner Line Permits (ILPs) to enter Arunachal Pradesh.[50]

The biggest anxiety which was constantly hovering in the background had to do with the proximity of underground insurgents in the area. Certain pockets of my field area were known to be bases of the ULFA (United Liberation Front of Assam) militants. There was also some NSCN (National Socialist Council of Nagaland) presence in the area, spilling over from Nagaland and Arunachal Pradesh. The KIA (Kachin Independence Army) were also believed to have some cadres stationed along the Buridihing river. And most recently, there have been reports of some major Maoist activity in that area. Given this scenario, there was also a lot of army and paramilitary forces stationed in the region and frequently one heard news of 'encounters' between militants and army personnel, often leading to a call of a *bandh* (Hin. strike, blockade) by some group or the other in protest.[51]

The town of Margherita is the Head Office of the Northeastern Coalfields of Coal India Limited and there are four operational coal mines in the Ledo area with many high-ranking officers and engineers living there. The nearby town of Digboi has an oil refinery and is the headquarters of the Assam Oil Division of Indian Oil Corporation Limited while the oil drilling company Oil India Limited has its headquarters in Duliajan, also close by. While this meant better infrastructure and facilities in the area, it also meant more money in the hands of the local people, hence making the officers prime targets of militants and underground activists operating in the region.[52]

Early on in the project, we decided that we would not go out of our way to meet or interview any militant or militant organization. We also did not ask to know more about their activities, nor even their reaction to our presence in their midst. At least one village where I have stayed is known to be home of some insurgents. Our Tangsa interlocutors would sometimes tell us about incidents involving some of these groups. There were often reports of the presence of insurgents in neighbouring areas and of army searches. We did try, as far as was possible, to find out whether a particular village was 'safe' before we arrived there; there have been a couple of close calls, but we have been lucky.

A Brahmin Assamese Woman Alone in Tangsaland

The fact that our field sites were mostly in Assam made me an almost 'native' researcher. Of course, that label is contested (cf. Narayan 1993), and there are problems in either case:

The outsider may enter the social situation armed with a battery of assumptions which he does not question and which guide him to certain types of conclusions; and the insider may depend too much on his own background, his own sentiments, his desires for what is good for his people. The insider, therefore, may distort the 'truth' as much as the outsider. (Jones 1970: 256)

This rang true, for there have been occasions in the field when I have jumped to conclusions too quickly, or misinterpreted things. Therefore, I did consciously try to be constantly aware of the importance of 'problematising my own cultural blindness' (Ruotsala 2001: 121).

For most Tangsa people, it was immediately clear (from my name) that I was an Assamese Hindu. What was not as clear was what an Assamese Hindu woman was doing in their midst. Initially, the very idea that such a woman could want to stay in their village simply to find out more about the day-to-day life of the people made some doubt my sincerity, and made them wonder if I was not a government spy or some undercover agent. Things got even more complicated when my Tangsa hosts found out that not only was I a Hindu, but also that I was a Brahmin, that is, I belonged to the highest Hindu caste (which is known for its strict rules for purity and impurity and so forth). So while it might have been conceivable for my Tangsa interlocutors to imagine that some Assamese people would not mind eating in their house, they would not expect a Hindu Brahmin to eat a meal with them, leave alone stay in their houses.[53] That fact, coupled with my urban, upper-middle-class family background, made it even harder for me to explain to my Tangsa interlocutors my reasons for desiring to work with them and how I could possibly live and eat with them without things going badly with me later back home.

Even otherwise, there were many occasions when our hosts were not sure what to make of me because even though as an Assamese I was not quite an outsider, I was not a complete insider either; what was more was that I was a woman, that too, a woman, apparently claiming to have a husband but one that none of them had ever met, roaming around all by myself, or with a bunch of men, none of whom was my husband!

In certain senses, it can be easier for a foreigner to do fieldwork in Assam than for an Assamese because of generations of distrust and the far from satisfactory nature of much research done in recent years by local academics. However, since they could speak to me easily in Asamiya, and could relate to me more easily because I was closer to home to them, my Tangsa interlocutors treated me with a little less formality than they did my foreigner colleagues in the project.

But it also came at a price. For although my foreign colleagues had the right to ask any question they wished to, as an almost native researcher, I did not have the permission to ask silly questions (Ruotsala 2001: 123). There was also this additional 'burden of a native researcher', where one is supposed to not only know what is the correct behaviour in certain situations but also to comply. So, for example, during a festival, they expected me to sit in my allotted place and not run around trying to record the event. I was also expected to know and tell my foreign colleagues about what they considered to be sensitive topics, and about the ethical issues involved. They automatically assumed I would know. Moreover, I was expected to conform to the village norms of decent behaviour; therefore, I did not try to hang around too long with the men once they started smoking opium or drinking. That implied that I did not really manage to get included into the men's domain. However, with the women the distance could sometimes be even greater—for the cultural differences are more obvious when one sits in a kitchen but does not know how to help with the cooking.

Following the rules of field ethics, I did try to explain to our interlocutors about our project and its aims but I am not entirely sure they believed me—after all, why should Germany pay for an Assamese woman to go and hang around with them for months on end, with apparently no other job but to just chat with people and make free video recordings of village events for them?

Coming to Terms with Writing Up

For me, the hardest part, at least in the initial periods of my fieldwork, was not so much coping with the Tangsa but with myself: I could not somehow accept the fact that although I was Assamese and had lived in Assam for most of my life, I did not know anything about the Tangsa (worse still, had not even heard of them) and had not cared to find out anything about any of these people, who lived so close by, till then.[54] I told myself that my Tangsa interlocutors had been right in treating me with that initial mistrust.

But they were the first ones to extend their hand of trust and of friendship, which I gratefully accepted. There were even a couple of incidents when I was asked to actually participate in decision-making by my host-families, and I turned into a circumstantial activist (see Marcus 1995: 113); at those times, my wish to want to be just an observer came into direct conflict with my obligation to respond to the request of my hosts, and I chose to follow my gut instincts about which role to take on depending on the context.[55]

Later, as familiarity turned into friendship, I realized that my attitude towards my Tangsa interlocutors had also changed with time (and especially towards the end of my six-month long field trip in the third field season). As I slowly began to really participate in their normal everyday life, I stopped thinking of them as objects of study. Their problems had started to become 'real' for me. I had become part of their families, as much as they had become part of my life.

And with this also changed the nature of how I looked at the project. For I was no longer doing it because I was paid to do so or for the sake of my PhD, but for 'their' sake as well. There was this growing sense of responsibility towards my field community—'people to whom we are bonded through ties of reciprocity' (Narayan 1993: 672), and this sense of obligation and responsibility grew stronger over time. I was terrified that like Lassiter's Kiowa interlocutor, my Tangsa interlocutors would also accuse my ethnography of having more relevance to other anthropologists than to them (Lassiter 2005: 18–19). For like Lassiter, I wanted to do an 'ethnography that could be read, discussed, and used at various levels by both academics and my interlocutors' in an effort 'to narrow the gap between anthropology and the communities' studied (Lassiter 2005: 18–19). But that seemed like a tall order.

And if that was not enough, came the next worry—did I know anything about the Tangsa at all that was worth writing about, that would bear scrutiny? Furthermore, was there anything that I could write about that even my Tangsa interlocutors would value? That worry had haunted me for a very long time. There were many moments during the course of my field stay when I really asked myself if my informants were simply telling me what they thought I wanted to hear, but which carried no real meaning to them. Were we (the team) then in danger of over-interpreting or misinterpreting what we had seen and what we had been told?[56] These questions became more and more relevant to

me over time as I sometimes had the feeling that our Tangsa interlocutors were beginning to use the fact of our presence for their own ends,
for instance, when they sought to raise the importance of their village
festival in the eyes of the local administration by mentioning the fact
that some foreign researchers had attended it.[57]

Coupled with my diffidence about my knowledge about the Tangsa,
there was another big question that bothered me to no end. It was the
question that I was asked mentioned at the beginning of the chapter:
Why study the Tangsa at all? For on most counts, the Tangsa story, or
that part of it that I had been able to unearth, apart from their mind-
boggling linguistic diversity, seemed very similar to stories of other
small ethnic groups in the region. There was this irritating sense of déjà
vu when I read works of other scholars working in the area, such as
Erik de Maaker's work on the Wangala dance of the Garos or Alban
von Stockhausen's description of the Naga Hornbill festival. Was there
any point in writing another book if there was nothing substantially
different to tell?

Why then must it be? The bottom line, of course, was that it is the
only story I had to tell, and secondly, for my Tangsa interlocutors it
did matter whether their story was told or not, whether there was a
book with their name on the cover; perhaps, not many Tangsa would
be able to read and make sense of my writing immediately, but as
Robbins Burling had pointed out to me a long time ago, the Garos
were just happy to hold his book (Burling 1963) about them in their
hand, look at the photos, and feel that someone at least had taken
them seriously. And since it bothered me so much, perhaps this could
be one way of making up to my Tangsa informants for all the indif-
ference and insensitivity they have had to suffer at the hands of my
fellow Assamese.

Added to all these worries related to the Tangsa, I also had some
problems with myself and with my discipline of anthropology.[58] Many
of my mentors in anthropology did not approve of the working methods (based on eliciting information) of our team (led by linguists) as
well as the basic idea of documenting 'endangered languages' and
'disappearing cultures'. I did see the problem with that, but it was also
hard to argue that a language should not be called 'endangered' in the
face of the certain fact that the only two speakers left of the language
were both over 80 years of age.

I also had problems with the anthropologists' endeavour to find deep meaning in everything and the need to be politically correct at all times. For working with the Tangsa had made me realize that, rather than having some deep unfathomable logic, most of their decisions were based on primarily pragmatic considerations; therefore, I felt that it was my duty to 'not build things up that aren't there' (Lassiter 2005: 14). In other words, I had to be careful not to explain away the Tangsa, but to describe them in a way that readers could get a faithful impression about them. To do that one should be allowed to comment about what was surprising or what was unpleasant, I felt. I was aware, of course, that my reactions could not be assumed to be typical or canonical in any way. Still I believed that as long as I made my position clear, adding my own reaction would make the description only 'thicker'.

Therefore, it was not just the 'what' but also the 'how' I would write that was bothering me. If it were not for Kirin Narayan's staunch defence of 'narrative ethnography' (Narayan 1993: 681) and Sanjib Baruah's timely prod to 'suspend disbelief and just write', I might have perhaps not made it this far. I have chosen to write in a more descriptive style primarily because I do not want my field to become invisible. Moreover, there is no single frame or format with which one can analyse or explain the immense diversity that I met in the field—by going into the details I want to present the full depth of the complexity of the situation. Moreover, by writing myself into the story at every stage, I wish to follow Michael Jackson's 1989 call for 'radical empiricism': a methodology and discursive style that emphasizes the subject's experience and involvement with others in the construction of knowledge (see Narayan 1993: 680).

Considering everything, I decided to use the 'language of everyday life', as recommended by Abu-Lughod (1991: 151). Jaarsma's words below came both as a challenge as well as an invitation.

> Taking this challenge seriously will profoundly change the way we work. Theoretical sophistication and exclusionary jargon will no longer be the measure of our work, but will be superseded by a demand for clarity and accessibility. Sophisticated analysis, however fruitful in its application, cannot serve any community's long term purpose if it virtually encrypts the knowledge it produces. In the long run, the production of ethnographic knowledge defeats its own purpose if it does not become

available and accessible to a wider audience, including the people we
study. (Jaarsma 2002: 12)

I wanted to test myself to see how far I would get.

Notes

1. The term 'state' will be used to mean the Indian state, as well as to refer to
the federal states (or provinces) of the Indian union, the sense in which it
is used here.

     The term 'tribe' is still used in South Asia (particularly in India) as part
of a broader repertoire applied by the state to classify people into groups.
The term 'tribe' will be used here as a label for any group which displays
the broad characteristics of 'tribal societies', as defined, for instance, by
Xaxa (1999: 1524); the point being that 'a tribe is seen as a distinctive type
of society' that marks it to be at variance from the mainstream population.
For more, see Béteille (1977, 1986).

     I use the term *community* for a set of people who share an idea of belong-
ing together, and the term *group* to refer to any set of people. Following
Cohen (2003), just like an ethnic group, a community exists in the minds
of its people and is connected through symbols that hold and perpetuate
its meaning for its members.

2. The region which is called northeast India comprises of eight states that
lie in the north-eastern corner of the country; the river Brahmaputra flows
through the heart of the region; the plains region lies mostly in Assam
with the hill states surrounding it. The region is connected to the rest of
India by a very thin corridor (22 km at its narrowest). Except for this very
short domestic boundary, the rest of the around 4,500 km long boundary
is international. It is bordered by Bhutan and Nepal in the west, China
(Tibet) in the north, Myanmar (Burma) in the east, and Bangladesh in the
south. Of late, there has been an increasing tendency, even in academic
discourse, to club all the northeastern states together as one entity called
the 'Northeast', for example, see Berger and Heidemann (2013). For a con-
cise but comprehensive introduction to northeast India, see De Maaker
and Joshi (2007: 384) and to the available literature on the region, see
Subba and Wouters (2013). For a gentle introduction to Assam and northeast India, to some of the special regulations in place there, and to some
locally situated issues, such as the claim that the Northeast is more part of
Southeast Asia than of South Asia, see Burling (1967).

     As Farrelly points out, the Northeast has been imagined 'in opposition
to the Indian "mainland", "mainstream", "centre", and "core"' (2009a:

284). Each of these phrases are regularly used to explain the differences that are perceived, on both sides, between the region and the rest of the country.

3. There seems to be no unanimity about the number of Tangsa groups. Simai (2008: 5) claims there are 17; Morang (2008: 17) divides them into six larger sub-tribes. There seems to be a list with as many as 32 different Tangsa communities approved by the Government of India. According to a latest count made by our DOBES project, linguistically, there could be as many as 69 groups on both sides of the Indo-Myanmar border who could be considered to be Tangsa/Tangshang/Heimi. (In Myanmar where the Tangsa also live, the terms 'Tangshang' or 'Heimi' are used for the Tangsa.)

   I will often use the term 'traditional' in this book, also a label, to refer to what people consider as coming from the past, whether it is objectively true or not. Depending on the context, it will refer back to a time when the Tangsa were still in the hills, or to a time when they had not converted (to one of the standard religions like Christianity or Buddhism) and were still following their older beliefs, of course, with the understanding that there was probably no agreement even in the past on what these practices were. This is particularly the sense in which I use, for example, the term 'traditional religion' later on. Sometimes, however, these terms will be used without marking so as not to break the flow of the argument.

4. The Naga, like the Tangsa, are also another linguistically diverse collection of tribal groups who live in Myanmar as well as in northeast India (see, for instance, Burling 2003). There were 16 officially recognized Naga tribes in India in 2001. There will be more about the Nagas in later sections.

5. I use Assamese to refer to the predominantly caste-Hindu, Asamiya-speaking (see note 48) community of the state of Assam who wield political and administrative power in the state. The question of who is Assamese is, however, hotly contested; other definitions could include people who consider Assam to be their 'homeland'. For debates on this issue, see Bhattacharjee (2008) and references therein. For more about the Assamese, see Cantile (1984).

6. The modern world, according to Duncan, 'include[s] fluency in the national language, conversion to a recognized religion, and entrance into the cash economy' (2004: 3). This, together with access to basic infrastructure, health care, and communications technology, could be taken as a rough description of what it means to be modern for the Tangsa if one qualified the national language to mean the official language of Assam.

   I use the term 'modern' in this work as a label to refer to the present, not so much because I believe that the Tangsa are all modern, but because my Tangsa interlocutors themselves wish to make this distinction between their life in the past and in the present, which is characterized by a move down to the plains and their acceptance of a lifestyle similar in many ways to that of the majority mainstream plains populations.

7. An ethnic group will generally refer to a group of people who claim to have the same identity (Eriksen 2010).

8. See Khilnani's *The Idea of India* (1999) where he argues that postcolonial conflicts are first and foremost contests over the ownership and access to state resources.

9. The past is also therefore a 'perceived' past—real, 'imagined' (Anderson 1983), or 'invented' (Hobsbawm and Ranger 1983)—on which much of the present-day discussions and deliberations of Tangsa culture and ethnicity are based.

10. I use the term 'caste-Hindu' to refer to the set of Hindus who follow a caste system similar to that in the rest of India. Many ethnic groups, especially in northeast India, have become Hindus but do not strictly follow the caste system. In particular, tribal people are not usually organized along caste lines, as are the caste Hindus. For more on this discussion, see Pathak (2010).

11. The project was funded by Volkswagen Foundation under the DOBES programme. My project colleagues were a linguist from La Trobe University, Australia (Dr Stephen Morey), a Tai expert (Professor Barend Terwiel), and a German ethnomusicologist (Dr Juergen Schöpf), and also students of linguistics from Gauhati University.

12. The use of the plural 'we' without clarification will refer to the project team of which I was a member. The name Stephen will refer to Stephen Morey, my Australian linguist colleague in our project team.

Burma came to be officially known as Myanmar from 1989. Throughout this text, I use the terms 'Burma' and 'Myanmar' interchangeably, using the term best suited for the context in which it is used.

13. Although the Tangsa varieties our team examined are being passed on to children, there is a gradual loss of the cultural richness, as texts like that of the Wihu song are not being passed on. For more reasons in support of language documentation, see Nick Evans' evocative book *Dying Words* (2009) and Bradley (2012).

14. The Wihu song, for example, was not recorded at all before we started with our project (see Barkataki-Ruscheweyh and Morey 2013). On one occasion, one of our principal interlocutors Aphu Tyanglam, explained to me why he had asked Stephen Morey to hoist the flag for the Wihu-kuh festival celebrations that year: Since many of the Tangsa people did not care for Wihu-kuh, he thought they might change their minds if they saw

that a foreigner was interested. By showing honour to the foreign guests, he also expected some political as well as financial return (Kharangkong, 30 December 2010).

15. This can be considered at best a kind of Boasian 'salvage ethnography', as discussed for instance in, Pachuau (2014: 68ff) and Nutini (2004: 23).

16. For instance, we shall never know in what form the Wihu-kuh festival would have been celebrated in the village of Kharangkong if Stephen Morey had not arrived there in January 2007 and Aphu Tyanglam, in his great enthusiasm to have a foreigner as guest, had not promised him to hold the festival in a much grander style the following year. I discuss this in detail in Chapter 4.

17. Another similar study has been done on the Khasis of Meghalaya by Lyndoh (1991).

18. Broadly speaking, *agency* can be understood as the capacity to make choices and impose those choices on others.

    A community can be called *marginalized* when they cease to matter to those in power, when they are not consulted about decisions that directly impact them, and when they are not given any choices but are forced to play along. Moreover, being marginalized is a trap because it is much more difficult for marginalized people to get to positions from where they can influence decision-making in order to get out of that condition. For another engaging and celebrated study of marginality (and its connotations and implications), see Tsing (1993).

19. Made famous by Leach's 1954 classic treatise on the Kachin groups living in Highland Burma, 'Kachin' is a cultural term while 'Jinghpaw' is a linguistic term. Kachins are not just Jinghpaw-speaking people, but a range of groups, several speaking distantly related Burmic languages, who form a cultural unit. The term 'Singpho' refers both to the people as well as their language in India. The language of the Singphos in Assam is similar (though not identical) to what Leach (1954) calls Jinghpaw. For more see Nath (2013), Sadan (2013), Chit Hlaing (2007), and Hanson (1906).

20. There are not many Singphos in India; Sadan (2013: 7) puts the number at around 10,000. But they have close links with their relatives and greater Singpho/Jinghpaw/Kachin organizations based in the Kachin state in Burma, in Yunnan, in Thailand, and elsewhere. Sadan's monograph gives many details of these connections and networks. She also points out that since the Kachin is Burma are Christian and the Jingpo in Yunnan are communists, these differences create tensions in their relations with the Buddhist Singphos in India.

21. Although I focus only on three Tangsa villages in Assam and a few in Arunachal Pradesh, my field visits have taken me to many Tangsa villages

in both the states and I have met a wide cross section of the Tangsa population living in India.

22. One could have also started much earlier with Durkheim (1912), Malinowski (1922), and Mauss (1925). A huge body of literature exists on these and related topics (see Bakhtin 1968; Falassi 1987; Gertz 1991; Guss 2000: Ch. 1; Schechner 1988; Stoeltje 1992; Turner 1982, 1986).

23. Following Longkumer (2015), by *performance*, I will mean that which is 'performed' for audiences (Ebron 2002: 1). Another important characteristic is that 'actions are deemed performances when they are not merely done but done to be seen' (Goffman 1974: 58).

24. Within the frame of this book, festivals at three different levels will be considered—first, the village level 'traditional' festival which comprises mostly of rituals; second, the community level 'ethnic' festivals which include not only rituals but also elements of self (re)presentation and entertainment, and finally, the trans-community mega festivals, such as the Hornbill Festival in Nagaland, in which the ritual part is more or less elided or enacted as mere performance, and the emphasis is on performing and presenting the 'culture' of different communities in staged presentations, and in displaying and selling 'traditional' food and handicrafts, thereby promoting business and tourism in that area.

25. *Rituals* will be assumed to be repetitive and established patterns of actions which convey some meaning to those performing them. Seen as a whole, they are formalized symbolic actions which have specific meaning for the community and often, but not necessarily, have some religious connotation, while festivals will be generally thought to be secular.

   For a good recent overview of the different meanings and definitions of ritual, see Handler (2011). For a discussion on the political implications of ritual, see Kertzer (1988). See also Brosius and Hüsken (2010).

   A 'cultural show' comprises a sequence of cultural performances (Singer 1959: xiii), mostly dances, but often also fashion shows, skits, and dance dramas, which are performed on a designated stage, by a set of performers who are suitably dressed, and who have rehearsed their parts beforehand.

26. I refer to the excellent literature already existing on these topics: For ethnicity—Banks (1996, 2013), Barth (1969), and Eriksen (2010); for identity—Brubaker and Cooper (2000), Hall (1991, 1996a, 1996b), Handler (1994), Sökefeld (2001), and Taylor (1989); and for culture—Baumann (1999), Clifford (1986, 1988), Sahlins (1999a), and Wimmer (2005).

27. On this subject, Shneiderman (2014: 285) points out: 'Both Scott and the Comaroffs touch upon the expressive aspects of ethnicity, but neither explores its implications fully. Scott suggests that "a person's ethnic

identity … would be the repertoire of possible performances and the contexts in which they are exhibited …."' (Scott 2009: 254–5).

28. Moreover, as I discuss presently, the state notions of ethnicity are also basically essentialist.

29. This is not necessarily true of all groups, for, as we will see later, 'Nagaland
for Christ' as a motto for the Naga, can be considered to be an attempt to
introduce religion into cultural identity.

30. The word 'articulated' in the sense of Hall (1986) can be used to mean to
express, as well as to link (as in an articulated lorry) and comprise different
elements which can be put together in different combinations at different
times according to the specific need and context (cf. Fiske 1996: 213).

31. A *Scheduled Tribe* is one which is mentioned in the scheduled list of the
Indian Constitution under Articles 342(i) and 342(ii). The Tangsa, if
and when they appear, are included as Other Naga tribes in these lists.
Therefore, all Tangsa living in Arunachal Pradesh are ST while only those
living in the Autonomous districts of Assam (as stated in the Sixth Schedule
of the Indian Constitution) are. For an account of the special provisions
made for the ethnic communities in the Northeast, the reorganization of
the states as well as the 6th Schedule Provisions, see Karlsson (2001: 18).

   See Nongkynrih (2010) for a discussion of tribe versus scheduled tribe.
See also Béteille (1998). For a detailed discussion of the many terms such
as 'tribe', 'adivasi', 'indigenous people', and so forth, and their various connotations, see Van Schendel and Bal (2002).

   The terms 'indigenous people' and 'tribal' are often used interchangeably (Karlsson 2001, Srikanth 2014), but to avoid confusion, I reserve the
term 'indigenous people' to mean the 'Bhumiputras', or the sons of the
soil. The Tangsa are not indigenous in this particular sense (see also Cobo
1986).

   De Maaker and Joshi define 'tribes' as 'a classification based on linguistic
and cultural criteria developed in colonial times, and which is still in use
today' (2007: 382). Bhagabati (1992: 500) is of the same view.

32. According to the 2011 Census data, there are more than 31 million
people living in Assam. With a population of more than 1.35 million in
2011, the Bodo are the biggest ST group in the state. Available at http://
censusindia.gov.in/2011census/censusinfodashboard/stock/profiles/en/
IND018_Assam.pdf (accessed 28 December 2013).

33. The People of India (2003) project has studied 115 such groups: see http://
www.ansi.gov.in/people_india.htm (accessed 6 August 2014).

34. For a detailed analysis of how new states were progressively carved out from
the state of Assam after Indian independence in order to meet the demand
for 'homelands' for different ethnic groups, see Van Schendel (2011). And

the struggle continues; the Bodos, the largest ethnic minority in Assam, have already won their fight to have their language recognized. They have also been awarded an autonomous territorial council but have still not given up their demand that the state of Assam be divided fifty-fifty to create a new state of Bodoland (see U. Goswami 2014; Deka 2014; Sharma 2007).

35. In the two introductory chapters (Chapters 2 and 3), I have included topics (such as descriptions of some of their past practices as told to me by elders from memory) because I am also interested in documenting the changes that have taken place in Tangsa society in recent years, and hence I consider an understanding of their past important to the understanding of their present. In so doing, I do not wish to 'objectify' their past, or be normative; rather I wish to give my analysis historical depth and record a small part of the cultural history of a few of these groups.

36. Many of the concerns expressed in the various Postscripts have been put together in (Barkakati-Ruscheweyh 2016).

37. Of course, in reality there is no territorial area that can be termed as Tangsaland, except for some small pockets in the Changlang district in Arunachal Pradesh since the Tangsa live scattered over a large area where many other communities live as well.

38. DOBES stands for 'Dokumentation Bedrohter Sprachen' or 'Document-ation of Endangered Languages'. Further details are available at http://www.mpi.nl/DOBES.

39. For my fourth and final year, I worked in an extension of the earlier project titled 'A Multifaceted Study of Tangsa—a Network of Linguistic Varieties in North East India'.

40. The project required all team members to make visual, audio, and pho-tographic recordings in the field, make comprehensive meta files for each media file, and then to upload and archive all our material in the open-access DOBES archive (http://www.mpi.nl/resources/data/dobes) at the Max Planck Institute for Psycholinguistics at Nijmegen, Netherlands.

41. Since my hometown Guwahati is not very far from the 'field' it was always problematic for me to physically demarcate and locate my 'field'. While for my project colleagues Guwahati was already part of the field, my field began only somewhere beyond it. For a very comprehensive analysis of the idea of 'field', see Gupta and Ferguson (1997).

42. This is due to several reasons: first, that most of the initial work was done by Stephen Morey, who is male; second, that in each village the men are usually from the tribe we were studying while the women were often from other groups and were not mother-tongue speakers of the language under investigation. Finally, the women had less time to spare for us. Of course, there were exceptions.

43. Periods of my fieldwork trips are February–March 2009, mid-September–mid-December 2009, mid-October 2010–mid-April 2011, January–March 2012, October–November 2012, and another trip in January–mid-April 2013.

44. While staying put with one community would have been fine as far as anthropology was concerned, it would not have served the basic purpose for which I was employed in the project—to make contact and, if possible, also language recordings from as many different Tangsa communities as possible.

45. I am aware of the dangers of misunderstanding and also misinterpreting while making such free translations.

46. Since I was part of a team and most of the textual work was done by the linguists in our team, I have not included any samples of language or of translation in this work, and concentrate mostly on my own contributions to the project.

47. I bought myself a smaller and hence much less conspicuous video camera after my first field trip.

48. Although the language spoken by the Assamese is also usually referred to as Assamese, I refer to it as Asamiya when I wish to make a distinction. *Asamiya* is an Indo-Aryan language, closely related to Bengali but which has many loan words from the many Tibeto-Burman languages spoken in the region. It is one of the official languages of the state of Assam.

49. Internet connectivity is still not good in that area; however, things have improved significantly even within the duration of our project. Today there is internet connectivity in even a few Tangsa homes and many of the English-educated younger Tangsa people, especially in Changlang, go to internet cafes regularly to check their e-mail.

50. Although ILP requirements are still in place for non-local Indians, recently the requirement of Restricted Area Permits (RAPs) for foreigners have been lifted from all other north-eastern states (except Arunachal Pradesh).

51. Sector 25 of Assam Rifles, a paramilitary force of the Indian state, under the command of a Brigadier, has its headquarters at Lekhapani near Ledo.

    The culture of bandhs is a legacy of the Students Agitation in Assam in the 1980s. For more, see Kimura (2013: Ch. 4).

52. There have been several cases of kidnappings of foreigners or high company (Oil or Coal) officials for a ransom often ending in harassment and in a couple of cases, even death.

53. Most of the Asamiya-speaking people who live in the same area are either Ahoms or Sonowal Kacharis; they are usually not Brahmin.

54. My master's thesis was on Assamese identity (Bhattacharjee 2008). But in that study I had only looked at the Assamese caste Hindu population.

The fact is that there is very little contact between the dominant majority Assamese population and the other groups living in Assam.

55. On one occasion I was asked by my host Tangsa family to intervene in order to persuade their young son to return to boarding school; the young boy had come home for his holidays and had met his other friends who had either stopped going to school or were attending the local village school, and told his parents that he would not go back to boarding school again.

56. One instance of this was when a red chicken was sacrificed one year at a festival, and we naturally assumed the red colour to have some meaning till a brown chicken was sacrificed the following year.

57. See Saikia (2004: xvii) for a similar discussion vis-à-vis the Tai Ahom community in Assam.

58. It was heartening, therefore, to discover that I was not the only one who had problems of this kind. See, for example, the discussion in Pelto (1970: Epilogue) and Borneman and Hammoudi (2009) not only about topics of research but also the language in which one writes up.

2 Introduction to the Tirap Area

The Tangsa and the other Naga tribes are like the five fingers in one hand, each a little different from the others, but all bound together.
—Aphu Tyanglam, Kharangkong

The Tangsa population is scattered over the trans-Patkai region. Most Tangsa in India live in the Changlang District of Arunachal Pradesh, mainly on the western slopes of the Patkai hills. Many more Tangsa live across the border in Myanmar (where they are called Tangshang or Heimi Naga). A handful of Tangsa also live in upper Assam, concentrated in its eastern most tip, in the Margherita subdivision of the Tinsukia district, capped by the Changlang District, as shown in Map 2.1, which also shows some Tangsa villages where I worked, both in Assam and in Arunachal. I call the area where the Tangsa live in Assam 'Tirap' since it contains the Tirap *mouza* and also because most of it lies between the Buridihing and Tirap Rivers (see Map 2.2).[1]

The first time I had heard the term 'Tirap' was in an Asamiya song by the Assamese music maestro Bhupen Hazarika titled 'Tirap Simanta' (The Tirap Frontier). As a child, places like Tirap and Sadiya were really at the outer boundaries of my Assamese world. During my first visit to the Tangsa village of Phulbari, I discovered that Tirap was the name of the beautiful river along which it was located; and it was the same river one crossed near Lekhapani at Tirap Gate. I had also seen the Tirap colliery near Ledo. Many other terms—the Tirap Frontier Tract, the Tirap Tribal Belt and the Tirap Transferred Area—also contained the word

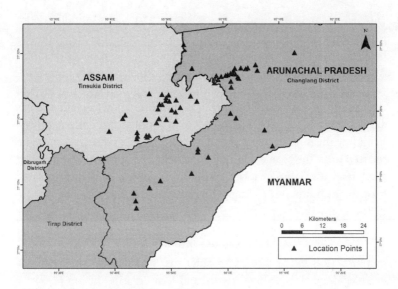

Map 2.1   Some of My Field Locations

Source: Sukanya Lehnhardt.
Note: Map not to scale and does not represent authentic international boundaries.

Tirap. Hence the name Tirap sounded just right for the area in Assam where I would base my work with the Tangsa. From now on, whenever I use the word Tirap, I will refer to this particular area, unless specified differently. Note that this area in Assam is not to be confused with the Tirap district in eastern Arunachal Pradesh.

Brief History of the Tirap Area

Although most of the Tangsa villages I worked in were beyond Ledo towards Lekhapani and Jagun, the Tirap area belonged to the Margherita subdivision with headquarters in the town of Margherita. During my first visit to 'Tangsaland' what had surprised me the most were the many industries, besides the tea gardens, that were to be seen in that supposedly 'remote and forgotten corner' of a state that did not have many industries to boast of in any case. I had imagined that the landscape beyond the urban centres of Dibrugarh and Tinsukia would be predominantly rural. Contrary to my expectations, the area looked almost 'cosmopolitan'. The little towns of the area—Digboi, Makum,

Duliajan, Margherita, and Ledo (see Map 2.2)—were populated not just by the Assamese and the tribal communities of the area, but also by Nepalis, Bengalis, as well as people from other parts of the country.[2] Also, the name Margherita sounded quite European—I was mystified!

To set the scene, I need to go back at least to British times, to the first quarter of the nineteenth century. It is common knowledge that it was a Singpho chieftain who first gave a wild tea plant to a British officer, heralding the birth of the tea industry in Assam. This led to what can be referred to as 'the great enclosure movement in Assam' when the British tried to acquire large areas of agricultural and forest land to set up large tea gardens in the vast rolling plains and valleys of upper Assam. More disturbingly, the establishment of tea gardens not only implied the 'entry of over a million labouring migrants' from central India, but, as J. Sharma argues, 'decisively transformed the region's social demographics' (2012: 17), because besides the 'tea coolies', Marwari traders, Nepali graziers, Sylhetti clerks, and East Bengali Muslim peasants' also came to settle in the region and to create new social and political identities (see also Dasgupta 1991). Some consequences of these demographic changes will be discussed later in this chapter.

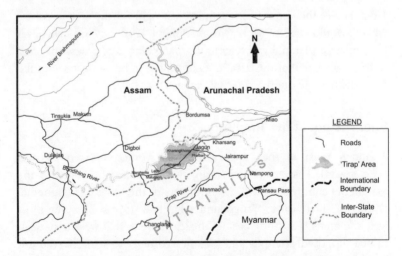

Map 2.2 Map Showing Some of the Places Named in the Text with the 'Tirap' Area Shaded

Source: Jayanta Laskar.
Note: Map not to scale and does not represent authentic international boundaries.

The existence of coal deposits in the area around Makum in Assam was already known to the British by then but since transportation was a problem nothing much happened till the middle of the nineteenth century. In 1867, oil was also discovered in the area by a group of British prospecting for coal.[3]

In the early years, tea—grown in upper Assam—was transported by big steamers down the river Brahmaputra to Calcutta, now known as Kolkata. Soon, however, the Assam Railways and Trading Company (AR&T Co.) was set up in 1881 to extend the railway beyond Dibrugarh. The Company was also given rights over coal and hence also oil prospecting in the area. An Italian engineer, Roberto Paganini stationed himself in Makum to supervise the work. The Ledo Colliery was started in 1882. In 1884, when the railway line, the bridge across the Dihing river and the Tikak coal mine were opened, it was mentioned in a company report that the company's settlement beyond Makum junction had been named Margherita in honour of the Queen of Italy.[4] And that tiny little settlement became so important for the British that during a visit in March 1900, the Viceroy Lord Curzon said, 'I find here a most interesting and enterprising corner of Her Majesty's Dominions'.[5]

The other industry apart from the flourishing tea industry was a very large wood industry producing plywood for wooden chests for the transportation of tea to Calcutta; wood was also necessary to produce berths for railways wagons. Timber was plentiful and was transported from the forests using elephants. A sawmill and plywood factory was set up in Margherita. The construction of the railway and collieries created substantial demand for bricks. By 1890, a brick kiln was set up at Ledo.

As far as the underlying objectives of the British were concerned, Rustomji remarks:

> The British interest was primarily commercial, the development of the tea industry and, later, the exploitation of oil, mineral, and forest resources. Their concern with the hill-men was strictly limited—that they should not come in the way of the acquisition of land and forest areas required for establishing tea gardens and not interfere with the functioning of such gardens when established. (1985: 23)

In those early days, work in the coal fields progressed rapidly with the use of local Naga workers who lived in the area and who were adept at cutting down trees and clearing forests, as they did that all the time for their *jhum* (swidden) cultivation.[6] But nothing would tempt the Naga to go down into the underground mines or to work in the oil wells. However, by then, the British had already learnt the trick of importing indentured labourers from other parts of India to work in their tea gardens, so they brought in men from Bengal, Bihar, and also from faraway Andhra Pradesh to work in their mines and in the oil fields.

Much earlier, the oil interests of the AR&T Co. were taken over by the Assam Oil Company (AOC) which was formed in 1899. Digboi refinery, commissioned in 1901, is the oldest refinery in India, and played an important role in making fuel available to run the Allied effort in the area during World War II. The coal mines were nationalized in the 1970s and restarted operations again in the early 1980s under the aegis of Coal India Limited (see Note 17 of Chapter 5). Many of the tea gardens in and around Digboi, Margherita, and Ledo now belong to huge conglomerates such as the Tata Group and Williamson Magor. The flourishing timber and plywood industry in the Margherita-Makum-Dumdooma area (and also elsewhere) collapsed after the ban on felling trees came in December 1996 by order of the Supreme Court (see Simai 2008: 18–19).

Margherita today is a bustling trading town of more than 25,000 people, a majority of them Bengali. Given the history of the area around Margherita, it is not difficult to explain the heterogeneity of its population and also the difference of this area in terms of having a concentration of so many industries in a small area compared to other parts of Assam where the picture is more homogeneously agricultural and rural. It is rumoured that, during some period in the early twentieth century, the undivided Dibrugarh district was supposed to have brought in the highest amount of excise revenue for any district in the country. The dilapidated 1890 brick kiln at Ledo and a rather inconspicuous signboard of a school in Margherita mentioning the AR&T Co. are the only reminders I found in the field of those old Company days.

Geographical Description and Political History of the Tirap Area

The old maps of the Tirap area tell the story of progressive migration and settlement in the area. A British map (Tandy 1927) shows vast tracts of the Lakhimpur Frontier Tract marked as Singpho areas in the north and Tikhak (Naga) and Ponthai (Naga) areas in the south (see Map 2.3).[7]

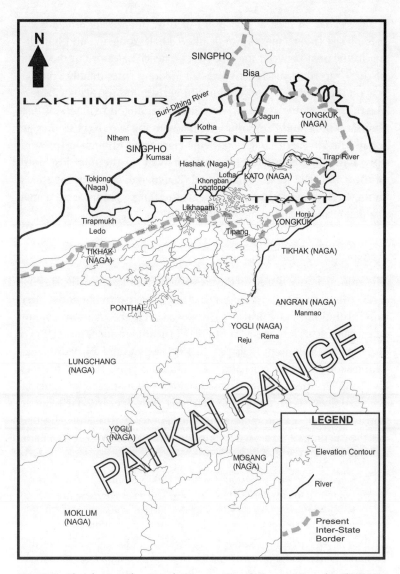

Map 2.3   Sketch Map Showing the Tangsa (Naga) Groups Named in the 1927 British Map

Source: Jayanta Laskar.
Note: Map not to scale and does not represent authentic international boundaries.

It shows that, at least at that point of time, there were Singpho and some Naga (now Tangsa) groups like Tikhak, Yongkuk, and Kato living in the area between the two rivers. The Tikhak were to the south of the Tirap river; the Naga village of Tokjong (presumably Ponthai) was on the north bank of the Buridihing river and the Naga village of Hasak (presumably Yongkuk) as well as the Singpho villages of Bisa, Kumsai, Kotha, and Pangshun were between the two rivers, as they are today. The village of Longtong (Sema Naga) and Khongban (presumably a Yongkuk clan name) are also marked on the map just north of the Tirap. The terms 'Tangsa' and 'Rangpang Naga' do not appear in the 1927 maps; in most documents the Tangsa groups were named separately and qualified by the term 'Naga'.[8]

Administrative History

The administrative history of the area is very complex. As early as 1903–4, the tribal tracts in the plains of Lakhimpur were brought under direct administration by the British.[9] The Tangsa were the main inhabitants of this area. This area was part of the Dibrugarh Frontier Tract (DFT) of the erstwhile Lakhimpur District till 1914, when the DFT became part of the Sadiya Frontier Tract and the Lakhimpur Frontier Tract. In 1943, the Tirap Frontier Tract was created (with Headquarters at Margherita) with certain areas from the Sadiya Frontier Tract mainly to facilitate the construction of a motorable road, later known as the Stillwell Road, for the opening of a passage to Burma during World War II (see Barua 2013 [1991]: 21).[10]

> The area which was carved out from the Sadiya Frontier Tract to form part of the Tirap Frontier Tract in 1943 was known as *Rangpang Area* ....
>
> From February 25, 1943, following the posting of a separate Political Officer, the Rangpang area with some parts carved out of the Lakhimpur Frontier Tract and the Excluded Area (1936) was formally constituted into a separate administrative unit to be known as Tirap Frontier Tract. (Barua 2013 [1991]: 366ff)

In 1951, some part of the Rangpang Area, which was in the plains, was transferred from the Tirap Frontier Tract to the jurisdiction of the erstwhile Lakhimpur district of Assam (Barua 2013 [1991]: 375).[11] It was named the Tirap Transferred Area. Although the reasons were not stated officially as such, the presence of the coal mines and the oil wells

in the Tirap Transferred Area was possibly the main reason for this area
to be transferred into Assam from the Tirap Frontier Tract which then
became part of the erstwhile North East Frontier Agency (NEFA) and
was subject to Inner Line Regulations. [12]

The Tirap mouza was created in 1953 with the portion taken out
from the Tirap Frontier Tract, that is, the Tirap Transferred Area (with
an area of over 100 square miles).[13] In 1976, when the Lakhimpur
District was split, with the creation of the Dibrugarh district, the Tirap
mouza became part of the Dibrugarh district, and when the Dibrugarh
district was split in 1989, it became part of the Tinsukia district. This is
the area where the Tangsa now live in Assam.

The Tirap Transferred Area was earlier part of the Abor-Mismi-
Tirap-Balipara Tribal Belts.[14] In 1951, this area was separated and
reconstituted as the Tirap Tribal Belt with a total geographical area of
about 290,400 bighas (about 96,000 acres or 150 square miles) and
62 villages.[15] Although these figures are still valid, as I show later in
this chapter, the demography of the area has changed drastically in the
period between then and the present.

Some Administrative and Terminological Details

Top-down, for administrative purposes, each of the 29 states (formerly
also called provinces) of the Indian union is divided into districts, and
the districts into subdivisions. Subdivisions, headed by Sub-Divisional
Officers (SDOs), are further divided into circles for revenue purposes
(headed by a Circle Officer) which are then again subdivided into mouzas under a *mouzadar*. Kharangkong, Phulbari, and Malugaon, about
which I say more in the following chapters, belong to the Margherita
subdivision of the Tinsukia district of Assam. Margherita subdivision has one revenue circle which is further subdivided into three
mouzas—Makum, Buri Dihing, and Tirap. Malugaon (as well as the
towns of Margherita and Ledo) belongs to the Makum mouza while
Kharangkong and Phulbari belong to the Tirap mouza. All villages in
the Tirap mouza belong to the Tirap Tribal Belt.

I have already used the term 'basti' (originally a Hindi word) to
mean settlement, village, or part of a village; for example, by the Cholim
basti in Kharangkong village I will mean that part or section of the
Kharangkong village area where most of the Cholim Tangsa people live.

Note also that besides the Cholim basti and the main Kharangkong basti, there is also a Nepali basti and an Asamiya (Ahom) basti, all of which belong to the village of Kharangkong. Village will mean an official administrative and revenue unit, often covering a much larger area than just the basti where the Tangsa live. For example, Parbatipur village (of which the Ronrang Tangsa basti of Upper Phulbari is only a very small part) extends technically all the way from 4-mile near Lekhapani to 10-mile beyond Jagun on one side of the national highway.

A (revenue) village often has a headman called 'Gaonbura' in Assam or simply GB. Gaonburas are selected and then appointed by the administration, but in the Tangsa area it is often hereditary, the current incumbents often being descendants of one of the first families who came to live in the area.[16] While Kharangkong and Parbatipur are revenue villages, in the above sense, Malugaon is not to date an officially recognized village and is referred to as an NC (non-cadastral) village. The Gaonbura of Malugaon, therefore, although he exists and performs more or less the same functions as the others, is not officially appointed and is called an honorary GB. I refer to Phulbari and Malugaon as villages (and sometimes also as bastis), even though they are not strictly officially recognized villages as defined above, and even though Phulbari actually comprises of two bastis—Upper and Lower (as described in Chapter 6). In the same sense, I refer to places like Ledo, Manmao, and Nampong as towns to make a difference between semi-urban settlements and villages (or bastis), even though they probably do not classify as towns in the strictly technical definition of the term, which is reserved for places which have a population of more than 5,000 inhabitants.

The Ethnic Mix

Some of the tribes that were living in the Tirap area by the first quarter of the twentieth century are mentioned in the quote from a British report below.[17]

> The tribes known as Nagas occupy the hills stretching south and east of the Sadiya, Lakhimpur, Sibsagar, and Nowgong districts from the Patkoi to North Cachar. In the northeast they merge into the Singphos and in the south (in the Manipur state) into Kukis …. East of the Tirap the ascendancy of the Singphos are said to be complete, but west of that their

influence in the past has probably been considerable. The Rangpang and the Tikhak Nagas, who live on the slopes of the Patkoi and west of the Hukong valley, are said to have been driven into their present area by pressure from the Kachins or Singphos. (*Report* 1921–2: 90)

As already mentioned, there were Singpho, Sema Naga, and some Naga (now Tangsa) groups living in the area between the Tirap and the Buridihing rivers by the late 1920s. A few new Tangsa, Singpho, and Sema Naga settlements came up in the area in the succeeding years, and a few Tai Phake villages (such as the one in Ninggam) were also established, mainly through the efforts of a few hardy and adventurous men in search of cultivable land.[18] Each of these groups was numerically very small, not more than a few hundred each, and lived in close proximity to one another. Henceforth I refer to these four groups—Tangsa, Singpho, Tai Phake, and Naga Sema—as the 'older' tribal groups living in the Tirap area.

As mentioned earlier, the coming and settling of people in the area from elsewhere in India had started at least by the middle of the nineteenth century when the British brought in large numbers of Adivasi people from central India to work in the tea gardens, Bengali clerks and officials to work in the railways, Nepali chowkidars or guards and also Telugu miners from as far as Andhra Pradesh to work in the newly established coal mines in the Ledo area.[19] Over the years, Marwari, Bhojpuri, and Bihari traders and businessmen have also come from the Indian 'mainland' to live in the region.[20] It is not without reason that today this area is often referred to as 'Mini India'.

In the words of one senior Assamese interlocutor from the area:

> Margherita was 'discovered' by the British because of the coal, tea, plywood, and minerals that were available in this region. Hence the local society at that time was based mainly on the British and the industrial workers who had come in from other parts of the country. Therefore, there was this immigrant (but economically and socially advanced) community in Margherita on the one hand and the tribal people who had always lived here and led relatively undisturbed (and hence relatively laid back) lives till the onset of World War II. (Dibrugarh, 26 February 2012)

There was a fresh wave of migration during World War II when many bases were set up in the Dibrugarh district at Chabua and at Lekhapani.[21] One of my older Assamese interlocutors recounted his memories of that time.

> During British times, the tribal people living in this area were protected
> and allowed to live life according to their own ways but all this collapsed
> during the World War II when many people came from abroad and from
> elsewhere to build the Stillwell Road. They camped in the Lekhapani
> cantonment and exploited, raped, and harassed the tribal women,
> who had to run further into the jungles to keep away from the soldiers.
> (Margherita, 8 January 2012)

See also Simai (2008: 10), Barua (2013 [1991]: 416–17). The onset of
World War II meant that many tribal people living in the hills were
displaced, and many highlanders, who had come down to work in the
construction sites, to build the Ledo road (see Note 10), for instance,
and as porters during the war, stayed on in the plains around Ledo and
established their own villages.[22] Some of the Sema Naga villages of the
area also came up in this manner.[23] There were many Nepali (Gurkha)
soldiers in the army who stayed back after the war in the Lekhapani
area. So there was a large Nepali population already in this area at the
time of Indian Independence.[24]

The earthquake of 1950, and the subsequent devastation of the
Sadiya-Saikhowa area, left thousands of people living in that area
homeless.[25] Five hundred and nine families were given settlement in
the Lekhapani area of which 394 were Nepali.[26] They were all settled on
both sides of the national highway 153 from 0-mile (near the bridge at
Tirap Gate) to 6-mile (at Rampur). At that time there were only forests
in the area and only about 15 tribal villages.[27] The Tikhak Gaonbura
of Tinsuti-Mullong recounted how the tribal chiefs and headmen of
that area were asked where they would prefer the victims of the Sadiya
flood to be settled (Tinsuti-Mullong, 4 January 2011). The tribal chiefs
together decided that they would move away from the main road leav-
ing the land along the highway for the refugees from Sadiya.[28]

But that was not the end of the influx. Over the years, many Asamiya-
speaking communities (mostly Ahom and Sonowal Kachari) have also
come to settle in the Tirap area, some in search of land, and others
in search of employment.[29] They now form a large group in the Tirap
mouza. Over time, many ex-tea-garden worker families have also come
into this region from elsewhere in the state.[30]

Some reserved forests in the Tirap Tribal Belt have been de-reserved
and given to new settler groups like the Misings while other areas have
been forcefully 'deforested' and occupied. In the last decade, about

600 Hajong families have come to settle in the reserved forests beyond Jagun in the direction of Namchik Gate. The forest cover has almost completely disappeared there. This is part of a more general phenomenon seen elsewhere in the state as well.

> Faced with the waves of land-hungry peasants coming in, enforcing these exclusionary rules proved extremely difficult. From time to time, governments in the colonial and postcolonial era have had to adapt to the reality of settlements in prohibited areas, and even to legalize them. Thus, forest reserves and grazing reserves have been 'de-reserved', and tribal belts and blocks have been turned into un-prohibited spaces. Over time, what were known as the grazing reserves of Assam almost disappeared, as have many forest reserves. (Baruah 2010)

Evidence of this is to be seen in many places in the Tirap area.

The population figures in Table 2.1 show that the 'older' tribal groups—Tangsa, Singpho, Tai Phake, and Naga Sema—have really become a small minority in the Tirap Tribal Belt today. Moreover, while the population of those 'older' tribal has not increased significantly, the rate of the increase of the Nepali, the Ahom, and the tea-garden communities have been phenomenal. Furthermore, many new tribal groups (like the Hajongs and the Misings) have come to settle in the area, while many of the older ones like the Khamptis and the Abor have more or less disappeared or relocated.

Table 2.1 Population Figures of the Tirap Mouza/Tirap Transferred Area

Community (Tribal)	2001 (1978)	Community (non-tribal)	2001 (1978)
Tangsa	1,299 (1,482)	Nepali	32,132 (9,304)
Singpho	1,341 (702)	Tea-tribes	10,323 (5,341)
Sema Naga	2,485 (855)	Asamiya Ahom	5,829
Tai Phake	598 (355)	Bihari	3,196 (1,399)
Sonowal Kachari	1,834	Muslim	502 (10)
Hajong	1,603	Telugu	365
Mising	820	Marowari	210 (157)
Khampti	0 (22)	Bengali	104 (576)
Total population		**62,967 (25,008)**	

Source: Circle Office, Margherita.

As is clear from the 2001 figures in Table 2.1, more than half of the population in the Tirap mouza was Nepali, while the four 'older' tribal groups added up to less than 10 per cent of the total population. For comparison, there were only eight villages in the mouza where the population had more than 50 Tangsa (see Table 3.1), and only seven such for the Singpho; the highest number of Tangsa in any one village was only 250 (at Lakla), whereas there were at least seven villages with more than 1,000 Nepali inhabitants, and the largest Nepali village (Udaipur) had a population of close to 5,000. Also, while the tribal communities were settled in only a few villages, the Nepali, the tea-tribes, and the Ahoms were to be found in almost every village in the mouza.

Coping with Diversity

As far as the complex population picture in the Tirap area is concerned, there are three main groups: the 'older' tribal groups, the Nepali, and the others (consisting of both the new settlers as well as the descendents of those who were brought in earlier by the British). The present population of the Tirap mouza could be close to 100,000 in 2011, the Nepali undoubtedly and by far the largest group in the area (more than half) and they are increasing by the day, while the total population of the four 'older' tribal groups will not add to more than 10,000.

There are increasing tensions among these different communities, also due to economic disparities (between the salaried class, the big businessmen, and the farmers) and increasing pressure on land with increasing population. The Nepali and the more recent settlers are generally more proactive and more enterprising and hence are getting richer relatively faster; the leaders of the 'older' tribal groups feel wronged as they believe this whole area originally belonged to them but they are now the weakest (in terms of population and income levels) amongst the different communities living there.

Apart from a few successful ventures by Singpho entrepreneurs (setting up ethnic cuisine restaurants and the Singpho Eco Lodge near Margherita), the situation had not changed much over the last decades for most of the 'older' tribal groups. Government efforts, so far, to improve educational and employment levels and to create awareness amongst the tribal groups about the possibilities of converting their skills into commercially viable and valued commodities, have been feeble and largely unsuccessful.[31] On the other hand, even those attempts were viewed by the non-tribal people with concern and apprehension as they felt that letting the tribals gain in importance would be to their disadvantage.

With growing encroachment, the new settlers—both tribal and non-tribal—were worried of being evicted from their lands, although the state machinery so far has been totally ineffective in stopping these settlers. Identity issues have also become increasingly important due to the growing political activism of the expanding educated middle class within the communities living in the region.

For all these reasons, recent years have seen a gradual polarization amongst the different groups living there. The four 'older' tribal groups have decided to come together and join forces mainly against the Nepali, but also against the new settler groups. Evidence of this polarization, as well as the state's response to it, are to be found both in how the Dihing-Patkai festival was organized as well as in the award of a Development Council to the 'older' tribal groups. I discuss both in the following sections.

Performing 'Unity in Diversity': The Dihing-Patkai Festival

In recent times, a three-day trans-community mega cultural event called the Dihing-Patkai Festival (hereafter referred to as the DPF) is held each January at the site of an abandoned World War II airstrip near Lekhapani. Close to the Indo-Burmese border, the airstrip is located along the historic Stillwell road and close to World War II monuments (like the War Cemeteries at Digboi and at Jairampur), thereby adding a sense of history to the area to attract tourists. Sponsored by the Assam government, this festival, like the much better known Hornbill Festival of Nagaland, aims at fostering 'communal harmony and understanding' among different indigenous groups of the region, as well as promoting tourism and commerce.[32] Culture is sought to be displayed as 'unique yet distinct' to the world beyond. However, for the many diverse communities living in the area, this festival has become a platform for publicly performing their presence in the region, which in turn enables them to advance claims on land and further dues.

Originally conceived of as a festival to showcase 'the social unity amidst ethnic diversity' of this area, to present the diverse lifestyles of the different tribes, as well as the ecological diversity and historical sites of the area, under pressure from the other communities living in the area, such as the Nepali, Telugu, Bhojpuri, and others, who also wanted to participate and display their cultural and material heritage in the festival, the festival has, over the years, assumed a pan-Tirap, if not a pan-Indian character, and the festival is not exclusively tribal anymore.

This transformation of the DPF has meant growing dissatisfaction amongst the 'older' tribal communities. Not only was the DPF no more exclusively tribal, it was also a very lucrative business proposition for mostly the non-tribals living in this area, because it was they, and not the tribals, who profited most from the whole exercise of staging the event as well as from the increased number of visitors to the area to attend the DPF. 'It is essentially a "business mela [fair]" to sell things', one tribal leader told me, 'The cultural show is just to attract people to come. But while the Burmese sellers, the Bengali contractors, and Nepali taxi-drivers make a big profit, we get nothing'. Therefore, although the DPF is seen as an attempt to connect with the discourses of tourism, development, and nation-building, many tribal leaders felt that the gains were not evenly distributed across the communities.

So the original idea of using the festival to appease the indigenous groups of the area seems to have boomeranged to some extent. Even if one were to believe that the state has the noble intention of bringing all communities together on a common platform, in order to increase understanding and dialogue between them, there is not much to show for that. In fact, if the comments made by some community leaders at the DPF 2011 are any indication then they go precisely in the other direction—'the Nepalis tried to hijack the show', 'look how the Ahoms have moved from mud houses to stilt houses', and so on.[33] Going by what one saw at the DPF in 2011, the Tirap area presents a highly fractured picture.

Dissatisfaction among the 'older' tribal groups has grown in recent years: the loudest voice of protest came from Manje La Singpho, who was the Organizing Secretary of the DPF, 2011.[34] 'The original character of the festival is gradually getting lost. The fate of the DPF is miming the fate of the Tirap Tribal Belt which is also being taken over by non-tribals,' claimed Manje La (see also his message in *Souvenir* 2011).

He believed that political considerations and population numbers had played a part in this process. Working on a policy of silencing through rewards and incentives, Manje La was made the Chairman of the Development Council which was announced soon after in March 2011 (see next section). But before that, I discuss some aspects of the DPF 2011 in a little more detail.

Some Cultural Aspects of the 2011 Festival

Cultural innovations such as the opening welcome song (sung by four girls from each of the Tai Phake, Singpho, Tangsa, Sema communities and six Assamese girls) were supposed to create new bonds of tradition and a sense of 'local common heritage' among the communities participating in the festival. Since these groups had no language in common, they sang in Asamiya. Moreover, since they had no rituals in common, a new common ritual called the 'Tipam pooja' was 'invented' for the occasion, 'invented' because although Tipam (or rather Dibam) is a place name in that area, no participating community has a deity/spirit named Tipam.[35] Interestingly, only the 'older' tribal groups and the Assamese were included in the welcome song, and the Tipam pooja was performed by a Singpho priest. Hence, perhaps, a subtle differentiation was sought to be made by the organizers among the different communities participating in the festival.

As for the format of the events, everything was reduced to the time-tested standard formula for such mega festivals everywhere in the region: Sports and official events in the mornings, traditional and 'folk dances' during the day, and the big attractions—the real crowd pullers—the fashion shows, the popular entertainers, and pop stars, who had been invited from the state and beyond to perform, in the evenings till late into the night, on a stage lit brightly with psychedelic lights and booming sound effects.

The demands of tourism and 'local sentiments' had to be taken into account while deciding the programme, I was told by the festival organizers: 'The idea is not to transform but just to transmit the reality of the region.' And if the response to the popular entertainers and pop stars dancing in Bollywood style at the event was any indication then the impact of the greater Assamese and even pan-Indian culture is a reality in that region.

'The DPF does not aim to safeguard but only to showcase and high-light indigenous cultures', the Working President of the Organizing Committee told me. But how was traditional culture 'showcased'? The rule seemed to be: 'You show us your culture, but according to our spec-ifications: so many slots per community, not more than so many danc-ers on stage at a time, and not more than so many minutes per dance item.' Everyone had to agree to be cast in that standard mould. Even the 'ethnic houses'—one house per group—set up in the Heritage Village had a look of inevitable uniformity: one long row of similar-looking, similar-sized, equally badly-constructed, mostly empty structures.

In other words, the culture of these communities was sought to be 'externalized' (Litzinger 2000: 231)—on the one hand, by presenting 'culture on stage' which means just song, dance, music, and costumes; and on the other, by presenting the 'typical' living style of a community by building 'typical' ethnic houses where 'typical' elements of every-day life of these communities (including their cuisine) were sought to be presented. But this too was at best another 'performance', another stereotyping, another labelling—'the Singphos smoke their meat, the Tangsa roast it'; the idea behind the organization of the heritage exhibi-tion to present the material culture of the participating groups was also along the same lines, hence reducing their culture to a few material objects and a set of distinguishable and highly performative practices and elements, which MacCannell (1976: 91) eloquently calls 'staged authenticity'.

Many of the costumes and accessories used in the Ethnic Costume Show, which tried to combine the ethnic and traditional with the popular and fashionable, were based on video images obtained via TV or from DVDs smuggled in from across the border from places like Nepal, Myanmar, Yunnan, and Thailand. Also evident was innovation and modification in the ways these communities presented themselves keeping pace with their counterparts in other countries.

A lot of uniformization and standardization in the cultural fare dished out by the ethnic communities was necessary in order to present it to the world: for the logistics of performing on stage are simply differ-ent—they have to look good even from a distance, and look colourful and attractive on TV; and with each community trying to outdo the other, the use of brightly coloured plastic twine around legs and arms, or the practice of sewing mirrors on shoulder bags in order to make them look more striking, have become commonplace.[36] The communities compete with one another and also learn from one another. What is more, some have even gone to the extent of deliberately 'exoticizing' their 'culture' to fit in with popular perceived notions about the tribal way of life, a kind of 'strategic essentialism' (Furniss 1998). Thus, not only are these communities smart enough to play to the gallery, they have also figured out that they can exploit the multiple avenues that exist in a 'modern' connected world to achieve those ends.

The long arm of the state was amply evident in the diverse symbols of the state—the flag hoisting, the tricoloured balloons, the brass band of the Gorkha Battalion—and in the format of the official part of the programme. The ubiquitous hand of the Assamese was evident in many subtle but unmistakable ways: The language used for moderation on stage was Asamiya, the entire festival was stage-managed by a set of Assamese government officers, journalists, and individuals; the choreographers of the welcome song and the costume show were also Assamese.[37] Furthermore, the participating communities did not seem to have much say in deciding whether the DPF would be held in a particular year or not. For instance, in 2012, when Ledo was selected to host a session of the Assam Sahitya Sabha, the biggest literary organization of the state, the DPF was reduced to just one evening's 'cultural show', that too, only as part of that Sahitya Sabha session.

What was also clear is the impact of other similar festivals on the DPF, notably the state-sponsored but much larger and much more 'exotic' Hornbill Festival in Nagaland in the artificially constructed Kisama village in the outskirts of the capital Kohima in December every year. Even at the Hornbill, the Nagas are also made to enact the same 'unity in diversity' slogan ostensibly to bring some sense of unity and cohesion amongst the very diverse Naga tribes—and to create a sense of 'Naga-ness'. At the DPF, however, since the participating communities are even more diverse (and include tribal as well as non-tribal groups) such a 'collective identity production' is not possible; but participating in it perhaps helped the Tangsa to create a sense of pan-Tangsa solidarity.

Minority Politics: The Formation of a Development Council

One tribal leader claimed that as early as in the early 1950s, seven tribal chiefs had written a memorandum to the then Political Officer at Margherita demanding that the land in the Tirap-Lekhapani area should be returned to the tribal people. Towards the end of the 1960s, tribal elders (belonging to the Singpho, Tangsa, and Tai Phake communities) from Kharangkong, Ninggam, Bisa, Hasak, and Kumsaigaon called for the formation of the 'Janajatiya Santi Parishad' (Tribal Peace Council) to mediate with the Assam Government on this issue (see Ningkhi 2009). They demanded that either the non-tribals be deported from the Tribal Belt or the Tirap Transferred Area be transferred back to Arunachal Pradesh.[38] However, nothing of the sort happened. So, on 15 December 1980, a delegation of tribal leaders met the then prime minister Indira Gandhi in Delhi and submitted a memorandum to her.[39] Her assassination soon afterwards, and the turbulences in Assam in the 1980s due to the Assam Agitation (see Baruah 2001: Ch. 6) kept matters on hold for a long time.

In 1995, the tribal groups came together again to form the Tirap Autonomous Council Demand Committee, with the hope that such a council would protect the rights of the tribals living in the Tribal Belt and prevent further influx of non-tribals.[40] Despite some setbacks, such as the alleged disappearance of one of their most prominent leaders, due to the sustained campaign of the Demand Committee, soon they were close to getting a council.[41] A meeting was called at the Patkai Festival grounds in November 2006 where the formal declaration of the council was supposed to be made by the Chief Minister. But the meeting could not take place as a large number of Nepalis laid siege on the roads.[42] The local Sub-Divisional Officer's car was burnt down by the mob. The Chief Minister had to cancel his visit and the announcement of the Council was never made.[43] The whole campaign petered out gradually.

On 1 March 2011 came the news that a Development Council had been awarded jointly to eight small ethnic communities including the Singpho, Naga Sema, Tangsa, and Tai Phake.[44] While it was seen by many as just an election sop offered by the outgoing government (since elections to the Assam Legislative Assembly were due in April 2011), most tribal leaders considered it to be a long-awaited breakthrough.[45] Aphu Tyanglam, Lemo Rara, and Gaonbura Hakhun (more about all of them later) became the Tangsa members in the Council. Manje La was nominated the Chairman and Aphu Tyanglam the Vice-Chairman of the Council.

The newly constituted Development Council was given a grant of 1 crore INR (roughly about 140,000 Euros) for the year 2011-12.[46] Compared with what they had originally demanded—an Autonomous Council with administrative and territorial powers, and what they could have possibly been given in November 2006—what they finally got, a Development Council with no administrative or territorial powers whatsoever, but with just some allocation of funds to carry out developmental work of their communities, is not very much; this is perhaps an indication that the 'older' tribal groups are slowly but surely losing the battle of control over their own area.[47] We will see more indications in this direction in the chapters that follow.

Two Crucial Developments

In this section, two separate issues, both relevant and necessary for an understanding of the communities living in the Tirap area, will be discussed. The first is the gradual process by which certain tribal groups living in the area have embraced Christianity. Since the Ahom and Nepali populations are still mostly Hindu, as more and more tribal groups convert to Christianity, religious difference has become an additional point of difference between the tribal and non-tribal communities living in the area. The second issue is the rise of militant nationalisms, which has become a disturbing feature, not just of this area, but of the entire Northeast, in the last few decades. Although there are many such groups operating in the region, I focus only on the two main insurgent groups operating in the Tirap area.

The Coming of Baptist Christianity

The first Baptist missionaries had already arrived in the neighbouring state of Nagaland in the 1870s.[48] The impact of their coming on the Naga was not much different from that on the upland communities of Southeast Asia:

> With the arrival of Christian missionaries in the hills around the turn of the century, upland people gained access to a new salvation religion. Many of them seized it. It had two great advantages: it had its own millenarian cosmology, and it was not associated with the lowland states from which they might want to maintain their distance. It was

a powerful alternate, and to some degree oppositional, to modernity. (Scott 2009: 319)

By embracing Christianity rather than Hinduism, the religion of most of the valley dwellers around them, the hill people of the Northeast wanted to assert their difference. Moreover, as mentioned by Pachuau (1997), the caste hierarchies inherent in Hinduism were not easy for the more egalitarian tribals to accept, and the fact that tribals could join the system only at the lower levels made it even less attractive to them.

However, contrary to Scott's reading, Christianity was and is not seen by my Tangsa interlocutors as being oppositional to modernity; it is rather their path to it (cf. Comaroff and Comaroff 1991). For instance, Christianity is clearly strongly associated with education, which is a big aspect of modernity, anywhere in the so-called Zomia area.

The Tangsa living in Assam and Arunachal first came into contact with Christianity at the time of World War II when British and American soldiers stationed in the area left behind small pocket Bibles for them (Ronrang 1997: 21). But at that time they were not educated enough to read them. Many new roads were also built in the remote areas of Arunachal during the war, and missionaries from Nagaland and elsewhere used those roads later to spread Christianity. The Tangsa living in Myanmar (where they are called Tangshang or Heimi/Hewe) had started to convert to Christianity from the middle of the twentieth century (Ronrang 1997: 23). As there was a lot of contact between the Tangsa living on both sides of the border, Christianity also spread through these mutual contacts.

The Ao Naga village in Tikok and the Sema Naga Baptist village in Lalpahar already existed in the 1950s.[49] A Sema Naga pastor, Yeluvi Sema, had been appointed for the Sema Baptist Christians in 1955 under the Upper Assam Sema Baptist Church Association. Initially, the Ao Naga and the Sema Naga Baptists had no plans to go to the Tangsa areas. But the Tangsa people from the neighbouring areas visited these villages at Christmas, and there were also a few Ao-Tangsa marriages; slowly the Tangsa began to convert. The process was always the same— first a few people converted when an evangelist visited their village, then a few converts got together and built a church. The Tikhak basti of New Kamlao and the Kimsing basti of Nongtham in Arunachal were among the first Tangsa villages to have churches.

Impur, near Mokukchung, was the headquarters of the Baptist Church in Nagaland. Rev. A. Temjen from the Impur Baptist Church visited Tikok and baptized some people (including three Tangsa women) there in 1965 (Ronrang 1997: 27). Yeluvi Sema baptized some Tangsa people (including two in Phulbari) in 1968, and, as the only licensed evangelist in the area, continued to do so in the following years, baptizing more than 500 Tangsa in Upper Assam and Arunachal.

The Tirap Baptist Church Council (TBCC) was formed in 1972 in New Khamlang (in Arunachal) with 21 village churches under its control (see *Souvenir* 1997). Following the centenary celebrations of the ABAM (Ao Baptist Arogo Mungdang, the central organization for the Ao Baptists in Nagaland), and in response to a request made by the TBCC, a decision was taken by the ABAM leaders to start a Tirap Mission Project (for 25 years) from 1974 to support the TBCC and to help the churches financially, spiritually, and otherwise from Impur. Tangsa pastors went for training to Impur and also to other places like Jorhat and Dimapur.[50] Kamthoi Mungrey of Phulbari described the situation accurately: it was the Sema Naga Baptists who sowed the seeds of Baptist Christianity amongst the Tangsa in Assam, while the Ao Naga Baptists built on that and took it forward.

In 1979, the TBCC was renamed the Tangsa Baptist Church Association (TBCA). In 2011, the TBCA had over 90 churches and about 10,000 members in Changlang and Assam. Thus, the Baptists are by far the largest of the Christian denominations that have a following amongst the Tangsa living in India.

Militant Nationalisms

According to a recent estimate of the Home Ministry, there are 79 insurgent groups, including splinter factions, which are active across six north-eastern states (*Assam Tribune*, 24 August 2011). Of these, five were active in Assam and three in Arunachal Pradesh. Militancy stemming from ethno-nationalistic demands has spawned in the Northeast ever since independence.[51]

The Many Factions of the NSCN

The National Socialist Council of Nagaland (NSCN) is a Naga militant underground outfit demanding sovereignty of the Naga state.[52] In 1975, the Naga leader Phizo's Naga National Council (NNC) signed the

Shillong Peace Accord with the Indian Government. Three members of the NNC, Muivah (Tangkhul Naga), Swu (Sema Naga), and Khaplang (Heimi Naga), disagreed with the Accord and broke away to form the National Socialist Council of Nagaland (NSCN) in 1980.

Since then, the NSCN has been running a parallel government of sorts in Nagaland.[53] The NSCN's Greater Nagalim demand is based on the territorial unification of all Naga-inhabited areas in Nagaland, Assam, Manipur, and Arunachal Pradesh.[54] But in 1988, the NSCN split into two factions, identified by the names of their leaders Khaplang (K) and Issac-Muivah (I-M).[55] Born in Pangsau very close to the present day Indo-Burmese border, Khaplang is a Burmese national. He is a Heimi Naga belonging to the Shangwan tribe, a Tangsa tribe in India. Hence the Tangsa are more inclined to support the NSCN (K).

Each faction has certain areas under its control where it has established bases. The NSCN (K) has links with a few Tangsa villages in Assam. They also collect taxes regularly from Tangsa villages in the Changlang district. Although there is a ceasefire in place between the Indian government and the NSCN (I-M), in recent times, there have been frequent clashes between rival factions, also in the Tangsa-inhabited areas of the Tinsukia and Changlang Districts, leading to a lot of disruption and uncertainty, with innocent villagers caught in the cross-fire.

There is certainly an established relationship between the NSCN and Baptist Christianity. Most of the NSCN cadres are Baptist Christians. With their motto, 'Nagaland for Christ', the NSCN (I-M) had been the main force behind mass-scale conversion to Baptist Christianity in the Nagalim areas.[56] There were many instances of entire villages in the Tirap District being forced to convert to Baptist Christianity 'at gunpoint' (Kumar 2005: 140).

The rather contradictory picture of the NSCN with an AK-47 gun in one hand and the Bible in the other is not the only problem many of my Tangsa interlocutors have with them. As strict Baptists, the NSCN formally oppose opium production and consumption. However, it is well known that the illegal sale of opium produced in Myanmar is one of their main sources of income.

The ULFA in Assam

Some writers believe that the ULFA, an acronym for the United Liberation Front of Assam, was formed on the advice of the NSCN (see, for instance,

Phadnis and Ganguly 2012 [1989]: 339). As Goswami observes, both the NSCN and the ULFA have common strategies of sustained armed struggle. Both outfits have training camps in Myanmar and Bangladesh. Moreover, both the rebel groups have strong connections with the Kachin Independence Organization (KIO) in Myanmar (Goswami 2011: 10).

Formed in 1979, the ULFA aims to liberate Assam from the 'Indian Colonial Rule' and to form a 'Swadhin' independent state with the help of armed insurgency (see Bhattacharyya 2014: 166ff). It was banned in 1990 by the Government of India. In the mid-1990s however, the closure of the timber business was a big blow to a large section of the people living in the Tirap–Margherita area; and, as a fall out, many young men from the Moran Muttocks communities of the Margherita Subdivision (led by the ULFA Commander-in-Chief, Paresh Barua, who hails from the area) joined the ULFA. The dense forested area around Kakopothar and Pengeri (close to Margherita) were hideouts of the militants for a long while.[57]

Basing their arguments on the idea of internal colonization of the Northeast by the Indian state and asserting the right to self-determination, the ULFA ideology had initially caught the imagination and also the support of a large section of the Assamese people. However, over time their support base has corroded due to the excessive violence that was unleashed on the population (both by the ULFA and the Indian state) and also because of several practices, including collecting funds by extortion from common people, business houses, and commercial establishments. Most of the ULFA leadership have surrendered now and are in talks with the government.

Many Tangsa elders have described to me occasions, mostly in the 1990s, when they had no option in the middle of the night but to open their doors to ULFA militants who arrived at their doorstep and asked for food and shelter for the night, at the point of a gun. Fearing for their lives, they did as they were told only to have to face the brunt of the army and police harassment and questioning the following days for having sheltered miscreants. Similar stories were also narrated by Naga village headmen with respect to the NSCN.

Postscript: Persistence of Colonial Attitudes

What the administrator Nari Rustomji claims was 'in the past' persists in the present with regard to the attitude of the plains people towards

the hills men: 'Hill people have been regarded in the past with an attitude of condescension, as simple folk with quaint and curious customs
which they will outgrow as they are progressively civilized. Much of
the discord on the borders is a reaction to this attitude of patronizing
condescension' (1985: 2). And he goes on to say that 'the failure has
been, for the most part, not so much in intention as in empathy and
sensitivity' (Rustomji 1985: 3).

This 'big brother' attitude of the Assamese towards the smaller
communities living in Assam, which some writers have termed as
'hegemonic Assamese nationalism', has caused disillusionment and
resentment amongst other groups and have led to their progressive
estrangement from Assam leading to its fragmentation (Baruah 2001).[58]
Today, even the tribals are speaking up against this. 'One of the most
responsible factors [sic] as to why the tribals have become alienated
from the mainstream of Assam is the attitude of the Assamese people.
The Assamese people have never accepted the tribals as part and parcel
of the Assamese community' (ABSU 1987).

Recent literature coming out of the region provide more evidence
of this well-meaning but subconsciously paternalizing attitude; for
instance, in the following remark about the Tangsa by the Assamese
editor of Morang (2008): 'They are the children of nature' (2008:
104). Not just in the written word, one saw this attitude also in practice. For instance, Mr Gogoi, the Assamese Headmaster of the primary
school in the Hakhun Tangsa basti of Malugaon tries, as best as he
can, to bring the Hakhun children of Malugaon in contact with the
Assamese living down in Ledo.[59] Having spent many years teaching
the Hakhun children, he has seen them from very close and also has
many Hakhun friends in the basti. Although he cares for and respects
the Hakhuns, and wishes them well, Mr Gogoi sees no other way
for the Hakhuns but to join the mainstream and become (like the)
Assamese. In their defence, it must be said that all of the Assamese
mentioned above only meant well. But although their wish to 'hold
them by the hand to show them the way' was sincere, it was paradoxi-
cally also paternalistic.

The ignorance and apathy shown by many well-to-do and educated
Assamese, who live in the towns and cities nearby, is harder to com-
prehend or condone. One day, a high-ranking Assamese officer of Oil
India from Digboi who had come with his family to spend the day at

the Singpho Eco Lodge, told Manje La, 'I thought you were a Singpho, but I'm surprised that you speak such good Asamiya'.

'Is that a contradiction?' Manje La shot back. 'I was born in Inthem, went to an Asamiya-medium school in Margherita, and went to college in Digboi. Why should my Asamiya be any worse than yours?'

The oil town of Digboi is around 10 kilometres away from Inthong where the Eco Lodge is located, yet, for that Assamese family, going to Inthong was like going to another planet.

Many of my own family and convent-educated school friends living in Guwahati also had similar ideas. Most had not heard of the Tangsa before. The word 'Tangsa' sounded strange and exotic to most: 'Are the Tangsa really Naga?' 'Do they also eat monkeys and snakes?' The better-informed among them would ask me knowledgeably. Many would beg me to tell them more about my field experiences but were ready to swoon when I described the kind of improvised toilets most Tangsa households had—'How can they live like that?' and then with even greater incredulity, 'How did you manage to live with them?' As Van Schendel rightly observes, 'Ignorance may not breed contempt, but it certainly breeds prejudice' (2005: 11).

And here it is not only the Assamese who are guilty of such misconceptions. During my time in the field, whenever I have met or visited some Nepali people also living in the area, they have never failed to be surprised, and at times, even upset, when I told them that I was staying at a Tangsa home. It was hard for them to imagine how that was possible, given how different the Tangsa food habits and everyday practices were. Then they would invariably invite me to stay with them, saying that since they were also Hindus like me, I would at least not have to worry about what I was eating and so on.

More or less the same story was repeated when I met non-tribal community leaders, government officials, or administrators in the field. When they heard what I was doing and where I was staying, they would express grave concern for my health (you need to eat and sleep properly in order to be able to do the kind of hard work you are doing), well-being (you can't be sure whom to trust), and security (the area is so dangerous), and would very solicitously offer to arrange accommodation in government guest houses and so forth for me. Some of them even went so far as to warn me about working with foreign researchers (you can't know what their hidden agendas are). They were kind, very concerned, and helpful, but I often had the unsettling feeling that we were talking in two rather different languages.

Of course, not everyone was like that. In fact, I would not have been able to sustain my work without the help and understanding of a few friends and acquaintances, with whom I could discuss problems and who were always ready to do for me what I wanted them to, even if they were not always convinced about the need of doing so. Most of them were working with other minority groups or were involved in other social causes, so many were in the same boat themselves. They were genuinely interested to learn more about the Tangsa, and unlike many others, did not feel the need to 'slot' them immediately. They also understood my sense of frustration and disappointment at the reactions of many of my own family and friends.

Nevertheless, the more I saw and read about the Assamese attitude towards the tribal 'other', the more I worried about whether my Tangsa interlocutors would accept me at all. While in the field, I tried to play down the fact that I was Assamese as much as I could. I also tried to avoid contact with other Assamese when I was in Tangsaland.[60] Moreover, I feared that they would hold the fact that I was not making an effort to learn any of their languages against me, and construe the fact that it was a foreigner (and not I) who was actually learning their language, as a sign of my Assamese arrogance. I was also afraid that once they came to know about my family background (and the fact that my mother was a politician and was once a minister in the union government) they would treat me like they treated Assamese officials—with respect and formality, but also with caution and mistrust. I did not want them to slot me before I had been given a chance. Because I felt it would be much harder to prove myself and to win their confidence if I had to carry the baggage of my background, I feared that it would be a lost case.

I knew I could not lie and that eventually they would come to know all, but I just hoped and wished that in the time it took them to find out, I would have established my own relations with them in such a manner that it would not matter anymore. The more Assamised Singpho and Nepali communities figured out my family background much faster, since they had much more contact with the Assamese world. My only hope was that my Tangsa informants would take longer.

Notes

1. A mouza (perhaps a term brought into use during the Mughal period) is the smallest revenue collection unit in the country, the revenue collectors being called mouzadars.
2. The original town of Makum was where Margherita is now, and the name Makum Junction was given to refer to the place where the trains headed off towards Makum. Now Makum Junction is called Makum.

   Approximate distances between some these towns: Dibrugarh to Tinsukia (NH 37): 50 kms; Tinsukia to Margherita, via Makum and Digboi (NH 37 and NH 38): 45 kms; Margherita to Ledo (NH 38): 10 kms; Ledo to Jagun, via Lekhapani (NH 38 and NH 153): 20 kms.
3. For another take on the economic history of this area, see Saikia (2004: 108ff). For more on the history of oil in the region, see Saikia (2011).
4. Margherita of Savoy (Margherita Maria Teresa Giovanna; 20 November 1851–4 January 1926) was the wife and Queen consort of the King of Italy, Umberto I, who reigned from 1878 to 1900. http://en.wikipedia.org/wiki/Margherita_of_Savoy (accessed 13 June 2013).
5. For this and many other delightful details of the first years of the AR&T Co., the reader is referred to Surita (1981) published during its centenary celebrations in 1981.
6. Most of these supposedly Naga people who used to live in this area must have been from some groups that are included as Tangsa now.
7. Map 2.3 is a sketch map based on the original 1927 British map showing the named Rangpang Naga groups.

   Although they are acknowledged to have arrived in the area earlier, the first mention of the Singpho in British records is around 1825, when a band of Singpho men invaded Sadiya (see Mackenzie 2012 [1884]: 62).
8. Some present-day Tangsa groups were also referred to as Trans-Patkoi Nagas in some British reports.
9. As mentioned in *Gazetteer* (1980: 39ff). The Tangsa were required to pay a tax of two rupees per house and the Singphos of Bordumsa three rupees per adult (see *Gazetteer* 1980: 41).
10. Vide Notification No. EX/15/43/108/G.E. Dated 25 February 1943. For the full notification, see Barua (2013 [1991]: 428ff, Appendix III).

    The Stillwell Road (known to the Allied Forces as the Ledo Road) extended from Ledo in upper Assam up to the Pangsau Pass in Arunachal Pradesh, and the Burma Road from the Indo-Myanmar border up to Kunming in China. Considered an engineering marvel, the road was built during World War II mainly by the Americans with the help of British, Indian, Burmese, and Chinese soldiers and labourers. Meant as a supply channel from India to China through Burma to support the Chinese troops fighting the Japanese Army, the road zigzags through the rugged mountainous region of northeastern India and the dense jungles of Burma. The full length of this route was 1,726 kilometres. Only about 60 kms of the Stillwell Road lie in India today, most of it in Assam. For more details on the Stillwell road, see Barua (2013 [1991]: 21ff.).

11. For the notification and a full description of the area, see Barua (2013 [1991]: 426–8, Appendix II, para 3).

12. As early as 3 May 1926, the then Political Officer of the Sadiya Frontier Tract, Mr T.P.M. O'Callaghan, had written a letter to the Deputy Commissioner, Lakhimpur, in which he wrote: 'In connection with the notification of the Inner Line of the Sadiya Frontier Tract consequent to the completion of the survey of this district, I have the honour to ask whether you do not consider if the time has not arrived for the revision, if not the abolition of the Lakhimpur Frontier Tract by absorption in the Lakhimpur District .... The Assam Railways and Trading Company have opened a colliery and it is for consideration whether this area should not, for administrative reasons, be absorbed in the Lakhimpur district together with the area occupied by the Nagas up to the Tirap river boundary of the Sadiya Frontier Tract' (see *Report* 1929).

    North East Frontier Agency was later renamed Arunachal Pradesh when it became a Union Territory in 1972.

13. As stated in a letter dated 25 July 1953, in which the appointment of Bisa Jokhong as the mouzadar of the newly created Tirap mouza is also mentioned. (The letter is currently with the son and current mouzadar of the Tirap Mouza, Bisanong Singpho and published in Changmai [2003: 51]). This area extended from Lekhapani right up to Jairampur.

14. The Abor/Mishmi and Tirap Tribal Belts were originally part of one belt but were separated into three different belts. Tribal Belt means that only certain notified protected classes of people can live here, besides the tribals: they are the tea-tribes, Nepali (graziers and cultivators), and Scheduled Castes (SCs). These Belts are administered under Section 161 of Chapter X (added in 1947) of the Assam Land and Revenue Regulation of 1886.

15. Vide Notification No. TAD/REV/73/50/43 dated 13.3.1951 (see *GoA* 1990: 57). One acre is roughly 3.025 *bighas*.

    The difference in area of the Tribal Belt and the Tirap mouza is explained by the fact that some parts of the Tirap Tribal Belt (for example, the area around Ketetong) do not belong to the Tirap mouza.

16. The GBs are essentially revenue functionaries and are accountable to the mouzadars at the mouza level and to the Circle Officer at the Circle level.

17. For more on these groups (see Barua 2013 [1991]).

There were also some other groups, such as the Morans, a big community living to the north of the Dihing (Gurdon 1904).

18. There are a few villages of Tai people, mainly the Tai Phake and the Tai Khamyang, scattered in the Tirap area. These Buddhist, Tai speaking, wet-rice growing, valley and plains dwelling people are what Leach (1954) defines as the Shan people of Highland Burma. The allied Tai communities in Assam are the Tai Phake, Tai Khamyang, Tai Khampti, Tai Aiton, and Tai Turung. For more on the Tai Phake, see Phukan (2005).

   For more about the Tai (Shan) communities living in Myanmar and the differences between the Thai people of Thailand, see Farrelly (2009b), according to whom 'Shan' is a Burmese term commonly applied to the Tai speaking people of northern and north-eastern Myanmar. They call themselves 'Tai', or derivatives of that word.

19. Earlier referred to as 'tea coolies' or indentured labourers, today they are officially referred to as 'tea-tribes', 'tea garden labourer community', or 'ex-tea-garden labourer community'; however, they prefer to call themselves Adivasis or (Ex) tea-tribes; For more, see J. Sharma (2012), Ananthanarayanan (2010), Behal (2014).

   The Nepali are Nepali-speaking people whose roots can be traced back to Nepal but many of whom have lived in India for several generations. Following the encouragement of migrations into both the valleys of the Brahmaputra and the Barak (Surma) by local authorities for the cultivation of waste lands, the Nepali came originally as immigrants to Assam from Siliguri (West Bengal) in about 1832. They were even financially assisted to move to Assam. They were mostly rubber collectors, buffalo dealers, dairy farmers, herders, graziers, sugarcane cultivators and jaggery producers. Many continue in those occupations even today. For more see Subba, Sinha, and Tandon (2000) and Baruah (2001: 63).

20. See Weiner (1988: Ch. 3) for details of the migrants. For another account, see Karlsson (2001: 8).

21. The operations in Assam were under the South East Asiatic Command (USA, Britain, and China) created in August 1943. For more details of the horrific impact of this war on the region, read Barua (2013 [1991]: Ch. 12).

22. For instance, the area where the town of Jairampur now is, was earlier a purely Singpho and Tikhak area known as Khatang Pani. The area was taken over during World War II operations and a base was established there which was converted later into a base camp of the 7th Assam Rifles Battalion.

23. The Sema Naga living in the Tirap area have come from the Zuhneboto district in the state of Nagaland. Today there are seven Sema Naga villages

in Assam, the oldest being Tsaliki followed by Lalpahar and Longtong, the latter close to Kharangkong.

24. So much so, that several Nepali leaders have been elected to the Assam Assembly from that area since.

25. An earthquake measuring 8.6 on the Richter scale with the epicentre located near Rima, Tibet, occurred on 15 August 1950, causing a lot of devastation, also from the massive flash floods that ensued. The earthquake was destructive in both Assam and Tibet, and thousands of people were killed (see, for instance, Kingdon-Ward 1955).

26. There were also 16 Asamiya (which later grew to 22), 62 Bihari, 28 tea community, and 3 Bengali families in that group. See Upadhyaya (2012: 173).

27. Upadhyaya (2012: 172) states that only the following villages existed in the Lekhapani-Tirap-Jagun area around 1950: Bisa, Toklong, Kumsai, Hasak, Ningam, Kharangkong, Kotha, Longtong, Lalpahar, Lekhapani Nepali village, Mullong, Tinsuiti, Phaneng, Keniya, and Jagun village.

28. This fact is seconded by Upadhyaya (2012: 172); some members present at that meeting were tribal chiefs Bisaladoi Singpho, Kothagam, and Jahabi Sema, besides Nepali leaders Sankardev Sharma and Prithviraj Chouhan, and the DC, Lakhimpur district, Sultan Ahmed.

The main reason behind this decision, according to my Tangsa consultants, was that since most of the tribal people took opium if they settled away from the main roads, there would be fewer police raids and so on. In a micro-scale, this is reminiscent of Scott's (2009) claim that the hill people retreat to the hills (read interiors) in order to evade the state.

29. Belonging to the larger Tai/Shan family, the Ahoms came into Assam over the Patkai Hills and ruled over it for several centuries till the British annexation in 1826 (see Chatterjee 1955: 10; Saikia 2004; Terwiel 1980). The Ahom buranjis or chronicles written at the Ahom court are rich historical sources (and are the earliest written records) of the region (Bhuyan 1932; Chatterjee 1955; Gait 1905; Hall 1955). The Ahom language is no longer spoken as a mother tongue, and is used only for ritual purposes. Unlike the other Tai groups in Assam, most of the Ahoms today are not Tai-speaking Buddhists but Asamiya-speaking Hindus.

The Sonowal Kacharis are a plains tribal community belonging to the large Bodo-Kachari family.

30. Many Ahom families also came to settle in Phaneng and a large number of tea-tribe families came from the Tengakhat area and settled in Parbatipur in 1957; whether they have official permission is contested.

31. Recently, another project of establishing an ethnographic museum in Margherita for the ethnic communities living in the area has been initiated

by the local MLA (Member of the [Assam] Legislative Assembly). There will
be further mention of this in the last chapter.

32. The festival was first held in the year 2002 at the initiative of the local
Congress MLA who is currently also a minister in the Assam Government.
The President of India APJ Abdul Kalam attended the DPF as the Chief
Guest in 2003.

   For more on festivals and their relationship to tourism and cultural representation, see, for example, the essays contained in Picard and Robinson
(2006). Many writers, such as Magliocco (2001) and Von Stockhausen
(2008), have alleged such mega festivals to be inauthentic and have called
them 'folkloric'. However, it is perhaps more productive to consider that
even these 'newly invented' and 'touristified' festivals remain expressions
of community participation and identity operating within different social
and spatial scopes (see Azara and Crouch 2006).

33. This is not entirely correct. For there are indications that the Ahoms traditionally did have stilt houses, but then they moved down to mud houses
with only the kitchen on a raised platform, before giving them up altogether. Our team members have visited and have photos of Ahom houses
on stilts—some even had mud floors and walls.

34. Manje La Singpho is one of the main leaders of the Singpho community in
Assam today. He and his wife run the Singpho Eco Lodge in Inthong. He
is very involved in many activities of the Singpho such as creating a new
Singpho orthography using the Roman script (see Nath 2013). He has also
composed an anthem for the Singpho to be sung at their annual festival,
the Shapawng Yawng Manau Poi.

35. There is a Tai village called Tipam in the Dibrugarh district, and some Tai
people say the word means 'place of battle'. Singphos use the term 'Dabam'
frequently in their traditional songs.

36. Some Jinghpaw bags were traditionally done this way, but not usually in
India.

37. While Assamese intervention might have been necessary to prevent the festival from getting hijacked by one or the other community, and to prevent
smaller communities from feeling ignored, it could also mean one or both
of two things: First, that that sort of trust does not exist between the communities and, second, that the local administration perhaps believed that
most of the participating communities have not reached the stage of being
able to manage the show by themselves.

38. This is a good illustration of the principle of 'negative solidarity' (Subba
1988: 169)—when a common lack or loss becomes a bond—that sometimes come into play among minority groups in the face of a common
threat. This also substantiates political scientist Sanjib Baruah's (2013: 71)

claim that 'territoriality is an idiom of resistance by "indigenous" ethnic groups against what is seen as a process of minoritization'.

39. The team members were: Haren Manje, from Mungong, Inthem, President of the Santi Parishad and Manje La Singpho's father; Aphu Tyanglam, Vice President (who we shall meet again later); Lilakanta Kiyang, Singpho leader from Kumsaigaon, General Secretary; and Khamau Larin, Singpho leader from Mungong, Inthem, and Member, Santi Parishad.

40. Their main demands, as stated in *Memorandum* (2004), included the creation of an Autonomous Council for 'the immediate political protection of the Buddhist, Christian religious and linguistic minorities and hill tribal groups like Singpho, Tangsa Nagas, Tai Phakey, Sema Naga, Man (Tai-speaking), Khampti, Hajong, Sonowal Kachari, Deori, Bodo, Maran, Motok etc. to protect the aforesaid tribal community groups from the salient encroachment of Nepali, Bangladeshi and other non-tribals in the tribal areas'.

41. The Central Bureau of Investigation inquiry into that disappearance was closed in 2010 due to insufficient evidence.

It was not clear what kind of a Council was going to be announced. The government claims that they would have been awarded a Satellite Council, while the Demand Committee leaders believed that they were going to be awarded a full-fledged Autonomous Council.

42. The Nepali version is that rumours were spread by some Right-wing Nepali leaders and some other non-tribals that the Chief Minister was coming to declare the area as a tribal belt, which meant that they would be evicted, or would have to pay tax to the tribals for their cows, or that they would have to marry tribal girls. Hence, every Nepali was asked to go out in protest to stop that from happening. Nepali leaders claimed that the situation got out of control largely because of a lack of communication—the local administration did not bother to explain what the real story was to the non-tribals beforehand. The police resorted to firing and three Nepalis were also seriously hurt.

On their part, the Nepali felt that it was unfair that land-settlement papers have not been given even to those Nepali families who have lived in the area for close to a hundred years; whenever they went to ask the local administration about it, the tribal leaders put in an objection and the matter just got stalled.

43. This kind of protest action is very common in northeast India. Baruah (2010) remarks: 'When a tribal political organization protests that a state government has failed to protect tribal lands, and demands separate statehood or greater autonomy, there is often a subtext: that territory in the hands of interlopers could be reclaimed as tribal lands under a reformed

pro-tribal political dispensation. Not surprisingly, popular movements for tribal autonomy in the Northeast, such as the Bodo movement, have often been accompanied by strong counter-mobilization by groups that fear being legally marked as interlopers in a new political dispensation.'

44. Notification Number TAD/BC/65/2010/26, dated 1 June 2011. The remaining four communities are Tai Khamiang, Tai Turung, Tai Khampti, and Tai Aiton.

45. There are 20 such Development Councils in total in Assam, all constituted after May 2010, which seems to imply a connection with the State Elections that were due in April 2011. Although the members of the Singpho-Tangsa-et al. Development Council were already sworn in in early March 2011, the swearing-in ceremony was a closed door affair and the Gazette Notification was published only in June 2011. For more on the different categories of councils and the politics of ethnic communities resulting in the award of these councils, see the essays contained in Prabhakara (2012: Section 11).

46. 1 crore is 10 million INR, where INR stands for Indian Rupees, the Indian currency, sometimes also written as Rs. One Euro is roughly equivalent to 70 INR (June 2015).

47. At present, there are 6 Autonomous Councils in Assam, one each for the Mising, Deuri, Sonowal Kachari, Thengal Kachari, Lalung (Tiwa), and Rabha Hasong communities; they were formed much earlier (see, for instance, Karlsson 2001: 32 ff).

According to a guideline issued by the Department of Welfare of Plain Tribes and Backward classes of the Government of Assam, the 'objective of setting up the Development Councils for these communities is to provide maximum peoples participation of various backward communities within the framework of the constitution of India for social, economic, educational, ethnic, and cultural advancement of the people belonging to these communities in the State of Assam' (TAD/BC/450/08, dated 7 January 2011).

48. For more details about the spread of Christianity in northeast India, see Downs (1976) and Eaton (1997). For more recent accounts of the spread of Christianity in the Angami areas of Nagaland, see Joshi (2007, 2012: Ch. 5).

49. The first Christian Fellowship was organized by the Ao Naga people in Tikok village near Malugaon on 20 October 1958. It was earlier called the Kohima basti, because at the time of World War II many Ao men had come from the Kohima area of Nagaland to work in road construction, got married to local tribal girls, and stayed on and established the basti there.

50. Most of the above is taken from an interview with Molem Ronrang, former Executive Secretary of the TBCA, on 11 January 2011. He also claimed

that missionaries did not come from Nagaland to convert the Tangsa as is commonly believed. Rather, people converted because of the contact with Christians and because of missionary and evangelist activity from within their own people, not from outside. The churches were run with the help of local evangelists. The motto of the Baptist Church is self support, self government, and self propaganda. In the beginning, around 1974–5, a pastor was paid a monthly honorarium of only Rs 30 per month, an evangelist something like Rs 300 per month from Impur. Later, after the Tirap mission came to an end, it was decided that the pastors would be paid by the local church and that only evangelists would be paid by the TBCA.

51. The *Assam Tribune* article of 24 August 2011, is titled '79 ultra groups active in NE' datelined New Delhi, 23 August 2011 and is by a Special Correspondent. While Assam has five active militant outfits including ULFA, NDFB, DHD, UPDS, and KLO, in Arunachal Pradesh, apart from the two factions of NSCN, another militant outfit, National Liberation Front of Arunachal has reared its head in the state.

    For more, refer to Baruah (2001, 2005), Hazarika (1995), Hussain (2005), Kotwal (2000), Misra (2000), Roy et al. (2007: Ch. 6). For more on armed ethnic movements in northeast India as well as to the Indian state's response to armed violence in the Northeast, see Goswami (2011), Bhaumik (2007), and Baruah 2009. For more on armed insurgencies and human rights issues in the Northeast, read Hayes (2012). For a good summary of the genesis, ideology, and impact of both the NSCN and the ULFA, see Biswas and Suklabaidya (2008). For an overview of the problems and issues related to the different ethnic groups and the militant organizations in the Northeast, see Baruah (2004), Jacob (1997), and Prabhakara (2012). For a comparative view between the insurgencies in the Northeast and Northern Myanmar, see Farrelly (2009a).

52. For a recent and comprehensive analysis of the genesis of the Naga problem, see Joshi (2013); for a pro-Naga reading, see Franke (2009). Refer to N.K. Das (2011), N. Goswami (2014), Iralu (2005) for other readings.

53. Moreover, all government departments in those areas pay 2 per cent of all developmental funds to NSCN separatists as an unofficial tax, a local MLA from Arunachal claimed (see http://scroll.in/article/719587/Arunachal-complains-that-it-was-not-even-consulted-on-AFSPA-notification, accessed 11 April 2015).

54. These include: Manipur's four hill districts of Churachandpur, Senapati, Tamenglong, and Ukhrul; Assam's Dima Hasau and Karbi Anglong Districts; and Arunachal Pradesh's Tirap and Changlang Districts (see Goswami 2011).

55. The split was caused mainly because the leaders belonged to different Naga tribes. Another split occurred in 2011 with the breakup of the NSCN (K). Kitovi Zhimoni, the Kilonser (Prime Minister) of the NSCN (K) faction, and Khole Konyak, a senior leader (co-founder) of the outfit, broke away to form a new group called NSCN (Khole and Kitovi). Khole is Konyak and Kitovi is a Sema Naga from the Mon district of Nagaland (Goswami 2012b).

    According to an informant from the Tirap district of Arunachal, there is another new front called the Arunachal Naga Federation (ANF) led by local leaders from Tirap and Changlang. This group is in alliance with the Khaplang faction, against the (I-M) group.

56. In continuation of the nation-building strategy envisioned by the NNC: 'one people [Naga], one nation [Nagalim], one religion [Christianity]'.

57. For a good overview of the debates surrounding the Assam Agitation, see the collection of papers in Ahmed (2006). For more on the ULFA see Baruah (2001: Ch. 7, 2005: Sec IV, 2009, 2012), Dutta (2009), Hazarika (1995: Sec II), Shekhawat (2007). For a recent account of the genesis of the ULFA and its present predicament, and face-to-face interviews with Paresh Barua as well as with Khaplang, see Bhattacharyya (2014).

58. Rustomji describes why that happened in his words: 'Assam, in her zeal to promote unity by prescribing Assamese as the official language for the entire state including the hill areas, succeeded in alienating and finally losing the hill areas' (1985: 152).

59. On one occasion, Gogoi and a few young Assamese college teachers from Ledo had organized for a group of school children from Malugaon to participate in an Asamiya dance-drama (for which Gogoi had written the script) as part of a cultural programme staged in Ledo.

60. On the few occasions when I did run into some Assamese while in a Tangsa basti, they would invariably slot me either as a journalist (if they saw me walking around by myself with a camera in my hand), or as an interpreter/ guide for my foreign project colleagues, if they happened to see us together.

3 Getting Acquainted with the Tangsa

'Without a history, without songs and stories, a human being is not human.'

—H.K. Morang, Nampong

'They have as much history as they require.'

—Scott (2009: 330)

As mentioned by Morey and Schöpf (under review), 'the ancestors of today's Tangsa people have been roaming the eastern part of the Patkai mountains on the India-Burma border for centuries, but in modern times some of them have moved into the lowlands on the Indian side'. Hence, apart from the Tirap area of Assam, the Tangsa in India also live in the Changlang district of Arunachal Pradesh, mainly on the western slopes of the Patkai, in the Miao, Kharsang, Nampong, Manmao, and Changlang subdivisions.[1] There are also many Tangsa (more accurately Tangshang or Heimi/Hewe Naga) in the Hkamti District, the Sagaing division of Myanmar.[2] Recently, all the Naga groups in Myanmar have been awarded a Naga Self-Administered Zone, with headquarters in the town of Lahe.[3] Although they live in two different countries and are subject to differing political systems, the Tangsa living in India still believe that culturally they belong to the same 'imagined community' as their fellow clansmen in Myanmar.

As discussed in the last chapter, the Tangsa in Assam are a tiny minority group in an area of great ethnic diversity. That diversity is matched by the great internal diversity amongst the various Tangsa groups in language and in their cultural traditions. In this chapter, I put together an account of that internal diversity; I also discuss some aspects of Tangsa life relevant to the understanding of the ethnographic chapters that follow. A section on the available literature on the Tangsa is included to help situate this work and to build on work done by others. I also give a brief overview of the linguistic classification of the different Tangsa groups; this grouping is also reflected in their cultural traditions and helps to define the Pangwa groups who are central to my work.

Survey of the Literature on the Tangsa

There is not much early literature on those Naga tribes who we call the Tangsa today. Even Edward Gait (1905), who wrote at great length about the Nagas and the Singphos, spared just a single sentence for them: 'further east, as far as the Patkai, there are various Naga tribes who are in complete subjection to the Singphos, and who seem to be quite harmless and inoffensive' (Gait 2003 [1905]: 377). Although several Tangsa tribe names are mentioned in the various tour diaries of several political officers of the area during British times, the term 'Tangsa' does not appear in them. They were referred to as the Patkoi Nagas and later also as the Rangpang Nagas. The first mention of Patkoi Nagas is found in British records in 1835.[4] Mackenzie (1884) describes the Rangpang Nagas as 'a people in no way impressive, living in unkempt hamlets', adjacent to the Singphos in Naga country.

In Political Officer O'Callaghan's 1923 tour diary, there is a mention of the 'Rangpang Mosang and Tikhak villages on the Patkoi slopes'.[5] Furthermore, he writes, 'human sacrifice was prevalent amongst the Rangpang Nagas (especially amongst the Ronrangs at Manmao)'.[6] They lived on the southern slopes and on the foothills of the Patkoi range in the basin of the Namphuk, Namchik, and the Tirap rivers, that is, south and southeast of Margherita and Ledo. At the time of Sir Harcourt Butler's slave release tours of Upper Burma in 1923–5, the Rangpang Nagas were branded as 'slave capturers' while other Nagas were declared as 'slave traders'. Both the Burmese campaign and the Pangsha anti-slavery expedition by J.P. Mills of 1936–37 (Mills 1995) mention this (see Das 2014). The fact that the Rangpangs practised human sacrifice is also mentioned in Butler's 1925 account as well as by Mitchell (1929).[7]

The word Tangsa appears for the first time in the 1952 tour diaries of Mr B.K. Borgohain, Political Officer, Tirap Frontier Tract. 'The Punyang people are Lungri by the Tangsa caste.'[8] He then talks about burial practices of the Lungris and says that 'the Lungris, like the Yogli and the Ronrung, bury their dead right under the chang [elevated platform] of their house, ... [while] the other Tangsa, viz. Mosang, Tikkhak, Moklum, Longchangs, and Ponthai burn their dead'.

Post Independence, some attempts were made by the research department of NEFA to write about the various tribes living in the region. Various articles on Tangsa language and culture appeared in the journal *Resarun* of the Department of Research, Directorate of Research, Government of Arunachal Pradesh. The efforts of Research Officer Parul Dutta (1969) resulted in the first ethnography to my knowledge on the Tangsa (or more specifically on five of the Pangwa groups). Thereafter, besides another monograph by Borah (1991), nothing more substantial than a couple of paragraphs in sundry compilations about tribes in the region appeared.[9]

The first PhD on the Tangsa was awarded from Gauhati University in 1987 to an Assamese, Chowdhury (1987), who had worked with the Mossang Tangsa in Arunachal Pradesh. To my knowledge, four PhDs and a few masters dissertations have been written so far on the Tangsa, mostly from Rajiv Gandhi University at Itanagar, Arunachal Pradesh. A few compilations have appeared in recent years, notably, an edited volume *Traditional Systems* (2005), and a monograph by Rao (2006).

There is some amount of literature in Asamiya about the Tangsa strewn in newspaper and magazine articles. A few older Tangsa (such as Kenglang Kengsang, Nong Tikhak, and others) have also written about their own people. There have been some very recent and learned attempts from within the Tangsa community to write about themselves. The best efforts in this direction are those by Morang (2008, in English translation) and Simai (2008). The latter, however, is just about the Tikhak, one of the Tangsa subtribes. Apart from these, sundry newspaper/magazine articles written in Asamiya by journalists like Rajiv Ningkhi and writers like Dibyalata Dutta, Christian literature on the Tangsa and allied groups, and a few research publications of researchers, including our team members, have also added to the pool of knowledge available.

As far as I could ascertain, although there is some literature on the Tangsa population living in Arunachal Pradesh, for instance Simai (2008) and Rao (2006), this present work is the first detailed study of the Tangsa in Assam. Moreover, it is surprising that most of these authors, as well as many authors writing about the Nagas, such as Saul (2005), almost completely ignore the Christian element, which is a big reality in the lives of most Tangsa I met in the field.

Literature on the Tangsa (Tangshang/Hewe) living in Myanmar is also scant and not easy to come by. Statezni (pers. comm. 8 September 2012) has shared with me a short write-up on the 'Tangshang Naga Migration History' as told to him by a Burmese Tangsa interlocutor, Shumaung.[10] A few accounts about the Nagas contain some mention of the Tangsa (see, for example, Saul 2005, Van Ham and Saul 2008). Also, some accounts of researchers, such as Goswami (2012a), working on the Naga independence movement and the various NSCN groups contain some mention of the Tangsa, especially since Khaplang, the leader of NSCN (K) faction, is himself a Heimi Naga from Myanmar. For a general overview of the ethnic diversity in Myanmar, see Gravers (2007).

Linguistic Classification of the Tangsa Groups

Just like the term 'Naga', the term 'Tangsa' is also a 'cluster-label' (Dasgupta 1997: 367) adopted by Indian administrators post Independence to club together about 35 different trans-Patkai 'tribes' who had come into India from Burma but were too small in numbers individually to merit a separate listing of their own.[11] The Political Officer, Mr B.K. Borgohain (Barua 2013 [1991]: x), of the Tirap Frontier Tract, claims that the word was coined by him and accepted by the tribe and government for official use during his tenure.[12] A few Tangsa elders have recounted how a meeting of the leaders of the different Naga groups living outside the Naga Hills area was called by the government in the 1950s where they were told that since 'they wore clothes and were less aggressive' they were different from the Nagas, and hence they should have a different name. They were asked to choose a name for themselves to replace Naga, and the elders agreed upon the word Tangsa which literally means 'children of the hills'.[13] One motivation for this was perhaps to keep the Tangsa separate from the Naga who had already started their struggle for sovereignty by then (see, for example, Barua 2013 [1991]: 34, Fn. 2).

According to Bhagabati (2004: 179–80), the term 'Tangsa' is only a 'formal label' since

> the traditional societal situation in the hills was never one which offered any scope for the Tangsa to act as a sort of corporate functional entity. The smaller units or the so-called sub-tribes were on the other hand, meaningful social universes, each possessing most of the characteristics of a tribe, such as cultural and linguistic homogeneity, territorial contiguity, a common pattern of social organisation though not organised as single political units under any sort of centralised leadership or chiefs.

However, I use the term 'tribe' to refer to the 'sub-tribes' as defined above; they will further be classified into different groups, such as the Pangwa. Although the Tangsa are tribal people, Tangsa is not the name of any single tribe. Today it is more of an ethnic label for the different tribes that are now included under the Tangsa umbrella.

As mentioned earlier, the word Tangsa means 'children of the hills' (or 'people of the high land'), from *tang* 'high land' and *sa* 'child' (Dutta 1969: 1). An alternative reading of the word suggests that Tangsa could mean 'people who do sacrifice', coming from *tang* meaning 'to sacrifice', because some Tangsa groups performed human sacrifice in the past.[14] It is worth noting here that when talking amongst themselves most Tangsa do not refer to themselves as Tangsa but mostly as Hawa (Hewa, Hewe, Hiwi, Heimi, Haimi), which is possibly an indigenous term for the whole group or for some part of it.[15]

The term used in Myanmar, 'Tangshang', appears to be etymologically unrelated. Statezni (unpublished) has reported that 'according to interviews with Tangshang leaders in Myanmar, in April 2003, the name *Tangshang* was inaugurated at a mass meeting in Nanyun town. The name Tangshang is derived from Tang Nyuwang and Shang Nyuwang, two siblings in the oral history. All the Tangshang are regarded to be the descendants of these two siblings'. According to interlocutors in India, however, the term 'Tangshang' applies to a wider group, including the Nocte, Tutsa, and Wancho (living in Changlang and Tirap) whereas Tangsa refers to a smaller subgroup. Yet another version goes that there are two groups amongst these tribes, the Sangwa who are democratic (who have elected and not hereditary heads) and the Tangwa who have hereditary kings.[16] Together they are now called Tangshang—an umbrella term for the Naga groups living in Nagaland, Myanmar, Manipur, Tirap, and Changlang.

Of the many Tangsa groups today, some—like the Ronrang, Tikhak, Longchang, Juglei, Muklom, Katoi, Yongkuk, and Ponthai—are found only in India while others, like the Kimsing (Chamchang), Tonglum (Cholim), Mossang, Longri, Langching (Locchang), and Hakhun, are found both in India and in Myanmar. According to Saul (2005: 28),

> In Arunachal Pradesh, other groups or sub-groups such as the Muklum, Longchang, and the Havi are loosely gathered under the umbrella title of Tangsa, a term coined in 1956 and embracing thirty-two identified sub-groups. The Tangsa are divided into two sections depending on their residence in India. The first group of settlers are known as Tangwa, while the later arrivals are known as Pangwa or Pangsa. Although it is possible that there are still villages in Myanmar that are directly related to Muklum and Havi, the Tangwa lived almost exclusively in Arunachal Pradesh and claimed a variety of different origins ranging from 'just over the border' to the Hukawng valley in Myanmar. The Pangsa people, on the other hand, have most of their villages on the Burmese side of the border, where they are known as Ha Chat, a northern branch of the Heimi.

The names of these tribes can be confusing because each of these groups is known by a number of different names. Each tribe had a name which tribe members used for themselves (*endonyms* or *autonyms*) which are usually different from the names that other groups call them by (*exonyms*). These terms are often cognate but not identical. *Ethnonyms* include both endonyms and exonyms. Furthermore, some of these tribes also had simplified names that the British gave them, often called the 'general names' which are usually different from the ethnonyms.[17] For instance, the group with the general name Tonglum has the endonym Cholim and exonyms Tyanglam, Tilim, and so forth. The Morangs call themselves Mungre (Mungrey); the Ronrangs call themselves Rera and the Langchings call themselves Locchang (and more recently, Lauxchang). I normally use the general name unless otherwise mentioned to refer to both the people and the language.

Tangsa Languages

According to Simai (2008: 1), 'in the Tangsa area, the dialect changes every five kilometres'. This is not surprising, as linguistically the Tangsa languages comprise a diverse group of linguistic varieties (see Dasgupta 1978; Morey 2012). The Tangsa languages are currently listed in the *Ethnologue* under *Naga, Tase*, which is an alternate pronunciation for Tangsa.[18] The nearest relative to Tangsa is Nocte which is also not a single language. Both of these, together with several other languages, make up the Konyak subgroup within a larger group sometimes called Sal (Burling 1982), or more frequently Bodo-Konyak-Jinghpaw (Burling 2003: 176). This in turn is a subgroup of Tibeto-Burmese.

Based on lexical differences (Barkataki-Ruscheweyh and Morey 2013, Table 4), the Tangsa languages can be broadly divided into a few clusters, as shown in Figure 3.1, where languages which are similar have been put closer to each other and have also been painted in shades of the same colour.[19]

The Tikhak group (shown on the right bottom corner of Figure 3.1) includes Longchang, Nokja, Yongkuk, and Kato, and is reasonably well-established; see Simai (2008: 25), Parker (under examination). The Pangwa cluster (shown in the middle) has many more language

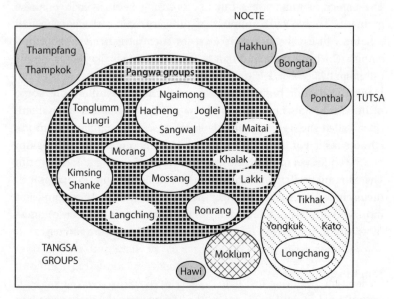

Figure 3.1   Linguistic Classification of Some Tangsa Groups

Source: Author.

groups including most of those that we met in the field, like Ronrang, Tonglum, Juglei, Kimsing, Langching, Lungri, and Mossang. The remaining groups represent a more divergent collection of languages including Ponthai, Moklum, and Hakhun. These languages are not mutually intelligible; Hakhun is very similar to Nocte, and Ponthai is close to Tutsa. There are yet others like the Thamkok and the Thamphang which are linguistically very different, where not much can be said at the moment. Morey believes that the Tangsa languages can be viewed as a 'dialect network' rather than a dialect continuum as there is no sense (so far, at least) in which there is a progression within the varieties.[20]

As Morey and Schöpf (under review) report, '[l]inguistic diversity amongst the Tangsa is so high that most language varieties are confined to less than ten villages'. Of the roughly 35 Tangsa groups within India, some of the languages vary so much that they need to use other languages to communicate not only with the outside world but also amongst themselves. Earlier, the lingua franca of the area was Singpho which is being slowly replaced by Asamiya (in Assam), Hindi, and pidgin versions of Asamiya, called Nefamese (in Arunachal) and Nagamese (in Nagaland).

Migration History and Connection with Other Groups

Colonial sources do not shed much light on the migration patterns of the trans-Patkoi groups. But it is clear that most of these groups had crossed the Patkai and come in from Myanmar at various points of time in the past. 'The Hukawng Valley is a historical route of invasion of India from the South-East and these Nagas are possibly early arrivals, pushed aside by the Ahoms and Kachin tides of movement, having been left behind by some pre-historic conquerors of Assam' (O'Callaghan 1926, see Appendix).

Another source specifically mentions the Rangpang Nagas:

East of the Tirap the ascendancy of the Singphos is said to be complete, but west of that their influence in the past has probably been considerable. The Rangpang and Tikhak Nagas, who live on the slopes of the Patkoi and west of the Hukong valley, are said to have been driven into their present area by pressure from the Kachins or Singphos. (*Report* 1921–2)

My account below is primarily based on interviews with Tangsa elders.[21] Although this method of uncritically using reported oral narratives as evidence can be accused of being based on 'methodological poverty' (Huber 2012), I still believe that information obtained from oral accounts, especially when they are corroborated by more than one informant independently, can still point to important facts about their past. Moreover, the information I have (for example, about Ronrang migration, referred to in Note 18 of Chapter 6) bears out Huber's main claim that migrations should be considered not so much as migration of entire tribes, but as micro-migrations—small numbers of individuals or smaller-sized groups moving relatively short distances (Huber 2012: 98).

Many Tangsa elders speak of a place called Masoi-Shingra (supposedly in the Myanmar/China border) as the common place where most of the tribal people in the Northeast used to once live.[22] Some then moved to the plains, while some talk about a war they had with the Siam Khamptis, after which some crossed the Tanai (Chindwin) river. Their migration stories speak of different places of origin and different routes of migration for the different tribes.[23] For example, the Mossangs believe that after crossing the Tanai river, all Mossangs stayed in a place called Sangkal (in Burma) from where they split into groups that took different routes to come into India. Some of course stayed back so that there are Mossang people still in Myanmar. Tangsa elders believed that there were essentially three *rasta* (Hindi, paths) through which the Tangsa came into India, the Pangsau road (also called *Ra-thun-pan-sa rasta*, before the pass was built), the road via Ranghill to Manmao called the Ranglom (or *Nyap-ket*) rasta, and the third was into Changlang with the Mukloms called the Lunglam (or *Walakto*) rasta.[24] The route of migration is an old one; however, migration from Myanmar into India still continues till the present day.

In any case, it is clear that the Tangsa have lived and moved about in the Patkai hills on what is now the India–Myanmar border for a very long time. But in the last several hundred years there has been a progressive movement of the Tangsa first into the Indian side of the present-day international border in Arunachal Pradesh and then further down to the plains areas of Assam, mainly in search of cultivable land. Different groups have moved at different times. The Tikhak, Yongkuk, Longchang, and Muklom appear to have arrived several centuries ago (see Simai 2008: 24ff for more details) while the Juglei and Mossang also have been in India since at least 1900 and probably before. Others like the Cholim and the Ronrang have arrived in the first half of the twentieth century, and the Hakhun even more recently.[25] Although not many Moklum live in Assam at present, some Muklom claim that they had lived in the plain areas around Margherita and beyond for a long time, and have receded back to the plain areas of Kharsang in Arunachal Pradesh in the last century due to various reasons such as illness and increased population pressure.

Connection with the Naga

Much is known and has been written about the different Naga tribes living in Nagaland and in Myanmar, for example, Hutton (1921), Von Fürer-Haimendorf (1939), and more recently, Saul (2005), Van Ham and Saul (2008), Oppitz et al. (2008), Von Stockhausen (2014), and many more. The Tangsa have traditionally and still today been clubbed officially under the 'Other Naga Tribes' category. Interestingly, however, in Nagaland, even among Naga elders and the educated elite, not many were aware of the existence of the Tangsa, leave alone know that they were related to the Naga. In Assam and Arunachal Pradesh, while some Tangsa were happy to acknowledge the Naga connection, others denied it vehemently.[26] This interesting situation illustrates how exonyms such as the term 'Naga' are differentially accepted or recognized by different group members and how relative and context dependent such constructions can be.

I was advised by my field interlocutors not to bring up this topic while talking to strangers. But it was not until I had asked this question many times to many different people that some patterns began to emerge. Those Tangsa who did not want to be associated with the negative connotations of being 'Naga' like their being aggressive, or primitive, or their desire to secede from the Indian union, were wary of admitting the Naga connection, and this was the case with most of the well-to-do Tangsa as well as with the Buddhist Tangsa like the Tikhak. Others, especially those who wanted to project their common (Baptist) Christian religious identity, as well as those who wished to claim a common heritage with some Naga groups, were happy to hold on to this link.

As my Tangsa-father, Aphu Tyanglam, explained so evocatively, 'the Tangsa and the other Naga tribes are like the five fingers in one hand, each a little different from the others, but all bound together'. Given the similarities in cultural symbols and in some of the traditional prac- tices as well as in their migration history, it is plausible that the Tangsa tribes are related in different and various ways to some Naga tribes. The Tangsa claim that they were the first to start wearing a *lungi* (Assamese/ Hindi, ankle-length cotton wrapper) instead of the *lengti* (Assamese, short loin cloth) and were supposed to be more docile and less aggres-sive than their Tangwa cousins in the hills.[27] In any case, all these tribes had probably lived in close proximity to each other in the Patkai hills and were even possibly hunting the same wild boars and hornbills, the teeth and feathers of which adorn both the Naga as well as Tangsa hats respectively (cf. Waddell 1901).

Most of the tribes belonging to the Pangwa subgroup of the Tangsa did not have hereditary leaders but had rich and powerful village chiefs (called Lowang/Lungwang in Mossang).[28] Barua (2013 [1991]: 308) goes one step further by arguing that it was perhaps precisely because the Pangwa groups saw the dangers and problems of having hereditary kings (as their neighbouring communities, such as the Noctes and Wanchos, did) that they decided to have a different system. This view supports Leach's (1954) thesis that societies oscillate between auto-cratic hereditary systems at one end and democratic republican systems on the other. The villagers turned to their Lungwangs (Lowang) in times of need; and the richest amongst the Lungwangs would also perform human sacrifices (or at least buffalo sacrifices) every few years. For more on the traditional village council, not much of which is evident today in the Tangsa villages in Assam, refer to Dutta (1969), Elwin (1965: Ch. 17), and Borgohain (1992).

I also saw no evidence among the Pangwa groups of the famous male (and female) dormitories (*deka-chang*s or *morung*s in Assamese) of the Naga tribes, which were believed to also exist amongst the Tangsa.[29] A few of the older Tangsa men did remember seeing or even living in such dormitories in their youth, and spoke about the role these dor-mitories played in courting and choosing their life-partners.[30] Only one interlocutor told me about the martial aspects normally associated with the men's dormitories.[31] These dormitories were called 'Papung' for young men and 'Likpah' for young girls in Cholim. But they used to exist a long time ago—my interlocutor had not seen a Papung, nor had his father, but he had seen Likpahs.[32] The Hakhuns, however, seem to have had them till more recently, reinforcing the argument that they are actually culturally more akin to the Nocte and the Naga than to the Pangwa groups; more on this in Chapter 5.

Relation to the Singpho

Many Tangsa elders (in the Kharangkong area) spoke of how Singpho village chiefs had first given them land and allowed them to settle there.[33] This shows that the Singpho had arrived in the plains much earlier than some of the Pangwa Tangsa groups at least. It is believed however that some other Tangsa tribes had come into the Tirap area before the arrival of the Singphos as some of them are said to have been conquered and subjugated by the Singphos (*Gazetteer* 1980: 34). The Tikhak Tangsa had probably come at the same time as the Singpho, and had developed and maintained close links with them over the centuries. It is not surprising then that most Tikhak living in the plains in Assam are Buddhist today, as are the Singpho.[34]

Relations between the Tangsa and Singpho were not always so cordial. As mentioned in the *Gazetteer* (1980), British records of 1836 allude to the fact that although the Tangsa of Namchik tried to maintain friendly relations with both the Dapha Gum and the Bisa Gum, the two Singpho chiefs, they were in need of protection. Consequently, they were given arms to defend themselves against the Singphos. However, Bhagabati (2004: 179) alludes to the fact that in pre-British times different sections of the Tangsa appear to have been under the strong influence of the Singpho since they adopted the Singpho language as a sort of lingua franca for inter-tribal communication.[35] But this influence did not last. According to Bhagabati (2004: 179), 'the weakening of Singpho influence, as well as loss of social contacts with trans-Patkoi tribes are both developments of the post-Independence period'.[36]

Today in Assam there is not much difference in terms of wealth and political influence, and in their economic situations, between the Singpho, the Tangsa, or their other 'tribal' neighbours like the Tai Phake or the Naga Sema. So much so that these older tribal groups (who are in this sense 'equal in weakness') have come together to put up a united front against their Nepali and Assamese neighbours and to demand political recognition from the state, as already discussed in the last chapter.

Hills versus Plains People

Just like the Naga (see Ao 2006: 6), with whom the Tangsa claim common descent, the remembered 'history' of the Tangsa is entangled with their myths of origin and their lores of ancestry, struggle, and conquest. For the Tangsa, the Singpho have lived in the valleys of rivers, while they have lived in the hills.[37] But as already mentioned, both these communities claim to have originated from the same place (see Morang 2008; Singpho 2000: 27). The hills–plains binary, applied more generally, implied the tribal–non-tribal binary. Even though the Tangsa have moved down from the hills for pragmatic reasons, their emotional and cultural homeland was still somewhere up in the hills of the Patkai range. Everything was better up there—less corrupted, more wholesome, and more pure. Moreover, the plains are associated with disease, and with cunning and deceit. In other words, the hills–plains binary could by extension also imply the good–bad or the innocent–corrupt binary.

The Tangsa have distinct terms for hill people, *ku-mih-se* (Cholim, hill-people-son), and for plains people, *kyom-mih-se* (Cholim, plains-people-son). In song language, the Pangwa call the people from the plains, Shamsa. This hills–plains binary shows up in various contexts such as in Wihu songs.[38] Another instance is the story below that was narrated to me by different people at different times.

> The story goes that once the Tangsa and the Shamsa brothers landed near the river. The elder Shamsa brother built rafts out of banana leaves and went down the river. The younger Tangsa brother called out to him but he could not hear as the voice was drowned in the noise of the water. But the younger one kept hearing what the elder one said—that is why even today the hills people understand the languages of the plains people but the other way around does not work.

Similar stories elucidate how the different Naga and Singpho tribes lived together as brothers till they got separated, the Singpho using the rivers to go down to the plains while the Naga went back up to the hills (see Morang 2008: 25).[39] The template of different brothers constituting the origin of different communities is well known (cf. Wellens

2012). Interesting, however, is the fact that in the narration of these tales of two brothers, the good (or elder) brother is invariably from the community to which the speaker belongs. This bears out the truth of Leach's claim: 'Every traditional tale will occur in several different versions, each tending to uphold the claims of a different vested interest' (Leach 1954: 266).

The somewhat unequivocal relation that some Pangwa groups share with the plains people can be best illustrated through the story that many Tangsa elders told me (at different times and places) to explain how the practice of doing human sacrifice became prevalent among the Pangwa groups. An extract from my field notes reads as follows:

> The motif of the two brothers mentioned earlier continues with the Tangsa brother living in the hills and the Shamsa one living in the plains. The mother lived with the Tangsa son and this made the younger son jealous. The younger one had already started doing wet rice cultivation. One day the elder brother went to ask the younger one to give him some rice grains to plant. The younger one gave him some paddy grains but cooked them before giving so that they did not germinate. The next year the elder brother came to ask again. The younger brother again gave him some rice grains but advised the elder to kill his mother and mix the paddy grain with her blood before sowing. That is how human sacrifice came into Tangsa society.[40]

And that is how, they believe, they first began to sacrifice humans; that is also why they do animal sacrifice even today for greater prosperity.

The Pangwa Group

About 20 of the Tangsa groups in India are clubbed together as the Pangwa (or Pangsa or Pawe), a term based on the word *pang* meaning 'spread all over'. This group was also called Rangpang by the British administration.[41] Amongst the Tangsa, only the Pangwa groups are believed to have performed human sacrifice in earlier times, although head-hunting was prevalent also among the Tangwa groups such as the Hakhuns.[42] As far as can be ascertained, cannibalism was not practised by any group. The British stopped these practices amongst the Tangsa by imposing heavy punishments.[43]

The Pangwa groups are mainly those tribes that are still to be found both in Myanmar and India and have crossed into India in the last hundred years or less (except the Juglei who have been in India for a longer time). There are around 28 Pangwa groups, some are mostly in India, and some mostly in Myanmar (see Morey 2012). According to another writer, herself a Mossang Pangwa,

> The Tangsa were those who had migrated from Myanmar to India long ago, including the sub-tribes of Lungchang, Muklom, Tikhak, Have, and Ponthai (Haqkhun). The Pangsa, in contrast, are those who were pang 'left behind' in Myanmar, which includes the sub-tribes of Moshang, Morang, Kimsing, Rongrang, Yogli, Longri, Shanke, and Longphi, in addition to the sub-tribes living exclusively in Myanmar. Thus, even though in some cases apparently all the members of certain sub-tribes (such as the Kimsing, Rongrang, Yogli, Longri and Longphi) have now moved to the India side, they are still considered Pangsa. (Mossang 1983 cited in Bhagabati 2004: 181)

Since two of the three villages where most of my fieldwork in Assam was based are majority Pangwa, most of the information in this work will relate to the Pangwa. However, I will continue to use the general term Tangsa both in the title and as a general label for the various groups because (a) my interlocutors were not all Pangwa, (b) because I agree with Bhagabati (2004: 181) that the 'distinction between the Tangsa and the Pangsa is considerably blurred today', and (c) because recent political developments in Assam, like the award of a Development Council to eight ethnic communities including the Tangsa, have further established the term Tangsa in the official vocabulary.

Today, most Pangwa groups have embraced Christianity. The Pangwa languages are more or less mutually intelligible though there are a few like the Ronrang and the Langching that most other Pangwa groups find hard to understand. However, they share a common heritage of the Wihu song and also the Sahpolo dance, and most elders claim that the song language of their traditional songs including the Wihu are the same or at least much closer to each other than the spoken language of today (see Barkataki-Ruscheweyh and Morey 2013). Culturally too, this grouping makes sense. For example, traditionally the Tikhak, Moklum, and Longchang would burn their dead while most of the Pangwa tribes would bury them.[44] Of course, there are differences within the Pangwa group as well. For example, unlike most of the other Pangwa groups, the Ronrangs do not have the practice of paying bride price at the time of marriage. However, both the Ronrangs as well as the non-Pangwa

Hakhuns claim to have a war dance, while the other Pangwa groups do not have it.

Many Pangwa elders gave me their reasons why their languages were distinct although their cultural traits were similar: Since they were headhunters in olden times, as headhunters they did not want their enemies (who were often their neighbours) to understand what they were saying, so their languages became very different, especially the languages of those communities who lived close to one another and were often at war with each other. This is in line with Jacquesson's (2008: 307) hypothesis in which he claims that amongst the Naga groups, relatively high population density has implied a high rate of change and differentiation in their languages.

Tangsa (Pangwa) Festivals

Many of our older informants told us that rich and powerful Tangsa chieftains (*Lowangs*) performed a kind of 'feast of merit' called the 'Wangjang-kuh' every few years, usually during the winter months, in order to demonstrate their wealth, to reaffirm their position within their community, and to seek blessings for more wealth and prosperity in the future. The date for the festival was not fixed and would depend on when the harvesting work would actually end. It involved doing ritual sacrifice of a large number of buffaloes (as is evident in Photograph 3.1), hence it was also called *nga/noi-tang* (nga/noi meaning buffalo, hence 'great buffalo sacrifice'), and in some Tangsa groups, also of slaves bought for the purpose, accompanied by feasting, singing, and merry-making lasting many days.[45] Other informants claim that after human sacrifice was abolished by the British, rich village chieftains started performing buffalo sacrifices instead.[46]

Being primarily rice-cultivators, the traditional festivals of the Tangsa were based on the agricultural cycle. Festivals accompanied each stage of activity—burning and clearing the forests, sowing the seeds, weeding, harvesting, storing, and so forth.[47] But the fact that many Tangsa have shifted to wet-rice cultivation and indeed to other occupations, as well as the fact that many have converted to other faiths, means that most of these festivals are not celebrated any more. Traditional festivals also had to do with the fact that they were hunters, but there were no large forests left in the plains where they could go hunting. Shortage of time, difficulty

Photograph 3.1 The Arrangement of Buffalo Skulls from *Nga-tangs*

Source: Author.

in finding the ingredients (as well as the priests) needed, as well as the high costs of holding these events are some more reasons cited by my Tangsa interlocutors for not celebrating their traditional festivals.

Consequently, the knowledge of songs and dances as well as of the rituals associated with these festivals have also declined—the orality of the Tangsa languages only aggravating the process. Fortunately, there are still many Tangsa elders, in bastis such as Kharangkong, who know how to do the rituals needed for the Wihu-kuh (Kouk) festival. The number of elders who can sing the Wihu song with some degree of competence, however, is smaller.

As I discuss at much greater length in later chapters, a growing awareness, also amongst the Christian Tangsa, about preservation of their traditional culture in their efforts to construct and project their ethnic identity has led to a sort of agreement to celebrate two festivals annually, the Moul (Mol/Moh/Moe) festival in the rainy summer season and the Kouk (Kuk/Kuh) festival in the dry winter season. However, since most of the Christians already celebrate Christmas and New Year in the winter, the Moul festival has become the official festival of the Tangsa in Arunachal Pradesh (it appears in the official calendar of festivals in Arunachal Pradesh and the date for the official celebration is 25 April, although village level celebrations are normally held later). As will be mentioned in the next chapter, the Tangsa in Kharangkong celebrate the Wihu/Shawi-kuh/Kouk on 5 January as their main festival.[48]

While the winter Kouk festival is mainly seen as a sort of thanksgiving, after the harvesting has been completed, with a lot of feasting and merry-making, the summer Moh/Moul/Meh festival is celebrated after the sowing and weeding has been completed, to pray for a good crop and also for better luck with hunting (by ritually honouring the skulls of animals hunted in the past).[49] Animals were not required to be sacrificed at Moul while animals (at least a chicken) were ritually sacrificed in every household for Kouk. The Wihu/Wihau song of the Pangwa Tangsa was sung only during the winter festival, while the Sahpolo dance (as seen in Photograph 4.3), which has assumed a pan-Tangsa character, used to be performed only during the summer Moul festival.

Photograph 3.2   A Tangsa *Chang-ghar*

Source: Jürgen Schöpf.

Life in the Plains

According to the 2001 Census, there are 40,086 Tangsa in total in India.[50] Table 3.1 gives the figures for the eight villages in the Tirap Mouza which has a Tangsa population of more than 50 persons in 2001. Note that there is only one village (Wara NC) in Assam which is purely Tangsa. In all the others, the Tangsa are in a small minority. Henceforth, by a Tangsa village I will mean a village where a significant number of Tangsa live, irrespective of their relative strength in relation to other groups living in the same village.

Not surprisingly, one Tangsa elder in Arunachal described the Tangsa living in Assam as a 'khichri samaj' (Assamese, a mixed/impure society), not only because many Tangsa groups lived together in the same village but also because they lived together with many other non-Tangsa groups as well, such as the Nepali, the Assamese, and the tea-tribes. Of the eight villages mentioned in Table 3.1, I take a closer look at Kharangkong and Parbatipur (Phulbari) in Chapters 4 and 6, respectively.

Some of the Changes

For many Tangsa groups, the move down to the plains from the hills have implied many changes to their lifestyles. The traditional Tangsa

Table 3.1 Population Breakup of the Tangsa Villages in Assam

Name of Village	Population	Tangsa	Nepali	Tea-tribes	Ahom
Lakla Pothar NC	1,352	250	957	25	30
Wara NC	221	221			
Parbatipur	4,280	200	3,345	250	250
Kharangkong	519	148	65	12	256
Kamba	734	142	275	310	3
Mullong	529	107	173	213	
2 Toklong Gaon	510	95	180	90	103
2 Ninggam Gaon	338	53	239	12	12
Total Population in the Tirap Mouza (2001)	62,967	1,299	32,132	10,323	5,829

Source: Circle Office, Margherita.

chang-ghars were easy to build when the village moved to a new location (see Photograph 3.2). Unlike the temporary nature of their settlements in the past, most Tangsa villages now are fixed and more and more Tangsa live in concrete Assam-type houses. The gradual disappearance of forests from their vicinity also means that the Tangsa have had to give up hunting and have begun to depend on markets to provide for their needs.

In terms of religion, almost all Tangsa were still practising their traditional beliefs when they first moved into present-day India.[51] Those Tangsa groups who came into India a long time ago (like the Katoi) have been Hinduized and have got assimilated into the Assamese population; those, such as the Tikhak (see Simai 2008: 70) who came about a couple of centuries ago along with the Singpho and the Tai Phake are mostly Theravada Buddhists today. There are Buddhist temples in many Tikhak and Yongkuk villages. A strong wave of missionary activity in the early 1970s resulted in many Tangsa, mostly amongst the Pangwa groups, converting to Christianity. Besides the Buddhists and the Christians, in Assam there are also a few households left in Kharangkong where the older traditions are still practised (see Chapter 4). There is much more to be said in terms of religious diversity with regard to the Tangsa living in Arunachal Pradesh. I postpone that discussion till Chapter 7.

Linguistic diversity amongst the Tangsa has already been discussed. But, since the Tangsa languages are oral, most Tangsa learn to read and write in Asamiya, Hindi, or English. The Tangsa living in Assam are forced to adopt Asamiya as their first language when they study in government schools, while those going to private schools or those studying in Arunachal Pradesh can choose to study in English or in Hindi.[52] As a result of that, and also because of the ethnic mix in the villages in which the Tangsa live today, many of the younger Tangsa are gradually giving up speaking their own languages even at home.

Despite the diversity in the languages they speak, what unites at least many of the Pangwa groups is their culture—their songs and dances, their 'ritual acts' (Leach 1954: 279), and their traditions such as their life cycle rituals, their festivals, their practices of healing disease, performing augury and divination, and so forth. But most of these older cultural practices were associated with their traditional beliefs, and with the fact that they were originally hunters and rice-cultivators. But there are not many Tangsa left who still practise their traditional religion; neither are there many who do shifting cultivation these days. Furthermore, conversion to Christianity (especially into the more strict denominations like Baptist Christianity) has implied that my Tangsa interlocutors have had to give up many of their older cultural practices (such as making offerings to spirits) which were considered to be associated with spirit worship. As already discussed, even the few festivals that are still celebrated, like the Wihu-kuh festival in Assam and the Mol festival in Arunachal Pradesh, have undergone drastic change in their relevance, significance, and cultural content, as will be investigated in detail in the following chapters.

Impact of 'Modernity'

Infrastructural development has come very late to the remote areas of northeast India compared to the rest of the country, but it is slowly beginning to happen. Recent governmental efforts in that direction, mainly in the form of better roads and a better communication network, have made remote areas more accessible. Most Tangsa villages today have access to electricity; others also have some facilities for basic childcare and health care. Moreover, improvements in transport facilities and greater governmental presence and support have enabled the Tangsa to participate more actively as citizens of a democratic state. Many of the Tangsa leaders are actively involved in party politics, and many others try to make the best of state welfare schemes and soft loans meant for members of 'backward' tribal communities.

With better access to and facilities for education, many more Tangsa are getting educated. The school- and college-educated Tangsa have better prospects for finding gainful employment; there are at least a few Tangsa with regular office jobs. This has meant moving away from the traditional occupations. Even those who have remained agriculturalists have stopped doing swidden cultivation and have taken to wet-rice cultivation in the plains and also increasingly to tea cultivation.

The mobile-phone revolution in India and the move down the hills have brought my Tangsa interlocutors in increased contact with other mainstream Indian communities. Increased exposure to the pan-Indian and 'Western' culture through cinema and television has meant that the younger generation of Tangsa are slowly opting for the new ways over their own traditional lifestyles. In the words of a native Tikhak Tangsa, 'the lifestyle of the Tikhaks has changed drastically' (Simai 2008: 128). He goes on to say that modern gadgets have replaced the old systems of counting, sending messages, weights and measures, and the calendar, and that greasy food has replaced boiled food.

Thus, according to some Tangsa, the changes have not been all for the better. Ongtang Thamphang, a Tangsa, has this to say about his own people:

> The Tangsa are gradually discarding the old beliefs calling them just superstition. Educated youth have forgotten their culture; they pollute their society by speaking in other languages. The changes is so sudden and fast that they get very little time for adjustment from traditional way of living to modern life. So modernization has brought mixed effect [sic] for this tribe. (Thamphang 1999: 21)

There is a perception among some community members that all change is bad; furthermore, they are not always ready to accept the fact that change—good or bad—is inevitable.

Conversion to Christianity

For my Tangsa interlocutors as well as for the other hill communities in northeast India, there is a strong link between thinking of oneself as 'modern' and being Christian. This is possibly because most Tangsa link Christianity with the English language and with the West, both of which are thought to be 'modern'. Hence, modifying slightly the title of a book by Van der Veer (1996), conversion to Christianity is seen by many Tangsa as 'conversion to modernity'.

Reasons for Conversion[53]

For many Pangwa, the decision to move down the hills in search of land suitable for wet-rice cultivation more or less coincided with their decision to convert to the Christian faith. The expenses that had to be incurred in performing the various rituals and sacrifices in order to keep the spirits in good humour were becoming a big strain on the finances of many Tangsa households.[54] Moreover, *shammas* (healers) and *dum-sas* (Singpho, priests) who knew their jobs were becoming impossible to find. Many plants and roots they needed for their traditional healing and rituals were simply not to be found in the plains; hunting animals was also not possible. Many told me that there was no choice for them but to convert after coming down to the plains.[55]

In fact, it was 'less risky' to become Christian, as the traditional rituals required strict observance of rules; many feared that if there were not performed correctly, then instead of healing they could even aggravate the problem. And with access to modern medicine and health care, most of it had also come to be seen as unnecessary. Although individuals might have different reasons for converting, usually villages or families converted en masse as these units tended to remain together. A Tangsa elder said that when most people of a village converted, single individuals did not feel 'secure'(whatever that might mean) to remain outside even if they were not entirely certain they wanted to convert. In any case, this is also a clear sign of shared group identity, as Bal (2007a: Ch. 7) points out with regard to the Garos.[56]

They also believed that in the plains they would be prone to attacks by many new unknown 'spirits'—a belief which sounds plausible considering that it is warmer in the plains and that many new illnesses like malaria and typhoid are prevalent there, and they had already caused many hill people to suffer and die or return to the hills.[57]

Another hypothesis offered was that the complete ban on human sacrifice imposed by the British had caused an imbalance amongst the Pangwa groups in the exercise of their older religious practices, leading to many falling seriously ill because they had angered the spirits, and there was no way for them to correct this imbalance except for quitting the system altogether.[58] In other words, people convert because the previous relationships have become bankrupt. Converting to a completely different faith was seen as one way of regaining control over their lives. Endorsing this view, another Ngaimong interlocutor further claimed that since the other non-Pangwa groups like the Tikhak, Moklum, and Longchang never practised human sacrifice, such acute imbalances were not created in their worlds by the ban and hence they did not feel the same pressure to convert to Christianity (Mullong, 16 February 2012).

Moreover, the increased presence of Baptist missionaries at their doorstep who had come to spread the word of the Lord and also to show them the positive attributes associated with a Christian way of life—a tidy and clean home, with better access to education, health facilities, and better prospects for employment—helped to gradually convince the people. In the words of one of my staunchly Baptist

Christian interlocutors, 'wars, opium and rice-beer drinking were exchanged for peace, brotherhood and strict abstinence from all intoxicants. Old animosities and rivalries were buried, the converts joined their new faith with a sense of respect and fraternity for the others'. Some more reasons were cited by Mr Molem Ronrang, former Executive Secretary, TBCA:

> When there was illness, they had to do expensive poojas [rituals] or had to fear the worst—so they converted. When lightning hit a house or a paddy field, the old religion required the people to abandon the house and the paddy of the whole field. When they became Christian they did prayers and then could use the house and the paddy of the field (except for a small portion where the lightning actually struck) again. Miracles and healing were some of the other reasons for people to be attracted to Christianity. Under traditional belief there were curses but these could be warded off by Christian prayer.[59] Christians take recourse to prayer when in distress; and they stand by one another in times of need because all the Christians feel they are part of one big family. If one member is hurt, all the others suffer with him.

The reasons cited for conversion differed, however, depending on whether one asked a Christian Tangsa or one who had not converted. For the non-Christians, the new converts got monetary incentives at the time of conversion as well as other gifts like piglets to rear, tea-saplings to plant, mosquito nets, medicine, and so forth. Also, facilities for education and health care are better for Christians, as they have their own schools and hospitals. For the non-Christians, economic grounds were the main reason for conversion (see also Joram 2001). While denying payments of money to converts, one Presbyterian preacher admitted that the main reason for conversion is economic; however, he denied that new converts were given money in cash.

Healing through prayer was also a very strong reason for conversion. Many told me that they had converted almost on their deathbed when the traditional methods of healing did not work but the prayers done by the Pastor and the grace of God did. Others simply could not afford the expenses involved in doing sacrifices when someone was ill, or when a new house was built. Now, after conversion, there was peace and less illness; their expenses had also gone down because as Christians, they needed to offer tea or just a prayer.[60] Some reasons were quite dramatic: one Tangsa interlocutor had converted, against the wishes of the elders in his own family, because his family was being harassed by an Assamese 'witch' neighbour.

But there were some curious twists to the tale. Some Tangsa Baptist interlocutors felt they had actually never converted. In fact, the stories of the deluge in the Old Testament was enough proof for many converted Tangsa to believe that their older practices, in which there are also stories of flood and destruction, were similar to those described in the Old Testament.[61] Another Mossang Tangsa interlocutor told me that since the Tangsa never had an image of God, their traditional belief system was similar to that of the Old Testament where they spoke only of a creator without an image. Hence, they had always been Christian, but had only not recognized it or known about the Lord till they came 'into the light'. Now after having recognized Christ they have begun to follow the New Testament.[62]

Some of those who had not converted had their own reasons for not converting: 'The church is like a schoolroom—everyone is forced to follow the rules, do as they are told', one Buddhist Tangsa woman said. Moreover, because it is forbidden to brew rice-beer in Baptist homes, the men went out and got drunk on cheap adulterated alcohol and fell sick. In that way, more money was wasted and their health was also damaged, she felt.

Impact of Christianity

Most of the Tangsa Christians in Assam are Baptists today. Baptist missionaries were the first they came in contact with in Assam, but over time some groups have also joined the Presbyterian Church, some have become Catholics while some others have joined smaller denominations like the Church of Christ and the Little Flock.

For many of the newly baptized, it was literally a completely new beginning (cf. Robbins 2004: 127). From all accounts, Pangwa society took to their new religion with great devotion and fervour.[63] Traditional practices, including songs, which were supposed to be associated with spirit worship, were summarily banned. The houses were cleansed of animal skulls and other symbols of their earlier beliefs. Valuable family heirlooms—dresses, gongs, jewellery, accessories like caps, and items of warfare—were burnt or destroyed. As Longkumer reports about the Zeme Nagas, 'Traditional clothes, necklaces, beads, wood carvings, and so on were burnt publicly as a sign of shedding of "old clothes" and taking on "the new body of Christ". This symbolic Christian imagery not only affirmed the religious solidarity of the Nagas but it also led to the overhauling and indeed the loss of traditional culture overnight' (2010: 146). Prayer and modern health care took care of illnesses; thus they had driven out or neutralized the bad spirits which were supposed to cause illness and misfortune. They embraced the good spirits in the Holy Spirit.

What my Tangsa informants told me about the changes Christianity had brought in their lives sounded repetitive and similar to what they had heard their Pastors tell them in church—earlier they had wars and enemies, now after becoming Christian they were all friends and broth-ers.[64] Their homes had also become cleaner and there was a greater sense of responsibility for the community. There was a sense of equality and of mutual respect and a large social network, connecting them to other Christian communities in other states of northeast India and beyond; moreover, most Christian denominations organized annual conferences every year where one could meet and interact with other Christians.[65]

Furthermore, many of my women interlocutors had become articulate and more assertive after taking on responsibilities in the church. They had thereby gained agency, even within their own families and circle (cf. Robbins 2004: 133). According to my Hakhun hostess in Malugaon:

> Becoming Baptists is the best thing that has happened to us—the men have stopped wasting their time and money drinking rice-beer and smok-ing opium—not everyone, she hastily added, but at least many. We don't have to spend money on sacrificing animals every time someone is sick and the church has brought us all together—it has given us a platform where we have learnt to become better people, to be able to take respon-sibility and to share our concern for others. Before we were like animals, only caring for ourselves—killing each other, going to war, sacrificing even human beings. (Malugaon, 9 January 2009)

In other words, just as in the Garo community in Meghalaya, 'the preva-lent local perception is that Christianity saved [them] from barbarism' (De Maaker 2012: 135).

About the impact of Christianity on the Tangsa way of life, Thamphang (1999: 93) writes: 'Christianity has given brotherhood and a sense of dignity. Christianity introduces a new kind of leadership and a new principle of social control among the Tangsa. The concept of sin and the fear of retribution become powerful instruments of social control in Tangsa society.'

The Present Scenario

The move of the Tangsa down from the hills, their conversion to Christianity, and their first contact with a modern lifestyle happened almost concurrently. The coming together of these three very crucial factors was like a watershed in their lives, marking a clear break with their lives before. (For a general view of the changes, see Bhagabati and Chaudhuri 2008.)

Considering everything, there has been a huge change in how most of the Tangsa live today, how they dress, what they eat, and also in their expectations from their lives, the state, and the people around them. While all this has impacted on their everyday business of living, conversion has brought about a change in their worldviews and also their opinions about their life in the past. For a while, many of the newly converted Tangsa had believed that their new religion could suffice also as their culture, but as time has gone on (most of the Tangsa converted after the 1970s), some have begun to see that religion alone cannot help them secure their ethnic identity.[66]

Moreover, creating a common pan-Tangsa identity is important for them if they wanted to remain (and be recognized as) a Scheduled Tribe. And this was desirable because of the concessions and privileges that came with it. In recent years, a certain section of the Tangsa leadership has therefore come to recognize the need to regroup and redefine themselves. Some Tangsa groups have adopted officially recognized strategies like forming societies and associations to work towards those goals. Others have started to do so also by observing and imitating the actions of other tribal groups in the area. Relative economic stability and growth of a middle class among them have aided these processes. It is precisely this question of how my Tangsa interlocutors attempt to redefine themselves as Tangsa—with or without their religious affiliations—that I will look into in the later chapters.

Societies and Associations

Developments have taken place in two distinct directions with regard to forming registered Tangsa associations and societies in Assam. The

Tangsa (Naga) National Council is the official representative body for the Tangsa in Assam.[67] Aphu Tyanglam is its president. He also established the Tangsa Naga Cultural Society in 1987 (registered in 1990) and has been its president since its inception; more about Aphu and the activities of the Society in the next chapter. Aphu's efforts have been more towards consolidation, towards creating a pan-Tangsa repertoire of songs and dances, which can create a sense of cultural unity amongst the different Tangsa tribes and also be presented to the world as 'Tangsa culture'. On the other hand, some Tangsa groups, noticeably the Langchings and the Hakhuns, who have a few strategically clever leaders, have started the process of forming their own associations for the welfare of their own tribe members. And this trend is slowly catching on among some Tangsa groups as well. In this case, the tendency is towards fragmentation, of forming smaller more cohesive units based on the older tribal divisions.

I shall say more about the aims and activities of the Hakhun Association in Chapter 5. The All Langching Welfare and Development Society was formed with the aim to record (in written form) their history, family genealogies, migration stories, the many clans and subclans, and all the 'lost' or 'fast disappearing' traditional practices. A general meeting of the society is held on 15 December each year. But they did not call it a festival and there was no cultural component to the programme, I was informed. Once when I expressed my interest in attending their next meeting (in December 2009), the Secretary of the Society told me not to bother as they had 'nothing to show' as yet. They were in the process of preparing the costumes necessary for the cultural programme: their traditional dress is almost the same as the other Tangsa groups, he told me, *but they are trying to make it a bit more colourful*; the other accessories—like spears, shields, caps, and ornaments—were also being procured; and the singers and dancers were being trained. He believed that in a year they would be able to stage a cultural programme as well. And in a couple of years they hoped to have their 'history' ready too.[68]

Of course, the phenomenon of political mobilization through forming cultural associations is well known (see, for instance, Colson 1996: 73). What is worth noting here is that while Aphu Tyanglam and his group are not Christian, most of the office bearers of these newly formed (Hakhun and Langching) associations are Christian (mostly Baptist). As such one gets a sense of growing urgency amongst the various Tangsa groups about trying to relocate themselves in the new scheme of things in a way that not everything of their past is lost without making too many compromises with their new religious beliefs and their 'modern' way of living. I discuss these issues in Chapters 5 and 6.

Postscript: My First Introduction to the Tangsa

When I had first started working with the Tangsa, there were quite a few things about them that struck me as different. Their villages looked different from what I was used to seeing in a typical Assamese village: there were chang-ghars and 'Tokou' palm trees, not mud houses and banana trees; they reared pigs, not cows; the sight of men wearing *lungis* and not *dhotis* (Assamese, loose cotton wrapper for men) or trousers, and of women wearing *mekhelas* (Assamese, ankle- length cotton wrappers for women) and blouses (*sam-tung*, Tangsa) but not *sadors* (Assamese, long strip of cloth normally used by Assamese women to cover the upper part of their body over a mekhela), often carrying heavy logs of firewood in baskets (*rhi-khya*, Cholim) resting on their backs (see Photograph 3.3), was not a familiar one. Soon the difference in the timings of their meals, and their food habits, with the almost complete absence of sugar, cooking oil, milk and milk products from their diet, made me feel the difference even more. Moreover, since toilets were always located away from the living areas and usually not close to sources of water, and with evening descending so early in 'Tangsaland', one had to get used to a different daily rhythm.

But that was not all. The Tangsa also had strong cultural differences from the Assamese community to which I belonged: Asymmetric cross-cousin marriages were the ideal matches for the Tangsa; most of the Pangwa groups had the practice of bride-price; many groups buried (but did not cremate) the dead. [69] Moreover, they had no special puberty rites, unlike the caste Hindu Assamese. I was also not used to people, especially women, drinking alcohol and rice-beer so freely. What was even more difficult for me to handle was the general permissiveness of their society towards pre-marital sex and what seemed to me to be a marked lack of inhibition of their women. The standards of decorum and propriety were different: for instance, although married Tangsa women often tucked their hair away under a scarf they usually do not use a scarf or sador to cover their bosoms, as Assamese women are often wont to do.

Photograph 3.3   Tangsa Woman Carrying Firewood

Source: Author.

Having had a pampered middle-class upbringing, I was constantly amazed at how hardworking most Tangsa women were. Although they are mostly confined to their homes, Tangsa women definitely contributed much more and played a bigger role in the affairs of the family than did their rural Assamese counterparts. Of course, normally they could not become village chiefs, and even today they have to do most of the work in the kitchen, but they were still permitted to participate in discussions and in some cases did not hesitate to come out to the outer area to talk to outsiders and strangers—noted Naga writer Temsula Ao (2013) calls this 'benevolent subordination'.

When I first began to interact with them I realized that their Asamiya was not easy to understand; first, because their style was quite different from the standard Asamiya I was used to. Secondly, certain Asamiya terms they used, such as *khub baru* (Assamese, meaning very nice), were quaint and almost obsolete in everyday spoken Asamiya.

Since I did not understand any of the Tangsa languages, I would often ask them in what language they were speaking (or singing)— Initially, I was invariably given the standard reply 'in Tangsa language', which irritated me quite a bit, as it meant that I would have to ask again before they told me which of the many Tangsa languages that meant.[70]

There was more confusion in store for me in the initial weeks: when one of my Tangsa hosts introduced somebody as his grandson or his daughter-in-law, I immediately started trying to figure out, most of the time unsuccessfully, whose son or whose wife the person was. It took me quite a long time to realize that when a Tangsa man referred to someone as his son, he could mean several other people besides his own biological sons, for all his brothers' sons were also his sons. When we sat down to draw up kinship tables, I got completely lost very quickly. For instance, the word 'eno' (in Cholim) can mean younger sister as well as one's younger brother's wife or even one's son's wife, while the word 'aphu' normally meant elder brother, but could also mean a cousin (father's brother's son) or wife's sister's husband.[71] More surprisingly, a man's mother's brother's daughter, if he did not marry her, was not his cousin but his maternal aunt!

With time, however, as the initial confusion settled, my worries also receded. I began to feel at home in Tangsaland, and grateful for their uncomplicated and unconditional affection. With time I also found out a little about what they thought of me. Many Tangsa found the fact that I often travelled alone to unknown places in the field so unlike what they imagined Assamese women from upper middle-class families to be capable of doing that they attributed my 'courage' to my many years of living in Germany. And by the end of my fourth season with them, they had gotten so used to hearing stories of my latest trips and exploits that they had begun to refer to me (between them) as the *pagli baidew* meaning the 'crazy sister' in Asamiya.

Notes

1. Changlang was inaugurated on 14 November 1987 as a district; earlier it was part of the Tirap district. According to the 1991 Census, there were

30,000 Tangsa in the district, out of a total of 92,891. In 2001, there were 20,431 Tangsa in Changlang district out of a total population of 125,422, while there were only 3,412 Singpho and 3,940 listed under 'Any Naga tribe'. The Tangsa population in Arunachal Pradesh in 2011 was more than 36,000 with another 12,338 listed under 'Any Naga tribe'. The Singpho population in Arunachal Pradesh is only 5,616 while the total population of the Changlang district in 2011 was 147,951.

2. Hkamti district or Khamti district (sometimes Naga Hills district). There are about 90,000 Tangshang living in Myanmar now according to Nathan Statezni (pers. comm., 3 July 2012).

3. This was officially declared on 20 August 2010; http://en.wikipedia.org/wiki/Naga_Self-Administered_Zone (accessed 4 July 2012).

4. See Mackenzie (2012 [1884]: 88–9). Mackenzie mentions that the Patkoi Nagas first came to the notice of the British because although the Nagas themselves were peaceably inclined, they were harassed and attacked by the Singphos. He then adds, 'From this point, notices of these Patkoi Nagas are few and unimportant, and in later years their very existence seems to have been lost sight of or to have been confusedly merged in that of the greater tribes to the west who are ordinarily communicated with through the officials of Seebsaugor.'

    For details of the relations of the British to the many hill tribes of Assam, see Chakravorty (1964).

5. Mr T.P.M. O'Callaghan, Political Officer, Sadiya Frontier Tract, wrote a separate 'Note on the Rangpang Nagas', as part of the Annual Administrative Report for the year 1925–6 of the Sadiya Frontier Tract (*Report* 1926). The 'Note' is cited as O'Callaghan (1926), and relevant excerpts are included as an Appendix. Mr T.P. Dewar's 1927 'Report on his expedition to the Hukawng valley' also contains a wealth of information about the practices of some Naga tribes, many of whom belong today under the Tangsa umbrella.

6. The Burmese Census of 1931 (Bennison 1933) lists the subtribes that performed human sacrifice. All were Pangwa groups. Since at that time most of the other Pangwa had not yet moved into India, that is presumably why the Ronrangs were singled out.

7. For more details, see Means (2000). See also Dewar (1927).

8. This entry is dated 2 January 1952. It is interesting to note how the Assamese Hindu Borgohain projected the Hindu caste system perhaps subconsciously into the tribal world.

9. Some linguistic analysis was done by Dasgupta (1978, 1980).

10. Shumaung's information is based on a book in Burmese containing this migration history. Our interlocutor, Aphu Tyanglam, in Kharangkong owns a draft version of the same book.

11. A label is a *cluster label* if within one presumed community/people there may be several communities/peoples. A similarly diverse group of varieties in the Tirap District of Arunachal got the name Nocte in an analogous way (see, for instance, Morey 2012).

12. Sebastian (1999) claims that the term 'Tangsa' has been used by other British administrators even earlier than that.

13. One elder told me that even a fine was threatened to be imposed on them if the Tangsa persisted in calling themselves Naga.

    Although I have not heard anyone explaining the choice of the word 'sa' (or child) as a diminutive, many have clearly made a distinction between the more 'civilized' Tangsa and the 'wilder and more aggressive' Tangwa ('wa' meaning father) groups among the Naga (see Note 16).

14. There is mention of human sacrifices being performed in 1929 (*Report* 1936: 3), and also in 1938–9 across the Patkoi range in the unadministered area of Burma (*Report* 1939: 1). The last mention I found is in the *Burma Report* (1942: 2) where it is stated that human sacrifices were carried out in 1940–1. Bhagabati (2004: 180) reports the last reported case of human sacrifice is said to have taken place in 1942.

    The fact that many Tangsa groups have specific terms to refer to human sacrifice (and also specific songs that are sung on such occasions) can also be indicative of its practice by some groups—*dah-tang* (Mossang)/*dawan* (Ronrang)/*di-ta* (Kimsing)/*kha-tang* (Juglei).

15. The term 'Haimi', also spelled Heimi, literally meaning 'good person', first appears in the literature in the *Census of India 1931*, which at that time included what was then called Burma (Bennison 1933). This was the first census of Burma to include the Naga; due to changes in politics, it has proved to be the only census to explicitly mention them (Statezni unpublished). In the *Burma Report* (1942: 3) the term is spelt as Haimyes and is considered distinct from the Rangpans.

    Another source states: The Heimi ethnic group belongs to the larger Tangsang Naga group including the Pangmi, Khaklak, and Tangan ethnic groups spread over contiguous territories in Sagaing and Kachin states of Myanmar. In India, the Tangsang group consists of the Tangsa, Muklom, and Tutsa in Arunachal Pradesh (N. Goswami 2014).

16. The term 'Tangwa' literally means 'father of the high land', and according to some Tangsa elders referred to the forefathers of the Tangsa, who wore loincloths.

17. According to some interlocutors, the general name is often the Singpho/Jinphaw term for them, for some others it is the term the Assamese used for them which the British adopted, and in many cases the two coincide.

18. *Ethnologue: Languages of the World* (www.ethnologue.com/) is a web-based publication that contains statistics for 7,105 languages and dialects in the 17th edition, released in 2013.

    For the connection between the Tangsa and the Naga languages, see Van Driem (2008).

    Tase is the Kimsing pronunciation of the term 'Tangsa'.

19. Note that the groups shown in Figure 3.1 are only those groups in India that we have been able to collect data on. But even there, some like Shangti and Lungkhi (Pangwa) are not included; Lungkhi and Khalak belong together. And this does not even begin to include the groups reported in Myanmar.

    Dewar's (1931: 295) list of the Rangpan tribe included only the following groups as subtribes: Mawshang, Sangche, Langshin, Myimu, Hkatak, Gashan, Tulim, Longri, Sangtai, Saukrang, Mawrang, Dongai, Maitai, and Sanri. The corresponding list for the Haimi tribe included Rangkhu, Lakai, Sanching, Longkhai, Rasa, Gaha, Samse, and many others; other groups like Gahki, Gakhun, and Bongtai are included under the Ku Wa tribe.

20. As evident in the title of our DOBES project extension (2011–2): 'A Multi-faceted Study of Tangsa—a Network of Linguistic Varieties in North East India'.

21. Based on interviews with Aphu Tyanglam and Phanglim Kimsing over extended periods of time during 2009–10 and 2010–11. See also Dutta (1969: 4–7) and Morang (2008).

22. Morang's 2008 book is titled *Tangsas—the Children of Masui Singrapum*. 'Pum' is the Singpho word for hill. Note also that other groups like the Singpho also claim the same place of origin (cf. Sadan 2012: 257).

    The Ronrangs go one step further backwards and start at a place called Rokachung (or Hookachung) where man and animals were created by the Supreme Being (*Traditional Systems* 2005: 151).

23. One version of the migration story of the Ronrang is described in Ronrang (1997: 5); another in Dutta (2011).

24. Interview with Lemkhum Mossang, 3 January 2012, Manmao. For another reading, see Rao (2003). The Mossangs are supposed to have taken the first two of the three paths into India mentioned above. According to some, those Mossangs who went with the Mukloms and followed the third path call themselves Lungphi today.

25. Proof of this fact could be easily seen from the fact that many Tikhak and Longchang elders we met were born in the area included in present-day India while elders we met from most of the Pangwa groups were born in Burma and had moved to India during their lifetime.

26. Haksar (2013: 84, 87) describes exactly the same ambivalence with regard to whether the Tangsa are Naga.

27. The practice of wearing lungis may in turn have been borrowed from the Burmans as traditionally Naga tribes did not wear lungis.

28. Here my findings are at variance with those reported by Bouchery (2007: 116) who claims that 'the Konyak, Wancho, Nocte and Tangsa groups, who occupy the northernmost part of the Naga Hills, have both stratified lineages and paramount chiefs (Ang, Lowang, Lungwang respectively) whose authority extends over a territorial domain consisting of a group of allied villages, and often behave like true autocrats'.

    Dewar (1931: 197), referring to people living right on the border of Kachin territory, contrasts Nagas, who have hereditary headmen, with those whose headmen were appointed by 'selection'.

29. O'Callaghan (1926) refers to *morungs* as 'meeting houses', see Appendix. For more details about the institution in general, refer to Nair (1985: Chapter 5) where he calls them 'bachelor dormitories' and 'virgin houses' respectively. Nair (1985: 112) also remarks that the dormitory system is not functioning well amongst the Tangsa. Of course, these dormitories still exist amongst the Wancho and the Nocte people in the Tirap and Longding districts even today.

30. They are also mentioned in their traditional love songs.

31. Kharangkong, 5 November 2009; see also Barua (2013 [1991]), Dutta (1969: 58), and Rao (2006: 167).

32. Roy Burman (1961: 97) seconds this fact (with respect to the Nocte and Wancho) when he states that the male dormitory 'has entirely disappeared though there is still a girls dormitory in some of the villages'.

33. The old Singpho GB at Kumsaigaon, adjacent to Kharangkong, told us that his grandfather had given land to the Tangsa to set up their own basti and showed us an old jackfruit tree that stood at the boundary of the land that was given away.

34. The Singpho living in India embraced Buddhism as early as in 1891.

35. The use of Singpho or Jinghpaw as lingua franca goes back a long time. As Leach notes, it is widely used as a lingua franca by groups who have some quite different mother tongues—this is the case with many Naga villages on the northwestern fringes of the Kachin Hills Area (Leach 1954: 46). Many Singpho words are still used in the area. Names of many villages and towns, like Ledo, Kumsai, Pansun, and so forth are also derived from Singpho words. For more on this, see Mahanta (2011: 30).

36. Sadan (2013: 184ff) claims smallness in numbers, their religious orientation towards Buddhism, and the loss of political and economic capital in Assam as the reasons for why the Singphos have not been able to assimilate non-Singpho groups in recent years.

37. Showing the relativity of the hills–plains binary that Leach had set out in his classic treatise in 1954. If the Kachins (read, Singphos) were highlanders in relation to the Shan lowlanders in Upland Burma, in relation to the Naga tribes they were valley-dwellers.

38. For instance, in the Wihu song sung by Dangkam Maitai on 9 November 2011 (and recorded and translated by Stephen Morey) they say:

> We fought with the Shamsa people of this world.
> We pierced them like the leg of a mother elephant.
> We fought with the Shamsa people of this world.
> We pierced them with an iron rod, like the leg of a mother elephant.

39. Since the Tangsa, while narrating stories, often refer to themselves simply as Naga, it is not clear whether, when a Tangsa narrator says Naga, he means all the Naga tribes or just the Tangsa subcollection within them.

    Lotha (2008: 54) alludes to a similar story where the younger brother is the ancestor of the Kachins and the elder brother to the Konyaks. For the Angami version of this story, see Wouters (2012: 43).

40. As told by a Tangsa elder in Manmao (6 November 2011).

41. The term 'Rangpan/Rangpang' first appears in the literature as a group of Nagas who raided settlements and waylaid travellers in 1875 (see, for instance, Statezni unpublished). According to Barua (2013 [1991]: 366 ff. 4), the term 'Rang-pang' comes from *Rang* which means sky or high up and *pang* meaning men of unknown character; the word then refers to people living higher up with unknown character, perhaps because they practised human sacrifice. Another interpretation is that Rangpang means 'people descended from heaven' as Rang means heaven (Sebastian 1999: 2); a third writer (Changmai 2012: 6) claims *pang* means dweller so 'Rangpang' means people dwelling on high ground or hill-dweller. Rangpang (in Burma) are also mentioned by Waddell (2000 [1901]: 63) as belonging to the Eastern Naga group of Nagas. The same list also includes the Moshang (Mossang) in the Eastern Naga list, mentioning that very little is known about the Eastern Nagas.

42. The Pangwa performed human sacrifice for primarily two reasons: either when a person was gravely ill, or as a sacrifice during a feast of merit. The Tangwa are more allied with the Nocte, Wancho, and Konyak Naga groups among whom the practice of headhunting is well documented (Von Fürer-Haimendorf 1962 [1939], Hutton 1928).

43. The British Frontier administration banned and stopped human sacrifices completely around 1926 (see, for instance, Ronrang 1997: 12). But Barua (2013 [1991]: 174) claims that it was still prevalent till as late as 1952. For

another description, see Dutta (1969: 77). The practice of headhunting was also banned by around the year 1945 (Barua 2013 [1991]: 263). Many elders spoke of how Pangwa men were forced to work by building roads as punishment for having indulged in such practices.

44. The old practice of burying the dead under their chang-ghars, for fear that the enemies might come and steal the head, and take it away as a trophy, has since been discontinued.

45. The buffalo skulls arranged in neat columns on the main wall of some Tangsa houses, one for each time such a feast was performed, on the wall (*nye-khring/nge-khurung*, separating the outer half enclosed area from the inner rooms and which is usually the side where the master of the house sits and presides over his household) is the only material evidence we have for these feasts having ever been conducted. I have not seen these columns of skulls, however, in any Tangsa home in Assam.

46. Taken from the written transcript of a talk delivered by a Tangsa spokesperson at Margherita College in November 2012.

47. The Hakhuns are supposed to have had twelve festivals, one for each month of the year.

48. Dutta (1969: 28) refers to this festival as 'bihukuk', perhaps inadvertently equating the Wihu festival of the Tangsa with the Bihu festival of the Assamese, as many other Assamese are also wont to do; more about this in the last section of Chapter 6.

49. The concept of thanksgiving is not used here in the Christian context but in the general sense of a harvest-end festival.

    For a comprehensive description of another such festival (Murung) to do with fertility amongst the Apatani people of northeast India, see Blackburn (2010).

50. Available at http://censusindia.gov.in/Census_Data_2001/Census_Data_Online/Language/Statement/htm (accessed on 14.9.2013).

51. Here the reference is to those Tangsa who have migrated into the region before the middle of the twentieth century. There is migration from Myanmar into India going on even today, but most Tangsa in Myanmar are now Christian.

52. Being the official language in most of Assam, Asamiya is the medium of instruction in government schools.

53. For a comparative view, see the reasons for conversion amongst the Angami Naga in Nagaland in Joshi (2007: 549); see also Mepfhü-o (2016) for further instances of conversion and its impact on Naga society.

54. For similar stories, elsewhere in India, see Boal (1982: 194).

55. This view is seconded by Maipa Kenglang in her M.Phil Dissertation (2002: 42): 'Christianity provided an answer to the vast groups of Tangsa who

found their traditional beliefs and customs too complex in nature and irrelevant to continue with anymore; had no other alternative but to abandon and embrace Christianity'.

It is interesting that not having a religion was never an option for any of my interlocutors.

56. According to Dr Nani Bath of RGU this was true for other communities in Arunachal as well, and this was borne out in my interviews with Tangsa elders.

57. It is commonly believed that malaria occurs more in the plains because there are more bamboo clumps in the plains where mosquitoes can breed. Cholera, dysentery, black fever, and malaria were quoted as the common ailments to which the hill people were often plagued by.

58. Dutta (1969: 77–8) referring to the ban on human sacrifice by the frontier administration says very much the same thing: 'Their belief is that nowadays they do not get good harvests, because they have abandoned this ceremony'. And again, 'According to the Ronrangs, their condition became deplorable from the time they gave up this festival'.

59. The Tangsa before they converted—and the fundamentalist missionaries who converted them—both believed in evil spirits, the devil or Satan, but animists and Christians differ in how to deal with them: The animists by placating, the Christians by fighting them off with prayer. For more on the massive impact of Baptist Christianity on Naga culture, see the essays contained in Longchar (1985).

60. For more about healing and conversion among the Angami Nagas in the neighbouring state of Nagaland, see Joshi (2012).

61. For instance, there is one such tale of a flood and destruction described in Khimhun (2006: 17).

62. Manmao, 2 January 2012. It is possible that Mr Mossang was only repeating to me an argument that he had heard from a preacher or an evangelist earlier, since the same argument has been recorded elsewhere before: 'It is often said by Christian Nagas that "actually" they were already Christians and believed in God before they received the true teachings from the Americans' (Oppitz et al. 2008: 23).

63. Although some residues from their older practices still surfaced from time to time, see section titled 'Residual Beliefs' in Chapter 6.

64. However, there were many instances which indicated that this peace had not been internalized completely yet. One instance was the reaction to the publication of and the subsequent resistance to the circulation of Uddi Ronrang's history of the Ronrang people, see Note 38 of Chapter 6.

65. For example, contact with Korean Baptist missionaries through their counterparts in Nagaland.

66. An Ao Baptist elder I met in Nagaland echoed the same thoughts when he said: 'a time will come when the Tangsa will realise that Christianity without their cultural value systems is meaningless. Religion is only *part* of our culture' (Impur, 21 November 2010, italics mine).

67. The Tangsa are not the only ones who have organized themselves in this manner. Other tribal groups also have their own organizations. The Singpho have a Singpho Development Society in Arunachal and a Singpho National Council in Assam.

68. They are not alone in trying to do this, as Schlemmer remarks about the Kirant people in Nepal: 'The wishes of ethnic minorities are founded on claims of a common identity and culture, and one of the privileged ways to express this is through possessing a proper history' (Schlemmer 2003/2004: 119). 'Subsequently inventing the past is inheriting the future' (Schlemmer 2003/4: 138).

69. Like many other tribes in the region and in Southeast Asia, including the Singpho, the Tangsa prefer (asymmetric) cross-cousin marriages. That means the most preferred marriage is when a boy marries his mother's brother's daughter, or a girl who can be considered to be in that relation to him.

70. Sökefeld (2001: 536–7) narrates a similar experience he had in the field in Pakistan.

    The local ethnic leader in Gilgit, Pakistan, explained why they did so in the following way: 'Of course, we speak many languages, but they are all the same because they are fundamentally different from the languages spoken by the surrounding nations (i.e., Kashmir and Pakistan).' The languages are the same—or identical—because they are characterized by a common difference distinguishing them from others that do not belong to this nation.

    This might well be the Tangsa explanation for it too.

71. Literally, the word means a younger sibling, and whoever stands in that relationship to you.

4 Kharangkong
The Last Bastion of the Old World

'If we do not know who we were, how will we figure out who we are?'

—Aphu Tyanglam, Kharangkong

The day begins early in the Tyanglam household; for Aphu even earlier, because he usually gets up before dawn and has a bath on the terrace with cold water (that one of the women of the family had fetched in a bucket from the deep tube well behind the house the previous evening); he then does exercises: as long as it takes for the water to dry on his body, he claims. Then he switches on his transistor radio to listen to the Burmese news; that is also the wake-up-alarm for the rest of the household. The Tyanglam household is large, comprising at any given moment, not just the immediate extended family (of the sons and daughters living at home and their families) but also nephews and nieces, relations and clan-relatives visiting from other villages, and anyone else who just happens to be there.

While the women (primarily his daughter-in-law, assisted by his wife and daughters) hurry to light the fire in the inner kitchen to start the process of cooking 'morning rice', Aphu leisurely lights the fire in the outer sitting area, waits for one of his daughters to fill the kettle with water, and then puts it on the metal tripod over the fire.[1] Then he seats himself in his customary place by the fire and waits for the morning tea (which usually has milk and sugar) to be made and served. While waiting, he plays with Cho-ong, his favourite grandchild. And, if by chance I was still asleep when the tea was ready, he

comes knocking at my door. 'Have you come here to sleep or to work? Get up,
or else the day will be over', he shouts through the closed door in Asamiya.

With good reason too, because early morning between morning tea and
morning rice was the best time to work with Aphu. Being an early riser,
Stephen usually spent those hours working with Aphu every morning, when he
was there. And so Aphu expected me to do the same. At times he would even
tease me saying he would inform Stephen how lazy I have been. Truth was
that Aphu really enjoyed talking and discussing Tangsa culture and history
with our project team. His view was that their older traditional practices were
getting lost (or at least getting diluted and corrupted) because of constant
interaction and intermixing of the Tangsa with other neighbouring communities, and because the Tangsa were obliged to learn to read and write in
Asamiya, English, or Hindi. Since he grew up in Burma, Aphu could read
and write only in Burmese. But he could speak many of the different Tangsa
languages, besides Singpho, some Asamiya, and a little Hindi.

The first time I met Aphu Tyanglam, then in his late seventies, I did not
understand much of what he said. He spoke in Asamiya but it was his very
own special brand of it.[2] What took me the longest to unravel was his repeated
reference to some 'kassa party'. Since he was a political leader of sorts, I initially believed this to be a reference to his political activities. It was much later
that I understood that 'kassa' was his way of pronouncing the word 'culture'
and his 'kassa party' was a group of young people from Kharangkong who he
had taught the 'traditional' Tangsa dances so that they could go and teach
other Tangsa their 'kassa'.

Tangsa 'kassa' was clearly very important for Aphu. Therefore the arrival
of our research team who wanted to (and had the wherewithal to) record and
document everything Aphu could tell, was welcomed with open arms by him.
He was very quick to understand the aims of our DOBES project and offered
his knowledge as well as his hospitality to the team. Besides providing us his
house to stay and work from, he took it upon himself to help us in every way
he could, by introducing us to others, and helping to translate our recordings
made with him and also elsewhere and giving us a lot of background information about the area as well as about the Tangsa. Very quickly he became one
of our main interlocutors, and his good voice and clear pronunciation in the
Tangsa languages he knew made him very valuable for linguistic work.

Once the morning rice was eaten, the day began for everyone. The women
of the house would vanish for the day, either to work in the fields or to collect
firewood, after sending the children to school. Aphu would normally stay at

home unless he had some work elsewhere. Since he was a local leader, on most days people from the area came to meet him with some request or the other. On some other days, he would help in the tea gardens, spraying pesticides or fertilizers on the patch of garden where they produced tea for sale.

Around 3 p.m., the women would return home to cook the evening meal, which would be served early, often before dusk. Sometimes fodder for the pigs (mostly chopped stems of yam and the arum plant) would be cooked in the outer area while Aphu and the children watched TV (if there was electricity) till it was bed time. When there was a power cut (and that was very often), Aphu spent his time either talking to people over his mobile phone (often till it ran out of power) or sitting at the kitchen hearth talking to his wife and others, or simply playing with his grandchildren. Sometimes, when he was in a good mood, he would even break into song, and sing old songs that most others did not recognize. At other times he would tell a story or recount some incident from his past life.

It had its charms, this sitting around the fire and listening to stories, for Aphu was a great storyteller. But sometimes it also made me feel very sorry for him, for, on many occasions, before starting to tell us a story or sing a song, Aphu would call out to his grandchildren and to his grandnieces and nephews to come and sit down and listen to him; he even used his mobile phone to call his niece and trusted assistant Bokja once. But rarely did any of them come voluntarily. They would usually find some excuse to not come.

As I listened to the grand old man describing the terrible war between the serpent king and the water spirit, or listened to his singing the tragic story of the two lovers who could not marry as they were from different tribes, I often wondered if anyone would be left who could tell us these things after he is gone. Our project was in some sense about documenting 'disappearing cultures'; I had been schooled to understand that cultures did not disappear. Perhaps, they didn't. But a lot would disappear in Kharangkong with the disappearance of Aphu Tyanglam. That much was clear.

In the rainy season, the part-metalled and part-dirt track to Kharangkong becomes impossible to use for cars. There is no regular public transport to Kharangkong from the main road. So on days he had to go out, Aphu would often ask a Nepali taxi driver living nearby, Rai, to fetch him in his ramshackle Maruti taxi. When Rai came, Aphu would insist that he come up to the front sitting area and have a cup of tea. Initially, to me it seemed quite odd that Aphu insisted that Rai sit at the same table with him and have tea. Back in my own home in Guwahati, I have never seen my mother do anything similar—drivers and gardeners do not sit in Ma's presence, leave alone be offered a cup of tea at the same table! Aphu and Ma are about the same age, they both are involved in politics, and are public leaders in their own ways. Yet, they were very different.

Rai, on his part, would always protest but give in quickly, because he knew that there was no saying 'no' to phelap (black tea) in a Tangsa home. Rai was always polite to Aphu and called him 'Baba' (Assamese/Hindi, father). Aphu was a good client. But privately Rai confessed to me that he found the standards of cleanliness in Aphu's house not entirely satisfactory and that he would prefer not to eat and drink there. Of course he would never eat a meal there, as he was a Hindu and he knew that the Tangsa eat all sorts of meat. Rai also told me that one of the main reasons why he did not like to go up to drink tea was that he was tired of hearing the same stories from Aphu over and over again.

And he was not the only one. Almost everyone I met confessed at some point or the other that the main reason why they avoided the old man was that once Aphu caught hold of them at least a half an hour or more would pass before one could hope to be released—Aphu loved to hold forth and just waited for an audience to get started.

Therefore Aphu was very pleased when I asked him to tell me the story of his life. He told me that he had even written down the main points, so that he did not forget them. He then went to fetch it—it was a single sheet of paper, densely written over in Burmese, from which he proceeded to tell me the story of his life. In the days that followed, Aphu told me much more than I will recount below—detailed accounts of his life in Burma before he came into India, numerous other public, cultural, and political activities that he had initiated or had taken part in, and a lot more about his various achievements as a leader of his people and of the area. Curiously, his version of his life story did not include any information about his family, how many children he had, when they were born, what they did, and so on. When I questioned him about that he told me that his family was his private matter but as a public leader he had to give me proof of what he had done for the public.

He had done all that only for his people, he did not tire of telling me, but it was clear that he was also very proud of what he had achieved, and that he enjoyed talking about it. But he also had his moods; sometimes he was stubborn and obstinate, at other times, he would pout and be offended when somebody defied him, and some other times he would rant and rave when *his pride was hurt. But it was always easy to read him. Over the years I have learnt to be able to predict his moods and reactions, and to love and respect this man, who was the first Tangsa I ever met, and who I have come to regard as my Tangsa father.*

Both the village of Kharangkong and Aphu Tyanglam are very important to the understanding of the Tangsa in Assam: Kharangkong, because it is perhaps the only Tangsa basti left in Assam where some people still follow their older traditional practices as they have not yet converted (to either Christianity or Buddhism), and also because it is the home of Aphu Tyanglam, who has been and still is, without doubt, the most important Tangsa leader in Assam, highly respected by all and considered by many to be one of the most knowledgeable Tangsa elders in India. As already mentioned, Aphu is currently the president of both the Tangsa Naga Council, as well as of the Tangsa (Naga) Cultural Society, the two apex Tangsa bodies in Assam. Furthermore, as will become presently clear, Aphu has been the moving force behind most of the recent efforts towards revitalization and re-articulation of Tangsa traditional culture, as part of the process of constructing a pan-Tangsa identity, based on both their past in the hills of the Patkai range as well as their present in the plains of Assam.

In this chapter, I want to present first, a partial biographical sketch of Aphu Tyanglam (largely as told to me by him) as an example of how a relatively uneducated and not-so-well off Tangsa young man from Burma came and settled in India and by the sheer strength of his personality and his involvement with various socially minded activities, rose to become a leader of his people. I will then describe the festival of Wihu-kuh that Aphu organizes every year in Kharangkong in order to arrive at an understanding of what 'kassa' means for Aphu and why he considers it to be important. Then, in the two following sections, I present a picture of the village of Kharangkong and also attempt to describe the Tangsa world as Aphu sees it and also how others around him see Aphu. In doing so, I will discuss the predicament of the Tangsa from Aphu's point of view in order to understand the reasons behind some of the steps he has taken in his attempts to secure their future. I end this chapter with a description of some issues involved in doing fieldwork with a person like Aphu.

Aphu Tyanglam: The Tired but Stubborn Campaigner

A Portrait of the Man

Aphu Tyanglam was born in 1931 in Mandang basti, now in north-eastern Myanmar (Bhamo district in Kachin state). He claims that a Burmese General had picked him up as a young boy from the hills and had taken him with him. He stayed with the General for a few years; there he learnt to read and write in Burmese as well as got some military training. He came to India (after having fought on the side of the Nagas against the Kachins) in 1965 following his family, and settled in the Udaipur/Kharangkong area.[3] Soon after he arrived in India, his mother got him married. Aphu's wife Renya is Khalak (Tangsa) and comes from a village called Likphan in Myanmar, two days walk away from Mandang. Her family had also moved to India a little earlier. Like many other of our older interlocutors, Aphu had started off in India as an opium dealer.[4] He came to live in Kharangkong only in the early 1970s and established the Cholim basti there, a little away from the main Kharangkong basti.[5]

Soon he became involved with issues regarding the development of their village and their area, together with other leaders of the neighbouring Ahom, Singpho, Tai Phake, and Nepali villages, playing a role in organizations like the Janajatiya Santi Parishad (as already mentioned in the section 'Minority Politics' in Chapter 2). In 1980, he went to Delhi as part of a four-member team to meet Mrs Indira Gandhi to demand greater autonomy and more political representation for the hill tribals in the Tirap area. He has been active with many developmental and welfare activities and projects that have been undertaken in the area, not hesitating to plead their case with the local administration whenever there was need. He has also played an active role in the maintenance of law and order in the village as part of the Village Defence Party (VDP). He took a lead in setting up the Friday weekly market in Kharangkong behind his home, and helped many new settlers to get their names included in the voters' lists.[6]

He has 30 puras (about 23 acres) of land, part of which is in Hewe Ninggam (another neighbouring Tangsa basti also known as Tangsa Ninggam), and the rest in Kharangkong. He has given most of the land in Hewe Ninggam to some Nepali families to do wet rice cultivation

(on a sharecropping basis); he and his family look after the tea plantations they have around their house. He also owns some pigs and poul-
try and also some 'Tokou' palm trees like most other Tangsa homes in
Kharangkong. He also takes up small government road-repair contracts
from time to time which he executes with the help of an Ahom contrac-
tor also living in Kharangkong.

He has six daughters and three sons. Although most of his grandchildren now go to school, none of his children except his youngest daughter ever finished school. Aphu's eldest son died some years ago and the
daughter-in-law lived with her children in a separate house in the basti.
The unmarried daughters and the two younger sons with their families
lived with him. Aphu's two brothers (one elder and one younger) and
a younger sister also lived in the basti in households of their own and,
although I have never seen his sister visit Aphu, there is a lot of contact
between the three brothers. Another family of a clan relative (comprising a widow, her unmarried daughter, Bokja, and a son with his family)
also live close by and are often seen in Aphu's house. The other families
living in the basti, although related to Aphu in some way or the other,
do not have as much contact with the Tyanglam household.

His house is the only concrete structure in the Cholim basti of
Kharangkong village—a rather ungainly structure on concrete pillars.
As with most other Tangsa, his kitchen is still a bamboo chang-ghar. A
small concrete outhouse comprises a small toilet and bath, although
the bathroom is rarely used and normally used to store the equipment
and fertilizers for spraying the fields. A schematic representation of his
house and the surroundings is given in Figure 4.1. His house is electri-
fied but the voltage is very low and there are frequent power cuts. A
deep tube well behind the kitchen is the source of water for domestic
use. Behind the kitchen there is a lake, some tea gardens, and a few
other smaller changs, all belonging to Aphu. His widowed elder sister
lived in one. The old chang-ghar in which Aphu had lived with his family before he built the concrete building was in bad shape. His second
son with family used to live in it before they built a chang-ghar of their
own nearby and moved out. Beyond the older house was a huge plantation of 'Tokou' palm trees also belonging to Aphu. In front of the house
is a relatively large field around which most of the other houses in the
basti are located.

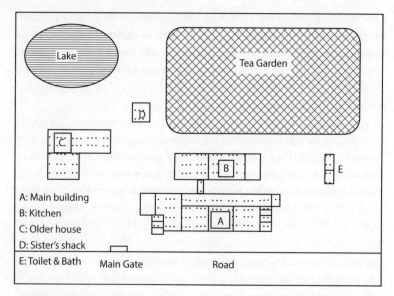

Figure 4.1   Schematic Representation of Aphu Tyanglam's House and
Compound

Source: Author.

Conflicting Loyalties

Politically, Aphu joined the Congress party in 1967 and has been a very
staunch and loyal supporter of the local Congress politicians ever since.[7]
The highest official position he has held was president of the local village council, the Kumsaigaon Gram Panchayat, in 1992 as a Congress
party candidate. Aphu knows the local Congress leaders personally. His
loyalty and persistence were rewarded when he was finally made the
Vice-Chairman of the Development Council constituted in 2011.

Despite the fact that he has been pro-establishment and an old
campaigner for the Congress party for most of his life, he was nevertheless very much a Naga at heart and still nursed hopes that someday
a united Naga state would come about.[8] He had no doubt that the
Tangsa were Naga, and that it was only the shrewd government policy
to separate the warring Nagas from Nagaland under Phizo soon after
Indian independence from the ones living in relative peace in Assam
and Arunachal that the term 'Tangsa' was coined in the first place. The

following incident, taken from my field notes, reveals how sensitive he
is about the whole issue.

> Once while recounting Aphu's history to someone in Aphu's presence,
> I said that Aphu had 'migrated' from Burma into India. Aphu flared up
> instantly and countered, 'Be careful with your choice of words. You are
> Assamese and now you live in Guwahati; suppose someday you decide
> to move to Dibrugarh, would you say that you would have *migrated* to
> Dibrugarh?' Seeing me shake my head, he continued, 'Then why do you
> say that I *migrated* from Burma? We Naga people have lived on both sides
> of the Patkai hills from times immemorial. Just because someday some
> British saheb decided to draw some lines to divide up our territory into
> two different countries does not mean that we will not go and settle
> wherever we wish to within our area, regardless of whether it is now in
> India or in Burma.[9] Do you understand that?'

Aphu's reaction reflects the predicament of many other Tangsa who find
it difficult to accept the fact that their natural homeland in the Patkai
hills now belongs to two different nation states.[10] Here was another
proof of Van Schendel's claim that 'borders not only join what is different but also divide what is similar' (2005: 9).

Some Tangsa are believed to have links with the outlawed Khaplang
faction of the NSCN in Myanmar. On the other hand, since the other
political parties in the area are either openly pro-Hindu (such as the
BJP) or pro-Assamese (such as the AGP), politically the Tangsa as
well as other small ethnic groups in the area have few options left but
to align with the Congress with the hope that their interests will be
secured.[11] However, their being pro-Naga and pro-establishment at the
same time is seen by many as mutually incompatible since the Naga,
who have been engaged in a long struggle for independence from the
Indian state, are assumed to be anti-Indian establishment by default.

Therefore, although Aphu's pro-Naga credentials are beyond doubt,
it was known that the NSCN was unhappy with him and some other
Tangsa elders who had not converted to Christianity. Perhaps, they also
do not like the fact that Aphu is friendly with some Congress leaders.
But that could not prevent Aphu getting beaten up by the Indian Army
some years back when he tried to defend some boys from the basti
the army had come looking for, suspecting them of having links with
the NSCN. Other Tangsa leaders have told me that it is mainly due to
Aphu's presence that the younger and more hot-headed ones amongst

the Tangsa leadership in Assam have so far refrained from resorting to violence to make their demands for political recognition heard.

The Wihu-kuh Festival at Kharangkong

Kharangkong is possibly the only Tangsa village in Assam where there are still a few families following their older traditional beliefs.[12] The founding fathers of the village had however embraced Buddhism soon after they settled in the area and came into contact with the Buddhist Tai Phake and Singpho communities of the neighbouring villages. As Buddhists, they began to follow the Buddhist calendar of rituals and celebrations and gave up celebrating their traditional Tangsa festivals till Aphu Tyanglam came along in the 1970s and tried to change that. Although traditionally there was no fixed date for the Wihu-kuh festival, Aphu Tyanglam fixed the date for 5 January.[13] Our research team happened to be present in Kharangkong for the first time during Wihu-kuh in 2008. While they were there, Aphu announced that Wihu-kuh would be celebrated on a much bigger scale in 2009. What follows is a description of what we saw in Kharangkong in January 2009 (when the festivities were a bit more elaborate than in the years 2008, 2011, 2012, at which we were also present).[14]

Description of the Festival

Wihu is the spirit of the earth and the festival of Wihu-kuh is a festival in honour of the earth spirit.[15] It is traditionally celebrated in a Tangsa home at dawn by sacrificing a chicken while saying the traditional ritual prayer called *rim-rim* at the ritual post (*men-ryo-chhung* in Cholim, see Photograph 4.1), holding a bamboo *khap* (container, *sunga* in Assamese) containing rice-beer (*chai* in Cholim) in one hand, thanking the spirit of the earth, and asking it to bring greater prosperity in the future.[16] The upper heads of the wooden notched ladders (*hija-chung*) at the entrance (and the back) of the house as well as the ritual post are nicely decorated with *chum-ki* flowers (*xo xo pyo*, in spoken Cholim) and *nyap-shak* (*koupat*, Assamese) leaves, and after the chicken has been sacrificed the post as well as the head of the ladders are smeared with blood, and a little prayer is said while pouring rice-beer over the flowers. This is done also at the chicken coop, the cattle pen, and the rice

Photograph 4.1   The *Men-ryo-chhung* (ritual altar) at Kharangkong
Source: Author.

granary. This is usually followed by performing augury with the claws of the chicken. The ritual basket (*ding-du-khya*) containing a khap with rice-beer, a packet of *chin-cha* (a spicy chutney made of rice, salt, ginger, and roasted meat) and some other items as well as the sacrificed chicken is then hung at the ritual post. The welcoming of Wihu, and hence by derivation also of the important guests, to a home is accompanied by singing of the Wihu song and the light dancing that accompanies it.

The rest of the celebration is mainly social, and comprises of visiting each other's homes, meeting up with relatives, drinking, and singing the Wihu/Shawi song together (as evident in Photograph 4.2). These social practices are aimed at maintaining family, clan, and community

Photograph 4.2   Celebrating Wihu-kuh at Kharangkong

Source: Author.

ties. It is also customary to send at least a bottle of rice-beer along with some select pieces of meat to one's maternal uncles at Wihu-kuh as a sign of respect, and in return for a blessing. Anyone who visits a Tangsa home on that day is given at least a small packet of roast meat to eat and rice-beer to drink. Guests, also from other communities, who come from afar, are often also offered a full meal with rice.[17] There is more singing throughout the day especially when the older people go to visit each other's homes but that is more or less the end of the rituals that takes place in most of the Tangsa homes in Kharangkong for Wihu-kuh.

However, a new 'secular ritual'—the flag hoisting—has been introduced by Aphu in Kharangkong. So in 2009, at exactly 7 a.m., the Tangsa flag, specially designed by Aphu, was hoisted in the field in front of Aphu's house by Aphu and Stephen in the presence of a few adults and children from the village.[18] It was followed by a short step-dance by a few girls from the 'kassa party', all wearing the colourful *mongnu khepa*—the special cloth that they wear at the time of the festival—to the sound of drums and gongs (see Photograph 4.3). Aphu, also dressed in a traditional attire, made a speech in Asamiya in which he explained the meaning of the flag and the various symbols depicted on it.[19] In most of the other years we were there, the flag-hoisting marked the end of the formalities. But in 2009, the festivities continued in Kharangkong. Most of what follows has already been described in Barkataki-Ruscheweyh (2013) but some of it is reproduced here for completeness. As the self-appointed host of the celebrations, Aphu had personally bought a pig and a cow and had them sacrificed at the *biri-chhung* (the sacrificial altar) set up at the village boundary (*hara-lim*) in the morning of Wihu-kuh.[20] He also invited (by sending out printed invitation cards in English) not only the entire village of Kharangkong and his relatives but also many Tangsa and non-Tangsa elders from elsewhere and government officials to attend the celebrations.[21]

Around 10 a.m., the traditional sports competition began—one-legged race, sack race, blindfolded race, musical chairs, pole-climbing, and so on. The most surprising element was the setting up of an elaborately decorated replica of the ritual post, in the middle of the field, next to the flag post, at the foot of which a large container of rice-beer was placed. This had not been done ever before and has not been done since in Kharangkong. Aphu told me that setting up of this post was mainly symbolic, and was meant to show outsiders what they normally would not get to see, as the actual rituals for the festival take place inside people's homes very early in the morning. In this manner, the first step towards dissociation of the older ritual from its actual site of performance was made.[22] The rim-rim, however, was not performed at this new outdoor post, although a few older Tangsa ladies later gathered around the post, drank rice-beer, and kept singing bits of the Wihu song for quite a long time.

Slowly the field started filling up with people, also from neighbouring villages, and the invited dignitaries also started arriving. A little stage—actually a small bamboo chang—(see Figure 4.2) had been erected at one end of the big field in front of Aphu's house where the dignitaries were ceremonially welcomed and from where they made their speeches. The public meeting, which was scheduled for 11 a.m., started more than an hour later as most of the invited dignitaries and government officials arrived late. The SDO and Sub-Divisional Police Officer arrived much later, at around 1 p.m., along with a large platoon of security guards. Others like the Singpho chief Bisa nong Singpho and a senior Assamese journalist from Ledo were already there. There were many speeches. Most speakers, including Aphu himself, spoke in Asamiya, except for Stephen

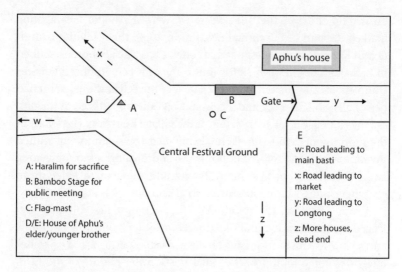

Figure 4.2   Layout of the Festival area for the Wihu-kuh Celebrations in 2009

Source: Author.

who spoke in Cholim. The speeches were interspersed with 'folk dances', the term used by Aphu in his invitation card.

This was followed by lunch served in the field to about two hundred guests. Tangsa elders and leaders from the Kharangkong main basti and elsewhere such as Gaonbura Hakhun (from Malugaon) and Lemo Rara (from Phulbari), as well as Singpho, Tai Phake, and Nepali leaders from neighbouring villages were present.[23]

The menu was rice balls (*cham-thop*) wrapped in *nyap-shak* (*koupat*, Assamese) leaves—which when opened up served as the plate—a mixed vegetable salad, fish, pork, beef, salad, and so forth, and rice-beer served in bamboo khaps.[24] Aphu left the dignitaries on the terrace of his house to drink rice-beer and munch on roasted pork to join the people seated on the ground in the field for the meal—a sign of a good host and a shrewd leader. While the people were eating, two Tangsa elders, one from the neighbouring village of Hewe Ninggam and the other from Kharangkong, went up to the stage, took a microphone each, and started to sing the Wihu song. Finally, there was another round of dances including the Sahpolo when the dignitaries also joined in. The whole event ended around 3:30 p.m. There were endless streams of guests to the Tyanglam household that evening and in the days that followed.

Modifying Traditions: (Re)articulating Culture

For Aphu, it was important that the tradition of festivals which they had grown up with in the hills should be carried on. But it was clear to him as well as to the others that it is not possible any longer to celebrate all the festivals that they had in the past in the way they had done while they were still in the hills.[25] Therefore, the Tangsa living in Kharangkong, goaded on by Aphu, have decided to celebrate at least the Wihu-kuh festival every year in their homes. Aphu claims he has been celebrating the Wihu-kuh, in its present form, in Kharangkong since 1985.

Surmising from what our team recorded in 2009, Aphu's version of the Wihu-kuh festival combined elements of a secular government meeting (with flag hoisting and a public meeting), the 'traditional' Wihu-kuh festival (with the rituals in the house and the singing), and the 'imagined' traditional feast-of-merit called the Wangjang-kuh mentioned in the last chapter (with Aphu hosting the festivities and arranging for the sacrifice of the pig and a cow followed by a community feast) to create a new kind of festival. But he called the festival Wihu-kuh, possibly in order to claim continuity with the older tradition; and also because it would have greater acceptance as a community festival than the Wangjang-kuh.

Many Pangwa elders, however, were confused when I referred to the winter festival as Wihu-kuh, following Aphu Tyanglam. The names for the winter festival differ with tribe, for instance, the Hakhun in Malugaon celebrate a festival called Seiju-kuh in mid December while the Ronrangs in Phulbari call their winter festival Shawi-kuh. While the Hakhuns do not have the Wihu-song, the Ronrangs are supposed to have only acquired it from other Pangwa groups over time.

In any case, Aphu Tyanglam has also brought in many modifications to the way the Wihu-kuh festival is celebrated today. We were told that in earlier times, among the Pangwa groups, drums (and also gongs) could be sounded only on occasions when blood would flow, either when they were going to war or when a buffalo (or a human being) was sacrificed; but Aphu claims he campaigned among his people for these rules to be relaxed. Today gongs and drums are often used as musical instruments accompanying the 'traditional' dances that are performed at Tangsa festivals. Moreover, although traditionally Tangsa dancers were mostly men, nowadays the dancers are predominantly girls and women. Furthermore, the Sahpolo dance, which was usually performed only during the summer Moh/Mol festival, was performed at almost every Tangsa festival we attended; so much so that it is fast becoming *the* Tangsa dance, just as the Bihu dance is for the Assamese.[26]

What then were the 'traditional' dances that Aphu had taught to his 'kassa party'? By his own admission, Aphu had choreographed and taught his own daughters and a few others from the village the older songs and dances, some of which he knew from the hills, but *modified and adapted to 'modern' times*. Just as was the case with the Panglhabsol dance in Sikkim when 'a ritual specialist from Ralang was requested to teach the dances to a dozen young men from the town' (Vandenhelsken 2011: 87), Aphu also taught the dances to his 'kassa party'.

Dances like the Sahpolo, according to some Tangsa elders, in the form that one saw it at present, were added to the Tangsa repertoire only after they came down the hills.[27] The most recent innovation has been to set the Wihu song to modern dance (Morey and Schöpf, under review). Aphu Tyanglam finds it easy to improvize, and although we were told that there were strict rules about how and when to sing the Wihu song, Aphu had no hesitation, on at least one occasion, to modify the lines a little to turn it into a farewell song to bid goodbye to our team. Moreover, even the performance of traditional songs like the Wihu had moved first from people's homes to the open field (in front of Aphu's house in Kharangkong) and later onto the stage (in Phulbari in 2010).

This is precisely the principle of 'emergent authenticity' (Cohen 1988: 371) according to which older traditions and events survive in more modern forms while new 'invented' ones become an integral part of the community's calendar. I wish to argue here that these new forms are still 'traditional' in the sense that, just like the Wihu-kuh festival that I witnessed in Kharangkong, they are based on older forms, either actually or simply imagined or perceived to be so. Linguistic analysis reveals that although the choreography is quite new, the words of the songs and the tune—at least of a song named 'Wang-shya'—are demonstrably related to the more 'traditional' forms. These older forms have been 'modified and adapted to "modern" times' no doubt, but into forms which the older Tangsa can still recognize and relate to.

This is also important because although cultural memory can be unreliable, it can still unify and give something in common to hold on to, even though actual practice can vary. Moreover they are 'traditional' relative to the newer forms which are also to be seen at Tangsa festivals, forms which had either been borrowed from the omnipresent Bollywood culture (as will be evident in the next chapter) or altogether new forms that have been put together, such as the newly created Tangsa anthem where each verse is sung in a different Tangsa language (which I recorded at the Pangsau Pass Winter Festival in Nampong, 2009).

For What Ends

For Aphu, celebrating the festival of Wihu-kuh is, above everything else, an assertion of his Tangsa-ness. The songs and dances are for him part of the Tangsa 'kassa'. So what did Aphu exactly mean by 'kassa'? The fact that he uses his variant of an English word and not any Tangsa word is telling because it implies that 'kassa' (or what he understands it to be) is something external, defined by others, and is therefore not integral to his understanding of being Tangsa. Chanwang, my Nocte assistant and constant companion in the field, helped me to formulate the definition of 'kassa' in this context, while we were at the Dihing-Patkai Festival. In his words, 'song, dance and costume as well as language, food and living habits constitute a community's culture'.[28]

For Aphu, however, being Tangsa meant much more than just being able to perform their 'kassa', for it included not only those elements mentioned above but also their rituals, their stories, their migration history, and also knowledge about how their forefathers used to live in the hills. Thus, Aphu could make a difference between their explicit culture (that which is seen or shown), which he called 'kassa', and their tacit culture (that which is felt) which he believed to be their Tangsa-ness. And it was very important for Aphu that the Tangsa should learn and know about both, otherwise there would be no difference between them and animals: 'If we do not know who we *were*, how will we define who we *are*?' he told me once. But why is there this need to go back to the past? Chanwang helped me achieve clarity also about this: 'Tribals have to look to their past to define their identity as in the present they all look the same as modern jeans-wearing, mobile-phone-wielding people.'[29]

Traditionally, Wihu-kuh could be held anytime in December–January after the harvesting was over (see also Rao 2006: 195). One of the main reasons for fixing the date was that the Tangsa in Assam

Photograph 4.3   Sahpolo Dance at Kharangkong during Wihu-kuh

Source: Author.

led by Aphu wanted to demand a local holiday for the Tangsa in that area on that day for the festival. They have made their demand to the local authorities, but it has not been granted since most of the Buddhist and Christian Tangsa living in other villages in Assam do not celebrate Wihu-kuh. For these and other reasons, the celebration of Wihu-kuh has been, by and large, restricted to Kharangkong and to Aphu's circle of family and followers.

Celebrating Wihu-kuh every year is part of a bigger agenda Aphu has for the revival and preservation, and for ensuring the continuity of their cultural traditions. He believed that the Tangsa living in Assam were on the verge of 'losing their identity' by getting assimilated into the greater Assamese population. The other aim that Aphu had was to spread the word around not just among the non-Christian Tangsa but also among those who had converted. His argument was that since everyone eats rice, regardless of religion, and since Wihu-kuh is about inviting the spirit of the earth (who gives us rice) to the home to thank it for a good harvest and to ask for a better one next time, the Christians should have no problems with joining in to celebrate it. He had even arranged for Wihu-kuh to be held in a Christian Arunachali village of Longtom one year, sometime around 2000.

In order to train more young people in the Tangsa dances, Aphu had sent a team from his 'kassa party' to Arunachal Pradesh one year during a Moh/Mol festival. He believed that being able to put up a 'cultural show' was important not only for those who came to see but also for those who actually performed, since each of the dancers in Aphu's 'kassa party' could at least now 'perform' a few Tangsa dances (even though they perhaps did not understand the meaning of the lyrics, or know how to sing the Wihu song), and hence it gave them an additional reason to feel happy about being Tangsa.

Although Aphu was aware of the instrumental aspects of having an identity, for him, first and foremost, knowing about one's own traditions had some intangible intrinsic value, which was more than enough reason in itself. But he felt that the younger generation did not share this view. Another elder from Phulbari echoed the same sentiments: 'The young people are not interested in any of the old customs, they are busy making money; they do not realise that they will also need it someday.' As to why they might need it in the future, the answer was always the same: to tell their children what it means to be Tangsa.

But what were the older customs and traditions that they were talking about? In the hills, the celebration of Kuh comprised mainly the rituals performed at home, the singing of the Wihu song, drinking rice-beer, eating roast meat, and visiting each other. But that did not correspond with the modern-day idea of a 'cultural festival' prevalent in northeast India, which also included a component of entertainment. Moreover, there were not many left who knew how to perform the rituals, nor many who could sing the Wihu song. And not many of the youngsters were too interested in participating in those older festivals, the problem aggravated by the fact that many had also converted to Christianity.

Hence, Aphu saw the need to suitably 'dress up' the traditional notion of a village festival in order to make it more attractive, both for those who participated and for the audience, and at the same time make it fit in better with other cultural festivals organized in that area. In other words, an official looking 'cultural programme' needed to be added. To achieve this, as already mentioned, Aphu came up with a few dances basing the steps and lyrics on older forms. The Sahpolo was there already, and it would be performed also at the winter festival; the drums, gongs, and the colourful dresses would add festivity to the proceedings, the rice-beer and roast meat would be served in any case, and all of this would together give the Tangsa people living in Kharangkong as well as outsiders an idea about Tangsa 'kassa'. This sounds remarkably similar to the process by which the Panglhabsol dance was woven into a full-scale festival in Sikkim as described by Vandenhelsken: 'Gradually, various lay elements were added to the celebration, such as volleyball matches, the "traditional" dances of various ethnic groups, which together were called the "cultural programme", and the market stands. The "neo-ritual" was soon institutionalised through the creation of an official organising committee' (2011: 87).

And in order to make it look more official and representative, elements from secular festivals like the flag-hoisting ceremony and a public meeting were added (a cultural procession was also added in Phulbari in 2010). Local administrative officials and political and tribal leaders were invited. This was done to gain visibility and legitimacy in order to be able to instrumentalize it for larger political ends; for, at the personal level, the successful organization of these festivals gained Aphu recognition in a wider circle, ranging from the Tangsa people, representatives of other neighbouring communities to the district and state administration, as the undisputed leader and representative of the Tangsa in Assam. But looking ahead, although Aphu exhorting his Tangsa people to know more about their past traditions was something he felt very strongly about and for which he had campaigned long and hard, as the following sections and chapters will reveal, it is far from clear whether all his efforts will be enough to secure for the Tangsa their identity, in a form that he would like them to.

The Village of Kharangkong

The word Kharangkong comes from the Singpho words *kharang* which means dry cultivation and *kong* (meaning 'slightly raised land'). The village of Kharangkong is located south of the Buri Dihing river, and very close to the Buddhist Tai Phake village of Ninggam and the old Singpho villages of Pangshun, Kumsaigaon, and Kotha, the Ahom village of Koyapani, the old Naga Sema village of Longtong as well as another old Tangsa village called Hewe Ninggam, as shown in Map 4.1.

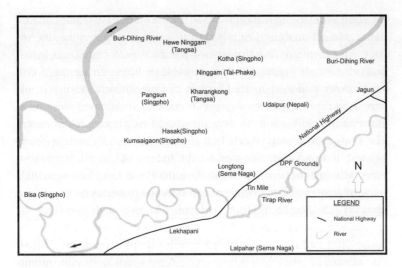

Map 4.1   Sketch Map of the Villages in the Area around Kharangkong

Source: Jayanta Laskar and Inez Ruscheweyh.

Note: Map not to scale and does not represent authentic international boundaries.

Kharangkong is not marked on the 1927 British maps. But the now predominantly Singpho-speaking village of Hasak is marked as Hasak (Naga). Hewe Ninggam is perhaps the oldest Tangsa settlement in the area, followed by Kharangkong, sometime in the late 1930s or early 1940s. The Cholim basti of Kharangkong was established much later in the early 1970s as already mentioned. By a rough count there are 37 Tangsa families in main Kharangkong (9 of them Mossang) and about 17 (9 Cholim) in the Cholim basti. But they are outnumbered by the 58 Ahom, 15 Nepali, 7 Adivasi, and 1 Bihari families who live in the Assamese and Nepali bastis that came up much later around the two older bastis and are all mostly Hindu. Official records state the population of Kharangkong to be 657 in 2011 and 519 in 2001. Being a mixed village, even in terms of the Tangsa groups living there, the lingua franca for the Tangsa living in the Main basti is Singpho (and increasingly also Asamiya).

Hindu-Buddhists: A Convenient Double-representation

The Singpho and Tai Phake living in the area around Kharangkong are Buddhists, the Naga Sema are Christian, and the Tangsa are

Hindu-Buddhists, according to Aphu. But who are Hindu-Buddhists? Aphu coined the term 'Hindu-Buddhist' for those living in the Cholim basti who continue to follow their traditional practices. But in actual practice they are neither Hindu nor Buddhist. Though they put themselves down officially as Buddhist in the government records, most Tangsa living in Kharangkong still do animal sacrifice on festive occasions such as Wihu-kuh; so they are not strictly Theravada Buddhists. The Tangsa are certainly not Hindu, in that they do not believe in any of the Hindu gods and goddesses. But Aphu and many other Tangsa elders whom I met in the hills use the term 'Hindu', for lack of a better term, to mean a follower of the older traditions (possibly because like a section of the Hindus, they also performed animal sacrifices).

There are other reasons too for claiming to be Hindu-Buddhists. Earlier they had no proper name for their traditional practices.[30] They also wanted to assert their difference from the majority Hindu community around them (comprising mostly of the Nepali and the Assamese Ahom). Moreover, Buddhism had already arrived in the area and was known to be a mild, non-demanding, non-assertive religion. They do exactly as Scott (2009: 319) predicted by 'adopt[ing] a religious identity at variance with that of the core-state populations, whose culture they associate with their stigmatisation'.

There were also historical reasons for adopting Buddhism. The Singpho village of Kotha and the Tai Phake village of Ninggam are very close to Kharangkong. A Buddhist monastery was built in Ninggam around 1960. Following the example of the Singpho and Tai Phake friends and neighbours, the Tangsa in Kharangkong also embraced Buddhism. Moreover, Tangsa traditional practices can easily be combined with Buddhism as is clear from the following excerpt from my field notes about a meeting with a Tangsa priest:[31]

> In the nearby Tangsa village of Hewe Ninggam I met one of the few remaining practising priests (*dumsa*) of the Tangsa traditional religion. He told me he is a Buddhist but that he still performs the duties of a dumsa (which he had learnt while assisting his father and other older dumsa in their work earlier) due to public pressure and on public request. People still invite him for housewarmings or when someone was ill, but those occasions are few and far between. No one else in the village knew those traditional practices, and the knowledge would die with him, he feared. Interestingly, he had pictures of both Buddha and Shiva hanging on the walls of the room of his house where he met us. When I asked him

how he could be both a Buddhist and a dumsa, he told me that he was Buddhist because they were all Buddhists in his village and he did not want to go against his own people, but all of them still followed their old religion in their everyday life. (Hewe Ninggam, 31 October 2009)

However, Aphu Tyanglam, as the foremost 'Hindu-Buddhist', did not always make it easy for others to understand how the system could work. Since he was a Buddhist he could not kill, so he usually gets his wife to sacrifice the chicken on the morning of Wihu-kuh while he sings the rim-rim and conducts the rest of the rituals in their house. He got his elder brother to sacrificially kill the pig and the cow in 2009; however, he did the augury with the chicken claws and the pig liver later. I have never seen Aphu visit the Buddhist temple in Ninggam.[32] It did seem that the degree of Hindu-ness or Buddhist-ness that a Hindu-Buddhist demonstrated varied, depending on who the person was.

I had once asked the rather young Buddhist monk (*bhante*) from the Ninggam monastery how someone could claim to be Buddhist when they still sacrificed animals for ritual purposes. The bhante did not seem too perturbed by my question, and replied,

Buddhism is not a religion that coerces anybody into doing anything. If anyone comes to ask me, I will surely tell him or her that drinking too much rice-beer or sacrificing animals are both bad actions, but as a Buddhist each individual is free to choose his or her own actions, a person's karma will reflect his or her actions—be they good or bad.

He went on to say that since there were so few Buddhists in India at present they were forced to make concessions about the practices of their followers if they wanted to survive at all.[33]

Mixed Ancestries, Fluid Identities

The villages surrounding Kharangkong (Tangsa, Assamese, Nepali) are Ninggam (Tai Phake, Bengali, Tangsa), Kothagaon (originally Singpho but now only 3 families are left, besides 35 Ahom families and 45 Nepali families), Udaipur (Nepali—very large), Pakhagaon (Tea-garden Hindu), and Navajyoti (Assamese, Tea tribes and some Nepali).[34] Beyond it are the Ahom village of Koyapani and the Sema Naga village at Longtong (see Map 4.1). So the ethnic picture of the greater area around Kharangkong was highly mixed to say the least.

Since there has been a fair number of intermarriages across communities, the mixed ancestries of many of the people living there at present is not difficult to explain. And this diversity has been a feature, even at the time of the establishment of the village. The three founding fathers of Kharangkong were not all from the same Tangsa tribe—they were Langching, Lungri, and Mossang. But that was not all. The mother of the Mossang Gaonbura of Kharangkong was Manipuri Hindu, from the neighbouring state of Manipur. That came about simply because a Manipuri family also happened to come to live in the village just like all the others, I was told.

Some ancestries were even more complex: one of our main interlocutors in Kharangkong has a Ronrang father and a Langching mother. Both his parents came from Burma; they separated at some point and the mother and child came away and settled in the Langching Tangsa village of Hewe Ninggam, where the mother married a Kachari elephant-catcher.[35] Our interlocutor married a Nepali woman and had two daughters. One daughter is married to a Singpho and lives in Miao. The other married a Sema Naga man from Hasak. All this is very confusing, but why did our interlocutor call himself a Langching? It is because he has always lived in the Langching village (of Hewe Ninggam), he told me simply.

From this and the many other examples it is clear that tribal affiliations are not as watertight as they are believed to be. What is more, changing membership from one Tangsa group to another was not only not difficult, but it was actually also the norm in certain situations, especially when a family or two of one Tangsa group came to live in a village where the majority community was from another group.[36] Moreover, the bigger Tangsa groups who have been in the area for a longer period, such as the Mossang, the Juglei, and the Yongkuk, had demarcated areas in the hills which were supposed to be their territories (khels). Permission to settle in a village in the territory of one of those groups implied or required adopting the ways of the group. The new settler families quickly learnt the language and soon also changed their names.

And this is prevalent also in other ethnic groups of the area as Ramirez reports about the Karbi community he works with:[37] 'The adoption of individuals or groups originating from a different ethnicity is far from being a marginal phenomenon and is often institutionalised …. As people move from one community to another, they adopt new cultural features and a new surname, but on a broader scale, prescribed alliances and relations of exogamy are preserved' (Ramirez 2013: 279).

And while this routinely happened amongst the different Tangsa groups, the degree of difficulty varied—the closer the groups were traditionally and historically, the easier it was. While Tangsa women, on marriage, routinely adopted the ways and language of their husband's group, it was also not uncommon to find examples where women from non-Tangsa communities became Tangsa after marriage. Instances of non-Tangsa men (from other neighbouring tribal communities like the Nocte and Singpho) becoming Tangsa were less frequent although not unknown.

As Burling very aptly comments, ethnic boundaries are neither 'permanent nor unambiguous. Rather, the boundaries are contested, constructed, negotiated, imagined. This allows ethnicity to be changed' (Burling 2012: 60–1). The Tangsa case also confirms what was observed by Leach (1954) about the neighbouring Kachins and the transformations that were possible in their social structures and the flexibility that was inherent in their cultural patterns and practices.

Looking behind the Curtains

The Grey Zones

The first impression one gets of the Kharangkong main basti is striking: The houses are large and look well-cared for, the tea gardens are lush and green and well-tended, and the pigs and fowls look fat and well-fed. These images are proof of how hardworking and enterprising Tangsa women in general are and how much pride they take in taking care of their homes and surroundings, but not of the general level of wealth or education in the village. There are a few enterprising families in the main basti who are reasonably well off because they have a lot of land which still yield good crops. Most of their children are studying in good schools and colleges, and are well on their way to a better material standard of life, even though it is not clear whether they would return to the village to live off their land like their parents or would prefer to go away and find employment elsewhere.

But apart from these few families, the others are not doing as well, even less so in the Cholim basti. The older generation is mostly illiterate. Most of the younger children go to the primary school more than a kilometre away at Koyapani. The middle-aged population have all had some education, but not many amongst the adults in Kharangkong have finished school and Kharangkong is still a largely illiterate society. Many gave up after primary school; those who made it to high school stopped at Class IX or X, as they were just not able to clear the end-of-school public exam.[38] The situation with the youngsters is not very different.[39] There was a very high dropout rate at the local village middle school. The standard reason given for this by many was that since one would have to work in the fields and had no chance of ever getting a job, they saw no reason to study further. Being a *jawan* (Hindi, soldier) in the army was the only job that seemed possible, for which not much education was necessary. And since they earned enough from their palm tree plantations, their rice fields, and their tea gardens, the status quo continued.

When I spoke to Aphu Tyanglam later about the low educational levels in the village, he had a lot to say: 'Unless the parents themselves become responsible nobody can do anything. When most fathers go to play cards and drink every evening and are addicted to alcohol and opium, when the mothers remain uneducated and do not know what is good for their children, then there was no way to stop the downward slide.[40] In such a situation nothing can be done to help anyone', he said and continued. 'They will just squander away their lives like that, or become "terrorists" because they wish to imitate all the fighting they see everyday on TV', he concluded. [41] That was Aphu's opinion; there were many others in Kharangkong, however, who argued that if Aphu had really shown the way, like a true leader, then Kharangkong should have and would have done much better.

Opium addiction is still prevalent to a very high degree in Kharangkong; drinking of alcohol and rice-beer is also common, especially amongst men. It is not uncommon to find Tangsa men in Kharangkong sitting around a fire, smoking opium all day while the women go out to work. Besides the impact on health, it was also a serious drain on the family resources. Gambling made things even worse. For these reasons, many in the neighbouring Tangsa village of Hewe Ninggam were either sick or bankrupt or both.

A vignette: Although almost illiterate, one of our interlocutors in Kharangkong was very good with languages. He spoke perfect Asamiya, and was Stephen's interlocutor for Langching. But he did not have any regular employment or work. On many occasions, I have found him in people's houses, sitting in the outer area with other men (and smoking opium, I was told). He had some land but had sold it all little by little and was now almost down to this last plot. His two daughters also had not studied very far. Although married, his younger daughter seemed to be back home again with her father. She had a little booth in the market area where she sells bottled 'sulai mod' (locally brewed alcohol), which she buys from the wholesale market and sells at a profit.

A visit to the Kharangkong weekly market on Fridays reveals many of these problems. On the face of it, it had the usual vendors—mostly Bihari, Nepali, and also Assamese—selling vegetables, provisions, clothes, shoes, and so forth. That was the section where women were seen buying essential items of food and clothing. On another side, however, there was a row of shops, all selling raw and roast meat, country liquor and with gambling and dicing counters set up in front. That was where most of the men gathered. And they played for money. A few policemen were also seen on duty but they did not seem to be doing much. They even looked a bit drunk, and seemed to be enjoying the fun.[42]

Another vignette: The women of the leading Christian family in the village had once told me that it was a blessing that their men don't drink. However, soon afterwards, during a festival in a nearby village, they put up stall to sell roast pork and rum/whisky/brandy. 'We are doing it only for the money', they told me, rather unabashedly, seeing the surprise written on my face.

Finally, the proximity of the larger Nepali and Assamese communities (with their large and influential networks) has become a big threat to my Tangsa interlocutors in Kharangkong. When the Nepalis first began to arrive, since the Tangsa owned a lot of land around the area, they allowed the Nepalis to work on their fields on a share-cropping basis. But over the years some Tangsa have (informally) sold their land to the Nepalis when they needed money for some event (such as an illness or a wedding). Most of my Tangsa friends have been no match for the more enterprising Nepalis, their inability to compete being aggravated by their relative illiteracy and deterioration in health due to addiction to opium and alcohol.

The Tangsa situation in Kharangkong is typical of other ethnic communities in the area, such as the Singpho, where opium addiction is also prevalent. The relatively small population of these communities have also been a disadvantage. As a result, the 'older' tribal groups who had first settled in the area are now gradually losing out to the relatively new settler communities who have greater bargaining power, higher levels of education, and are also more competitive.

Fissures and Fault Lines in Kharangkong

The first non-tribal person to settle in that area was an Ahom teacher from Sibsagar named Upen Konwar. Ironically, although the tribal leaders wanted all the settlers to leave the area now, Konwar was actually invited by the tribal village chiefs to settle there to teach their children.[43] The first primary school was started in Kharangkong in 1955 with Konwar as the teacher. But those were different times. In the words of the present village schoolmaster, Toseshwar Gogoi, another Ahom:

> In the 1960s, Kharangkong, Ninggam, Kothagaon and the Sema Naga village of Longtong were much larger villages than they are now, and there was a very good system of village administration in place to resolve all problems, including judicial ones such as elopement or theft. Five puras of land was kept aside as public land and the produce of that land was put in public granaries, for distribution to the villagers in time of need. With increase in the number of people living in the area, the forests have shrunk and the animals, birds, fish, even the trees have disappeared.
> (Kharangkong, 6 January 2012)

If all that was not enough, there were new problems in the present. The Tangsa population in Kharangkong is physically divided, since the Cholim basti is not part of the main basti, but this divide has over time assumed a bigger dimension as it has spread to other factors beyond geography: the Cholim–non-Cholim divide implies that Cholim is spoken in the Cholim basti while Singpho is spoken in the main basti; this divide also has become a religious divide—while most Tangsa in the main basti are practising Buddhists, those in the Cholim basti are Hindu-Buddhists. But the most significant difference between the two bastis is the presence of Aphu Tyanglam in one and not in the other.

There are a few leaders in the main basti too, descendants of the founding fathers of the village, but they are younger and no match for Aphu. While they are willing to concede that Aphu has done a lot to make Tangsa 'culture' known to the world outside, their main objection was to Aphu's style of functioning—he never gave others a chance, and tended to speak on behalf of the whole community. They resented the fact that Aphu presented himself as the one and only Tangsa leader.

Moreover, many Buddhists in the main basti had problems with Aphu's interpretation of religious beliefs and Buddhist practices. This did not bother Aphu in the least. He had much bigger concerns about the Christian converts in the village. One of the front ranking members of his 'kassa party' was banned from visiting the Aphu household after he joined the village Presbyterian Church.[44] Such acts have only isolated Aphu further, as more and more Tangsa are gradually turning to Christianity. But for Aphu, his reasons for disliking Christianity were clear—it was a religion of rules (one *must* go to church every Sunday), of force (one must *not* drink rice-beer), and of 'business' (the church actually *buys* converts by giving them money and other things but the tithes one has to pay over the next years to the church eventually takes everything back and more). Moreover, according to him, the converts had no freedom and had to organize their lives as the church leaders told them to.

For all these reasons, in recent years, there has been a subtle parting of ways; for example, on New Year's Day there are two picnic parties organized in Kharangkong—one in the main basti and the other in Aphu's back garden. Although there is a lot of contact among the people living in the two bastis and they still help and support each other, strong feelings surface as soon as Aphu comes into the picture.[45] In many ways, Aphu Tyanglam has become the one single factor that plays a role in almost all that happens in Kharangkong at present. Furthermore, as will be evident in Chapter 6, his presence and his proactive role might be creating at least as many problems as it is solving for the Tangsa in Assam in general and for those living in the village of Kharangkong in particular. What will happen after Aphu Tyanglam is gone is hard to predict. But, for the moment, there is a forced uneasy calm.

A Proud but Beaten Man

In a sense, Aphu was already of the past. The younger lot barely suffered him; one felt that there would be no holding them back, once he was gone. Many things would change and that change had already started in the main Kharangkong basti.[46] As already mentioned, many believed that Aphu had done very little for his own village. Many accused Aphu for the sorry state of education levels in the village. He did not value education, I was told, since he could not read and write himself—that he could read and write in Burmese was not taken into account.[47] Although many were scared of this proud Tangsa 'Raja' (king)—as Aphu was sometimes referred to—it was always sad to see his helplessness when a letter (written in English or Asamiya) arrived in his name and he was not able to read it. And this inability did cost him heavy at times, for instance, he always seemed to make losses on road-repair contracts which he executed jointly with an Assamese man from the main basti. Of course, he would explain it off, in his characteristic style, by saying that he wanted to do the job properly irrespective of the costs.

But after having seen Aphu Tyanglam in action all these years, one can sense the change—he is gradually growing old and losing his hold over his people. Many signs of this were evident. The first sign came when he was not able to prevent Christianity from coming to the village despite his being so vehemently opposed to it. Having all his life held the view that Christianity was responsible for the decay of Tangsa traditional culture, he had sternly forbidden everyone to become Christian. Yet, it had arrived in his own basti during his lifetime. And the number of Christian converts from Kharangkong is going up steadily.

Then there was the problem regarding the organization of the Wihu-kuh festival. It was Aphu's wish that Wihu-kuh should be celebrated centrally by all Tangsa living in Assam on 5 January every year, and that the location should keep changing. To this effect, he organized it in 2009 in Kharangkong and persuaded Tangsa elders in Phulbari to host it in 2010. And although Phulbari hosted it and organized a big festival as will be clear in Chapter 6, Aphu annoyed everyone by not respecting certain agreements made earlier. Consequently, most other Christian Tangsa villages were reluctant to come forward to host future festivals.

This has hurt Aphu very much. In a very emotional moment, he told me once that he knew that a time will come when every Tangsa would have become Christian, and when all his people would only speak in Asamiya. But still he tried and did what he could; he travelled everywhere to exhort the Tangsa to do something about preserving their language and traditions. He wanted people to remember that at least he tried. However, he knew that many others did not agree with him and hence the battle would eventually be lost. But still that could not be reason for him to not do what he thought was right, and he would continue to do so till his last breath, even if it meant having to celebrate Wihu-kuh by himself in his own home only.

If he was upset that other Tangsa were no longer acting according to his wishes, defiance from within his own family hurt him even more. One by one, two of his unmarried daughters eloped within the space of a year; one of them with a Christian. Not being able to keep even his own house in order has been a big blow to Aphu's self-respect and also his standing in society. In his effort to recover face, in March 2012, Aphu got his youngest son married, very traditionally, to a Mossang girl from the neighbouring village of Hasak. Even the news of his being made the Vice-President of the Development Council did not help much to raise the spirits of the old man. 'I am tired of having to do everything alone', he told me, referring to his lifelong campaign to tell the Tangsa the importance of remembering what it means to be Tangsa, 'if others don't want it, then let it be'.

Before I end this chapter, it is important to look back and work out why this one man's experiences and reflections are important to the research questions under investigation. First of all, by taking a closer look at Aphu's home, family, and daily routine, the intention was to convey an impression of how most Tangsa live in Assam at the present time. It is true that Aphu is not a 'typical' Tangsa in any sense, but many Tangsa homes look like his. Furthermore, it is also important to understand Aphu's personal biography and development as a Tangsa leader. Because, as the foremost Tangsa leader in Assam, at least for the present, Aphu's understanding of what Tangsa-ness means or ought to mean definitely impacts on current Tangsa representations of their identity; and also because by figuring out what his priorities are at present, one might gain some insight into how things might evolve for the Tangsa in Assam in the next few years.

Postscript: Doing Fieldwork with Aphu

For a long time, Aphu Tyanglam mistook my being Assamese to mean that I was Ahom; perhaps it was because most of the Assamese who lived near Kharangkong were Ahom. He also asked me about my family—and I replied as truthfully as I could without saying more than was necessary. Every time I would visit, as is usual in Tangsa society, the first questions would always be about the well-being of my family. It never occurred to Aphu to ask me if my mother worked, and hence I did not feel the need to tell him more. By the time he came to visit me in Guwahati for the first time, I had already been working with him and the Tangsa for more than three years, and although he was surprised to meet my mother and to learn about her past career in politics (and he later jokingly accused me of not telling him the whole truth), it did not seem to make any difference anymore to how he or the others in his family treated me. That was a very big relief.

My German connection was also a constant source of confusion. Aphu introduced me everywhere as the 'baideo (Assamese, sister) from Germany' because for him it was clear that I was German since I was married to one—such were the rules of the Tangsa world. When I would protest he would reluctantly add that I was also 'a daughter of Assam'. Although I called him 'aphu' (elder brother), I was quickly inducted into the family as a daughter and was treated as such.

But then, like a true concerned father, Aphu would insist that I call him every few days, even when I was not actually working in the area, and tell him my whereabouts and about my travel plans—I found it a bit of a burden at times, but I found myself reporting back to him every now and then as it somehow felt safer when I had told him. There were often reports of firing, army searches, and police operations to uncover underground activities of various militant groups and there were a couple of very close calls, but fortunately, I never came face-to-face with any real danger even once during any of my field trips. One reason for this could be the fact that Aphu claimed to be on very good terms with some of the different factions of 'ultras' (or underground insurgents) active in the area, and that he had told them about the work our project was doing towards preservation of Tangsa culture and had asked them to leave me alone. In fact, he even went further to say that he had requested them to keep an eye on me to see that no harm came to me. Although I have no way of verifying this claim made by Aphu, some incidents that happened during my stay in Tangsaland make me inclined to believe him.

Aphu expected me to obey him, just as he expected everyone else to obey him. When I was staying with him in Kharangkong the rule was that I could go anywhere I wished to during the day, preferably with one of the girls but also alone if no one had the time to accompany me, but that I should definitely get back home at dusk and not venture out anymore till the next morning. However, the fact that in winter dusk came very early to those parts of Assam (around 5 p.m.) meant that I essentially had only half a day to work outside the home. So I usually landed up spending a lot of time chatting with Aphu and his family in the evenings.

That in turn essentially implied chatting with Aphu alone, for he would seldom let the women speak up in his presence. Aphu's wife, Renya, was a rather frail-looking elderly woman who was always busy working and keeping an eye over everything. I slowly got used to Aphu answering for her. It was not that Renya was not capable of doing so; on the contrary, she knew a lot, and had a very sharp memory. Aphu would often ask for her help when he forgot something, for example, what the name of some village or some person was. But Aphu would just not let her speak for herself. And she actually allowed him to have his way. Of course that did not stop me from talking to her, often when Aphu was away. From what I understood, it was more out of habit and less out of fear or admiration that Renya allowed Aphu to answer for her. But that, in turn, allowed Aphu to continue to believe that he was the cleverest person around and the only one competent enough to talk to his 'learned' guests.

Aphu's pride about his knowledge also created some other problems, for example, it made him a very possessive interlocutor. Since he believed that he was the most knowledgeable amongst our Tangsa interlocutors, he felt there was no need for us to go and talk to anyone else. Aphu was not happy when I expressed the wish to stay in the main basti and to meet other Tangsa people—'what more can they tell you that I have not told you already', he would pout. He would be offended when I would say I was going away or when I would first go somewhere and come back and tell him about having met some other knowledgeable elder. He would then immediately tell me some story about him which would either prove that what that elder had told me was only what Aphu had told him earlier, or he would try to somehow illustrate that his knowledge was deeper.

And sometimes it was clear that he misunderstood some of our project aims: for instance, Aphu confided in me a couple of times that he was hoping that Stephen's linguistic work would one day help the Tangsa to develop a common Tangsa language, taking words from the various Tangsa languages! Stephen, however, was not as hopeful, not so much because of the difference in the pronunciation of words, but also because of the different grammatical structures of the different Tangsa languages.

Nevertheless, Aphu did know a lot and he was by far also the most resourceful and supportive amongst our field interlocutors. Moreover, he was our first real Tangsa contact, and till date, also the most valuable one. In terms of linguistic and cultural data, what Aphu has given us remains unsurpassed, both in qualitative and quantitative terms. After several years of working intensively with him, we have heard more or less all that he wanted to tell us, but for me his home is still my first stop every time I go to the field. And over the years my Tangsa father Aphu has not only helped me understand the Tangsa better but also my own Assamese people; more about that in Chapter 6.

Notes

1. Most Tangsa eat two rice-meals per day—morning rice is usually served around 7:30 a.m. and the evening meal is usually around dusk, somewhere around 5:00 p.m.

2. Even when he pronounced words correctly, in some instances there could be confusion in the meaning; for example, Aphu would say that a food item was *mitha* (sweet in Assamese) to mean that something was tasty or delicious, even when the food in question was not sweet at all.

3. The fight of the Nagas against the Kachins probably refers to the incident in 1964 when thousands of tribal people from Burma had to flee to India after the conflict with the Kachin Independence Army fighters. For further details, see Barua (2013 [1991]: 314–15). Also mentioned in Ronrang (1997: 24) and Bhattacharyya (2014: 220).

4. In those days, Aphu used to sell *kapur-kani* (opium rolled on cloth) at the rate of Rs 30/35 per kg. He would carry around 10–15 kgs of opium to sell. Once he was arrested and had to spend 15 days in jail. Opium was grown in Arunachal Pradesh and in the Naga hills in those times. Every village had a *kani-mahajan* (an opium-merchant).

It is the British who are supposed to have first introduced opium to the hills of northeast India as a way to keep the aggressive hill tribes under control (cf. Mahanta-Kalita 2012: 185). For more on opium addiction in the region, see *Report* (1924).

5. Although Cholim is more of an endonym than a general name, I refer to the basti as the Cholim basti as that is how it is referred to by the Tangsa living there (see the section 'Linguistic Classification of the Tangsa Groups' in Chapter 3). In this chapter, Cholim will also refer to the language spoken by the Cholim (Tonglum) people.

6. Of course it was convenient, and also perhaps brought his immediate family some economic advantage, to have the market close to his house.

    Helping people to get their names included in the voters' lists reveals how far-sighted he is, given that the question of illegal infiltration into northeast India across the porous borders is a very sensitive issue in Assam.

7. The Congress is a national political party that has been in power in Assam almost without a break till the 1980s when the student-led Asom Gana Parishad party came to power. The Congress is again in power in Assam at present (2013) and the local MLA (Member of the Legislative Assembly) is also from the Congress.

8. As Douglas (2013: 190) points out, such incidents also illustrate another important idea: the continuity of ethnic cultures across international borders which provides a counter-narrative to the dominant story of state formation and indeed of modernity itself: namely that once people are exposed to the conveniences of the modern state (technology, education, and so forth) they will assimilate. See also Bal and Chambugong (2014).

9. Aphu feels that all the Nagas should have been put on one side of the international border; in his opinion, since people living west of the Tanai (Chindwin) river have 'eaten Indian salt', the international border should have been drawn along that river. It is worth noting that in colonial times, the unadministered Naga Hills district of Burma was precisely the area lying between the Patkai hills in the west and north and the Chindwin river to the east (cf. *Burma Report* 1942: 1). So, Aphu perhaps had a point there.

10. For instance, one eastern Naga leader recently said, 'The British had no right to draw the borderline in the heart of Naga country'. Available at http://www.burmalink.org/british-right-draw-borderline-heart-naga-country-eastern-naga-leader/ (accessed 30.8.2014).

11. BJP stands for the right wing pro-Hindu Bharatiya Janata Party while AGP stands for the regional party called Asom Gana Parishad which had come into existence in the 1980s in Assam.

12. Such practices are still followed by people living in some parts of Arunachal and also (at least) among the Donghi (Jiingi) tribe in Myanmar.

13. Since most others leaders in Kharangkong were practising Buddhists and Aphu Tyanglam was perhaps the only person interested in celebrating the festival initially, his decision to fix a date for the festival was accepted without much dissent or discussion, although many Tangsa, especially those

who have now converted to Christianity, have often said that it was very inconvenient for them to celebrate another festival so close to Christmas and the New Year. The Wihu in Myanmar is now celebrated as a large festival, moving from one major location within the Tangshang area to another, from one year to the next. It is held on 15 January, as far as I have been able to ascertain.

14. For another description of the Wihu festival in Kharangkong, see Morey and Schöpf (under review).

15. 'Wi' is the Tangsa word for grandmother and 'kuh' means to gather or to assemble. The term 'kuh' is a general term for festivals but traditionally the Wihu-kuh festival was often referred to as kuh. According to one interlocutor Wihu was their equivalent of the Hindu Goddess of prosperity, Lakshmi. Cf. Lyngdoh (2016: 37) describing the Pynhir Myndhan ritual of the Khasis.

16. While chicken sacrifice was done in many of the other houses in the Cholim basti in the morning of Wihu-kuh, many families in the main Kharangkong basti (which is closer to the Buddhist Tai Phake village of Ninggam) performed the same rituals but omitted the chicken sacrifice, and used cooked instead of raw meat for the rituals.

    The *men-ryo-chhung* is a specific inner post of the house, often located in the kitchen, at which the rituals are done.

    The brewing of rice-beer for the event had begun many days in advance, as had the rehearsals for the dances.

17. Many groups of Nepali young men, as well as some Biharis, also came to visit from the surrounding villages.

18. It shows the sun, the moon, and the Naga hat with the wild boar teeth and the hornbill feathers.

19. The married and older ladies usually dress in their traditional long wrappers (*khya-se/ningwats*) and blouses (*sam-tung*), many using Assamese *gamochas* (Assamese) to cover their heads, while others use the traditional Tangsa chequered scarves (*jeship khepop*); they also often wore beautiful traditional jewellery made of shells and beads. The men also usually wear their traditional violet and green *lungi*s (*rhii*, closed wrappers) with a shirt. During festival time, Tangsa men often sport a turban on their heads with the trademark purple and green scarf (*nairi-khepop*), and wear a Naga jacket (*kot-sam-tung*) of some kind over their shirts. Most men carry a hacking knife (*jang* in Cholim, *dao* in Assamese) in a shoulder bag (*khaang*) when they go out.

20. According to Aphu, about Rs 40,000 (roughly 550 euros) was spent for the Wihu-kuh celebrations in 2009, most of which he had spent from his own pocket. Our team, as well as some Nepali men, also contributed.

21. The fact that the invitation card was printed in English can have many reasons: the most obvious being that it was easy and also perhaps cheap to get something printed in English. It also made the whole programme look more formal and official. To print in a Tangsa language would be problematic because (*a*) there is no standard spelling system in use, and (*b*) each Tangsa tribe has a different language.

    The other option would have been to print the card in Asamiya. But since the invitation card was sent out to many who did not speak (and most importantly read) Asamiya (like the Tangsa leaders in Arunachal Pradesh), and since most of the Christian Tangsa could read some English, it was the obvious option. Moreover, perhaps a difference was also sought to be maintained from the dominant Assamese community around them.

22. This is precisely the sense in which Shneiderman (2011: 207) defines performance: 'performances take place in the open, in public domains with the express purpose of demonstrating to both selves and various others what practices [rituals] look like'.

23. During lunch, Lemo and a few others were seen busily trying to write a short press release about the festival. Lemo requested me to give him a few photos from my camera. He believed that giving publicity to the event through the local media and press every year was important to strengthen their demand for the declaration of a local holiday on 5 January, and also for requesting funds to hold the event in the future.

24. Some men from the basti were in charge of cooking the cow and the pig that had been sacrificed earlier while the women cooked the rice and the vegetables.

25. For a complete list of Tangsa festivals, see Morey and Schöpf (under review).

26. Bihu is the main festival of the Assamese people; there are three Bihus. Rongali Bihu is celebrated in mid-April to mark the Assamese New Year, and the Bihu dance has become a cultural symbol for the Assamese.

27. According to Khapshom Juglei, the Sahpolo dance is also relatively new, first performed at the Mol festival in Changlang in 1969 (see also Morey and Schöpf, under review).

28. Karlsson observes much the same tendency among the Rabhas when he writes, 'metonymically the dancing or the dress represents the entire Rabha culture' (Karlsson 2000: xvi).

29. This reminded me of the Naga student in Mokukuchung who had given a similar pithy answer when asked to define culture: 'culture means roots'.

30. Some Tangsa told me later that their traditional religion could be called the 'ajanti' religion, the religion they followed before they came in contact with civilization.

31. As we shall see in the section titled 'The Residual Beliefs' in Chapter 6, some Tangsa who are Christian now still follow some of their traditional practices. But none of them have continued as a priest (*dumsa*) after conversion. See also Spiro (1967: 3).

32. Aphu explained this to me by saying that since Phraa (the Buddha) was everywhere there was no need to go to a temple looking for him.

33. Main Kharangkong basti, 3 November 2009. Today, the maximum number of Buddhists in India is to be found in the western Indian state of Maharashtra due to the conversion of large numbers of Dalits (untouchables) to Buddhism in the second half of the twentieth century.

34. By Assamese I mean Asamiya-speaking people who are mostly Ahom and Sonowal Kachari in that area.

35. Kachari is a generic term and refers to a plains tribal community, belonging to the larger Bodo-Kachari group. For more details, see Endle (1911).

36. I have recorded many examples of this: In the Ronrang village of Balinong, a few Thamkok families have become Ronrang; in the Juglei basti of Kantang, many Morang (Munre) families had become Juglei. There were even instances of Nepali men becoming Ronrang after marrying Ronrang women. Another interesting case is that of the Tangsa Lungphi—while some Lungphi claim they are a Mossang clan, others claim they were Tikhak (cf. Simai 2008: 27).

37. For more, see Ramirez (2014: Chapter 3), Bal (2007a: Chapter 6) and all the essays contained in Vandenhelsken et al. (2016).

38. According to the 10+2+3 system of education present in Assam, a student goes to school for 10 years: Class I to Class X, of which the first 4 years belong to the primary section. There is a public end-of-school examination called Matriculation at the end of Class X, after which there are two years of Higher Secondary Education before one can go to college to do a 3-year graduation.

39. Till 2010 they were only about 6–7 students who have cleared their Matriculation exams at the end of Class X, exactly one who has cleared the Higher Secondary stage at the end of Class XII and only one who is going to college to do his graduation. As a result, there are not many with regular jobs in the village except for the few who were soldiers in the army.

40. For a historical account of the use of opium in the region, see Sharma (2012: 62ff).

41. Kharangkong, 29 October 2009. On another occasion, Aphu had also explained why young men joined underground organizations: They did so only because they were poor and needed money and it was impossible to get a regular job without bribing someone, and they did not have the

money to pay for bribes. On the other hand, the underground outfits paid quite handsome salaries to their cadres.

42. I visited the market on 30 October 2009 and also later.

When I asked government officials about the police non-intervention I was told that gambling was officially allowed by the government in the month after Diwali, the Indian festival of lights, which normally takes place sometime in the autumn.

43. In those days, the Tangsa leaders Nowang Mossang (also called Mossang Gam) and Sekhip Lungri from Kharangkong, the Singpho Kotha Gam of Kotha village, and Aikya Chekhap of Ninggam were very close friends and they acted together on most issues.

44. The Presbyterian Church is controlled by the Mizo missionaries and has a much smaller presence amongst the Tangsa. In Assam they are mainly in Kharangkong and in the villages of Lakla near Phulbari and Mullong 1 near Malugaon.

45. In fact, our team was not invited to a housewarming ceremony in the main basti once, despite the fact that everyone knew we were interested in recording such events, possibly because we were staying with Aphu at that time and the hosts probably felt that if they invited us they would then have to also invite Aphu who would then come and take on the job of telling everyone what to do.

46. One of the oldest families in the main basti was also contemplating converting to Christianity soon. Having to face Aphu's wrath was one of the main reasons for their not having done so already.

47. Aphu had once told me that there was no use in learning Asamiya, the children should learn either Hindi or English. He had supported the setting up of a Hindi medium school at Tin-mile. The younger girls in Aphu's greater family, however, have all gone to government-run Asamiya schools.

Only when it came to sending his grandsons to school that Aphu began to believe that education was important. And he sent them to an English medium school in Lakla run by Presbyterians, at a considerable expense and even when it meant having to set up another establishment to make it possible for them to attend school.

5 Malugaon
Striking a Fine Balance

'The modern does not belong to anyone, the modern is the same across
tribes and people. Nobody had heard of the Hakhuns, not even the other
Tangsa groups, till they began to celebrate this festival. Now, because of
this festival, at least the Hakhun are known within Tangsa society.'

—Gaonbura Hakhun, Malugaon

*It is not easy to get to Malugaon from the railway station at Ledo. There is
a walking track winding up the hill to Malugaon but I was not sure I would
find my way. Also, since the narrow dirt track went steeply uphill most of the
time, it was impossible for me to manage to get to Malugaon with my heavy
luggage, without help. Theoretically, it is also possible to go to Malugaon by
car, but the road is very bad in patches, and it is a very long detour. Therefore
I had called the Gaonbura of Malugaon, and had asked him to send someone
to meet me. A provision store owned by a Bengali man, on the edge of the
railway track, was our usual meeting point.*

*Two young boys from the village were waiting there for me. They knew me
from the previous year. We started off immediately, after thanking the shop
owner. There was a little crowded stretch in the plains, with small mud houses
and the odd concrete one on both sides of the path. It was a Bengali basti, I
was told. But soon the path turned away and led to a little stream. The boys
crossed with habituated ease and waited politely for me to either make it on
my own or ask for help. There was a dense bamboo bush on the other side, the
last bit of shadow, before the skies opened up before us and the uphill climb
started. The town was quickly left behind and the densely inhabited areas gave
way to large open stretches of green tea gardens.*

I tried to chat with the two boys; both were wearing stylish jeans and T-shirts—their hair had also been done up to stand upright as was the current fashion. One of them I recognized as Khejong, the son of one of our consultants in Malugaon. Khejong had a rather large and heavy watch on his wrist. He looked taller and seemed to have grown both in height and in confidence since I had last seen him the previous year. He was also more forthcoming in his replies. Yes, he was still studying in the boarding school in Lakla, close to Jagun at the Assam–Arunachal border. No, they were not having vacations; he had come home from school only for the festival, and would have to go back immediately afterwards. He and his friend had studied together when he was still going to school in Ledo. But his friend had stopped going to school after failing to pass his class VIII exam. He now worked as a helper in a car-repair shop in Ledo and was already earning some money besides learning on the job. When I asked Khejong whether he was happy with his boarding school he did not reply. Yes, he had been promoted this year, he responded, to my next query.

I remembered the tough time the family had the previous year convincing Khejong to go back to school after his vacations. His parents had decided to send him to a Christian boarding school at Lakla after they found out that he was getting into bad company and was missing school and spending the day loitering about in the town in Ledo. Khejong had gone to Lakla but was soon very unhappy with the rules and restrictions of his new school. And he found his studies even harder than before since he had moved from an Asamiya medium school to an English medium one. After he had failed in his class VII exams, he had come home on vacation and had told his parents that he was not going back to school anymore and that he would find some job or the other in Ledo, like most of his other friends from Malugaon. It required a marathon sitting, where not only his parents, relatives, and village elders were present but also outsiders like me were roped in, before the boy could be persuaded to give his expensive new school another try.

As we neared the village I recognized some people from the basti; they recognized me too and waved. They were busy tending their patches of tea garden. Tea saplings had been planted all over the slope. Not all of it belongs to people from Malugaon, Khejong told me; some Bengali families living in the basti we had just crossed had also started growing tea. And the Marwari tea planter was still there. As I turned around to look back at Ledo it was astonishing to see how high we had climbed so quickly.

The village, when we finally arrived there, looked somewhat different from the previous year. At first I could not make out exactly what was different. But soon it was clear—there were just many more houses all over the compound where Limhang, my host in Malugaon, lived. And this was the case not just in Limhang's compound. As the days progressed, I found out that the 30 families that were living in Malugaon the previous year had grown to 45 this year. So the movement down from Myanmar continued unabated. 'What can one do', Limhang said, shaking his head when I asked him about this later. 'After all they are also part of my family, I have to help them when they are in need. And the conditions in Myanmar are so difficult that it is becoming almost impossible for them to continue to live there'.

Limhang commented that he was having a tough time having to provide for so many extra people, but by all counts his home looked much more prosperous than before. There was much more furniture in the house—also a refrigerator in the front room. Limhang had also built a concrete water tank next to the old rice mill, as the water connection had been extended recently all the way to Limhang's house. To have running water at the turn of a tap seemed like a dream when one reminded oneself of how difficult it had been when the family had to carry water (in usually big plastic Jerri cans carried in wicker baskets) from the water tank at least 500 metres up the hill.

'In trying to help others we have not been able to build the concrete toilet and bath that I had promised you last time', Limhang added. Well, that was fine, after all, being able to stay in Limhang's concrete Assam type house in Malugaon was already in itself a luxury. The toilet was still rather basic but functional—a smooth curved piece of tin, placed on an incline leading to a hole at the back. They were easy to construct on slopes. The toilet, however, had moved from its position of last time to a little further away. Like always it was clean—Nyamlik, Limhang's wife, was very particular about that, a 5-litre used plastic Jerri can served as the water reservoir. I also found a broken mug next to it. An empty sack served as a curtain as well as a door. No big surprises there.

There were a few women crowded around the kitchen hearth, cooking. Junglum—Limhang's 75-year-old father and by far the most knowledgeable man of the village—was not to be found; he was busy with the preparations for the festival, I was told. Junglum's wife, who was slightly older than her husband, looked pale and unwell but went about her chores as usual. I could only nod my head to her by way of greeting as she spoke only Burmese and perhaps also Hakhun but no Assamese or Hindi.

I was shown into the same room where I had stayed on previous occasions but was rather surprised to find that Nyamlik now ran a little shop from out

of the window of that room. So the room was filled with little plastic jars con-
taining toffees, cookies, biscuits, small sachets of shampoo, toothpaste, slabs
of soap, and so forth. 'This won't disturb you', she said, 'I don't have many
customers. There are so many small shops in the village now'. That was hard
to believe; last time there was not a single shop in the village. I decided to go
for a little walk of the village before it got dark.

On my way I saw quite a few new houses—some concrete Assam type, some
bamboo-changs—at various stages of construction. Some looked even bigger
than Limhang's. The tiny bamboo and tin shacks along the roadside were
shops; in the following days I discovered that these shops did good business
during the day, selling tobacco, toffees, and small snacks to the men carrying
coal on their backs down the hill. Khothing was one of our main interlocutors
in Malugaon. His sister lived at the end of the road. After her husband died,
her husband's brother had taken her as his wife. Their new house also looked
complete. It was a grand sprawling bungalow now. I had never met the man
but wondered what he must do to be so rich. I also wondered whether she
would let me bathe in her concrete bath-house this time as I had done the
last few times.

But the biggest surprise came when I saw the village church, completely
rebuilt with bricks and concrete and freshly painted; the old mud and tin
structure in which I had attended services the previous year had disappeared.
The signboard told me that it had been inaugurated only a few months ago.
I walked on. As I reached the school compound, I could see that the school
building had also been extended. The Gaonbura and some villagers were hav-
ing a meeting in the school field. Some of them greeted me—a meeting of
the core committee of the festival was in progress. When I congratulated the
Gaonbura on the many positive changes in the village in the past year, he told
me that things were on their way to getting even better.

Not desiring to disturb the meeting, I walked on, past the Pastor's house,
till I came to the Gaonbura's double-storey wooden house. It looked more or
less the same. On the other side of the road was the recently built Assam type
house. There was a large coal dump in front of the house—it was large, dark,
and ugly.

Another time, I walked on further along the winding road, past the
Gaonbura's house, leading to the coal mine, which is less than a kilometre
away. The smell and feel of dust and the heavy grimy atmosphere around an
open-cast coal mine became stronger. The vegetation thinned out; no more
trees, just straggling weed-like plants growing out of the pale, pulpy soil. Soon

I came up to the ridge from where one could see the mines. They looked dark and forbidding, even from the distance. One could see the layered formation along the steep edges. Big Volvo dredgers were at work, digging out the coal. Many trucks were stationed next to them to carry the coal to the coal loading station down at Ledo. There the coal would be loaded into train wagons and transported out of the region. The digging process created a huge pool, and as the dredgers continued to nibble away on one steep edge of the lake and

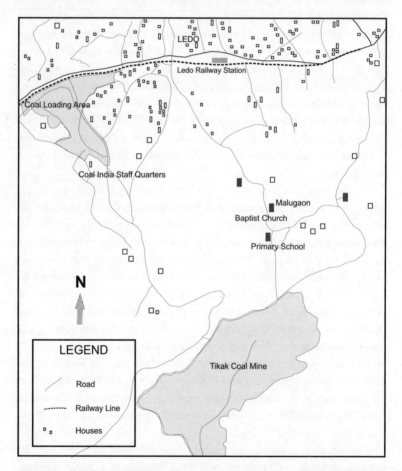

Map 5.1   Sketch Map Showing Malugaon in Relation to Ledo and the Tikak Coal Mines

Source: Jayanta Laskar and Inez Ruscheweyh.
Note: Map not to scale and does not represent authentic international boundaries.

spitting out the soil which did not contain enough coal on the other side, the lake gradually moved, literally. As a consequence the hills on one side got 'eaten up', while new unreal-looking pale hills sprang up on the other side. For what they 'spat' out was a totally barren, lifeless matter which had nothing of any value left in it that could support any life.

As I stood there, looking at the deep gorge created by the mine, a young man joined me—he was Bengali and worked there as a guard, he told me; he was not an employee of Coal India but of a private company that had been given the contract of digging and transporting the coal from the mines. When I expressed my surprise at finding a young Bengali working there, he informed me that there were many Bengali people working there—his father had come from West Bengal to settle in Ledo and work for Coal India in the 1980s when the mines started functioning again after being shut down after the British left. As we chatted, he said that not only were there many Bengali people working there, there were lots of Telugu-speaking people from distant Andhra Pradesh also living in Ledo—they had also come to work in the mines in British times and had stayed on. So much so that there was even a Telugu-medium school in Ledo. Just beyond the hill in front of us, behind the mines was the Tangsa basti of Rhan-rhing-kan; it was in Arunachal Pradesh but was not too far. He offered to show me the way if I wished to visit it someday. But the day was getting on, I decided to return.

On my way back to Malugaon, I met Lumren, a Hakhun who lived in Nongtham in Arunachal Pradesh. He had just arrived and had decided to walk up the road to accompany me back. At a certain point on the road, Lumren told me that he would show me something very pretty—we left the road and walked through the forests, climbing uphill for a while till we reached an opening, and then suddenly in front of us the view opened up; it was as if we had suddenly come out into the open from a tunnel—we were almost at the top of a hilly slope covered with lush green tea plants, when one looked up one saw the sparkling blue sky and between them a mountain range in several overlapping and interlacing layers. That was the Patkai range straddling the Indo-Myanmar border. The home of the forefathers of many of my Tangsa friends was somewhere there in the hills in front of me. The sight was majestic and sublime; to see those mountains that I had heard so much about, to have nothing between them and me—I looked on in silence.

And as we turned to go back to the road I gasped again, for in front of me was a view that extended for quite a few kilometres. In the distance, past the village, beyond the railway track and the town below, there were vast expanses *of plains—mainly golden with paddy, green with tea at some places, dark and forested elsewhere—they were the fertile flood plains of the Tirap and the Buridihing rivers. The rivers were too shrunken at that time of the year for me to be able to see them, but one could see their looped and wavy courses clearly—our land is so beautiful, I heard myself saying aloud.*

The picturesque Tangsa village of Malugaon is located up the hill very close to the busy town of Ledo near Margherita.[1] Malugaon is very close to the Assam–Arunachal border and not too far from the international border with Myanmar. There are two large open coal mines—the Tirap and the Tikak Coal Mines—very close to Malugaon (as is evident from Map 5.1). In fact, the Tikak mine is less than a kilometre away. Most of the Tangsa living in Malugaon are Hakhun, which is not a Pangwa tribe.

In this chapter, I describe the landscape around the basti of Malugaon and the livelihood patterns of the Hakhun people living there, in order to understand better the reasons that make it necessary for them to negotiate their existence not only with their clan-relatives in Myanmar, but also with the Assamese living down in the town of Ledo, as well as with the officials of Coal India and the local state administration, including the police and the army. The connection between the Hakhun and the Nocte, and issues related to insurgent activity in the area, informal trade in coal and opium as well as environmental problems related to living close to a coal mine will also be discussed. I will also describe and discuss a Hakhun festival in order to understand the underlying compulsions and intentions, and to show that the much closer contact the people of Malugaon have with the plains and the state machinery have enabled them to work out more efficient strategies for survival and also to present themselves as 'modern tribals'.

Hakhun: The Burma Connection

The Hakhun are a Tangsa tribe with only about 110 families in India (in 2010). Malugaon is the largest Hakhun village in India.[2] I was told that about 80 per cent of the Hakhuns are still in Myanmar. Since most of the Hakhuns in India today have only very recently migrated from Myanmar (many within the last 20–5 years), their links with Myanmar are still very strong; for instance, they prefer to use the term 'Tangshang' which is more generally used in Myanmar, rather than Tangsa.[3] It was pretty normal for people from Myanmar to come visit their friends and relatives in Malugaon. Some Hakhuns from Malugaon still played an active role in their ancestral villages back in Myanmar.[4]

Similarity with the Nocte

Although the Hakhun are non-Pangwa, the lingua franca of the village was Hacheng, a Pangwa language.[5] There were some Thamphang (non-Pangwa) speakers in Malugaon as well. The picture was even more complex because, linguistically, the language of the Hakhun resembled that of the Nocte community very closely, while it was almost completely unintelligible to most of the other Tangsa groups.[6] Today, the Nocte live in the Tirap district of Arunachal. According to Hakhun elders, the Hakhun also used to live in the area around Khonsa, the capital of the Tirap district, about hundred years ago from where they had to flee to Burma after having a fight with the Wakka people also living there over the ownership of a salt mine.[7] The five Hakhun bastis in Myanmar are located close to the Indo-Burmese border. In recent years, many Hakhuns have moved downhill from Myanmar to Malugaon and to a few other places in Assam and Arunachal Pradesh.

The fact that their traditional practices were also somewhat different from the other Tangsa groups reinforced the popular belief amongst many Tangsa that not only were the Hakhun not Pangwa, but that they actually belonged to the Tangwa tribes, which include the Northern Naga tribes like the Wancho and the Konyak.[8] Of course, the Konyak in Nagaland live right across the border to the Nocte and Wancho in the Tirap (and the recently created Longding) district of Arunachal Pradesh, so all the different strands seemed to fit together quite nicely.

In any case, the Hakhuns in Malugaon, both in terms of their language and some of their traditional practices which we recorded, seem to be rather special and different from the Pangwa. They do not have the Sahpolo dance; Junglum Hakhun did not know how to sing the Wihu song but said they had a similar song called Phon-tu-si.[9] At the village organizational level, unlike the Pangwa groups who usually had elected chieftains, the Hakhuns used to have hereditary kings (*Angs*). However there seems to be no obvious connection between those 'Angs' and the present-day Gaonburas;[10] the present Hakhun Gaonbura of Malugaon does not belong to the kingly clan—he had simply inherited the job from his father.

Culturally and linguistically there were many reasons to believe that the Hakhun are more Nocte than Tangsa. However, the Hakhun were officially included as a Tangsa group, and consider themselves to be Tangsa today. And the Gaonbura of Malugaon has been so successful in projecting himself as a Tangsa leader that he was one of the three Tangsa members nominated to the newly-formed Development Council, although there might also be other reasons for this, as I discuss later.

Ongoing Migration from Myanmar

Junglum Hakhun came away from Myanmar because of the atrocities of the Burmese army who were supposed to clear that area of insurgents in the 1970s (see, for instance, Bhattacharyya 2014). The rebels were hiding in the jungles but the army would come into their villages, burn houses, kill and eat the cows, pigs, and other animals, and beat and torture the villagers; unable to cope with all that, he ran away and came to India. The army would come in every year and create a lot of trouble, so many people fled to India. Junglum believes that the situation had improved since 2000, but the villagers were always supposed to be ready to provide the army with men whenever they needed some to perform various tasks like transporting rations (the nearest town is more than two weeks by foot away from the village where he used to live) and for other hard work. Life was very difficult there. So it did seem that there were quite a few reasons why the flow of settlers from Myanmar into Malugaon continued unabated.

Junglum Hakhun and his wife came to India in the 1970s. Their son Limhang, who was born in Burma, came to India as a young man. He married Nyamlik when she moved to India with her family in the 1990s. Nyamlik could read and write in Burmese, like Aphu Tyanglam, but had recently started learning to read English by herself at home; she spoke reasonable Assamese, like her husband.

Junglum's nephew, Yedim, described to me the route to go from Malugaon to his home in Vanruk in Myanmar via Khonsa and Lajo and then across the border on foot.[11] And he had done it at least once a month to visit his children who were living with Junglum and going to school. But in 2011 when his wife fell ill, they moved to Malugaon because there were no medical facilities available anywhere near their basti in Myanmar.

In just the three consecutive years (2009–11) that I visited Malugaon, the number of houses in the compound where Limhang and Junglum live had nearly doubled.[12] In 2010, a new chang-ghar was built right in front of Junglum's original chang-ghar and Limhang's sister's family moved in there. Yedim had moved with the rest of his family into Limhang's former kitchen chang-ghar, which had been dismantled and redone, and Junglum and his wife lived there in 2011. A new kitchen had been set up in the chang-ghar on the other side of Limhang's concrete house. The chang-ghar where Junglum used to live till 2010 was occupied by Limhang's newly married younger brother, his wife, and little child. Limhang's brother-in-law had moved in 2011 to the house across the road facing the rice mill. A schematic presentation is shown in Figure 5.1.

Politics of Survival

Sitting on a Coal Mine

Originally, the slopes of the hills on which the bastis of Malugaon, Mullong, and Rhan-rhing-kan are presently located was a Tikhak Tangsa area and the village was named after Malo, a Tikhak community leader.[13] The village of Rhan-rhing-kan still has a Tikhak Gaonbura, although most of the Tikhak people living in the hills have since moved down to the plains around Ledo.[14] Rhan-rhing-kan means 'smelling or odorous mountain' in the Tikhak language (see also Simai 2008: 21). The entire area has coal quite close to the surface. The story goes that it was the Tikhaks who first discovered coal in that area while they were clearing land for *jhum* cultivation.[15] Later, the British started mining in the area. However, the people living in those hills consider the coal to be rightfully theirs, and hence believe that they are within their rights to mine and sell it.[16]

In the 1880s, the British established six underground mines in the area.[17] The Tikak and Tirap mines were recast as open-cast mines and started operations from the 1980s. These mines presently produce 1 million tonnes of coal per year. Since the ban on the plywood and timber industries in the early 1990s, coal mining is the biggest industry in that area.[18]

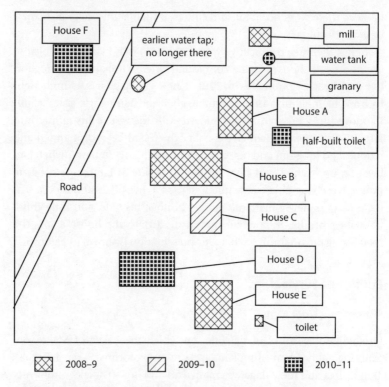

House A: The chang-ghar where Limhang and family earlier used to live with Junglum's wife, also kitchen; in 2010, Junglum's wife lives in the front part, and Limhang's cousin Yedim (with his wife and four children) live in the back part; Junglum moved back in with his wife in 2011.

House B: The concrete house where Limhang lives with his family; his nephew stays on the roof and runs the mill.

House C: Limhang's new kitchen (earlier the kitchen was in House A).

House D: Junglum's daughter's chang-ghar, she lives there with her husband and four children.

House E: Junglum's original chang-ghar; his youngest son also lives there with his family since 2011.

House F: Limhang's brother-in-law lives in this chang-ghar with three children, mother, and wife.

Figure 5.1   Layout of the Area around Junglum's House

Source: Author.

The Gaonbura of Malugaon claims that the village has had to move five times in the last 50 years. The village, in its present location, exists only for about 10 years. There was an earlier basti further up the hill which was destroyed when the empty underground mining chambers of the old Tikak mine collapsed; the date of the disaster is contested—Coal India sources claim it was in 2001, local residents claim it was earlier in 1999 (cf. M. Das 2011; Gogoi 2012). There were 30–35 families living in that (upper) Malugaon basti then. Coal India gave compensation and took the responsibility of rehabilitating all of them, some were temporarily housed (and are still living) in Coal India quarters, many others decided to move and settle in the village of Rhanrhing-kan, while 10–15 families eventually came to settle in the present location of Malugaon.[19] The rest of the people living in Malugaon now are even more recent arrivals, and most of them are from Myanmar. According to a Coal India official, around 2005, there were at most 20–25 families living in Malugaon. The population more than doubled in the next five years, mostly due to migration from Myanmar. Official records state the population of Malugaon to be 317 adults in 2011.

The villagers have an uneasy relationship with Coal India because of the sheer proximity of the coal mines although Coal India is their principal benefactor, and descendants of about 25 'Naga' employees who joined the mines during British times are still employed by Coal India at present. Many more 'tribals' are employed directly or indirectly by Coal India as drivers and machine-men. Moreover, in Malugaon the company also bore the expenses of running the village primary school, providing water reservoirs, and free electric supply, and paving the main village roads. Confirming all this, the Gaonbura added, 'We have now requested Coal India to pave *all* the roads in the basti'. He also told me that half of the total amount of Rs 8 lakhs (800,000 INR) spent on rebuilding the village church had been provided by Coal India. They had also provided for the extension of the school building and the renovation of the school toilets. Two new water reservoirs had been built in the basti by Coal India so that by 2011 there was some kind of water supply to all houses.

When I asked a Coal India official how they showed all this in their records, he explained that as part of the Corporate Social Responsibility (CSR) Scheme, Coal India was obliged to distribute 5 per cent of its profits to people living within 8 kilometres of their area of operation.[20]

Furthermore, when the company needed to acquire some land, instead of going into long drawn-out negotiations, they would often just give the Gaonbura a lump sum say of about 10 lakhs (in INR) to be distributed amongst the villagers. The lower part of the neighbouring Tangsa village of Mullong I near the adjoining Tirap mine had been relocated just in the last few months; they have been compensated by Coal India and have been assured that they would not have to move again.[21] This is what another researcher working in the Hacheng village of Mullong II had to say:

> The coal industry was an ambivalent issue for the villagers. There were many people working in or for the mine, and they were sure happy about the money they could earn. Also the mine provided electricity and water, much more reliable than the government would have done. On the other hand the acquisition of the plots now being mined was seen more or less as a scam. It seems the land was bought by the British from the people living there, much undervalued, as they were using the ignorance of the locals of what the black stone lying everywhere on the ground was used for. (E-mail: 20 May 2013)

These issues, however, did not seem to bother those living in the village of Lekhapani further down the national highway from Ledo. The people I could talk to were quite enthusiastic about the fact that the newly commissioned Lekhapani Open Cast Mine would go operational soon, barely a kilometre away from their basti. Coal India has already built a community hall and had promised jobs, water, electricity, and roads in their village.[22]

In any case, the fact remained that those who were living so close to a coal mine might have to move again any day. And that was not an empty threat. Knowing all that, why was it that more and more people were coming to settle in Malugaon? Why were they not bothered about the health hazards associated with constantly inhaling coal-dust or fumes from the coal fires? And while earlier they used to live in bamboo changs which could easily be dismantled and moved, why were more and more cement concrete houses being built in Malugaon? 'We cannot just stop living just because we might have to move someday', the Gaonbura told me. 'Moreover, the better the houses we have to leave behind the bigger the compensation we will get.' Although this logic might sound rather perverse, it was quite sound as a strategy—they were making the best of the hen that laid the golden eggs while it lasted.

Insurgency, Coal Mafia, and Opium Trafficking

Most people living in Malugaon still do jhum cultivation in their fields further up in the hills. But that could not be the only source of income in the village. For, economically, Malugaon today is visibly on its way up—there were signs of prosperity and affluence, and better infrastructure everywhere. Quite a few new houses—some of concrete, some bamboo chang-ghars—had come up. Elsewhere, chang-ghars were being replaced by brick and cement constructions. Most houses in Malugaon have at least a motorcycle; many also have small transporters to transport coal. The roadside shops were flourishing; there was just more money going around.

Compared to Tangsa youth in other villages, those in Malugaon looked surprisingly 'modern'—fashionable tattered jeans, big flashy watches, spiky hairstyles, a 'cool' attitude—with Ipods or MP3 players stuffed into ears playing western pop music. Since most of these young men were school dropouts with no visible sources of income, it was not easy to explain this new affluence.

Although nobody told me anything in so many words, the evidence was all around me. One of the village elders was arrested and had to spend a few months in prison when he was caught in an army raid while selling opium. Many, especially older people in the village, still take opium quite openly. The illegal trade of opium smuggled in from Myanmar had made some people rich, I was told.

Some others had become rich from the informal sale of coal. Men, slowly walking down the hill, carrying heavy sacks of coal on their backs, is a common sight in Malugaon (see Photograph 5.1). Coal, collected from the mines manually by such hired hands, was collected in the coal dumps in the basti during the day; the sacks were then loaded in medium-sized pickup vans and transported to distant places during the night. The commotion created by these loading operations had kept me up many nights.

Moreover, it is known that some of the villagers have links with insurgents active in the area. In fact, it is believed that the local area commandant of one of the insurgent outfits is a Hakhun from Malugaon, and that the area around the hills of Malugaon and beyond even up to the Kharsang and Miao in Changlang is under the control of this group. Relations between Coal India and the Hakhuns in Malugaon

Photograph 5.1   Porters Carrying Sacks of Coal Down from the Mines
Source: Author.

had become very tense after the kidnapping and suspected murder, allegedly by the same insurgent faction, of the manager of the Tikak Mines in 2003. The Coal India workers from outside the state were terrorized with fear after the manager was killed. According to Coal India sources, the tribals exploited this fear to the maximum. They would sometimes waylay workers, beat them up, or throw stones to damage the costly Volvo machines used in the mines. 'Moreover', the visibly unhappy official continued,

> [T]heir nuisance value has gone up in recent years since the insurgents arrived in Malugaon around the year 2000. So now they have to be paid to not create trouble and this suits them very well since they need to do nothing to earn their living. And if they want more there is always enough coal to steal and opium to smuggle.

However, although that new affluence had brought about an improvement in the housing and living standards in Malugaon, it had not created a greater awareness for education. Some well-to-do parents, such as Khejong's, have sent their children to boarding schools elsewhere. But left to himself, Khejong would prefer to roam the hills with his friends on his brand new motorbike. There were only two girls from the village who had managed to get as far as graduation. The highest educated amongst the boys had studied only till class XII.

There is only one primary school in the village; the children had to go down to schools in Ledo when they finished the primary level. The headmaster of the primary school is the Assamese Gogoi, who has been introduced in Chapter 2. He and his two Manipuri assistants lived down in the town of Ledo; they trudged up and down the hill everyday in order to keep the primary school going. Gogoi is the only Assamese I know who can actually speak a few words of a Tangsa language. But his opinion was clear—as long as the Hakhuns continued to smoke opium, drink rice-beer, shelter insurgents, and resort to illegal means of making money, there was no way forward. He told me that the children of the basti were not interested in education as they saw their parents earning a lot even though they were uneducated. Easy money coming in from so many illegal sources had already and was going to ruin the village completely, he felt.

Culture as Expedient

The Hakhun Association and the Hakhun Festival

The banner on the gate, beautifully decorated with hornbill feathers and images of wild boar teeth, leading up to the festival grounds proclaimed it to be the 2nd Tangshang Hakhun (Naga) Development and Welfare Association (THDWA) Foundation Day Celebration on 8 November 2009 (see Photograph 5.2). The venue was the playground of the primary school at Malugaon. They were celebrating the foundation day for the second time in this manner; the first time was exactly a year ago, although the THDWA was formed already in 2006. The Gaonbura, in his welcome speech, however, claimed that they were celebrating the traditional Hakhun festival of Seiju-kuh which was the Hakhun thanksgiving festival for a good harvest, like the Wihu-kuh of the Pangwa groups; traditionally, it would be celebrated in mid-December.

Lumren Hakhun, who we have met before, is the President of THDWA. He stated their aims and objectives as follows: (a) to promote unity amongst the Hakhun people, (b) to preserve their older

Photograph 5.2   The Decorated Gate of the Malugaon Festival

Source: Author.

traditional dances and dresses, and (*c*) to strengthen Hakhun identity. Organizing a festival was a good way to achieve those aims, he added.[23] His own personal hope was 'to organise culture through religion' and one of the first steps in that direction was to show that it is possible to participate in a traditional festival *in a suitably modified form* even while remaining a practising Baptist.

He believed that there was no need for forgetting one's culture and traditions just because one had become Christian. Of course that did not mean, he continued, that one should start drinking rice-beer again or start fighting with one's neighbours, just as in former times. So although, as Baptist Christians, they do not sacrifice animals any longer, they would set up the sacrificial altar in the festival area, and the ritual prayer that would usually have been said before sacrificing animals would be enacted by Junglum as a 'performance' at the festival.[24] Junglum had also trained a band of dancers who would perform some of the 'traditional' dances they had danced in the hills in Myanmar (as seen in Photograph 5.3). In this way, the children would learn about

Photograph 5.3   Performing at the Malugaon Festival

Source: Author.

their older traditions as well as get to see their traditional dresses, songs, and dances, he told me.

The Baptist church of the basti was very actively involved in organizing the festival. The Hacheng pastor was present all through the celebrations and the church building had been converted into a sort of temporary green-room-cum-store where many of the rehearsals were held and most of the hired equipment was stored. Lumren Hakhun made sure that their new religion would also be in evidence at the festival. Besides the prayer and blessing to mark the beginning and the end of the festivities, three songs, sung by a church group comprising five girls (wearing conservative but 'westernized' outfits and accompanied by a guitarist) who were specially invited from the neighbouring village of Relang in Arunachal Pradesh, were also included in the 'cultural programme'.[25]

Moreover, a few modern songs, composed by a girl from the village and choreographed by her brother, were also performed in some sort of Bollywood style by a group of about 20 teenagers from the village (accompanied by a guitar and drums) dressed in colourful semi-traditional dresses. Similar events have been recorded at other festivals elsewhere (see, for instance, Vandenhelsken 2011: 85). And this is even to be expected, for the presentation of 'Bollywood-style number[s] … carr[ies] the weight of "culture" in the generic South Asian sense' (Shneiderman 2011: 203).

Up to this point, there was no similarity of the 'cultural programme' on offer in Malugaon with that which I had witnessed at Kharangkong earlier. But towards the end of the programme, two Tangsa elders from some other village came up and began to sing the Wihu-song; the Sahpolo dance was conspicuous by its absence in Malugaon. Given the differences in the songs, dances, and dresses that were on show that day in Malugaon, one could surmise that the projected Hakhun 'culture' (or 'kassa') was somewhat different from that presented at Kharangkong.[26]

When asked, the Gaonbura explained that the 'modern' dances and songs had been added only to attract the younger lot; they were not part of their culture or identity because 'the modern does not belong to anyone, the modern is the same across tribes and people', echoing what Chanwang had already told me. Only the traditional songs/dances/dress would define their identity, he went on to say. They would allow modern songs and dances to be performed only within the village; outside they would present only their traditional dances as their culture. And Junglum Hakhun's troupe was already going to various places to present their Hakhun 'culture' to the world.[27]

But how traditional was the 'traditional'? Junglum Hakhun had spent the day before the festival at Ledo market trying to find coloured plastic twine, small mirrors, large beads, and other such things for use as accessories. Nyamlik had cleverly produced very striking ear-ornaments for the dancers using cheap colourful plastic beads and tufts of paper. Since they did not have much of their traditional ornaments any more, they were forced to resort to 'fakes'—such as using a twisted metal rod to make bangles for the girls to wear, she told me (see Photographs 5.4 and 5.5).

The Pastor felt that what they were doing at their festivals was 'just an attempt to keep things from getting lost'; they were doing the best they could, but it was not much more than 'poor imitations'. Earlier they would use ornaments made of ivory and beads, silver-handled daggers, and real shields. Wild boar horns and teeth, heads of monkeys

Photographs 5.4 and 5.5   Ornaments: Some Old, Some Imitated

Source: Author.

and dogs, even tiger teeth had to be placed on the sacrificial altar, in olden times.

Lumren confirmed what Nyamlik had told me earlier: When they converted to Christianity, they were encouraged to burn their traditional dresses, headgear, and ornaments.[28] So they would have to go back to the hills—their imagined homeland—to 'find' their traditional costumes and accessories. Once found, they would have to be *suitably modernized and then mass-produced*. That was what their Association planned to do, he told me. Moreover, their history would have to be written down, but first it would have to be collected properly, by asking elders in Myanmar and also in India. Oral history must not only be collected, it would have to be carefully cross-checked before anything could be written down, Lumren continued. It was clear that he took his job as President very seriously. There was so much work to be done, Lumren added, that they had decided to hold the festival, in such a big way, only every two years.

Instrumentalizing festivals

The Gaonbura and his group, however, had other plans and went ahead with the festival also in 2010. But why was the Gaonbura so keen to hold the event again in 2010, even though the Association had decided against it? 'First of all, because a gap of two years is too long for the children and youth to remember the songs and dances they had learnt', he claimed. But it was clear from the way he said it that there were other bigger reasons; and it did not take long for the Gaonbura, assisted and prompted by the Village Secretary, to continue: 'Nobody had heard of the Hakhuns, not even the other Tangsa groups, till we began to celebrate this festival.[29] Now, because of this festival, the Hakhun are known at least within Tangsa society.'[30]

When I asked him why they did not then hold the festival in the big field down in Ledo town, which was much more accessible and hence many more people would be able to attend, the Gaonbura told me, rather mysteriously, that they would hold it there once they were 'ready', but they were not ready yet. As far as their identity was concerned, they want to be known as a 'developed tribe who had come out from the darkness to light'.[31] Earlier they were ignorant and celebrated their festivals only at home, they told me, but now they wanted to celebrate it centrally at one place to show the government that they also exist, in the same way as the Biharis and the Asamiyas also exist!

There were a few voices of dissent to the above statements, noticeably from Lumren Hakhun who said that the festival was not just to show others their 'culture' and thereby to make the Hakhun well known, as claimed by the Gaonbura; it was also supposed to have some value for the Hakhun themselves—it was supposed to help them get to know themselves better. In response to that, the Gaonbura added that festivals should also be a record of their culture for later generations, since the younger lot was forgetting everything.

The Gaonbura's views about the role of the THDWA were also different from Lumren's: 'The main reason for forming the association was to be able to make demands and claims from the government.' That was perhaps a hint that the crucial reason behind the decision to hold the festival again in November 2010 could have been the fact that the state elections were around the corner in April 2011.[32] Besides the Tangsa leaders and elders, almost all the non-Tangsa VIPs invited for the festival in 2010 were politicians, journalists, or Coal India officials.[33] The politicians who attended the festival took it as a platform to campaign for the forthcoming elections thereby instrumentalizing the occasion for their own ends, besides praising the Gaonbura for having put up such an impressive show.[34] The Coal India officials made many new promises of help. The local media gave the festival some coverage in the local television channels. For the media-savvy and ambitious Gaonbura the festival was a big opportunity to demonstrate his organizational and leadership capacities.

The Gaonbura had organized the festival, in a form that was not only meaningful to the Hakhuns but which was also recognized as a festival by outsiders; the Hakhun becoming, in the process, a 'mimetic minority' in the sense of Jonsson (2010). By doing so, the Gaonbura had demonstrated what a village head can do, almost single-handedly, for the welfare of his village and towards the preservation and projection (read articulation) of the 'culture' of his tribe. He had also proved, by getting so many important people to attend, that he was a modern village head capable of dealing with politicians, administrators, and journalists on behalf of his people besides being a leader of the Hakhun in India. While projecting himself, he had also carefully nurtured his relationship with other Tangsa tribal leaders such as Aphu Tyanglam and Lemo Rara from Phulbari, as well as with Baptist church leaders such as the Executive Committee Members of the TBCA.

Were these enough reasons for him to be included as one of three Tangsa members of the Development Council? The fact that Malugaon is very close to Ledo and the sub-divisional headquarters at Margherita must have certainly been a factor for consideration in the selection—since the Gaonbura lived so close by and was mobile (since he had a motorbike), he could be summoned at short notice whenever needed by the civil administration. On the other hand, since he had good contacts with the local civil and police administration it was useful for the Tangsa to have him as their representative. The fact that a high-level insurgent cadre was from Malugaon was also perhaps another reason for his consideration. Whatever the reasons were, the Gaonbura succeeded in getting what he wanted—recognition and political power.

The inhabitants of Malugaon, however, have a much more urgent and substantive reason for organizing such festivals. It is the threat of displacement looming over their heads because of their proximity to the coal mine, their recent arrival in Malugaon, and their somewhat illegal status there. Therefore they have to keep reasserting their presence (and inviting outsiders to witness their presence there) in order to make sure that if and when the time comes for them to have to relocate then there will be enough witnesses ready to vouch for them to ensure that they get suitable compensation. Holding a festival is a good strategy for a small community like the Hakhun to be seen by others, especially by those who matter.

Different Rituals, Culture on Show

Therefore, there were many reasons for holding a festival, both for the Gaonbura and also for the community. But was that all? What were Junglum Hakhun's reasons for participation? Let me next look at the nature of the rituals and the 'cultural programme' presented in order to investigate these questions further.

Basically, three kinds of rituals were performed at Malugaon: (a) the secular ones like the hoisting of the festival flag and holding of a public meeting which we have already seen at Kharangkong, (b) the Christian rituals comprising the blessing and prayer at the beginning and the end of the day's events conducted by the Pastor and Lumren Hakhun, and (c) the traditional rituals which were enacted by Junglum Hakhun with the help of two women assistants. Some characteristic material symbols of Hakhun-ness—the hornbill feathers, the teeth of the wild boar, cowrie necklaces, their dresses and ornaments, their traditional bamboo mugs and cane baskets—were also on display.

This is precisely an example of the 'ritualised celebrations of custom' (where custom is the same as tradition in my context) in the form of the music, dance, and 'traditional' dress, as dramatically enacted in art festivals, tourist events, and rituals of the state (Keesing 1989), as well as a kind of 'objectification and commodification of culture' defined as follows: 'In the process of objectification, a culture is (at the level of ideology) imagined to consist of "traditional" music, dances, costumes, or artefacts. Periodically performing or exhibiting these fetishized representations of their cultures, the elites of the new Pacific ritually affirm (to themselves, tourists, the village voters) that the ancestral cultural heritage lives on' (Keesing 1989: 23).

Although animal sacrifice and drinking rice-beer (*kham* in Hakhun) are forbidden among the Baptist Christians, Junglum presented the rituals associated with the animal sacrifice (which was an integral part of any village festival in olden times) as part of their tradition; the whole ritual was performed, including constructing the sacrificial altar (*kham-khit*, see Photograph 5.6), adorning it with all the necessary paraphernalia and symbols, and enacting the whole process right up to

Photograph 5.6   The *Kham-khit*
(ritual altar) at Malugaon

Source: Author.

the point of pouring rice-beer over the 'hypothetical' animal, drinking to its painless release, and praying for its soul (before it is sacrificed), all ostensibly for the younger generation of Hakhuns to witness. The striking point, however, was the fact that, contrary to the Christian prayer during which every Baptist I asked told me they 'really' prayed, the traditional rituals were seen as just 'hollow' performance, without any performative force, even by the Hakhun themselves.

Hence there was a difference, the Hakhun themselves admitted to, in the degree of efficacy or meaningfulness of the three sets of rituals: the secular ones were seen as enacted only to make the event look official and without any special significance to most, the Christian ones were necessary for getting God's blessings on the whole event, and the traditional ones were considered to be empty rituals (Harth 2006: 29), done 'just for show'.[35] In fact, it was precisely under the condition that the traditional rituals would be done only as performance that the church leaders had given permission for their enactment in the first place. Just like the Ao Pastor mentioned by Longkumer (2015: 56), the Tangsa church leaders also believed that 'Christians performing in the festival are merely acting; no one would go back and revert to their pre-Christian beliefs'.

It was hard to know whether Junglum Hakhun actually believed in the performative power of his actions while performing the rituals, or if he also felt that he was only enacting them just for show. In any case, there is a paradox inherent in the question of 'authenticity' of the performance of rituals described above because a ritual from their pre-Christian past performed by a Hakhun person (Junglum) who had converted to Christianity can never be 'authentic' or 'genuine' (Longkumer (2015: 59) aptly describes such a performance to be 'authentic in image, inauthentic in practice'); on the other hand, an 'authentic' ritual can never be performed 'just for show' by a real practitioner.[36]

Next, it is interesting to explore what aspects of their culture the Hakhun perceived they were presenting at the festival. After all, many people like Junglum Hakhun sincerely believed that holding a festival was important in order to transmit their 'traditional culture' from the older to the younger generation of Hakhun. But how much of their 'traditional culture' was on show at the festival? And how much of that was being transmitted? Presenting their 'culture'—as a sequence of dances—had become a set routine exercise for Junglum's 'kassa party'; they had performed the same dances at so many places and so many times in the past that they did not have to put in too much effort to re-enact them one more time. Although it was clear that the troupe clearly enjoyed performing, the impression they gave was that they were only playing at being 'exotic', at achieving some sort of 'staged authenticity' (MacCannell 1976: 91) for the benefit of the audience. And since his troupe comprised a more or less fixed older group of adults, the aim of transmission to the younger lot did not seem to be really happening.

Moreover, the 'cultural programme' was not much more than a few song and dance items put together from what was possible to present without too much effort. The Christian group was brought in from elsewhere by Lumren Hakhun; Junglum Hakhun took charge of the traditional part and the village youngsters tried their best to add a few items of their own taste to the programme.[37] Considering everything, it seemed as if it did not matter too much *what* cultural traditions they were presenting as long as they could establish that they *had* something to present (see also Bräuchler and Widlok 2007). This also explains the improvised and tentative quality of some of the dances presented.

Given the enthusiastic response from the non-tribal guests who had come from Ledo and further afield to attend the event, the enactment of the 'traditional' rituals associated with the sacrifice and the 'traditional' dances that Junglum had got his troupe to perform were 'exotic' and 'tribal' enough for the guests to be convinced that the Hakhun have a distinctive 'tribal culture', different from that of the plains people. And establishing their credentials as a tribal group is important for the Hakhun in order to create their cultural identity as an ethnic group.

Although Baptist Christianity is part of their new modern image, there was very little participation from the people of Malugaon in the Christian part of the programme, as the singers from Relang as well as Lumren Hakhun were all from Arunachal Pradesh. So, how important was their religion, after all, to the organizers? Let me describe a telling moment which came almost at the very end of the festival. Lumren had delivered his vote of thanks and was reciting a Christian prayer to bring the proceedings to an end. At the same time, Gaonbura Hakhun was captured on camera, busy, with his back turned to Lumren, giving interviews to a couple of reporters from the media. Later, I found Junglum Hakhun foregoing lunch to give an interview to a press reporter.

This serves to support my claim that at Malugaon, the Gaonbura, and other leaders wanted to present the Hakhun not only as exotic tribals but also as normal, capable, and modern individuals who have learnt the ways of the plains people in terms of how to behave in public, how to handle the press and modern technology, how to conduct and organize big festivals, and so on. Moreover, from the professional manner in which the festival was conducted at Malugaon, it was not just their ethnic credentials that they sought to establish but also their modernity—albeit a sort of indigenised modernity (Sahlins 1999b) which included their Baptist Christian present. As Brosius and Polit (2011: 1) remark, their efforts are to be understood 'as actions through which they actively seek to create alternative modernities and useable pasts'.

Of course, conformism is always a part of any identity politics—in that sense the Hakhun effort to make their festival look like festivals organized by other communities around them is not surprising. For, 'basically, the ideas of those who dominate become the ideas of the dominated' (Babadzan 2000: 131). What is surprising, however, is the implied fact that they have actually already come that far. They used the festival to demonstrate that they can still draw upon elements from their 'traditional culture' but are equally at ease with their new religion and the demands of a modern present.

Summing up, their festival was not just a platform to show their traditions to their younger generation but also to present themselves before a carefully selected group of outsiders, who were invited specifically because each one of them could be of some use to them in the future. And they did this not only to claim brotherhood with the rest of the country but also as a sort of declaration that although they could still boast of their uniqueness as a tribal group, they were not 'dumb' or 'primitive' as tribal people are assumed to be by most non-tribals.

Postscript: Two Aspects of Malugaon

Modern Technology and Community Researchers

Khothing, who we have briefly met before, was training to be a Baptist pastor. He felt the need to preserve and present their culture so strongly that he had actually joined Junglum's dance troupe. He saw no contradiction in his roles as a trainee pastor and as a tribal Hakhun. He is also perhaps one of our most skilled language assistants from within the community. Khothing speaks and writes reasonable English and is acutely aware of the need for language documentation and preservation. And since his parents and family were still in Myanmar initially, and he still held a Burmese passport, he would often walk over the hills, across the border to Myanmar.

Early on in our project, Khothing was given a small video recorder which he took with him to Myanmar; over the years, Khothing has made some amazing recordings of songs and dances of the Tangsa in Myanmar. Later on a laptop was also given to him and he started to write down the stories that he had recorded, both in English translation and in Hakhun, using the Roman script. While doing so, he felt the need to develop an orthography for the Hakhun language. Rather than adopting the Kimsing orthography of the (Baptist) Tangsa Bible, Khothing and Lumren decided to develop their own for the Hakhun language, which looks demonstrably different, with some technical guidance from Stephen Morey. In consultation with community elders, Khothing has been busily working on writing down the stories and migration history of the Hakhun in the last couple of years.[38]

Perhaps, it is due to the proximity of the urban areas of Ledo and Margherita that Malugaon was also the first Tangsa village where community members themselves took on the job of recording their own festivals and other social events (like house-opening) using handycams handled and owned by someone in the village. Almost everyone in Malugaon has a mobile phone, and besides using them to call others or to listen to music, many also regularly use the inbuilt cameras to take photos of special occasions. Perhaps it is the greater exposure to the media via television and contact with journalists and reporters, but the Gaonbura once even told me that he wanted to invite the National Geographic to make a film on Malugaon.[39]

In the last year of our project, we organized two 3-day workshops to train young volunteers from different Tangsa groups to record and document their songs and stories. Khothing was far ahead of all the others in that respect. He was also the first amongst our Tangsa interlocutors who we could reach over e-mail. But technology has improved dramatically, even within the years that I have been going to the field, and Internet is now so widely available and in use that many of our interlocutors are now also on Facebook. There are at present several Facebook Tangsa groups, some of which carry frequent updates of news related to the community. It is clear that the younger generation of technology-savvy Tangsa will have their own notions of how they want to define themselves as Tangsa, and their own special methods of doing so.

Hakhun and Coal India, and My Friends in Both

In all these years, my Tangsa interlocutors have never asked me to hoist a flag or make a speech at any event, although they have often asked my colleague Stephen to do the honours, whenever and wherever he has been present. Of course they have often invited me to sit on stage and feted me with a memento, but that was all. There are many obvious reasons one could think of for this—that Stephen is a foreigner, that he is a man, or simply that I was just too close to them to be considered a VIP.[40] Perhaps they thought I preferred not to speak or that their asking me to speak would disrupt my efforts to record the event. Whatever the reasons, the fact was that I was never asked, and I did not want to embarrass them by asking why not.

Although he did not attend many such events, my friend, Bolin, as a high official of Coal India, was invited as an honoured guest to every event that was organized in Malugaon. The Hakhun knew about my link with Bolin. I tried not to flaunt the connection, but I did not try to hide it either. I tried to make it clear, however, that my connection to Bolin was personal, and had nothing to do with the fact that I was working with the Hakhuns or that he was working with Coal India. Nonetheless, since Bolin had a lot to do with the Gaonbura and the others in the basti, there have been occasions when I have asked Bolin for help. In the other direction, when they wanted to get in touch with me, the Gaonbura would often ask Bolin about my whereabouts.

A mining engineer by profession, Bolin was a loyal and dedicated employee of Coal India—his whole life seemed to revolve around his job, and what is more, he seemed to love his work, and spent almost all his time, even his weekends, in the mines. Having lived and worked for many years in the area around Ledo populated by so many different ethnic groups, Bolin knew much more about the tribals than many other Assamese. His practical good sense and friendly unimposing manner also helped him to maintain good relations with them.[41]

Since Bolin's official quarters was very close to Malugaon, his home was a convenient base camp for me whenever I had work in the basti. Of course, it was a bit complicated for me to change roles every time I would go up to Malugaon after spending a day at Bolin's, or vice versa. For these were two sides of the same story. But often the positions were different: for instance, while Bolin told me how much Coal India was doing for the welfare of those living on their hills, the Hakhun felt it was much too little. While Coal India considered the informal trade in coal that was rampant in Malugaon as theft, the Hakhun felt that they have every right to take what was on their land. And while the Hakhun still considered those affected by the mining disaster as victims, Coal India felt that they had done more than enough to compensate, and that if they were still complaining then they were just trying to exploit the company. It was hard to take sides. And at times I could also feel the simmering tensions between them. At such times, I thought it best not to ask too many questions.

Notes

1. As mentioned in Chapter 2, Ledo is the starting point of the Stillwell (Ledo) Road; it is also the last stop of the railway line which was built in British times to carry coal from the coal mines that had been set up around Ledo in the 1880s.

2. There are also a few Hakhun families in Mullong 1 in Assam, and also in Nongtham (3 families), Febiro (6 families), and Rhang-rhin-kan (10–15 families) in Arunachal Pradesh.

3. Some people in the village also still use Burmese titles, for example, Junglum is usually addressed as U Junglum Hakhun while many women in Malugaon were addressed as Daw/Do, the Burmese title for lady/woman.

4. One of our interlocutors went to Myanmar frequently and played an active part in campaigning during the election time in Myanmar. Since he belonged to the kingly 'Ang' clan of the Hakhun, the villagers there still looked up to his family for guidance and advice.

5. This is largely because Hakhun and Thamphang, although both non-Pangwa languages, are very different from each other. Thamphang speakers can speak Hakhun but not vice-versa—one more example of linguistic non-intelligibility between Tangsa groups.

6. The similarity between Hakhun and Nocte has been established as part of the work done by the linguists in our project; see, for instance, the work Krishna Boro (a student of linguistics from Gauhati University pursuing his PhD at the University of Oregon).

7. Wakka is a large Wancho village, about 64 kms from Khonsa. It is now a circle of the Tirap district of Arunachal Pradesh.

8. For example, although the Hakhun were known to be headhunters and would bring home the head of enemies they had killed in battle (and do certain rituals with it), according to the *Burma Report* (1942) the Hakhun did not perform human sacrifice. Moreover, until recently, the male dormitories called *Po* played a more significant role in the life of Hakhun men than they did for the Pangwa.

   The Hakhun traditional dress is more like that of the Tangwa/Naga than that of the Tangsa. The men led by Junglum Hakhun dressed in *lengti*s and not lungis in Malugaon for their traditional dances, and they traditionally used drums and gongs in many of their dances, unlike the Pangwa groups.

9. Much like the Wihu-song, the Phon-tu-si is supposedly a very long song and is usually sung as a duet—it describes how to build a house, and narrates the different stages in a long journey, according to Junglum, who could sing it in parts.

10. There were no Ang elder in Malugaon till an elderly Ang couple came to live with his son in Malugaon in 2010 from Myanmar. But that does not seem to have affected the authority of the Gaonbura in any way.

11. Since the border is through dense forests there is hardly any border-control on that route. And since the nearest hospital in Myanmar from Vanruk was much further away, many had no choice but take this route to India when someone was sick.

12. According to the Gaonbura, there were less than 90 Hakhun families in India in 2009 and this had gone up to 110 in 2010. The Pastor told me that 12 new houses had been built in Malugaon in the year 2010–11.

13. The village is called both Malopahar and Malu/Malo gaon. *Pahar* means hill and *gaon* means village in Asamiya. Following general usage, I write Tikhak for the group name as well as for the language they speak and Tikak for the name of the village and the mine.

14. 'Kan' is a typical Tangsa word for mountain. There were about 150 families in Rhan-rhing-kan (mostly Hakhi, Longchang, Hacheng) in 2012.

15. Although I could find no official records corroborating this story, there is proof that some Rangpang (Pangwa) groups lived in the area around Ledo (see for instance, *Report* 1921–2: 93).

16. The Gaonbura showed me a faded photocopy of an official document from 1952 addressed to the Gaonbura Malogaon from the APO, Tirap Division, stating that their village was in a protected area meant for *janajatiya* (tribal) people only, apparently a reference to the fact that the area belonged to a Tribal belt.

    Unlike the 6th Schedule areas of the Indian union where the local communities have a claim over the mineral wealth of their land, it is not so in the Tirap area where it belongs to the government. The legal rights to extract coal in that area have been leased out to Coal India which is a public sector undertaking of the Government of India. Coal India is in fact a 'Navaratna' company, meaning one of the top 9 highest profit-making ventures of the state.

17. The six underground mines were located at Jaipur, Borgolai, Tikok, Ledo, Tirap, and Tipong. Only three of them are operational at Tikok, (Ledo), Tirap, and Tipong, of which only the last is still an underground mine. These mines are today under the Northeastern Coalfields with Headquarters at Margherita, headed by a Chief General Manager, who is directly under the Director, Technical, Coal India and ultimately under the Chairman Coal India with Headquarters in Calcutta.

18. According to Coal India officials, through Coal India about 5 crores INR was paid out as salaries every month to its direct employees and another 1.5 crores INR through indirect employees. Hence the whole economy of the area was heavily dependent on Coal India (1 crore INR = 10 million INR is about 150,000 Euros).

19. For reasons that I discuss in Chapter 7, there was the general feeling among the tribal communities that those who went to Arunachal Pradesh got a much better deal than those who stayed on in Assam.

20. All these villages get a so-called annual compensation from Coal India besides a one-time compensation whenever new land is acquired by the company and also when the contracts with private companies are renewed.

Besides, at least one person per family is included in the payroll of the
private companies which have contracts to work in the mines. Therefore,
on any average each family gets Rs 3,000–4,000 per month either directly
or indirectly from the company.

21. Mullong I had two parts—a lower and an upper basti with a Presbyterian
Church in the middle. It is reported that 3 houses from the lower basti collapsed in a landslide caused by blasting in the mine, and I saw a few houses
perched right on the edge when I visited the basti in February 2014. Some
of the 26 families from the lower part have relocated to the upper part even
higher up, at the top of the hill, where there were some Thamphang and
Lakki families from before. The church has been rebuilt with the help of
people from Lakla.

22. Till March 2014, environmental clearance had not yet been obtained.

23. This view is also shared by the Baptist Nagas in Nagaland: 'One view is
that the Festival educates the younger Nagas to appreciate their traditions
and customs such as dance, clothes, ornaments, food, stories, or as one
participant put it "how our ancestors once lived"' (Longkumer 2015: 57).

24. As Baptists, sacrificing animals was forbidden. He told me that he had heard
and was deeply upset about Junglum Hakhun having performed an animal
sacrifice for our DOBES team to record in December the previous year.

25. These songs had been especially composed for the occasion and were
celebratory in content. Even though there were Christian allusions in the
songs, they would not normally be sung in church, I was told.

    For another discussion of similar processes in Mizoram, see Zama (2006).

26. The dress of one of the Hakhun dances presented looked definitely Burmese.

    Another difference from the Wihu-kuh was that although there was
some amount of drinking of alcohol in the evening after the programme
got over, rice-beer was not served during the event.

27. Junglum's troupe performed at the DPF Festival in 2011, as well as in the
Phulbari festival in January 2010.

28. This was contested and explained by Baptist Church leaders as a misunderstanding. It could also be explained as a change in people's views once
control of the church passed to the hands of the people themselves.

29. This refers to the situation amongst the Tangsa in India, particularly in
Assam. The Hakhun are fairly well-known amongst the Tangshang groups
in Myanmar.

30. Although I have no proof directly, I was told that there was also some pressure from the local leader of the insurgent organization who encourages
and also financially supports the organization of these festivals.

31. The Christian overtones of this remark reveal the manner in which
Christian missionaries working in northeast India have depicted the tribal
past of the people. As Haksar (2013: 47) remarks, 'the more fundamental

versions of Christianity in vogue in the region call tribal history a "dark period" and thus condemn traditional culture and society as being barbaric'. That, according to Haksar, is one of the obvious reasons why young people from northeast India feel a deep conflict between their Christian and tribal identities.

32. This explanation is supported by the fact that no festival was held in November 2011, after the elections were over and Gaonbura Hakhun had become a member of the Development Council.

33. VIPs are very important persons or the dignitaries.

    In fact, the Gaonbura had even vetoed inviting some young college lecturers from Ledo College who were very interested in attending the festival, saying that there was no point inviting people who had no power or influence.

34. In a blatant demonstration of how little these politicians knew about the Hakhun and Malugaon, these leaders spoke about how 'foreigners' coming into the Northeast posed a threat to the region, not realizing that many in their audience were Burmese nationals.

35. Although such a ritual is empty of performative force (in the sense of Austin 1975) it perhaps still had some symbolic relevance to some in the audience.

36. I use the term' authenticity' here in the sense that 'authenticity encodes the expectation of truthful representation' (Theodossopoulos 2013: 339), where 'truthful' again means 'genuine' or close to how it was in earlier times which is again open to further interpretation.

37. This was also proof of their creativity, their versatility, and their adaptability: they were able to create new forms and adapt to create Hakhun lyrics set to disco music choreographed in Bollywood style. The fact that they were able to do so illustrated that they are not 'stuck in the past', as one of them told me.

38. Khothing has since produced a couple of small books for the Hakhun community, introducing the alphabet and also a book of illustrated short stories (*Tangsa Haqkun Likpuq*).

39. During my last visit to the field, the Hakhun were busy dubbing an English film (about the life of Christ) into Hakhun. In fact they had set up a 'Bible office' down in Ledo for the purpose.

40. The fact is that I have never seen a woman—Tangsa or non-Tangsa—being given any official task in any of their events so far.

41. Ironically, although completely integrated into the Assamese society now, Bolin's family also had some tribal roots. And this was an advantage at times; for instance, Bolin had no problems with eating pork or other kinds of animal meat, which most Assamese caste Hindus would hesitate to do.

6 Phulbari
Christianity as a Way of Life

'The Bible is to do with sin and going to heaven, but it does not tell you if you will be successful in a deer-hunt today. As for choosing partners from the right clans for a marriage—that is to do with family history, not with religion.'

—H.K. Morang, Nampong

'Even if we want to preserve our traditional culture, we cannot go too deep as it would mean getting into all kinds of contradictions.'

—Bimol Ronrang, Phulbari

It was almost dusk when I arrived at Phulbari on the evening of 23 December. My hostess, Timlin, had just got back from somewhere and everyone seemed very busy with various things. There was also a power cut. Normally, there were only four people—Timlin, her parents, and her younger brother, Nongkrem (who was a graduate but was unemployed)—living in the house. But another brother (who was in the army in Manipur) and his wife (who is a teacher at Jairampur), and the two college-going daughters of a distant aunt had also come visiting for Christmas, and their house was full. The mother left for the Thursday evening ladies church service soon after and I was left chatting with the father and Nongkrem who told me that the youth wing of the Phulbari Baptist Church had been very active in the last few weeks. They have been busy cleaning up the village, putting up banners and lights besides practising carols, and preparing for the games and the cultural items in the Christmas programme.

They had gone 'carol singing' till late the previous night and would do the same again that evening. I decided to join them. It was a group of about twenty young men drawn from various parts of Phulbari (but not all Tangsa—there were a few Adivasi and Wancho too).[1] One of the young men was dressed as Father Christmas, another had a drum around his neck, yet another carried a large plastic bag to carry back the rice and other things people would offer them. They started out around 6:30 p.m. A bright hand-held lantern showed them the way. They began with the houses of the three Adivasi families living at the far end of the Lower basti followed by the three Nepali families, who attend a Gurkha Church elsewhere. Then they came up towards the Tangsa Upper basti.

The following routine was repeated at every house. The group would stop before a house, gather around in a circle in the front courtyard, put the lamp in the middle, and start singing carols, mostly in English but also a few in Hindi, but not in any Tangsa language (although at one point, the drummer began to drum the Sahpolo beat, and a few others started humming along, while they were walking through the tea gardens between houses). They would sing 4–5 carols at each house by which time the hosts would come out with the offerings: mostly a plateful of rice and some money; they then would do a prayer for the well-being of the hosts. The hosts then offered the whole group cups of hot tea and some snacks—snacks like home-made pitha (Assamese, rice-cakes), biscuits, bhujiya (Assamese/Hindi, crispy savouries), and so forth. Each member of the group would take turns to shake hands with the host and his family and wish them 'Merry Christmas'. Then they would move to the next house. This went on till well past midnight.

The next morning, as usual, the ladies started with their daily chores early; Timlin's mother tending her cows and pigs, Timlin, who was very particular about keeping the house spotlessly clean, sweeping and dusting the house, and the sister-in-law, busy cooking in the kitchen. As for the men, only Timlin's father was up and was cleaning the front yard.

There was not much happening in the morning so after having my morning rice I went for a walk in the village. Lemo Rara (who we met briefly in Chapter 4) was sponsoring the Christmas lunch for the whole village that year, while the Assistant Pastor was financing the New Year's Day lunch. While I was sitting in Lemo's kitchen, a pig (weighing about 80 kg) was brought in by Timlin's eldest brother. It would have to be killed and the meat got ready for cooking for the feast the next day. They had killed another smaller pig already the previous day to feed everyone who was helping out. The pork had already been cooked, the vegetable dish was being cooked in Lemo's kitchen, and the rice was being cooked by some basti ladies in their own homes.

I passed by the church on my way back. A Christmas tree was being assembled with Tokou leaves, cotton, and balloons (see Photograph 6.1). The inside was being decorated by a group of young girls with balloons, plastic flowers, and coloured paper, while outside a group of young boys were making a gate with bamboo and ferns to frame the cloth banner announcing Christmas. Around 1 p.m., tea and snacks were taken from Lemo's house for all the young people working in the church. In the afternoon, Timlin's teacher-colleagues from the private English school where she worked came to visit, on her invitation, and were treated to a lavish meal. In that entire bustle, Timlin missed the evening church service.

Attendance at the evening church service on Christmas Eve was not very high. As usual, the preaching was in broken Asamiya, but lines from the English Bible were also read out. The congregation said their prayers aloud simultaneously in their own languages with their eyes closed and hands raised.[2] When they sang, they all sang together in Kimsing, the language of the Tangsa Bible and Hymn Book.[3]

On our way back, Timlin's mother went to collect rice from Lemo's house to cook for the Christmas lunch the next morning. As is the usual custom, the rice balls would be made by the ladies in their own homes and would be

Photograph 6.1   The Christmas Tree in the Phulbari Baptist Church

Source: Author.

brought directly to the church field where the lunch would be served. The rest of the menu would be cooked centrally in the church field where a temporary shed had already been put up.

On Christmas day, the day began even earlier for the ladies as they had to get all the morning chores done before the morning church service. Additionally, rice for the community feast also had to be cooked—Timlin's mother was doing that over a fire outside, while her sister-in-law was making the morning rice for the family in the kitchen. Timlin was cleaning the house and one of the girls was chopping vegetables while the other was washing clothes. The men were not to be seen. I went around 9 a.m., towards the church and found the all-male cooking-team eating their morning rice—they had cooked some of the to-be-discarded parts of the second pig for their morning meal, and would start cooking for lunch soon after. They told me they were up till 1 a.m., the night before playing badminton and had got up again at 4 a.m., to start cooking.

At the church, people took their time to come, and the service which was supposed to start at 9:30 a.m., started only around 10:30 a.m. Attendance was very good. Everyone was dressed in their best—ladies in the traditional Tangsa attire, men mostly in freshly ironed trousers and shirts, and children in smart new dresses. There was a short message, after which the Gaonbura gave a welcome speech. Both the sermon and the singing were fairly routine—there was not much special that was on offer for Christmas. The service got over before noon.

The next event was the sports competitions where many participated. The tug-of-war as well as the musical chairs items generated a lot of entertainment and fun for both participants and onlookers. Lunch was served to about 250 people. Invited guests were mainly from neighbouring villages—the Nepali Gaonbura of Bishnupur across the main road as well as Aphu Tyanglam and one of his Singpho associates. The meal was rice balls, salad, papad (Assamese/Hindi, a thin flat pancake), salt/chillies/lemon, dal (Assamese/Hindi, a lentil curry), and chicken or pork curry. Unlike in Kharangkong, where people ate sitting on the ground, in Phulbari there were chairs and benches for everyone; the furniture belonged to the village church committee. The young people served the food. It was around 2 p.m., when the last batch finished eating.

There was a church service again in the evening which I did not attend—I used the time of 'load-shedding' (power cut) to chat with Timlin's mother in the kitchen where she was cooking the evening meal. She told me about the *hardships they had faced in bringing up the children, of their time when they lived in the hills in Manmao, and of converting and moving to Phulbari. Timlin had got many marriage offers in the past but had turned them all down because the potential suitors were not Baptists. I found out later that Timlin's sister-in-law, who is a Bachelor in Theology from a Theological Seminary in Kerala, had read the 'Message' at the evening service and that the village youth group had performed some entertaining song-with-action numbers. At the end of the service, many of the congregation, including Timlin, went to Lemo's house for a 'Fellowship' (a prayer-service) and were asked to stay for dinner; the heads of the two pigs were being cooked for that meal. Since 26 December happened to be a Sunday, there was the usual Sunday service the next morning as well, where the year-end expense and income accounts for the church were read out.*

The village of Phulbari is located on the north bank of the Tirap river, about 10 kilometres from the border between Assam and Arunachal Pradesh. Phulbari is the only Ronrang Tangsa basti in Assam, there being six more in Arunachal—Balinong, Jorong, and New Lisen close by in the Kharsang area, and Manmao, Walaktoi, and Longchang a little further away. Although they used to live across the hills in Burma earlier, almost all Ronrang live in India today, and almost all of them, except a few families living in New Lisen, are Baptist Christian. Culturally, the Ronrang are somewhat different from the other Pangwa groups.[4]

Located very close to the busy commercial town of Jagun, Phulbari is very well-connected by public transport. As is clear from Map 6.1, Phulbari comprises two parts, Upper and Lower, with almost all the Tangsa families now living in the Upper part. Both parts of Phulbari (as well as a much larger area called Parbatipur) are under one Tangsa (Ronrang) Gaonbura who lives in Upper Phulbari. In this chapter, I wish to introduce the Ronrang people living in Phulbari in order to give an idea of life in the village and to highlight the special relation most villagers have with the village Baptist Church. This will also demonstrate how their lives and lifestyles have changed after conversion to Christianity. Next, I describe the Shawi-kuh festival that was celebrated in Phulbari in 2010 and discuss the Tangsa efforts towards ethnic consolidation, transcending religious differences. I end this chapter with a look at the attitudes of a section of the Assamese with respect to the Tangsa and other ethnic communities living in Assam.

Life in Phulbari

The Establishment of Phulbari

A few Tangsa men had worked in the Ledo area as porters during World War II and after it ended they did not want to go back to the hills and decided to stay somewhere near Tin-mile in the village of Khongman.[5] That entire area had been cleared during the war. But when the Nepalis were settled in that area after the 1950 earthquake, the Tangsa moved back towards the hills and established their village in Lower Phulbari in the early 1950s. There were 20–25 families in Phulbari then. Slowly others came down from Manmao and Lisen and the village grew. The basti was given an Assamese name—Phulbari, meaning 'garden of flowers'—in 1955–7 by the village elders.

According to the present Gaonbura, Bimon Ronrang, his father was among the first ones to come and settle, some 60–70 years ago, in Lower Phulbari, which was then a dense bamboo (*kakobah*, Assamese) forest. Another version of the story came from Onkham Singpho, who lives in Lower Phulbari and has a Singpho father and a Tangsa mother. He claims his father came from Titabor (near Jorhat) and 'opened' the Lower Phulbari village in 1950.[6] Gradually, most of the Tangsa families moved to (Upper) Phulbari where they live today.

The Arrival of Christianity

When Phulbari was first established, most of the inhabitants were still following their traditional beliefs (and a few had embraced Buddhism). The forefathers of the Tangsa living in Phulbari came into contact with Christianity for the first time during World War II when many Bibles were distributed in the area. A period of acute hardship with food shortages and disease followed the war. Many Ronrang came to settle in Phulbari after World War II. By the time the 1950 earthquake occurred in the area, many were beginning to have doubts about the efficacy of their traditional practices. Many roads had been built during that time so the area became more accessible and Baptist Christian missionaries came from Nagaland and from Burma.

By the time the village of Phulbari was established, Christianity had already arrived in this area. However, Baptist Christianity came to Phulbari only in the late 1960s. A Sema Naga Baptist evangelist, Yellowi

Sema, baptized the first person in the village in 1968. Nya-pho, popularly known as Morangkam, is widely acknowledged to be the person mainly responsible for bringing in Christianity to Phulbari. He was amongst the first to come to settle in Phulbari, and became a Buddhist. Morangkam's mother, wife, and sisters were among the first converts (see *Souvenir* 1997). Although missionary activity started in earnest in the region from around 1972–3, most people in Phulbari converted only in the 1990s (see also Ronrang 1997).

Village Statistics[7]

Phulbari (9-mile, Upper, Natun) has 55 families with a population of 220 (mostly Tangsa (Ronrang) with a few Nocte and Wancho families). Phulbari (Lower, Parbatipur Phulbari) has 60–70 Nepali families, 60–70 Ahom families, 10 families each of the Marwaris and Biharis, about 30 Adivasi families, and 3 Singpho families with a total population of more than 1000. Both parts of Phulbari are part of Parbatipur village. Official records give the population figures for Parbatipur to be 4,407 in 2011 and 4,280 in 2001.

Nepali and Assamese are the main languages in Phulbari. Although most of the Tangsa living in Phulbari are Ronrang, many of the younger generation prefer to speak in Hindi or in Nepali. This is because of the great mix of communities living in Phulbari but also because of the high incidence of intermarriage across communities: For example, there are at least two Nepali, one Sema Naga, and one Mizo women married to Ronrang men, and one Wancho man with a Ronrang wife in the village.

Lower Phulbari is closer to Jagun and also older, therefore, the Government High School, the government-run *anganwadi* (kindergarten) and the primary and middle schools are located there. Moreover, there are good private schools (run by the Baptists and Presbyterian missionaries) in Jagun and also in the Tangsa village of Lakla, both within striking distance of Phulbari. The nearest police station and primary health centre are in Jagun which is also a bustling commercial centre with many shops and a large open market. Phulbari has a Baptist and a Catholic Church, besides a Buddhist temple, a Hindu temple, and a Naamghar (a Vaishnavite Hindu prayer house); there are 43 Baptist, 15 Catholic, and 10–20 Buddhist families, and the rest are Hindu. Almost all the Tangsa families in Phulbari are Baptist Christian.

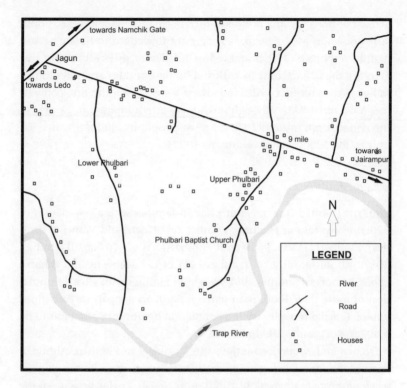

Map 6.1   Sketch Map Showing the Layout of (Upper and Lower) Phulbari

Source: Jayanta Laskar and Inez Ruscheweyh.
Note: Map not to scale and does not represent authentic international boundaries.

Among the Tangsa, there are 15 persons with regular jobs (including those in the army, many working in the forest department as guards), and about 10 graduates and a single postgraduate. There are no science graduates, no engineers, and no doctors as yet. After finishing school, most Ronrang go either to Itanagar (in Arunachal Pradesh) or to Ledo, Margherita, and beyond for further education.

Most Ronrang families living in Phulbari have some tea plantations around their houses in Upper Phulbari and some rice fields in Lower Phulbari which are looked after by Nepali or Adivasi families living in the fields.

There is a brick kiln very close to the Baptist Church in Upper Phulbari. The land belongs to a Ronrang person from Jorong who has given it on lease to a Bihari gentleman who lives elsewhere. The kiln employs 50–60 workers, mostly Biharis. A little colony for the workers had sprung up near it. The Tangsa living in Phulbari have very little to do with it—even their request to the owner that local residents be given a concession when they buy bricks has not been entertained.

Nearby, the dredging of the Tirap riverbed, to collect stones with large dredgers called JCPs, owned by non-Tangsa contractors, continues unabated. Some Ronrang men also tried to earn a little by selling pebbles and stones they piled along the river bank, gathered by wading in the water all day. Those stones were bought at very low rates by the contractors and carried away in trucks, for sale as construction material. For all these reasons, many in Phulbari felt that many people were getting rich from projects which were located in Phulbari, but from which the people living in Phulbari gained very little.

Three Faces of Phulbari

By way of introducing the reader to the people of the village, I present here three of our principal interlocutors, very different from each other but very special in their own ways, in order to give a sense of why we chose Phulbari as a fieldwork site in the first place.

Vignette 1

The smart, handsome, and resourceful Lemo Rara was our main contact in Phulbari. Lemo is the present Phulbari GB's paternal uncle. According to Lemo's mother, the family had gone to live in the Six-mile area in 1939 and had moved to the Lower basti in 1950. About 50 years of age, Lemo spoke perfect Asamiya, had finished his higher secondary education, and could read, write, and also speak some English. He was very polite and diplomatic and, much like the Singpho leader, Manje La, knew very well how to make the world around him work. He was shrewd and sophisticated, and was often chosen to represent the Tangsa in Assam.[8] Lemo has five daughters and a son. All his children had finished school. In fact, his eldest daughter was the only MA from Phulbari. Lemo's elder brother Molem, who lives in Jorong now, was the first Ronrang graduate. He then went to Bible College, did his

Masters in Theology and had held the post of the Executive Secretary of the TBCA till his retirement in 2011.

Lemo was a very active member of the church, and was perhaps one of the very few people in Phulbari who could really sing from the Tangsa (Kimsing) Hymn Book; he was also a natural leader of his community, who cared and could initiate change. For instance, almost the first thing he told us when we met him for the very first time in 2009 was that the name of their community (and the language they speak) should be changed to Rera/Roera since the term Ronrang was a British 'invention'.[9] Lemo was on very good terms with Aphu Tyanglam as well as with church leaders. He was the Organizing Secretary for the Shawi-kuh celebrations that were held at Phulbari in 2010. It was not surprising therefore that Lemo was chosen to be one of the three Tangsa members in the Development Council.

Vignette 2

In sharp contrast, the illiterate and much older Mohen Ronrang was essentially a 'misfit' as he belonged to another era and stood for a world that had almost vanished. He claims he had seen it all, from British times and human sacrifice, through many wars and difficult times, to moving to the plains and conversion to Christianity.[10]

Initially, he had owned a lot of land in Phulbari but he gradually sold most of it (in times of illness and also to get his daughters married) and was now classified to be BPL (Below Poverty Line). He had only one *pura* of land left on which he had 80 betel nut plants. He lived with his second (Nepali) wife in a tiny concrete BPL house given to them by the state.[11] On normal days he still went out to work, either to the forest to collect firewood or to the river to gather stones from the riverbed. So he was happy when our team visited the village because he could earn some extra money as our interlocutor.

Very small in build, he was very fit and could begin to dance or walk to the next village at a moment's notice. When we had first asked him about the songs and dances of the past, he told us that he had not thought about them for more than forty years since he became a Christian and hence he was badly out of practice.[12] But it did not take him long to get started. Over the years, he has told me many long, complicated, and wonderful stories—ancient stories about where they came from, from the time of the beginning of creation, the migration history of the Ronrang, about their life in the hills, their wars with neighbours, how they used to make gunpowder and salt in olden times; he also sang many different songs and narrated the stories around them and showed us many different dances as well as demonstrated the different beats of the gongs (*namnu/rajo*); although completely illiterate, he rarely mixed up sequences or got confused. Even though he was a little hard of hearing, his memory was prodigious.

I asked him once whether he was worried about telling us those old stories, and singing and dancing for us—in fact, doing exactly those things which were actually banned by the Baptist Church—he replied that he knew Jesus would forgive him because he was doing so only because he did not want their past to get completely lost.

Vignette 3

Surprisingly, the son—Kamthoi—of Morangkam, the person who brought Baptist Christianity to Phulbari is not a Baptist.[13] Kamthoi (born 1965) has a Nepali wife, and has made a name locally as a singer and an entertainer. He joined another congregation called the Little Flock, along with his father in 2002. He did not learn music formally but since his father was involved with the spread of Baptist Christianity in the village in the early stages, Ao preachers from Nagaland would come and stay in their house when he was a little boy. They would often bring their guitars along and sing together. Kamthoi learnt by watching them play and hearing them sing. He found it easiest to sing in Nepali and Hindi, then in Assamese, and finally in three Tangsa languages at least. He could sing in Morang (because his father was Morang), in Kimsing (his mother was Kimsing), and in Ronrang (because he lives in Phulbari).

Kamthoi represents a typical face of Phulbari today: A person with a tangled Tangsa background who has married a non-Tangsa and has tried to gain acceptance and recognition from the people of that area, both tribal and non-tribal, simply on the strength of something universal—his music. Although he had not finished school, he was perhaps the one who understood our project aims (and also my worries about writing a dissertation) the best amongst our Tangsa interlocutors in Assam. He was 'modern' in his attitude to life, very modest and soft-spoken, but with a mind of his own. Aware of the fact that his music brought in very little, he helped his wife to rear and sell broiler chickens, while taking care of their tea gardens and 'Tokou' palm plantation. He was serious about his religious practices, but did not feel the need to convince others to join his group since he believed that religion was an individual's personal choice. He was also quite interested in Buddhism, possibly having inherited his curiosity for other religions from his father. In any case, Kamthoi was quite open-minded in his attitude towards religion—perhaps a symptom of the fact that he was a second-generation convert.

A Glimpse of the Village

The first impression one got of Phulbari was of order. The village was incredibly clean and beautifully laid out: Houses with pretty front and back gardens neatly arranged on both sides of a straight road, leading from the national highway all the way to the Baptist Church compound very close to the Tirap river. The houses were well-spaced out with lush green tea gardens and betel nut plantations filling the spaces. Most of the Tangsa houses in Upper Phulbari were of the Assam type (not chang-ghars), built with cement and bricks with asbestos roofs.[14] Of course, many still had their kitchens in a chang or a mud hut at the side or the back, and most houses still had no proper toilets or bathrooms. But some, like the house of the revenue collector, Shimo Ronrang, not only had proper concrete toilets with running water, but also a sink with running water in the kitchen.

The Assam-type houses (see Sketches 6.1 and 6.2) and the way of living of most of the Tangsa in Phulbari was in stark contrast to the picture in Kharangkong. Most of the Ronrangs had some education; many spoke perfect Asamiya. Their living rooms had chairs and sofas; many also had dining tables which they regularly used. Most houses had a TV and a refrigerator, cooking-gas connections, and so forth, and many families had a private car or at least a motorcycle. There was not much opium or alcohol addiction to be seen in the village. All these features reflected their desire to live like the plains-people.

In any case, the difference in living standards, cleanliness, education, and outlook to life between a Christian Tangsa village like Phulbari and a predominantly non-Christian one like Kharangkong is striking

Sketch 6.1   A Recently Built Concrete House in Phulbari
Source: Inez Ruscheweyh.

although it was hard to ascertain whether the differences were due to the fact that Phulbari was such a mixed village or because of the proximity to the semi-urban life in Jagun, higher levels of education, economic prosperity, or simply because of the positive impact of Christianity amongst the Ronrangs.[15]

The fact that the Ronrangs were among the first of the later Pangwa groups to come into India is supplemented by the evidence that most Ronrang elders I met were born in India while Aphu Tyanglam and his brother, as well as almost all the Hakhun elders, were born in Burma. Moreover, the Ronrang moved down to the plains long before the other Pangwa groups, and hence had access to school education earlier than most other Tangsa groups. They had first settled in the Manmao area where there were schools from very early on.[16] Since they lived in the foothills, the Ronrang, along with the Mossang, were among the earliest of the various Pangwa groups to come into contact with the people in the plains.[17] At least three Ronrang *kotoky*s (Ass. mediator, interpreter) were appointed by the British to assist in translating and mediating between the administration and the tribal groups.[18]

Another factor to explain the difference was that as the only Ronrang village in Assam there was a lot of contact and competition between Phulbari and the older and more prosperous Ronrang villages of Balinong and Jorong in Arunachal. They wished to model Upper Phulbari along the lines of Balinong and Jorong. However, the constant competition with the Ronrang in Arunachal, and the comparison with the non-Tangsa inhabitants of Parbatipur village (of which Phulbari is a tiny part), did not make life easier for the Ronrang in Phulbari. Furthermore, since all the Ronrang villages in Arunachal are still almost 'purely' Ronrang, they have been able to preserve their language much better than the Ronrang in Phulbari who have not been able to keep their language from getting corrupted with Nepali and Asamiya words. In addition, my interlocutors felt that there was a 'dilution of traditions' that resulted from marriages across communities in a mixed village like Phulbari.[19]

For all these reasons and more, many amongst the Ronrang, especially among the younger lot, were convinced that it might be better if they too moved 'behind the fence', the allusion being to the Inner Line Regulations which are still in place in the hill state of Arunachal. They believed that the Tangsa in Arunachal have a better deal, mainly because of the security of land and property—while in Assam they were slowly losing out to the more enterprising Nepalis and Adivasis. However, some Tangsa, like Aphu Tyanglam, argued that they were more secure in Assam at least at the present time since it was believed that the NSCN leaders had told their ULFA friends not to bother the Tangsa as they were 'their' people. The NSCN did collect taxes from the Tangsa but they were much lower than the demands made by the ULFA.[20]

Christianity in Phulbari

A Christian Community

Apart from cleanliness, Christianity had brought other advantages to Phulbari too: the Ronrangs had access to better education, better health care, and a much better support network through the church. Christians have to learn to read in order to be able to read the Bible and the Hymn book—that forced them to go to school; that also meant that everyone was expected to have some basic education. Moreover, there were some very good private English-medium Christian schools close by. In addition, after finishing school, they could go to study in a Bible school—that was an additional source of employment for Christians, and also an incentive to finish school.

In any case, it was clear that the Ronrang considered it important to educate their children, and have been doing so for quite some time now. Consequently, there are many Ronrangs with regular jobs, and most Ronrang families were reasonably well-off. The other Ronrang villages in Arunachal Pradesh were even more so except for New Lisen which is not Baptist Christian.[21] Therefore, the connection between religion and the living standards of a village was hard to overlook. Not just Bible schools, other Christian organizations, such as World Vision, also offered employment to quite a few people from Phulbari. Many of the village ladies were employed as teachers or helpers in the many Christian schools in that area.

If Aphu Tyanglam was the single most important factor defining and dictating the conduct of normal life and events in Kharangkong, it was Baptist Christianity around which events and decisions in Phulbari revolved. For the Tangsa in Phulbari, religion had become a part of their lives. Most attended church regularly and participated in church events and activities and paid their tithes on time; and that was the case, not just for the older and middle-aged people but also for the youth in the village as well.[22]

The Phulbari Baptist Church was planning to celebrate its golden jubilee in 2018 in a grand manner. Constructing a new church building was part of the plans since the present Baptist church in Phulbari was a rather modest structure (see Sketch 6.2). There was a service in the church every day of the week except on Mondays.[23]

The Sunday services were almost always well-attended, and the singing of the congregation very enthusiastic. The discussions ranged from encouraging others to convert, and about setting up a Sunday school facility to making donations and praying that God gave everyone prosperity (so that they could in turn donate larger amounts to the church). Guests were introduced and were invited to say a few words.[24] Going by the numbers (and this is probably true in many other places of the world as well), the womenfolk in Phulbari seemed to be more serious about church attendance than the men, and also stricter about observances. Ladies generally did not miss church, no matter what other work they might have, and they also sang the loudest.

Sketch 6.2   The Assam-type Baptist Church in Phulbari
Source: Inez Ruscheweyh.

Besides the regular services, 'Fellowships' were often organized at people's homes when congregation members came together to bless the hosts and prayers were said to ward off future danger or illness; moreover, there were larger occasions like when church members were baptized, or when 'Prabhu Bhoj' (Assamese, Communion) was organized in the church, once every few months. Furthermore, 'Revival' groups were occasionally invited by the church leaders to Phulbari. These Revivalists went to people's houses to motivate them to attend church regularly and in more difficult cases they used their special powers of prophesying to foretell what harm might befall the defaulters. Church services were held almost every day during the period of their stay in the village and there was a lot of singing and 'revivalising', I was told, although I have never been in Phulbari at such a time.[25]

Besides the Baptists, in Phulbari, some 6–7 Tangsa families had joined the Little Flock and they met at houses of followers in turn for Sunday worship which was conducted in Hindi, English, or Asamiya.[26]

The Residual Beliefs

After a big storm created havoc and caused large scale destruction at the Dihing-Patkai Festival grounds in 2011, Timlin's father, a practising

Baptist Christian, explained the devastation to me by saying that the Tipam pooja, which was performed by a Singpho priest in the DPF grounds, had not been done properly. Many others in Phulbari and elsewhere were of the same opinion, and, as I found out later, this kind of belief was not rare. One other time, when a person from Phulbari died in a road accident, family members told me that very strong winds had begun to blow around their house even before they got the bad news. They sincerely believed that the spirit of the dead man had come to say goodbye to them.

Furthermore, some Christians still believed in the effectiveness of curses based on deeds done during their non-Christian past. I was told by a Baptist informant from Balinong that there was still a kind of a curse on a family in Phulbari because they had offered human sacrifices in the past. As a consequence of this curse, one of the brothers had lost a young son a few years ago, then another brother had died very suddenly, and the youngest brother had been having a lot of bad luck in recent times, including being kept in custody at the local police station for a fortnight for suspected links with insurgents and opium dealers.

There seemed to be set procedures in Baptist Christianity to get rid of such curses—through prayer and fasting. Moreover, many still believed there were illnesses that could not be cured by modern medicine. There were special Prayer Centres for these purposes where the sick or family members could go and stay to fast and pray.

From what I understood from discussions with my interlocutors, their older traditional Tangsa belief system was a complete way of life encompassing everything that was needed to make sense of the world around them; but Christianity fell short of that. In the words of one senior Tangsa interlocutor, H.K. Morang,

> The Bible is to do with sin and going to heaven, but it does not tell you if you will be successful in a deer-hunt today—there is no contradiction if one follows the old rules in one's daily life. As for choosing partners from the right clans for a marriage—that is to do with family history, not with religion. (Nampong, 26 November 2009)

So they still depended on their older beliefs to resolve questions for which their new religion did not give any definite answers.

As my Kimsing interlocutor summarized for me, all those traditional practices which do not come into direct conflict with Christian principles continue to be followed by the Christian Tangsa even today. De Maaker's argument below supports that view.

> Conversion, then, involves a process by which people convince themselves that certain assumptions about the superhuman are more persuasive than the ones that they previously held. This does not imply, however, that these previously held ideas become otiose. Rather, explanatory theories that gain ground do so because they merge with ones that preexist. And, until proven wrong or rendered obsolete pre-existing theories must remain valid. (De Maaker 2012: 159)

In that sense, the older belief system even complements the new religious beliefs of the Tangsa in order to give completeness to their worldview. This confirms De Maaker's view 'that conversion is best seen in terms of cultural continuity than as a rupture with the past' (2012: 136). Thus, while many Pangwa believe that conversion to Christianity was a complete rupture that was necessary when they were prohibited to do human sacrifices (as discussed in Section: Conversion to Christianity of Chapter 3), continuity is still evident in some of their everyday practices.

Culture Balancing the Old and the New

The Conservatism of Christianity

We were told at Malugaon (and also at Phulbari) that when the Tangsa had converted to Baptist Christianity in the 1970s and 1980s, they were asked to burn their traditional dresses, their heirlooms, their traditional items of war, and other accessories. Moreover, they were also forbidden from performing their traditional songs and dances.[27]

Given this, it was very surprising, and also a sign of the change in attitude, that a few Tangsa Baptist pastors were amongst the keenest to assist us in documenting traditional Tangsa life and culture. Some of them have since been very prolific in recording, transcribing, and translating their stories and migrations histories. Christian missionaries have been the first ones to try to develop a script for writing in a Tangsa language. Admittedly, it was for the express purpose of translating the Bible; however, the fact remains that the Church literature in Kimsing, Mossang, and Juglei languages are almost all that exist at present (at least in India) in terms of the written literature of the Tangsa. Therefore, even though Baptist Christianity has been accused of destroying and banning many elements of traditional Tangsa culture, it has actually been instrumental in the preservation of some of the oral languages.

Not only the pastors but also most of our Tangsa interlocutors were Christian. Many were respected church leaders and community leaders. Most of them have openly supported our efforts since they were very interested in having some record of their past. Therefore, it is not clear whether the 'felt' loss of traditional culture can be attributed only to conversion to Christianity or whether there are other factors as well. For as we have already seen in Kharangkong, the loss has more to do with the change in the Tangsa world which accompanied their move down to the plains and also with their coming in contact with and the adoption of a 'modern' lifestyle. Moreover, as was evident at the Malugaon festival, changes to and 'loss' of traditional culture have also occurred because the younger Tangsa are more interested in imitating Western or the pan-Indian Bollywood traditions.

On the other hand, Buddhist Tangsa villages in Assam (like Kamba and Tinsuti-Mullong) have also given up celebrating their traditional festivals altogether ever since they became Buddhist. The picture was the same in New Lisen, the only non-Baptist Ronrang village in Arunachal. The youngsters in any case, were not interested, the old GB of New Lisen told me, and sang only modern Hindi songs and other songs. While New Lisen did not have any dance troupes who could present their traditional songs and dances, the nearby Baptist Ronrang village of Balinong did.[28] In that respect, some Baptist Christian villages had a lot more to show than the Buddhist ones, in terms of their concern for their 'traditions'.[29]

The Executive Secretary of the TBCA at Nongtham listed some more ways in which the Church was helping to preserve 'traditional culture', which I reproduce here, in summarized translation, from my field notes.

Christians are involved in organising the winter festivals, but of course no rice beer is allowed. The new generation is trying for the preservation of culture and to revive what is lost. Of course everything related to spirit worship has been abandoned.[30] The TBCA has encouraged Baptists to take the tunes of traditional Tangsa songs, change the words and form new songs keeping the old tunes. The Secretary's wife was trying to reinvent the traditional dress. She has brought samples of their traditional dress from Myanmar but has modified them a bit (by making the

wrapper longer).[31] She started a craft centre in Lakla where she trained
Tangsa women to weave wrappers, jackets and scarves with traditional
patterns. They are spreading the word about preserving dance and dress
even through the Church and want to perform their traditional dances
even in their annual conferences. They are trying to preserve and produce other traditional items like bags, hunting equipment and weapons
of war, headgear and other items. Moreover, they are also encouraging
couples to get married in the traditional dress in church.[32] (Nongtham,
12 January 2011)

Over the years, the TBCA have gradually come around to the view
that their Christian religion and certain aspects of traditional Tangsa
culture can go together.[33] They could not, however, allow the older rituals invoking spirits to be performed (for example, the *rim-rim* prayer at
Wihu-kuh), since, as one pastor explained to me, 'now as Christians we
believe that there is only one Holy Spirit, hence we cannot allow other
spirits'.

'Therefore', one Baptist interlocutor from Phulbari, Bimol Ronrang,
told me, 'even if we want to preserve our traditional culture, we cannot go too deep as it would mean getting into all kinds of contradictions'. When asked what would be left of their culture if all the rituals
were left out, he said, 'Song, dance, dress and language will represent
our culture', shortening Chanwang's list. 'We cannot afford to do
more', he continued, 'as some balance with our new religion also has
to be maintained'. Nonetheless, he believed that it was possible to
achieve such a balance and that striving to achieve it would be good
for Tangsa society.

Tangsa Festivals and Baptist Christianity

The Tangsa in Arunachal have already made the first steps in that direction and had started celebrating the 'traditional' Mol/Moh festival in
April/May every year, albeit in a modified form. Since many of the
Tangsa in Arunachal are Christian, they kill (but do not sacrifice) animals for the feast and they drink tea instead of rice-beer.[34] Traditional
songs and dances are performed, in a suitably modified form. As such
the Mol festival is a secular festival which fits in with the Christian tradition. It has now become the official annual Tangsa festival (like the
Singpho Shapawng Yawng Manau Poi) in the Changlang District.

Perhaps wishing to replicate that in Assam, the people of Phulbari, led by Lemo and Shimo Ronrang, and goaded on by Aphu Tyanglam, decided to celebrate Wihu-kuh in their village. In doing so, the Tangsa in Phulbari were going along almost the same path as the Garos: 'With the disappearance of the traditional Sangsarek religion, Sangsarek rituals had lost much of their relevance and appeal. Only in the 1990s, the Christian churches had revived its celebration in "a Christian way", in order to bring Garos from different denominational backgrounds together, and to emphasize their distinct Garo cultural and religious (read: Christian) identity' (Bal 2010: 24).

But there were other reasons too; the most important factor was Aphu Tyanglam's request and continued insistence that Phulbari should host the festival, which Lemo Rara found difficult to ignore. Moreover, since the younger generation of Ronrang in Phulbari could hardly speak their language, and had no idea about their traditional dress and customs, some of the village elders felt that organizing a festival could be a way to get the youth interested. Therefore they agreed to hold the Shawi-kuh festival, the traditional Ronrang winter festival, in Phulbari on 5 January 2010.

But it was not easy to agree upon how it would be celebrated: non-Christian Tangsa leaders like Aphu Tyanglam insisted that there could be no festival without animal sacrifice and the consumption of rice-beer; both were, however, forbidden in Baptist Christianity.[35] Lemo Rara used his incredible negotiating skills to make both sides agree that some rice-beer could be brought in from Kharangkong but only for ritual purposes; what is more he succeeded in raising the celebrations at Phulbari from the level of a village festival that it was in Kharangkong, or even a community level one that we saw in Malugaon, to that of a pan-Tangsa festival of the Tangsa in Assam. Aphu Tyanglam, on his part, despatched a couple of members from his 'kassa party' to Phulbari a week before the event to train the Phulbari youth to be able to perform their 'traditional' dances. Consequently, a number of Christian young boys and girls from Phulbari wore traditional dresses and participated in the dances, many for the first time in their lives—Tangsa for a day.[36]

More details of the Phulbari festival are to be found in Barkataki-Ruscheweyh (2013: 247ff) and hence omitted here. In any case, the Phulbari event, in its scale and composition, had elements from both Tangsa festivals as well as larger mainstream cultural events, and was a good illustration of an instance of 'performance of identity' (Longkumer 2015: 52), where identity is taken to mean the cultural expressions of ethnicity, as seen in festivals like this one.

While the various elements of the festival programme can be thought of, at one level, as fabrications, 'inventions', and even manipulations, they are better understood by relating them to the politics of cultural performances as well as to the politics behind ethnic identity constructions of small communities fighting for recognition. Moreover, since the term Tangsa is itself of recent origin, attempts to give flesh, culturally, to the term must necessarily involve some amount of cultural innovation and reformulation or at least prioritization or selection of some elements of their older constituent cultural traditions over others. As Roosens notes, 'Ethnic groups are affirming themselves more and more. They promote their own, new cultural identity, even as their old identity is eroded .... To be sure, the process of acculturation will continue to cause many cultural differences to fade away. But new cultural differences will be introduced, sometimes in a deliberate manner' (1989: 9).

So what did they wish to achieve through this process? First, they wished to establish their uniqueness and cultural difference from other groups in the area. That is why it was important to establish their traditional dress, and their traditional songs and dances. However, there was more to it than just the construction of a unique pan-Tangsa identity. Let me discuss this in greater detail below.

Festivals for Consolidation of Tangsa Identity

Everything considered, the Shawi-kuh festival celebrated at Phulbari in 2010 was a huge success because the primary objective—of mobilizing all the Tangsa living in remote and far-flung villages of Assam under one banner—was realized. According to the President of the Organizing Committee, the main reason for celebrating the festival in such a big way was that there were many Tangsa families scattered over several villages in the Tirap Transferred Area, many of whom had no idea about their traditions and festivals. By celebrating Wihu-kuh/ Shawi-kuh together, a sense of unity was achieved amongst the Tangsa people of Assam, and they had become aware of their own 'traditions'. He hoped that, just as the Moh/Mol festival in Arunachal had been given official recognition, they would also succeed in getting a local holiday in Assam on 5 January to celebrate the Kuh festival. Thus, at Phulbari, the Tangsa leaders, led by Lemo Rara, wished to use the festival not only to construct and consolidate a pan-Tangsa identity for the Tangsa living in Assam but also to instrumentalize the ethnic mobilization of the Tangsa to gain political agency and visibility.

At the end of it all, one message was clear to all my Tangsa interlocutors in Assam who were hitherto so deeply divided along religious, linguistic, and also cultural lines—that it was possible to act together as one and present a common unified image to the rest of the world. Compromises needed to be made by everyone, some accommodation was called for, but it was still possible for the Christian Tangsa to project a common identity with the non-Christian Tangsa in Assam.

However, the above analysis begs the question: What was this common Tangsa identity that was projected at Phulbari? The older Tangsa image of drinking rice-beer and sacrificing animals was no longer acceptable, and even if some Tangsa would still like to project that image, the Baptist Christians have rejected that outright. The youth in Phulbari had learnt to dance a few Tangsa dances like the Sahpolo, and perhaps they would be able to recognize a Wihu song when they heard one the next time. Besides this, Tangsa 'kassa' amounted to some (still not so clearly established) differences in dress and ornaments, traditional Tangsa food, and in the display of certain material symbols of their identity such as the ritual altar (see Photograph 6.2), the trademark Naga hat decorated with wild boar teeth and hornbill feathers, and some Tangsa handmade artefacts such as baskets and bamboo mugs.

Just as in Malugaon, what happened in Phulbari is yet another example of the 'objectification of culture' (Cohn 1987: 224–54) through which a culture is reified and consciously used in the political mobilization of a community. However, as Cohn and others give examples of, even though culture in this form might not seem to amount to very much, it is roughly in line with what culture or tradition means to many other Indians as well (see Singer 1959: xiii). So, in that sense, it was not much different from what could otherwise be expected.

Both the Christian and the non-Christian hosts did put up a united common front to their guests. Fissures erupted, however, almost immediately afterwards, with the Phulbari elders and Baptist Church leaders taking strong exception to the free flow of rice-beer during the festival,

Photograph 6.2   The *Ru-chong* (ritual altar) at Phulbari

Source: Stephen Morey.

abetted by Aphu Tyanglam. Given the unhappiness of the Church leaders, an event in this form would perhaps never be organized again in another Christian village in the future.[37] That did not augur well for fostering internal cohesion and unity.

Moreover, there is a subtle difference in the degree to which these cultural elements have been internalized by different Tangsa groups: so, for example, although the Sahpolo dance was projected at the Phulbari festival and at various other occasions as *the* Tangsa dance, we have not seen it performed at other village events at Phulbari, such as the New Year's Day celebrations. But at Kharangkong, both the Wihu song and the Sahpolo dance are usually performed at other village events as well. Hence, while for the Tangsa living in Kharangkong both the Sahpolo and the Wihu song are 'sharply tagged as ethnic and employed for moments when ethnicity needs to be performed: festivals, independence days, New Year celebrations and moments of political motivation' (Douglas 2013: 199), that is not the case for the Christian Tangsa of Phulbari (and also at Malugaon).

In any case, just celebrating a festival for a day once a year might not be enough to bring about unity amongst the Tangsa, deeply divided as they are along ethnic, linguistic, and religious lines. And while returning to the hills to rediscover their traditional costumes and in an effort to retrace their migration history might be worthwhile things to do, they cannot help much in their project to construct a pan-Tangsa cultural identity, simply because in the past the Tangsa tribes were not one but many different groups, many of whom were constantly at war with one another. However, claims to peoplehood or nationhood always need to be based on a perception of a shared distinct culture (Karlsson 2001: 28–9). Unless such a shared perception can be created, the inherent differences amongst the different Tangsa groups might prove to be the Achilles' heel to put paid to all the efforts at pan-Tangsa consolidation.[38]

Postscript: The Assamese in Relation to the Tangsa

Unusual Data Collection Methods in Tangsaland

A young Assamese lady lecturer from Ledo has written her M.Phil. dissertation about the Hakhun of Malugaon without having visited the basti even once. She has depended solely on Mr Gogoi, the Assamese Headmaster of the Malugaon primary school, to provide her with the data. Mr Gogoi was also the link some journalists and occasional writers based in Ledo and Margherita had to Malugaon since most of them found it hard to trek up the hill to actually visit the place. Sometimes they would also request Gaonbura Hakhun to visit them in their homes in and around Margherita when they needed some input. Since the Gaonbura had a motorcycle and was often in Margherita for other reasons, it was easy for him to comply.

Some Assamese wrote occasional pieces on the Tangsa in Asamiya newspapers, based on impressions collected when they visited a Tangsa basti briefly to attend a festival or to attend a wedding. They wanted to tell their readers about the Tangsa, they told me. That was their reason for writing those pieces. Most of these pieces usually began by describing Tangsa food, houses, clothing, and so on, in order to first establish difference; then they went on to give examples of Tangsa kindness and hospitability, despite being neglected and sidelined by the state and by mainstream society. While there was much truth in their allegations, there was a general inclination to draw quick conclusions (which served only to confirm set stereotypical images) in the writings of the non-Tangsa, and a tendency to exaggerate or play down (depending on the context) in the writings of the Tangsa.[39]

'Your style of working is more similar to that of the missionaries', more than one of our Tangsa interlocutors have told us, referring to the manner in which our project team functioned in the field. It took me a while to understand why we were not bracketed with other researchers they had met. Over the years, we learnt that most researchers from the nearby universities have very different ideas about how to do fieldwork and collect field data. They mostly went on very short field trips, staying overnight at the nearest town if absolutely necessary. Most anthropologists from those universities just 'collected data, they did not conduct fieldwork' (Srivastava 2000: 36). Therefore, many of my Tangsa informants felt that the local scholars lacked the interest, the sincerity, and also the perseverance which they saw in the foreign scholars who came to work with them.

I learnt another method of doing fieldwork when I was staying with Manje La Singpho at the Eco Lodge. It was a Tuesday morning when Manje La Singpho's phone rang: a young researcher from a nearby university was on the line. She introduced herself and said that she was working on the Singpho and was due to present a paper on Friday about Singpho fishing and agricultural implements at a conference in Shillong. As she did not have much time left and would have to leave for Shillong soon, she asked Manje La if he could kindly tell her something about such implements over the phone right away!

At some point I wondered if I should try to establish direct contact with researchers at the local universities. Of course, our DOBES team had a lot of contact and interaction with the members of the very active Linguistics Department of Gauhati University, and many students of linguistics of that department have gone with us in the field from time to time, but we had no real contact with any of the university anthropology departments in Assam.[40] I had been put off trying to establish contact once after I was asked about the size of my research package.[41] Another time, a senior anthropologist had (perhaps jokingly) asked if collaborating with me could get one a free trip to Germany. Apart from Professor A.C. Bhagabati, no other senior anthropologist in Assam seemed to be really interested in knowing more about what I was doing in the field. This bothered me because as I was a 'local' it did not feel right for me to use Guwahati or Dibrugarh as just transit points on a field trip. I would have been happier if I could tell someone there what I had done in the field, what I had recorded, and what new data I was taking back with me to Europe. I cannot explain why nobody wanted to listen.

But even if others were not interested in my work, I was keen to know what others were doing. I was certain some work on the ethnic communities of the area must be going on in the neighbouring universities. So once I called up a young lecturer who was part of a 2-year major research project (awarded by the University Grants Commission) to write a descriptive grammar of the Tangsa language. He told me that they believed that there was one Tangsa language and what the Tangsa actually spoke were different dialects of that one Tangsa language— their aim was to discover this standard Tangsa language and write a grammar for it. I could not get much specific information about where and with whom they had worked. In any case, they normally asked their Tangsa consultants to come to their 'Language Lab' at the university since they couldn't get away from their teaching duties, I was told. He declined my offer to share our field data with them, nor did he want to discuss the matter any further with us. They wanted to finish their own research and analysis first, so as not to get biased, I was curtly informed. I decided to leave it at that.[42]

The Arrogance of the 'Big Brother'

Initially, the clear sense of difference with which most Assamese I knew treated the tribal population had taken me by surprise. The Tangsa, the Singpho, and the others were different—they were 'tribal'. But I was not sure what exactly their being 'tribal' meant in that context till I met a young Assamese photographer on New Year's Day 2011 in Phulbari. I was trying to gather a few of the nicely-dressed Ronrang ladies for a photo, when he came up to me and suggested that I should ask the Ronrang ladies to take off their watches and sandals before I took the photo!

Burling (1967: 219) had written a long time ago about 'the condescending way in which plains men sometimes refer to the hills as backward, as primitive and as lagging many centuries behind the more progressive and civilized plains'. The problem is that many plains men, including that upstart photographer, think along the same lines even today even though the actual reality, if they would only care to open their eyes and see it, is very different.

I couldn't help telling Aphu Tyanglam when I met him later that evening about the incident. Aphu reacted very calmly—instead of getting angry himself he tried to calm me down by saying that different people would have different opinions and that there was no point my getting agitated if someone had a different opinion from mine. As we sat there talking, he also told me that he believed most Assamese people still thought that the tribals were like 'monkeys sitting on trees eating bananas'. Since monkeys do not wear watches and sandals, the young man was right to expect the ladies to take them off, he concluded. His lack of surprise told me that he had heard similar statements before; his lack of anger pointed possibly at some sort of resignation.

In any case, that was the very first time I had heard him speak out against the Assamese. My other Tangsa informants were even more polite. There were not many occasions when I could get much insight into what they thought of the Assamese. But from their involuntary reactions and some of their accidental comments I could surmise that their general impression was that the Assamese (and the local Babus in the administration) did not really care about them or their fate, and that although they might make a cursory show of interest, they were not really serious about listening to them, or about making any real effort to get to know more about them.

I could also see good reasons for them to think that way. For, while in Tangsaland, I have often witnessed the absolute arrogance and total disregard for the local people demonstrated by some administrators and police officers. Most tribal people, on the other hand, treated them like royalty. One year, a young SDO, invited to the Wihu-kuh festival in Kharangkong as the honoured chief guest, spent all the time that he was not speaking into the microphone to deliver his speech, talking into his mobile phone, paying scant attention to what was going on around him. And when it was his turn to speak, he made it clear that he had not the slightest clue about who the Tangsa were or what the occasion was. Not only did he not know, he also did not want to know.

Other Assamese guests when called upon to speak at the same meeting made it clear that they knew everything better: a senior Assamese journalist spoke with considerable conviction about the connection between the Wihu festival of the Tangsa and the Assamese Bihu festival.[43] The same gentleman had also remarked to me in private that he felt that there was very little difference between animals and birds and 'those people', referring to the tribals. And as proof he told me that one such tribal person had told him that if they read and write and get photographed, their lifespan would go down, hence they did not encourage their children to study.[44]

Mercifully, there were a few redeeming exceptions—like the old retired Sonowal Kachari school teacher in Kothagaon who had spent all his life trying to educate Tangsa children, and who knew no other way to refer to the Tangsa but in terms of equality and respect. Of course, he would not eat anything or drink a drop of water in any Tangsa home, but he wouldn't in mine either for that matter, being a strict Vaishnavite Hindu.

Notes

1. The village church youth leader is an Adivasi, which means he belongs to the ex-tea garden labour community. I use the term 'Adivasi' in this chapter because it is more commonly used in Phulbari.

2. One gets an idea of the incredible diversity of the languages spoken by the Tangsa during such a Baptist church service when the congregation say their prayers aloud in their own languages. Otherwise, it is difficult for an outsider, who does not understand any of these languages, to imagine what this diversity could mean.

3. Many in Phulbari did not understand the Kimsing hymns, as the language of the Ronrang Tangsa people who live in Phulbari is quite different from Kimsing.

4. As already mentioned, the Ronrang language is somewhat different from the other Pangwa languages; Fish plays a big role in Ronrang (and also in Langching) marriages, and they have many stories about their relationship with tigers. Ronrang festivals were also different (see also *Traditional Systems* 2005: 80ff); moreover, they did not always have the Wihu song but have acquired it over time. Hence although the Ronrang are considered to be Pangwa, they are somewhat special in many ways. See also the section on the Pangwa groups in Chapter 3.

5. Khongman/Khongban is marked on the 1927 British map just north of the Tirap river, see Map 2.3. The place was possibly named after a Yongkuk man.
   Tin-mile (or Three-mile) means at a distance of 3 miles from Lekhapani along the national highway. Similarly for Six-mile and so forth. Upper Phulbari is approximately at Nine-mile.

6. Onkam claims to be descended from Ningru, one of the three Singpho chiefs—Kotha, Bisa and Ningru—in India. He claims they donated 200 puras of land to the village. Three of his brothers still live in Lower Phulbari.

   The Asamiya verb for 'open' (*khula*) is normally used by the Tangsa to refer to the act of clearing a forest and setting up a village in a new location.

7. As given to me by the Gaonbura in early 2012.

8. For example, Lemo went to Delhi in 2009 as the sole Tangsa representative in the ULFA pro-talks delegation for talks with the Central Government.

9. According to Stephen Morey, the original Ronrang village in present-day Myanmar has been identified, on the old maps, under the name Rara.

10. He claimed he was born in 1918 in Lisen, and that he was sure about it because it was in the year of his birth that the British had sent his father to work (digging drains) as punishment for performing human sacrifices. Another calculation showed that he had come to Phulbari in 1959 and was born probably around 1925 which sounded more plausible.

11. There were quite a few families also classified as BPL in Kharangkong.

12. Similar stories have been reported elsewhere. Referring to an Ao village in Nagaland, Von Stockhausen (2008: 67) writes:

    The population there had been forbidden for a number of decades to sing their traditional songs. Even love-songs were banned on account of their non-Christian origins. Since the ban has been maintained for a long while, there is almost no one left in the village who can still recall parts of the traditional songs. The oral tradition and thus the basis of the traditional culture has literally been hushed up.

13. Morangkam had converted to Baptist Christianity in 1973, but he later left the Baptist Church and joined the Baptist Revival Sect in 1996.

14. The same is the case in the Ronrang villages of Balinong and Jorong. Bamboo and wood had become increasingly difficult to find as building material, was more expensive and needed more frequent repair—hence they had decided to not build chang-ghars anymore.

    One Assamese interlocutor told me that since bamboo and Tokou palm groves have been replaced by tea-cultivation everywhere in the Tirap area, the tribal people who need both bamboo and Tokou palm leaves to build their homes would have to either get Assamised and build Assam-type houses or move back into Changlang and Myanmar in search of these raw materials. These thoughts were echoed by a Ronrang elder in Phulbari.

15. (See also Ronrang 1997: 90). For an interesting discussion about the connection between Christianity, and the association between material cleanliness and moral uprightness, refer to Chua (unpublished).

Of course, the Baptist village of Malugaon was not quite at par with the standards at Phulbari. This could be explained by the fact that Malugaon at its present location exists only for about 10 years.

16. A Base Superintendent of the army was posted at Manmao and there has been a school in Manmao since the 1950s at least. The language of instruction in schools in Arunachal at that time was Asamiya.

17. As mentioned in the British *Report* (1921–2), some Rangpang villages were in regular communication with the plains and some even paid an annual tribute to the Ahom kings.

18. The Assamese word *kotoky* or *kotoki*, in the meaning in which it was used by the Ahoms and later by the British, roughly translates to political interpreter. For more, see Mibang (1989). Even when Parul Dutta was collecting material for his Tangsa monograph in 1959, a Ronrang person (curiously called Mr Rifle), was his interpreter (Dutta 1969: Preface). One of the three Ronrang kotokys, Uddi Ronrang, had in fact even written a history of the Ronrang people in the 1940s in Asamiya (see Note 38 for more).

19. This intermixing of different communities seems to be a feature of most of the Tangsa bastis we have visited in Assam.

20. According to a Tangsa informant, Rs 150 is collected as 'tax' per house by the NSCN per year, but in recent years they have been forced to pay both the NSCN factions active in their area.

21. In the Ronrang village of Balinong, for example, there are 70 houses, and 83 families, all Ronrang, of which 42 people are in government service, so it is quite an affluent village.

22. Of course, this sometimes led to some degree of intolerance. I was told many stories of how marriages could not take place because of difference in denomination or religion, even though Tangsa clan rules permitted the marriage. But there were signs that those strict rules were gradually changing—one girl from the village had recently (December 2012) got married to a non-Christian Mising boy.

23. The general services are on Sundays and Wednesdays, the only ladies service is on Thursday, for the youth on Saturday, for mothers on Tuesdays, and general (only prayer) service on Friday.

24. Unlike in Malugaon, I have been invited to speak a couple of times during service in the Phulbari church. On one occasion, after a service, villagers told me that they were unhappy with my linguist colleague Stephen Morey because when called upon to speak, he used the chance to tell the congregation about the need to preserve their languages. 'He did not mention God even once', the baffled villagers told me, 'it seemed as if he did not care. But we thought he was Christian'. Nothing special was expected of me

because they knew I was not Christian. So they did not even expect me to go to church, although they were happy when I did.

25. The Revivalists were a group of Baptist Church members who claimed special powers of seeing visions and the ability to prophesize. The Revivalists amongst the Baptists are not to be confused with the Baptist Revival Church, which is a separate denomination; for more on the Revival Movement amongst the Angami Naga, see Joshi (2007: 551ff).

   Some incidents reported to have happened during Revival sessions were disturbing: For instance, it is reported that in 1996 a young Baptist Christian girl from a basti in Changlang was burnt to death, in the presence of some senior TBCA Church leaders, because one of the 'Revivalists' from the village declared the girl to be a witch; see *Report* 1996.

26. The Little Flock denomination has its headquarters in Dimapur, Nagaland, under a Sema Naga pastor.

27. Many writers, including Von Fürer-Haimendorf, have written about the lack of appreciation and understanding of the early American Baptist missionaries in Nagaland for the valuable elements in Naga culture; see Kumar (2005: Chapter 12) for instance for one account. Government officials such as Hutton and Mills and anthropologists such as Elwin and von Fürer-Haimendorf have accused the American Baptists of demoralizing and destroying Naga solidarity by forbidding the joys of drinking and feasting, and the decorations and romance of communal life. However, latter-day American missionaries switched to a more realistic policy which supported preservation of all that was good in the old customs as long as it was not inconsistent with Christian teaching (as reported by Sir Rober Reid, a former British Governor of Assam, in 1944, and stated in Barpujari [1984]).

   Haksar (2013: 225) also confirms the difference in attitude among different Christian denominations: 'The Baptist Church allows the Garos to participate in their traditional drum festival as long as they do not involve themselves in the rites and rituals but in the Khasi Hills, the Presbyterian Church forbids the Khasis from participating in any of the traditional festivals'.

28. A few Ronrang leaders in Balinong have also taken the lead in trying to record and write up their history and traditional systems.

29. One more ground in support of this view are the comments made by many of our Tangsa interlocutors to the effect that although the Tangsa groups in Myanmar are largely Christian (Baptist), the traditional Tangsa culture is still vibrant and alive there. Tangsa sang and danced during the 'Yuja' festival in Myanmar; even young married women could sing the *Shawi-shi* (Wihu song) there, contrary to the situation in India. The Tangsa students

union in Myanmar were making Tangsa dresses (in fact, the dresses worn by a section of the ladies at the festival in Malugaon—long skirts with a white stripe in the middle—have been brought from Myanmar).

30. As observed by Ketholenuo Mepfhü-o (2016: 373), both festivals and rice-beer were prohibited for Christian Baptists in the earlier stages of missionary activity in Nagaland:

> One major project of the missionaries was to teach the Nagas the sinfulness of drinking rice-beer. They felt that the Naga habit of drinking rice beer was an impediment to the Nagas becoming 'true Christian'…. Abstinence from rice-beer was advocated because rice-beer was used during rituals and festivities, which the missionaries defined as 'devil worship' and they considered the Naga festivals as occasions where they propitiated the 'devil'. The converts were restricted from any sort of association with the festivals. Abstinence from both rice-beer and festivals was made into a condition for Baptism and admittance into the church as a member.

31. Many other interlocutors confirmed this; some of our non-Christian interlocutors, however, told me that the original Tangsa wrapper was white with stripes and short (knee-length) and called *khesi*. But the version created by the TBCA is purple in colour with white stripes and black square patches, taking the design from the Naga *khepoh*. It is called the *khepoh-khesang*. See Photograph 7.2.

32. The motivation to get married wearing traditional dresses, however, was not just concern for 'traditions'; it was because the poor Tangsa, who could not afford to buy western clothes to get married in, were resorting to eloping to get around the problem.

33. Lumren Hakhun, who we met in Malugaon, was also of the same opinion. These aspects were also mentioned (in November 2010) by the Head of the Baptist Mission Headquarters for the Ao Naga at Impur, Nagaland. This has also been seen in Africa; see, for instance, Comaroff and Comaroff (1991, 1997).

34. Presbyterian elders in the Juglei Lungvi basti told me that they did not take any interest in the traditional songs and dances any more as they did not think it was necessary. Also earlier, the people would sing those songs during the Kuk festival when they would drink rice-beer; nowadays, since they don't drink rice-beer anymore, that kind of atmosphere with everyone singing and dancing has also disappeared.

35. Some of these Baptist Christian leaders, however, had had no problems with consuming rice-beer at the Wihu-kuh festival in Kharangkong.

The pig that Aphu Tyanglam had bought for sacrifice at Phulbari disappeared under mysterious circumstances and the issue of animal sacrifice got resolved by itself.

36. This is precisely an instance of the 'externalisation of culture' when 'the ethnic minority become ... an object to be displayed, an identity to be tried on, a cultural world to be momentarily inhabited' (Litzinger 2000: 231).

37. As reported in the *Assam Tribune* on 8 January 2014, in article titled 'Wihu Kum fest of Tangsa Nagas Celebrated.' datelined Tinsukia, 7 January 2014, by a Correspondent, the Wihu-kuh festival was celebrated in Malugaon on 5 January 2014, after a gap of 4 years.

38. Even within a single group, history-writing can prove to be tricky. To give an example: the short migration history of the Ronrang written by Uddi Ronrang in the 1940s (as mentioned in Note 18) was published, with minor corrections of language as a book (Dutta 2011) by our project. However, even though nobody showed much interest in reading or checking the contents before it was published, once it was published, Lemo Rara told us that the book must not be distributed or sold. The reason he gave was that at some point the writer mentions some fights between two Ronrang clans; 'Since all those clans have since converted to Christianity and live in peace with each other today', Lemo felt no good would come out of reminding them of their bloody past feuds.

39. For example, the village of Kharangkong is supposed to have been established as early as in 1802 according to a Tangsa writer in Borun Bora's 2012 Asamiya collection. However, she gives no reasons for the choice of date; neither do the editors bother to verify such details before the articles are published.

40. I have also had contact with the Folklore Department in Gauhati University, and also with the Tribal Studies Institute of the Rajiv Gandhi University at Itanagar.

41. I was told research projects are usually understood in terms of the 'package', meaning the total amount of money that is available for it; the topic to be researched did not matter as much, I was given to understand.

42. If they succeed, Aphu's dream of someone creating a common Tangsa language, as mentioned in the Postscript of Chapter 4, might come true after all.
    Despite repeated requests and attempts, I have not been able to get (or even see) a copy of their final report, although the project is long over.

43. See Changmai (2012: 16). Bihu is the major festival of the Assamese and is celebrated three times in a year, once in mid-April, another time in mid-October, and finally in mid-January.

44. Van Schendel has usefully coined the term 'tribalist discourse', which points to the remarkable resilience of images of tribes based on the presumption that all tribes share characteristics that are fundamentally different from, even opposite to, those of civilized people. They are considered to be 'isolated remnants' of some hoary past that have preserved their culture from time immemorial. They are backward and childlike, and therefore need to be protected, educated and disciplined by those who are advanced socially.' (Van Schendel 1992: 103).

7 The Tangsa in Arunachal
Life beyond the Fence

'Everything is much better beyond the fence.'
— Bimol Ronrang, Phulbari

'Just singing and dancing without maintaining any link to our older traditions are like flowers and fruits which have been separated from the
parent tree; they will slowly shrivel up and die.'
— Dr Jungdang Mungrey, Changlang

*The Kuh festival is held on a different date each year. We shall be able to fix
the date for this year's festival at Renuk only after the construction of all the
"new" houses in the village is completed', Lemkhum Mossang told me. 'It will
be sometime in February. I will keep you informed.' With 30 families, Renuk
was one of the largest Mossang bastis in Arunachal and one where more than
half the population had not converted to Christianity. I had been told that the
traditional festivals were still celebrated in Renuk and was keen to attend the
Kuh festival.*

*Lemkhum Mossang called me later to tell me the date of the festival. He
also informed me that the local MLA, who was currently a minister in the
state government, would also be visiting Renuk on the day of the festival.
Since the rituals would be performed very early in the morning, and the road
between Manmao and Renuk was very bad, we would have to get there at least
by the previous evening. We arranged to go together.*

*Though originally from Renuk, businessman Lemkhum was based in
Manmao, the nearest larger settlement. But since Jairampur, closer to the
Assam plains, had better schools, he also had another house in Jairampur*

where his wife and children stayed most of the year. That was not unusual; many other Tangsa living in the hills have a second establishment elsewhere for their children's education.

On the appointed day, I arrived at Lemkhum Mossang's home in Jairampur in my hired Maruti car. Seeing the small vehicle, Lemkhum looked a little sceptical, but the driver had assured me that he knew that area very well and had gone up and down to Renuk many times in that car. As we started on our journey and the ramshackle Maruti began to smoke and reek of burnt fuel, I was no longer so sure. We managed the 40 kilometres to Manmao in about two hours. Then after a brief stop at Lemkhum's house we started out for Renuk. The 10 kilometres took us more than an hour to negotiate. We crossed the Ronrang basti of Shingwan on the way. There were at least a couple of places on that narrow and steep road where I thought we would have to give up. But we made in just as dusk was falling over the very beautiful basti.

The Christians in Renuk were divided into two denominations—Catholic and Hewa Baptist. A huge Catholic church was being built in the village. Renuk has a primary and a middle school; the nearest high school was in Manmao. The Mossang basti at Renuk was earlier located in Borsatam (which presently has only 9 families); from there it moved to Sarusatam and then to a basti 3 miles uphill from their present location (where it was also called Renuk) before coming down to the present Renuk basti in 1979. This was originally a Ronrang area, and the Mossang moved in when the Ronrang moved further down to Jorong and Balinong. Slowly, the bits of my jigsaw puzzle were beginning to fit.

Lemkhum's brother was the Gaonbura of the village. Two articulate and friendly lady gaon panchayat (village council) members were entrusted to show me around, as Lemkhum had to organize the preparations for the minister's visit. I told the ladies how pretty and peaceful I found the village; they didn't seem too convinced. 'Look's nice if you are visiting here for the first time', they told me, 'but you would get bored very quickly here—this place is so cut off from everywhere else. That is why only school dropouts are left in Renuk now. Whoever could get away has left the village and gone to bigger places'. There was no mobile phone connectivity in Renuk but there were three wireless landline phones installed in the homes of three village leaders.[1] That was their only contact with the world outside.

First we went to the brand new house of the Circle Officer of the Manmao Circle, Wathai, where they had arranged for me to stay.[2] His elderly parents lived in the adjacent chang-ghar. His quiet and reserved father had studied till Class VII. In 1955, Wathai's father had become a teacher at the primary school in Reema, 7 kilometres away. But it was a dangerous and tortuous trip to Reema everyday through dense forests in those days, he told me. Wathai's grandfather had performed the last Nga-tang (Great Buffalo sacrifice) in the family in 1966 when six buffaloes were sacrificed.

That implied that Wathai's ancestors must have been rich and powerful village chieftains in the past. Continuing the tradition, the Kuh rituals would be performed in Wathai's parents' home the next morning. But Wathai's father did not know how to do the ritual prayer (rim-rim). There were only two people left in the village who still knew how to do that. Wathai's father's elder brother, the oldest person in the village, was one of them and would come and do the rituals in their house. Wathai's wife was Tangsa but belonged to the Longchang community, and hence she did not know much about the Kuh festival. Wathai and his wife had recently embraced Rangfraism and one of the rooms of their new house also served as the Rangfraa temple of the village. His parents had also become Rangfraites earlier that year.

How then could they be doing all the rituals as they used to, I asked?

No problem, I was told. Rangfraism was only a new name for the traditional Tangsa practices—nothing had changed.

There was a lot of activity in the village that evening. People were preparing for the festival as well as for the minister's visit. Every house had guests—mostly people from the village who were working elsewhere, or friends and relatives from other villages. Later in the evening, some people gathered around the fire in my host's home. At a certain point, Wathai's mother and a nephew started to sing the Wihau song, the Mossang version of the Wihu song. They sang from memory, and continued to sing till late into the night.

Hardly had we gone to bed, when it started to rain—very quickly it got stronger, and it did not stop raining the whole night. The lightning, the loud thunder-bursts, and the sound of rain splashing onto the new tin roof kept me awake all night. In the morning, it was impossible to walk the ten steps or so from Wathai's house to his parents'. I slipped and slid, and got there, completely muddy, but on time to record the morning's proceedings. It was not even 5 a.m.—they had started even earlier than usual to be finished and ready by the time the minister arrived. The rituals at the house post in the kitchen were similar to what I had seen Aphu do in Kharangkong. The pig that was sacrificed would be cooked later.

'No way for anyone to come here in this rain this morning,' Lemkhum said, when I saw him later.

'Very true. Will the Minister come?' I asked.

'He will manage—he has a sturdy 4-wheel drive all-weather vehicle. Maybe he will be a little delayed, but he will come. However, many others will probably not be able to, because of the weather.'

When the rain stopped around eight in the morning, they hastily redid the bamboo gate that had been erected at the entrance to the village to welcome the minister, which had been shredded overnight by the wind and rain. When the minister (who was not Mossang), his wife, and their entourage arrived around 10:30 a.m., the sun was shining and things were looking up again. I had met the minister and his wife a couple of times before.

The Minister was Baptist, 'how could he participate in a traditional festival?'

'So what? So am I,' said Lemkhum. 'Our community festivals have nothing to do with our religion.'

The Minister's wife was Assamese. She had converted and become Baptist after marriage, but had left the Baptist Church a few years back to found her 'own' church in Jairampur.

I was not sure what would happen when the Minister arrived—guessing from my experiences in Assam, I imagined there would be a public meeting, with many speeches. But as it turned out, the minister visited the houses of some of the village elders in turn, and at every stop chatted with his hosts, asked after the health and well-being, discussed their problems, drank some rice-beer, and ate some roasted meat before moving on. He also made gifts in cash to some families. There was no big formality, people were not bending over backwards to please the minister, but they looked pleased that he had come to visit them on the day of their festival. This was rather different from how a minister was treated or behaved in Assam, and it was not even election time! The hierarchies, which are so present in everything in Assam, were less obvious there. Only two vehicles and just a couple of security guards had accompanied the minister on the trip—that was unthinkable in Assam.[3]

Around midday, the whole village gathered at the lam-roeh, a place at the top of a hill, a sort of village crossroads, where another ritual was done at the ra-chuk, a conical structure made of bamboo, special leaves, and filled with earth (see Photograph 7.1). The ladies were dressed in their traditional best, most carried the special ritual baskets (sang-yi) on their backs (as in Photograph 7.3). Many were humming the Wihau song, but only in snatches. The ones who really knew how to sing the Wihau song were all dead, Lemkhum told me. The minister made a short speech, wishing everyone on the occasion. Everybody acknowledged the minister's presence, but celebrating the festival was what it was all about that day.

As the afternoon sun got weaker, my spirits began to drop. I realised I had a big problem—how would I go back? There was no way my little Maruti taxi could take me back that day. And given the amount of rain that had fallen in the night, I would have to wait for days till the roads were dry enough. The minister came to my rescue. He was going to drive back himself, he told me, and I was welcome to join them. I gratefully accepted his offer. The trip back was an absolute roller-coaster ride, but we arrived safely in Jairampur. I was completely worn out by the time we arrived, but apparently not the minister, for he offered to then come with me all the way to Lakla to honour our invitation to visit a documentation workshop we were currently holding there. From my previous meetings with the minister, I knew that he was interested and cared about preservation of Tangsa culture and tradition. He had already extended a lot of help to facilitate my work. But I had not expected so much.

In this chapter, the focus is on the Tangsa living in Arunachal Pradesh. But I will restrict myself to discussing only those aspects which are relevant to understanding the difference between the Tangsa situation in Arunachal and what has been described in the preceding chapters with regard to the Tangsa in Assam. I begin with a description of life for some Tangsa in the urban as well as rural areas of Changlang, followed by a discussion of the much greater diversity in religion prevalent amongst the Tangsa, and the many denominations amongst the Christian Tangsa. Some Tangsa festivals which I attended in Changlang will be discussed next. The advantages as well as problems faced by the Tangsa living in Arunachal, and some larger issues that stand in the way of forging a pan-Tangsa identity, will be discussed to put the Tangsa situation is perspective. I end with describing how my visit to some remote areas as well as to the state capital in Arunachal first made me see black, but eventually helped me find clarity in and closure to my work with the Tangsa. For the location of most of the places named in this chapter, refer to Map 2.2 as well as to the larger map of the whole area, Map (frontispiece).[4] For the names of the new Tangsa groups mentioned in this chapter, refer to Figure 3.1.

The Tangsa in Arunachal Pradesh

The sparsely populated and densely-forested hilly frontier northeast Indian state of Arunachal is home to more than a hundred recognized

ethnic groups.[5] Part of the excluded and semi-excluded areas in British
times, this area was known as the Frontier Tracts and administered by
British officials from Assam. It was renamed NEFA (North-East Frontier
Agency) and was placed under the administration of the Union
Government in 1948. It became a Union Territory in 20 January 1972
and a full-fledged state of the Indian union on 20 February 1987. The
tribal groups account for about two-thirds of the population and hence
it is a tribal-majority state. As such, special land ownership rules are in
force which imply that only tribal people can buy and own land in the
state.

I concentrate only on the tiny portion of the state in the southern
half of the Changlang district where the Tangsa live. Although there
are increasing numbers of temporary migrant workers (like Muslim
migrant workers working in construction sites and brick kilns), about
1,700 Tibetan refugees who were settled near Miao in 1975 (they
number about 3,000 now), and a huge number of Buddhist Chakma
refugees from Bangladesh who were settled in the Miao-Kharsang area
in the mid 1970s (and are still continuing to come), the area still has
a very low population density.[6] Hence, a lot of land is still under forest cover and the existing villages are well-spaced out. Although a very
impressive programme of road building is currently in progress in
Arunachal, large parts of Arunachal are still not connected by road, and
even where they exist, their condition is often very bad.

Changlang in the Tribal State of Arunachal

The Tangsa are numerically very small compared to the many other bigger groups living in Arunachal Pradesh. But in the district of Changlang
where almost all the Tangsa live, they are the biggest ethnic group.[7]
Within Changlang, they are concentrated in three areas—Kharsang-
Miao, Nampong-Manmao, and Changlang town, the district capital,
and hence have control over four of the five Assembly constituencies
of the district (the fifth constituency, Bordumsa, is a predominantly
Singpho area). The Tangsa have the Singpho as their immediate neighbours to the north while the Tutsa, Nocte, and Wancho communities
live in the area bordering the Tangsa area to the southwest.

Contrary to the picture in Assam, the Tangsa in Arunachal wield
administrative and political power in Changlang—educated Tangsa

professionals are in charge not only of running the local administration but also their hospitals, schools, and colleges (cf. Bhagabati 2004: 183). Education in Arunachal is largely imparted in English and in Hindi. The presence of Christian missionaries (of various denominations) and Hindu activists (like those working for the Vivekananda Kendra Vidyalaya (VKV) schools and rural welfare projects, such as Arunjyoti) in the area automatically imply that there are some (but not enough) private educational and health facilities available.

The Kharsang area of Changlang is in the plains. The Ronrang villages of Balinong and Jorong located there replicated the Upper Phulbari model—well spaced out houses, arranged along a central link road. My wish to visit all the Ronrang villages in India at least once took me to New Lisen and also up the hills to Manmao to the few Ronrang bastis there. Manmao town looked really sleepy; the town centre did not have more than five shops, and most of them looked permanently closed. Nampong, the other hill town on the Ledo (Stillwell) road close to Pangsau on the Indo-Burmese border, was not any bigger. There are several bastis perched on the hill slopes near these towns, many hard to reach. Although there are exceptions, many Tangsa villages in Changlang follow the pattern of Balinong and Jorong—one village, one tribe, one language, and often one religion. Many of the Arunachali bastis are very large, with population exceeding a thousand.

Given the high level of insurgent activity in the area, the Armed Forces (Special Powers) Act is in force in the two easternmost 'problem' districts of Tirap and Changlang.[8] So it is more difficult for outsiders to get permission to enter those districts. Moreover, there is a massive army presence there and many check gates.[9]

There were as many as three army gates on way to Changlang town, the district headquarters of the Changlang district.[10] The 40 kilometres from Margherita can take up to three hours to negotiate. Dense forests alternate with tea gardens and orange plantations all along the way. At one point on the roadside, there is a quaint twin temple—one with a statue of the Hindu God Shiva, the other with a statue of Rangfraa, the 'new' Tangsa god. Although not as small as Manmao or Nampong, the difference of Changlang town from the busy bustling plains town of Margherita is palpable.[11] It is small and quiet, and very spread out with lots of offices and government buildings concentrated on one side and a huge army base on the other, ostensibly to contain the growing

insurgent activity and to protect the border region.[12] Many small bastis
are perched on the nearby hills with a river flowing down the middle.
These bastis extend all the way to the Indo-Myanmar border and
beyond.

The Tangsa in Changlang

The Tangsa in Arunachal Pradesh belong to a much more diverse set of
tribes than in Assam. Although the Moklum or Longchang Tangsa are
hard to find in Assam, they are amongst the largest Tangsa groups in
India. Even amongst the Pangwa groups, the Mossang and the Juglei
are by far the largest in Arunachal, but not many from those groups
live in Assam.

Economically too, the variation is much greater. There are a handful of wealthy and well-heeled Tangsa politicians and businessmen in
Arunachal Pradesh who can well afford to send their children outside
the region for higher studies, and who have travelled to Europe and
America for business and for pleasure. Road building contracts, tea
gardens, and political clout had made a few Tangsa families very rich.
They were followed by a larger group of educated and salaried middle
class of professionals, teachers, and administrators.[13] I met self-assured
and well-to-do Tangsa doctors and engineers, teachers, lawyers, writers, civil servants, and administrators whose lives and concerns did not
seem very different from middle-class Indians elsewhere.[14] I also met
a few educated and capable Tangsa women who were leaders in their
own right—politicians, principals of high schools, and activists. The
picture was very different from the one I had seen amongst the Tangsa
in Assam.

Those were the people one met in the towns and larger villages that
were connected by road. The conditions for the Tangsa living in remote
and rather inaccessible bastis in the hills of Changlang, however, were
very different.[15] They were still swidden cultivators and hunters, many
had to walk for hours, sometimes even days, through forest trails to get
to the nearest town; education and health care had still not reached
many parts. In Assam, one did not find many Tangsa living in bigger
towns. But most of the bastis in Assam were not so remote. Hence, the
contrast to Assam was very great, in both directions. Moreover, although
many of the bastis in Arunachal look so well-established today, they

were set up not so very long ago—the Ronrang village of Balinong, for instance, was established as recently as in the 1970s. The stories I was told of the conditions prevalent in the area when they first came to 'open' the village bears evidence of how quickly things have changed on the ground as well as in people's lives and ways of living.

The Question of Religion

From the time the erstwhile North-East Frontier Agency (NEFA) came into existence, efforts had been made to obstruct the activities of Baptist and other missionaries who had been active in different parts of Arunachal.[16] Soon after Arunachal became a state, the Arunachal Pradesh Freedom of Religion Act, 1978, was promulgated 'to protect those who have faith in their own tradition' and to provide legal and constitutional protection against conversion by force, fraud, or induce-ment. In other words, it was aimed to stop conversions to Christianity, and I was told of many instances when the first Baptist evangelists, missionaries, and the first converts, were arrested, tortured, and even forced to revert back to their original faith during the initial years of missionary activity in the hills of Arunachal Pradesh (Ronrang 1997).

But all that stopped some time ago, and today many of the politi-cians and higher-ranking officers in government are Christian. In any case, most of the Pangwa groups I met in Assam and in the Kharsang-Jairampur-Manmao were Christian. Of course, being Christian did not mean one thing and sometimes there were acute denominational differences between the groups. There were also some Buddhists mostly amongst the Tikhak and Yongkuk groups both in Assam and in Arunachal Pradesh.[17] Among the Longchang and the Moklum, some had embraced Christianity, but a majority from these two groups had not converted and still followed their older practices, or had embraced Rangfraism.

In its present form, Rangfraism is a reformed, systematized, and institutionalised form of the traditional belief system of the Tangsa. It started in the late 1990s as a reaction to the ever increasing wave of Tangsa conversion to Christianity (see also Bhagabati and Chaudhuri 2008: 21). I do not go into Rangfraism in any further detail here as it has no followers amongst the Tangsa in Assam.[18] However, a Rangfraite elder from the Moklum village of Kuttum, where there are also many

Baptists, claimed that Rangfraism and Christianity were more or less the same—both had done away with the bad spirits and with sacrifices, both ask their followers to keep their houses clean, both ask their followers to pray to God and fast when they are ill, and so on. There was no more trouble and expenditure in having to please the evil spirits—if they were ill they prayed, and if that didn't work, they went to hospital, just like the Christians, he added.

The rule 'one village-one ethnic group-one language-one religion' followed by most of the Tangsa bastis in Arunachal implied that when groups from within a village community decided to convert to Christianity they often moved away and founded a new village, as I saw happen in the Kantang basti (see Note 21). Moreover, when members of the same tribe are divided by religion, then relations between them can sometimes become somewhat strained, as was evident in the Ronrang case. In any case, the religious diversity amongst the Tangsa in Arunachal is much greater than that in Assam, and this is true even if one restricted attention just to the Christian Tangsa.

Fractured Christianity amongst the Arunachali Tangsa

The lines along which Christianity spread amongst the Tangsa is very similar to that described by De Maaker (2012) for the Garo community in Meghalaya. Most Tangsa who had first converted in the 1960s and 70s had become Baptists as the other groups did not exist then. Even today, the Tangsa Baptist Church Association (TBCA) has the largest number of members among the different denominations in the Changlang district.

The New Testament has been translated into Kimsing and is officially the Bible that is supposed to be used in the churches under the TBCA. But, as a matter of fact, we have never seen it in use anywhere. One Baptist pastor told us that the Kimsing Bible was 'useless'. As already seen in Phulbari, most Tangsa do not understand Kimsing well. Denying this, the Executive Secretary of the TBCA, himself a Tangsa (Mossang), claimed that most Tangsa do understand Kimsing, as it was a sort of lingua franca amongst the Tangsa (Tangshang) in Myanmar.[19] The TBCA, he informed me, has always resisted division on the basis of language. However, even the former Executive Secretary of the TBCA, Mr Molem Ronrang, admits that there are not many Kimsing speakers in India: 'Still many have yet to master over this language .... Even the educated people hardly read the Tangsa New Testament (Ronrang 1997: 117).

In any case, it is a fact that the Presbyterians and the Hewa (Naga) Baptist Church Association (HBCA) are splinter groups that have broken away from the TBCA on the issue of the language of the Bible. The Presbyterians use the Juglei language and the HBCA use Mossang for their services. And that is not all. The Moklum and the Longchang Baptists are now threatening to break away from the TBCA if they are not allowed to have Bibles in their own languages. The Catholic Tangsa are not so strict about the language of their Bibles. However, I did not meet any Catholic Tangsa in Assam.[20]

But the Baptist Church is still attractive possibly because it is controlled locally by the Tangsa themselves. It also perhaps explains the greater interest the Tangsa Baptist church leaders had in questions about their cultural identity. In contrast, the Presbyterian Church is dominated by Mizo missionaries and most of the Catholic priests are from outside the state. Moreover, as Pruett points out, 'the Baptist polity meshes happily with Naga tribal polity .... Both polities are "congregational" and solidly committed to the concept of local autonomy' (Pruett 1974: 60).

Besides, there are other smaller groups like the Christian Revival Church (CRC), Church of Christ, the Church of Grace, and the Little Flock that we have already met in Phulbari. As mentioned earlier, the wife of the Tangsa Baptist minister has set up her own church called the Abundant Life Church in Jairampur. Given the huge number of different denominations existing in Arunachal and the fact that not many followers have some clarity about why they belong to one and not to the other, this general tendency to fracture, split, and regroup seems to be nothing unusual for the Tangsa. It is possible that the fragmenting nature of Protestantism really quite suits the Tangsa temperament, given the immense internal ethnic and linguistic divisions and subdivisions that already exist in their midst.

Summing up, the Tangsa community in the Changlang District are now split into two major groups, the Christian Tangsa (mainly among the Pangwa tribes) and the Rangfraites (mainly among the Moklum and the Longchang groups). According to Maipa Kenglang, also a Longchang Tangsa, 'both groups have now evolved a common platform in various aspects where they can re-establish the old pattern of interaction. Celebration of the common Moh/Mol festival has served as the most vital element in instilling the "we" feelings regardless of religion or group differences' (Kenglang 2002: 63). So let me turn to festivals next.

Festivals in Arunachali Villages

According to my interlocutors, the reason why the Tangsa community in Arunachal celebrate the Moh/Mol festival rather than the winter Kuk/Kuh festival is because the Longchang, Tikhak, and Moklum groups (that one finds in large numbers in Arunachal) do not have the Kuk/Kuh festival, while the Pangwa groups have both the festivals. The twin name 'Moh/Mol' was so chosen because the Moklum call the summer festival Mol while the Longchangs call it Moh. Moreover, since the time of the winter Kuh festival is close to Christmas, it is not convenient for the Christian Tangsa.

In any case, I was curious to know whether and how each of the two groups (Christians and Rangfraites) celebrated their 'traditional' festivals in their bastis. As I have described in the beginning of this chapter, I attended the Wihau-kuh celebrations at the Mossang village of Renuk. The only event there that was new (or different from what I had already seen at Kharangkong) was the communal gathering of the villagers at the lam-roeh, the village crossroads, around midday. The rituals, however, were familiar—making offerings of rice-beer and the meat-rice mixture and singing the Wihau song—as was the intention, which was to thank the Wihau spirit for its bounty and praying for a good harvest in the next season.

Inhabitants of the largest Mossang village (46 families) in the Manmao circle, Tengman, have converted to Christianity (Catholic and CRC) around 2004–5. But they have not stopped celebrating the Moul and Kouk festivals, as the Mossang call the Moh/Mol and Kuh/Kuk festivals respectively, and do so till the present day. For Kouk, they no longer sacrifice animals, nor do they have a ritual post in their homes. They also do not have a ceremonial ritual basket kept aside for those special occasions but they do decorate a basket with chum-ki flowers 'just for show' and hang it in front of their houses. Instead of going to the lam-roeh, they go to church and give their thanks with a prayer.

Photographs 7.1 and 7.2   The *Ra-chuk* Erected at the *Lam-roeh* at Renuk, and Different Kinds of Wrappers Worn by Tangsa Ladies

Source: Author.

But, much like in Kharangkong, they sing the Wihau song, dance, drink rice-beer, visit each other, and make merry the whole day. This much was possible in Tengman perhaps because most of the villagers are Catholic. I do not know of any Baptist Christian village in Arunachal where any of the 'traditional' festivals are celebrated in a similar way.

The Festival at Kantang

Attending the Wihau-kuh celebrations at the Juglei basti of Kantang, beyond Changlang town, was a different experience altogether.[21] I travelled with my hosts—a couple who normally lived in Changlang town but who also had a home in the basti where my host's old mother lived. Like most people in the basti, they were Rangfraites.[22]

Pigs were sacrificed only in three households in the basti that year— one at the home of my host, the second at a home where the (notched tree) ladder to the house had been renewed. In order to reduce costs, a pig (bought with contributions from all the families in the village) was sacrificed at the home of the *rimwa* (village priest) on behalf of the whole village, and all the rituals were done in his house. My hosts sacrificed a pig that year because they felt that the new road that had been recently laid by the government right through the village might have upset the presiding spirit of the village and disturbed the forest spirits living in the area; usually villagers did not make such major changes to their village area without giving the spirits due notice. Hence, they were offering the pig to appease them. Apart from those three houses, all the other families sacrificed a chicken at their ritual post in the morning, as in Kharangkong.

The village priest told me that if they had to do all the rituals involved in Kuk properly, they would have to start about a week before the actual beginning of the festival, when a group of hunters would have to go in search of large rats (that eat the roots of bamboo plants; they are usually caught in groups of 20–25 in one place), as well as monkeys and wild fowl to hang at the ritual post. Without those things, one could not perform the rituals necessary for Kuk. But all those animals were almost impossible to find these days, so these days they did a simpler ritual called 'Cham-kong-rok' in the village, to honour the rice-spirit Wihau, and to give thanks and pray for a good harvest next time. Every house has the ritual post (*sa-man-thong*, Kimsing) where the rituals are done. That year, a group of six people had gone hunting the previous day and had killed a monkey (which is essential also for the 'Cham-kong-rok' rituals) and a little deer. The monkey meat had already been distributed to all the families in the village.

The festival in the 'original' form called 'Rung-ri' was performed these days only when there was some grave misfortune in the village. Moreover, no one in the village except the priest knew how to perform the rituals; but they needed at least two persons who knew the rules to perform the rituals for Rung-ri so that they could constantly keep a check on each other. When I asked what kind of misfortune would require performing a Rung-ri these days I was told that it would have to be done if they killed creatures that they considered to be kings such as the tiger, the hornbill, or the elephant. Earlier, people would really avoid killing a tiger because of the huge expenses involved in perform-ing the Rung-ri. 'But nowadays, people have become smart', added my host, 'even if someone kills a tiger these days, "Rung-ri" would not necessarily be performed. Since it is believed that as long as the animal is not brought back to the village, no harm would come to anyone; so the body would simply be left to rot in the forest'.[23]

After the morning rituals were complete, the cutting up of the pig, dis-tribution of the different parts meant for different clan relatives, and then roasting the meat took up most of the morning in my host's home. At the home of the village priest, however, the rituals were performed only around 2 p.m. to allow for all the villagers to gather there after finishing their rituals in their own homes. Two bamboo containers (khaps) were hung at the ritual post, one for the priest's family called rim-rim-khap and the other that they would later carry around called the rung-khap. A mix-ture (called cham-cham) was made of cooked rice, the leftover squeezed rice (called chosi) after extracting the rice-beer, rice-beer (chol), and the pig and monkey meat, and ritually blessed by the priest.

This much was not entirely new. But then a group of young men from the basti accompanied by the Gaonbura (who is the priest's brother-in-law) went to each house in turn, carrying the rice mixture on a large round bamboo tray (also called rung-ri; dola in Assamese), singing the Wihau song and being offered rice-beer at every home.[24] Another young man carried the rung-khap filled with rice-beer into which the host in every house was supposed to add some more in order to make the rice-beer overflow, a sign of plenty. This went on till past

5 p.m. as they visited every house in both Kantang and Chimsu bastis and stayed for at least 5–10 minutes at each house.

Many have told me that real Wihau singers have the power to make a length of twine rolled out from the fibres of the *reiben* (wild jute) plant bend to drink rice-beer and to make the chum-ki flowers dance, just by singing the Wihau song. The Gaonbura's sister is the wife of the village priest. She was reputed to be a *shamma* (diviner) from the old times, and one of the last remaining persons who could 'really' sing the Wihau song. She had gone visiting people in the basti and had later gone off with a group of guests from Changlang to the next basti, and had got back home only around 11 p.m. Later that night, she invited me over to her house and sang the Wihau song again at their ritual post. That was the one and only time in my entire time in the field that I actually saw the reiben twine bend to drink rice-beer and the chum-ki flowers dance to the singing of the Wihau song.[25]

Continuing a Tradition

Guests had started to arrive in Kantang basti already around 11 a.m. and everyone was offered rice-beer and meat in every house he/she visited. Quite a few older Tangsa men came walking over the hills from other bastis and several groups came by car from Changlang and beyond during the course of the day.[26] There were also some important politicians and high ranking officers among them, but that did not seem to make much of a difference; everyone was treated more or less equally. There was no formality; people would just come in and sit down around the outer fireplace and start talking to each other (even if the master of the house was absent); some would start singing the Wihau-song, they would then eat and drink what was offered by the hosts, and then after a while get up and leave.

The atmosphere in the village that day is difficult to describe. It was as if the entire village was singing, and the festive mood was evident everywhere. People had simply let go, in most cases with the help of the rice-beer, and were out to just enjoy the occasion. Strains of the Wihau song was heard throughout the day and people visited each other's homes, ate meat and drank rice-beer, and kept singing and talking. It was the spirit of the festival—spontaneous, happy, unhurried, and in some sense, also rejuvenating.

There was no dancing in traditional dresses; no drums or gongs were sounded. In fact, no other song was sung except for the Shawi/Wihu/Wihau song. And unlike the gathering of villagers at the lam-roeh in Renuk and at the festival grounds in Kharangkong and Phulbari, there was no focal point for the festival in Kantang, except for the gathering at the priest's home for the ritual sacrifice. There was also no flag-hoisting, no public meeting, no communal feasting. People just came and went, much like they had done in the Wihu-kuh celebrations in Kharangkong in the years 2008 and 2011. However, there was a palpable difference in intention and in the level of self-consciousness I sensed in the Aphu Tyanglam household on the day of the festival and that in the home of my hosts in Kantang.

Much has already been said about Aphu Tyanglam's intentions and his expectations from organizing the Wihu-kuh festival at Kharangkong. My hosts at Kantang, and also possibly most of the other villagers in Kantang, celebrated their festival for no other reason than that they do so every year, and they did it essentially for themselves—whether people from outside were present or not did not seem to play a big role in their conduct of the festival. In that remote part of the frontier hills, the villagers were very much at home in their own territory; the state or outsiders have not yet arrived there to ask the villagers questions about their identity, hence they did not feel threatened, nor were they under any pressure to 'present' themselves and to consciously project their ethnicity. They did not also bother to explain themselves, they sang by themselves, regardless of whether somebody was listening or not, they did what they did because they felt the need to do it, because it meant something to them; they were not concerned about how it might look or how it might be interpreted by others. It was an occasion for social and cultural bonding, and held some intrinsic meaning and significance for each of the villagers—young or old, man or woman.

It was also clear that embracing Rangfraism had not changed much of their ritual practices at least as far as that festival was concerned. When I asked the village priest about it, he said that as followers of Rangfraa they no longer made sacrifices and offerings to bad/evil spirits that used to cause illness and misfortune; but the spirit of Wihau was a benevolent spirit, and they were performing the sacrifice only in celebration, in thanksgiving. He claimed that as long as they were in the 'older' system at least he, as the village priest, would have to do the rituals every year, even if in a much reduced scale, otherwise he would fall ill. I did not manage to find out who or what would make him ill. Nor could he tell me what could happen if the forest spirits or that of the village got angry as my hosts feared.

The Genesis of Festivals

I have not attended a Moh/Mol festival in Arunachal. However, I was shown videos of the official celebrations of the Moh/Mol festival in Changlang town on 25 April 2011. They looked very much like any cultural festival as described by Singer (1959: xiii). Traditional clothes, jewellery, accessories, and headgear were to be seen everywhere and dances of many different Tangsa groups were presented at the festival. The feeling that Tangsa 'kassa' was dying or dead, that one often got in Assam and that people like Aphu Tyanglam are trying to fight against, was certainly not valid in Arunachal. There were many reasons for that: Firstly, there were simply many more Tangsa in Arunachal, and secondly, the fact that most Longchangs and Moklums living in the area continued to practise their traditions as before (even though many now have adopted Rangfraism). Modernity might have arrived in the lives of some Tangsa there but the link to some of their older traditions did not seem to be as tenuous in Arunachal as it seemed to be in Assam.

A senior scholar from the university at Itanagar told me that the tradition of celebrating festivals to mark different stages in the agricultural cycle had got weakened during World War II when there was a lot of disruption, displacement, and acute poverty. It was further weakened by the advent of Christianity in the mid-1960s. The practice of having a common platform 'to showcase and preserve traditional culture' was initiated by the state government in the late 1960s as a reaction to Christian proselytization. As for the Moh/Mol festival, a group of Tangsa leaders had explored the possibility of the Tangsa having a common festival at a meeting in the early 1980s. That is how it first began to be celebrated for three days in April/May, and has become an officially recognized festival today.

And in keeping with modern times, state-sponsored mega festivals were also being organized in Arunachal regularly mainly to promote tourism. The Pangsau Pass Winter Festival (PPWF) in Nampong in January each year is predominantly a pan-Tangsa festival for Tangsa living both in India and in Myanmar. The Tangsa (more appropriately, Tangshang) from across the border with Myanmar come not as tourists but as participants.[27] The Chairman of the PPWF Organizing Committee that year, a Kimsing, told me that although the festival is about presenting Tangsa culture, not everything about their culture can be shown in a festival, so they concentrated on presenting their traditional dance and handicrafts, in other words, their 'kassa'. Of course, a lot also depended on the preferences of the tourists who came to attend, he continued, for example, bamboo items were in great demand, and hence he made sure they were available in plenty.

With regard to the sticky question of which Tangsa language should be used in a pan-Tangsa event like the PPWF, he told me that although a Tangsa anthem had been composed with one verse from each tribe, in the end, a Kimsing song was sung. He went on to say that the dances have been 'modernized', by which he meant that they have tried to modify the traditional dresses in order to make the new costumes look more colourful and attractive. But the 'traditional' is still there, he insisted. 'The Sahpolo dance is still the same, only the dress has been modernized.'

A non-Christian Tangsa couple I met in Changlang, however, was not too excited about the modifications that had been made, as this extract from my field notes show:

> Regarding the Tangsa dances that are presented on stage in the big festivals: the sequences were all wrong and he hated to see them performed, it made him very angry. Even the Pangwa Sahpolo dance had been distorted to look like some strange dance, keeping the song the same. He could not stand it. They had been modified by the Christians to make everything look beautiful on stage. Then his wife spoke about the modifications made to the ornaments—earlier 'Four anna' coins would be used as buttons in dresses, never as necklaces; now they use coins for everything—bangles too. People who watch these dances therefore get the wrong impression. Also the blue and white wrapper for women with red blocks produced by the TBCA was typically Naga, but certainly not Tangsa. Tangsa people traditionally did not know how to make block designs; Tangsa wrappers are either striped vertically or horizontally (called *raipang* or *raitu* in Joglei), now they are all Nagaland copies. The typical red shoulder bag (*khaak shaang* in Moklum) of the Tangsa was usually used only by senior, respected elders like Luwangs and GBs; normal men and women never carried those red bags, but now one could buy them in the market freely (Changlang, 29 January 2012).

Photograph 7.3   A Mossang Lady Wearing a Traditional Tangsa Wrapper at
the *Lam-roeh* Carrying a Basket with her Ritual Offerings

Source: Jürgen Schöpf.

Listening to them reminded me of what the wife of the TBCA Secretary
had told me earlier (in the Section: The Conservatism of Christianity of
Chapter 6) as well as of the Tangsa dress I had seen at the Don Bosco
Museum in Shillong—the ladies wrapper was blue and white with red
woven blocks (see Photograph 7.2).[28] 'Only Christian Tangsa wear such
wrappers', my interlocutor had told me. At least I had proof that some
Christian Tangsa wore them.

In any case, in Arunachal, I saw the whole range of festivals, from
the traditional old-style basti festival at Kantang and the newer modified village festivals of the Christian Tangsa to the PPWF, which was in
line with other state-sponsored mega festivals like the Dihing-Patkai
Festival in Assam and the Hornbill Festival in Nagaland.

Everything Considered

Factors Impeding Tangsa Unity

Repeatedly, Tangsa leaders told me that the only way to forge unity amongst the Tangsa was to use their culture as the common basis. Festivals could create solidarity among communities bound by common cultural traditions. But as we had discovered during the course of our project, in the case of the different communities who are clubbed together under Tangsa, even if we discounted the recent origins of some of those traditions, there was not much in their cultural traditions that they can boast of as being 'common'. Although the Pangwa groups among the Tangsa share many common cultural traits, they have very little in common with the Hakhun or with the Longchang-Tikhak group; bringing in other diverse groups like the Moklum and the Ponthai skewed the picture even further.

Furthermore, language disunity is another major stumbling block on the road towards pan-Tangsa consolidation.[29] The Baptist Tangsa in India have a Kimsing Bible and wish to project Kimsing/Shanke as their common language. But there are very few Kimsing in India and we have seen how divisions have appeared amongst the Christian Tangsa in India over the issue of Bible translation. Moreover, certain groups, such as the Longchang, the Tikhak, and the Moklum, who have been in India for much longer than the Pangwa groups, seem to have established a kind of precedence when it came to representing the whole community.[30]

And the fact that the Tangsa languages are all oral languages just complicates the issue even further. Since they cannot agree on a common language, some Tangsa leaders felt that having a common script might be a step in the right direction. Of course, the Bible has been translated into at least three Tangsa languages using suitably modified versions of the Roman script but in the process not one but three systems of orthography have been developed. Since Tangsa languages have sounds which do not exist in any of the other languages in circulation in the area like Hindi, English, or Asamiya, and have sounds different from each other, many Tangsa felt that a separate Tangsa script was required which could also become a part of their new pan-Tangsa identity.[31] At a meeting held in Kharsang recently, two different scripts were presented but neither was accepted, not on any technical grounds, but because one person was Mossang (and hence Pangwa) and the other was Moklum (and also had the support of the Longchang) and the leaders of neither of these groups were ready to give in to the other.[32] This case illustrates the rather tribe-driven politics of the Tangsa leaders and the Tangsa elite.

A case in point is Komoli Mossang's (Mossang 1983) consistent use of the word 'Pangsa' and not 'Tangsa' while reviewing Parul Dutta's 1969 book. Bhagabati (2004: 181) mentions this 'as an indication of another emerging orientation of identity even while the process of wider Tangsa identity crystallization is in process'. Therefore, it seems not inconceivable that someday the pressures of trying to forge a pan-Tangsa identity (which historically never existed) could well make the Pangwa groups decide to break away from the Tangsa umbrella. And such divisions have occurred before. For instance, the Tutsa community, which had hitherto been clubbed with the Nocte, have recently broken away and have received recognition as a separate group in Arunachal Pradesh.

In case such a regrouping were to happen on common linguistic and cultural grounds, besides the Pangwa group (which will be mostly Christian), another group comprising the Longchang-Tikhak-Yongkuk family (which will remain part Buddhist part Rangfraa) and a third comprising the Moklum and the Hawi could emerge. Whether that will turn out to be a good strategy for self-preservation remains to be seen, but at least it will be easier for those smaller groups to define a common identity.

In another direction, taking the cue from the increasing participation of neighbouring groups, such as the Bodo (Karlsson 2001), the Garo (Bal 2010), and the Naga (Karlsson 2003), in the indigenous peoples' movements, the Tangsa might also decide to join the bandwagon. The Secretary General of the Rangfraa movement is already a member of the World Indigenous Faith Preservation Forum which has membership of 60 countries worldwide.

Everything Is Much Better behind the Fence

If the condition of the Pansau area of Myanmar (which I have visited) and that of the Tangshang people from Myanmar who come to sell their wares (mainly woven cloth and typically Tangsa food items) in the Nampong Bazaar every Friday are any indication, then living conditions are better in Arunachal than in Myanmar. In any case, as we have seen in Malugaon, it is a fact that people are coming from Myanmar even today to settle in India mainly because of the better facilities in terms of health care and education.

There was also plenty of evidence that communities are also moving back to the hills of Arunachal from the plains of Assam. While on the face of it this might look like confirmation of Scott's (2009) thesis of hill people moving deliberately back to the hills to evade the state, most Tangsa are doing so not to 'evade' but to 'avail' the facilities provided by the tribal state of Arunachal. Although I do not address the issue directly here, my field data show that my Tangsa interlocutors, rather than being non-state people, are pro-establishment and proactively pro-state. Not only do they *not* evade the state, they try to exploit the state for achieving their own ends. For a similar reading, see Wouters (2012).

Many tribals moved 'beyond the gate' into Arunachal once the Transferred Areas were declared to belong to Assam. Most of the Ronrang now living in New Lisen, for instance, moved there from Phulbari (*a*) due to dearth of land in Phulbari, (*b*) because they wanted to remain Buddhist while those in Phulbari were converting to Baptist Christianity, and (*c*) because of better facilities for education in Arunachal.

With the influx of settlers from other communities (who have also come to the Tirap area in Assam in search of cultivable land) some tribal people have chosen to go back to the hills. Official statistics (Table 2.1) show that the population in Assam of certain communities like the Khampti is actually down to almost nil at present. The Singpho elder Bisa Nong told me that the Singpho were beginning to go back into Arunachal as they did not have to pay taxes there and had many other benefits. Two of his own brothers had moved back after floods submerged the village of Bisa in Assam some years back. Earlier there were 20 Singpho families in Bisa, now there are only seven or eight left. Even they are planning to move to Arunachal.[33]

Another story that I heard repeatedly was of border villages unilaterally deciding that they belonged to Arunachal and not to Assam; this has been the case with the bastis of Hanju, Warra, and Mungkam. The reasons given are always the same: better facilities, better schools, roads, electricity, and water supply. Hanju claims no official of the Assam government has ever visited them.[34]

One interlocutor from Phulbari told me that he was planning to eventually move 'beyond the gate' to Jairampur because 'the tribals were given no dignity in Assam and were treated like refugees'. They could also not claim any rights over their land in Assam and would not be able to do anything if all the non-tribals (who have already become a majority in the Tirap area) were to stand up as one and ask them to leave. At least in Arunachal the land belonged only to the tribals.[35] He was also happy that the Inner Line Regulations were still in place there.[36] Moreover, while the Tangsa are recognized as a Scheduled Tribe in Arunachal Pradesh, in Assam they are clubbed under the 'Other Naga groups' category.

Hence moving back 'beyond the fence' looks attractive to many young Tangsa in Assam today, especially amongst the Christian Pangwa groups. Of course, that question did not arise for some sections of the Tangsa population in Assam like the Tikhak and the Yongkuk because they are Buddhist, have lived in Assam for a very long time already, have studied in Asamiya-medium schools, and have been assimilated to a greater extent into Assamese society.

'Boundaries are markers as well as makers of difference', Townsend Middleton (2013: 16) writes, with respect to the situation in and around Darjeeling. But he could have well been talking about the Tangsa situation with respect to the inter-state boundary between Assam and Arunachal. The fact that Arunachal is a tribal-majority state where non-tribals are not allowed to buy land and settle, where the rights and privileges of ethnic communities are protected, and that the Tangsa, by virtue of being the majority population in the Changlang District, also wield political and administrative power at the district level, make Arunachal attractive for the Tangsa. By contrast, in Assam, they are a tiny minority group, forgotten and marginal even within the collection of ethnic groups in the state, where the land rights vested on tribals in Tribal Belts exist only on paper but have long since been superseded by vested interests of powerful non-tribal players.

Of course, there have been some positive developments in Assam in recent times: the award of the Development Council, for instance; however, the fact that it is only a Development Council with no territorial or administrative powers means that it does not amount to very much. Moreover, the couple of initiatives made by the local administration in Assam to work together with the tribal communities do not seem to have really taken off. The proposal for the establishment of three eco-lodges in that area is a case in point.[37] And we have already seen how the Dihing-Patkai festival which was supposed to be only for the tribal people of the Tirap area has been 'hijacked' by non-tribals.

Problems for the Tangsa in Arunachal Pradesh

However, it is also not true that everything is fine for the Tangsa living in the state of Arunachal. For one, the rapid change in lifestyles has brought in some imbalances and new dependencies. Moreover, underneath the picture of middle class well-being there are strong internal divisions amongst the Tangsa in Arunachal: some groups who came in much earlier to that area like the Longchang, Moklum, Mossang, and Juglei have had a headstart over the more recent arrivals.[38] Further divisions were caused due to differences in religion.

In terms of infrastructure, this easternmost tip of Arunachal is less developed in comparison to the neighbouring areas in Assam.[39] Since China poses a greater threat than Myanmar, the Indian government worries more about the western districts of Arunachal bordering China than about the eastern districts of Tirap and Changlang.[40] Furthermore, being so far away from the centre of power at the state capital, Itanagar, and being so numerically weak, the Tangsa as well as the others living in those districts do not really have much say at the state level.[41] State resources are distributed unevenly in Arunachal among the different districts and most of it is used up in the Itanagar–Tawang area. And this, despite the fact that there is a separate department for the development of Tirap and Changlang (DTC) headed by a minister.[42]

The growing unrest bred by the infiltration of the NSCN into the eastern districts has become a major cause for concern (see also Dai 2013). While Changlang is mainly in the hands of the NSCN (K), the NSCN (I-M) has a larger base in Tirap. According to a senior scholar who worked with the Tangsa in Arunachal, the fate of the Tangsa in Changlang is really in the hands of the NSCN (K) (which he interestingly believed to have been created by the Indian army in the first place); and hence there was no hope of any change for the better as long as the NSCN problem was not resolved.

This takes us back to the question of the relation between the Tangsa and the Naga; although, culturally and linguistically, there seems to be a continuum of sorts from the Konyak areas of Nagaland to the Wancho,

Nocte, Tutsa, and then Tangsa areas of Arunachal, the main link now of the Tangsa to Nagaland is via Baptist Christianity, the NSCN, and their underground insurgent movement.[43] It is ironical that while there is a ceasefire, and hence relative peace, in Nagaland, the fighting continues in Tirap and Changlang, not so much between the army and the insurgents but amongst different insurgent factions, and this is a constant source of tension and danger for the inhabitants of the area.[44]

Furthermore, Baptist Christianity is making rapid inroads into the districts of Tirap and Changlang. There are reports of forced conversions and extortion in those areas although people prefer not to talk about it. Many villages in the Tirap District had been forced to convert 'at gunpoint' by the NSCN.[45] A senior Rangfraa office-bearer told me that by asking the people not to convert to Christianity, the Rangfraa leaders had come into direct confrontation with the NSCN.[46] It is widely believed that the NSCN is also involved in opium trafficking from Myanmar, which is still widely prevalent in some pockets of the state, at least where opium addiction is high.

Returning to the Tangsa, another senior Tangsa leader named three factors that, in his opinion, had ruined the Tangsa in Arunachal in recent years and explained how they were connected: first, the 'kunda' timber business which had made some Tangsa rich overnight.[47] That made many believe that they did not need to study or look for jobs or others means of livelihood. But when the 'kunda' business came to an halt abruptly (with a Supreme Court ruling banning the felling of trees), many young men had no choice but to join the NSCN. That was the second factor in his list. Many could not, however, cope with the tension involved and started using not only opium but also other stronger drugs like brown sugar and heroin. That was the third factor. The use of alcohol and rice-beer was already prevalent; all these factors have impacted heavily on the well-being and future prospects of the Tangsa. Simai (2008) is also of a similar view.

So the situation for the Arunachali Tangsa is not so rosy either, trapped as they are between the uncaring state government and the NSCN 'ultras'. There is also resentment because there is very little development in the two eastern districts in contrast to other parts of the state, and my Tangsa interlocutors feel alienated also in Arunachal. The relative advantages that the Tangsa in Arunachal might have at present over those living in Assam might also disappear over time—the population in Arunachal is not so high now, but more and more non-tribals are settling there despite the Inner Line Restrictions, and in a few years time the demographic situation there could well become similar to that in Assam where many of the smaller ethnic groups feel threatened for their very existence and survival; even in Nagaland, there were reports that some Naga tribes were not treated at par with the others. It did seem as if there were not really many choices.

Postscript: Crisis and Closure in My Own Personal Journey

At some point, right in the middle of my fieldwork period in Arunachal, I was faced with a huge crisis. I had been travelling into some interior parts of Arunachal for the first time, and had just attended the Wihau festival in the breathtakingly beautiful Kantang basti where, before my eyes, I had seen the reiben thread bend over, obeying the Wihau singer's appeal, to drink rice-beer. I had also seen the chum-ki flowers bob their heads in tune with the singing. Visiting the remote but large and well-laid out, mostly single-tribe Tangsa bastis in Arunachal where people predominantly spoke to each other in their own languages, lived their lives at a completely different pace, continued to practise many rituals in more or less the same way as their forefathers had also practised before them, and where old village rules still seemed to regulate daily life, I was faced with a dilemma. For it became clear to me that our documentation of older Tangsa customs and traditions should have been done in Arunachal and not in Assam. The feeling that I had wasted a lot of time and valuable resources and that it was too late to start all over again was just so overwhelming that I was almost ready to throw in the towel and return to Germany.

By then I had also met wise and discerning Tangsa elders who could teach me a thing or two about doing fieldwork; for instance, one elder had advised me, 'Never take one person's word for the truth unless you hear the same story from someone else'. I had also understood that there was often nothing dramatic or singular about how matters evolved in Tangsaland, that decisions made by my Tangsa interlocutors were often ad-hoc and based on pragmatic considerations, that things or events did not always carry deep meanings, and that I had to learn not to expect more. Added to all the above was an irritating feeling that my Tangsa informants themselves seemed to be amused (rather than happy) about my desire to work with them and that they were probably having the last laugh behind my back. I wondered for whom and for what I was punishing myself by persisting.

Unable to see my way forward and not wanting to stay on in Tangsaland, I decided to go to Itanagar, at the other end of the state, just to get away from it all for a while. A different set of Tangsa—well-to-do, influential, and successful—lived there. Some of them had made it big in state politics. Others held high positions in the state administration. For me, it was very good to have a chance to see how far some Tangsa have made it on the one hand while also observing how they still retained their strong sense of belonging and responsibility for their own community. I also understood that for them there was only one way forward, the one that came with education, development, and modernization; they had come too far already down that path; soon they would become like the rest of us.

Chatting with a few of them over tea in a nice and comfortably furnished living room of my Tangsa host, I realized that their concerns were not very different from mine—they wanted a good education for their children, they worried about the damage travelling on the bad roads was doing to their backs, they wanted to know about possible places in Europe where they could go on holiday, they were concerned about the general state of the Indian economy, and so on. As we became friends, I also got to know them better as individuals, and found nothing surprising in their confidences either—they also fell in love and got married (quite a few of them have non-Tangsa spouses), they also worried about their aging parents, they also gossiped about the scandals caused by extra-marital affairs, but the day one of them asked me whether I could recommend a place in Europe where his daughter could go to learn baking, I realized that I could have just as well been sitting in my living room in Guwahati talking to my convent-educated Assamese friends.

That was a difficult realization to cope with initially, for when I had set out to work with them, I had imagined that the Tangsa would be 'different'. But being in the field with them and becoming friends with some of them had made me see that even if some of their worldviews or ways of life were different from mine, at the individual level, there was not much to set us apart. In other words, I could see 'the similarity in all our lives' that Abu Lughod (1991: 157) was referring to when she was recommending writing 'ethnographies about the particular'. In a certain sense, this realization brought me full circle and gave closure to my fieldwork. Curiously, one final incident, when I was unfairly but soundly rebuked by a Tangsa woman leader, helped me see that I had been in the field long enough; I had seen and experienced enough. It was time for me to start writing up, as best as I could. But it was also equally clear to me that 'their' story could not be told separately, that 'my' story had to be part of what I was going to write up, if any of it had to make any sense at all.

Notes

1. Every village in Arunachal Pradesh is supposed to have at least one such satellite phone connection at the house of the village headman.
2. Wathai had done his post-graduation from Rajiv Gandhi University, Itanagar, and was one of two Tangsa who had made the grade in the State Civil Services (APPSC) exam in 2003.
3. I had to remind myself of what I had seen during my visit to the minister's official residence in the state capital in Itanagar some time back to be able to make sense of what I was seeing. Many Tangsa, mostly students who were studying in Itanagar but also people who happened to come to Itanagar for some work, actually stayed in the minister's house, for days or months on end. As the elected representative of his people, as well as the only Tangsa minister in the government, he was expected to take care of the Tangsa who came to Itanagar in just the same way as the Tangsa would stay with a clan relative when he visits another basti.
4. Approximate distances between some of the larger named places: Margherita to Changlang: 40 kms; Jagun to Jairampur (NH 153): 14 kms; Jairampur to Nampong: 20 kms; Jairampur to Manmao: 40 kms.
5. Officially, there are at least 26 major tribes and more than 100 sub-tribes in Arunachal; see Census of India 2001.
6. It has a total population of roughly 1.4 million (as of 2011) in an area of 84,000 sq. km, amounting to a population density of about 17 per sq. km (far below the Indian average of 370 per sq. km).
   In 1980, the Chakma population in the district was about 15,000 (see *Gazetteer* 1980: 92). More recent figures for Arunachal are not available, although more than 175,000 Chakmas live in the states of Mizoram and Tripura in the Northeast according to the 2011 Census. For more on the Chakma problem, see Prasad (2008).
7. According to the 2011 Census, Changlang District has a population of 147,951. Though the community figures were not available, the Tangsa

are the single biggest tribal community in Changlang, followed by the Singpho and the Tutsa groups.

8. The Armed Forces (Special Powers) Act (AFSPA) is an Act of the Parliament of India (passed on 11 September 1958) granting special powers to the Indian Armed Forces in what the Act terms as 'disturbed areas'. In 1991, the districts of Tirap and Changlang were put in the 'disturbed' list as a reaction to intensified activity by the two factions of the NSCN.

   The district of Longding, which was carved out of Tirap, was added to the 'disturbed' list in 2012. In addition, AFSPA is already applied to areas falling within 20-kilometre radius in Arunachal bordering Assam.

9. Two units of the 25 Sector of Assam Rifles, a paramilitary force, are based at Jairampur and on the way to Changlang town, both headed by a colonel as the Commanding Officer. For more about how the Indian government asserts it presence and exerts its control in such border areas, read Farrelly (2013).

10. The Namchik gate leading to Kharsang and Miao was relatively easier to negotiate than the gate at Jairampur (on way to Manmao and Nampong) because of the large Assam Rifles base camp at Jairampur.

11. The people of Changlang town depended on Margherita for almost everything but curiously most people from Margherita seemed to know nothing about Changlang town, except that they had heard it was a dangerous place.

12. Officially, Changlang town had a population of 6,469 in 2001 although unofficially I was told that 20,000–30,000 people live in the town area which is managed by an Urban Council.

13. As evident elsewhere in the Northeast (see, for instance, Karlsson 2011), the differences in wealth and differential access to education and resources have also led to the formation of classes within Tangsa society in Arunachal, but that is not so evident among the Tangsa in Assam. For more on the apparent contradictions of globalization in Arunachal, see Nayak (2011).

14. At the house of my host in Changlang town, there was running water and electricity, computers, internet and a land telephone, sturdy cars, and the usual modern amenities. People in the Changlang town area seemed to lead reasonably comfortable lives, even though physically it was a world completely cut off from everywhere else.

15. I once met an old man who had moved with one of his granddaughters from an interior basti (which had no access to health care) to the side of the nearest road. They had simply built a small bamboo chang by the roadside and were living there—all they had, as far as I could see, were a few pots and pans, a sack of rice, a kettle, a couple of plastic mats, and a few pieces of clothing. For a discussion of these differences between the

educated and well-to-do section of society and those living in the remote villages, see Borthakur (2006).

16. Already in 1953, the Union cabinet had taken steps to ban the entry of Christianity to Arunachal (Ronrang 1997: 26). For a general introduction to the spread of Christianity in Arunachal, read Chaudhuri (2013).

17. I say very little about the Buddhist Tangsa in India; for more see Simai (2008) and the work of Karen Parker (under examination).

18. For more details, see Barkataki-Ruscheweyh (2015). Today there are about 70 Rangfraa temples in Changlang and the number of followers is going up amongst the Tangsa, as well as the Tutsa who live in the area bordering the districts of Changlang and Tirap.

19. Technically speaking, it is Shanke, which is lexically very similar to Kimsing, which is the language of wider communication and is some sort of a 'prestige' language among at least the Pangwa groups in Myanmar. It is believed that the NSCN leader Khaplang was in favour of recognizing Shanke/Kimsing as the common language for all the Tangshang groups.

20. For more about the 'inculturation theory' of the Catholics, see (Cannell 2006: 26). For more about the Catholic Tangsa in India see (Barkataki-Ruscheweyh in process).

21. Kantang basti is about 15 kms away from Changlang town and has about 15 families, of which only about 2 were originally Juglei; all the others are Moklum, Mungrey, and so forth. Even the Gaonbura is actually a Mungrey but the village is in an area which traditionally belonged to the Juglei people, therefore they all speak Juglei in the village and consider themselves to be Juglei. Earlier, they had lived up the hill in a village also called Kantang. But then a section moved down and settled in Hadap when they converted to Christianity. Then another group of mostly Moklum people broke away and formed another village called Chimsu just below the present-day Kantang basti. So now the old Kantang basti has been split into three smaller bastis, each with about 15 families.

22. My host worked as a veterinary doctor in the government-run veterinary hospital in Changlang town. His wife was an MA from a premier institute in the country, and had worked in the government before she gave it up to raise their children who were now both studying in boarding schools elsewhere. But she was very active socially and was Secretary of the All Arunachal Women's Welfare Society for many terms, and was presently the leader of the women's group in her local Rangfraa temple. They were also very enterprising: my host told me that they have a lot of pineapples growing in their land in the village. He was building a large concrete pig pen (with the help of Muslim masons, who had set up camp to live in their house) and wanted to start a real piggery.

23. Times were changing and nowadays some would even kill tigers deliberately by poisoning them for the hide which still fetched a lot of money, my host informed me. Earlier, no one would dare to do such a thing.

24. The entire event is called *Rung-ri-hun* (meaning 'carrying the bamboo tray' or literally *dola-loi-phura* in Assamese).

25. The shamma lady is supposed to have a tiger spirit as her companion which makes her very powerful.

    We have played this video to Tangsa (Christians) in both India and Myanmar, to their considerable fascination.

26. Among them was one group of Longchang Tangsa people from Changlang, who had come armed with sophisticated cameras and camcorders as they were very keen to see what the Pangwa did at their festival.

27. About a week before the Pangsau Pass festival in Nampong, a similar festival is also held in the Burmese side; the timing has been coordinated for the benefit of tourists.

28. Don Bosco Centre for Indigenous Cultures, DBCIC, Shillong. Available at http://www.dbcic.org/ (accessed 7 September 2014).

29. For a detailed analysis of this problem and a description of the various attempts that have been made at finding a common language, see Morey (2012).

30. For example, the Tangsa news broadcasted from the Dibrugarh radio station every morning is in Longchang.

31. For instance, see Morey (2011).

32. The meeting, held on 28 December 2010, was organized by the Tangsa Cultural and Literary Society, Arunachal Pradesh.

    What Sharma (2007: 206) says with reference to the Bodos is true also for the Tangsa in Assam—their rejection or acceptance of one or the other script could have reasons which have not only to do with reason and common sense. Hence the script issue could soon also become a site for Tangsa nationalist assertion. See also Prabhakara (2012: 11ff) for an overview of the politics of script of the Bodo language.

33. This movement is confirmed by Sadan (2013: 6), which she explains as a fear amongst the Tangsa elites that the eventual opening up of the Stillwell Road could result in many more non-Scheduled people coming to live in that area. Hence better to be officially a rural Tribal (in Arunachal) than an urban citizen (in Assam).

34. Warra has been persuaded to 'return' to Assam largely through the efforts of some Assamese NGOs active in the area

35. Similar sentiments are echoed by the people living in Mizoram (see Pachuau 2014:15).

    As Baruah (2010) points out,

If customary law governs land rights, and land rights favour particular Scheduled Tribe communities legally identified as natives in one state and not in the other, the consequences of where the border is drawn can be significant. Since ethnicity marks some claimants as native and others as non-native, the border could make all the difference as to how competing land claims are, ultimately, sorted out.

36. Other scholars have noted this fact too. Baruah (2010) below gives a reason why some Arunachalis might prefer to have the ILP in place: 'In the case of the Inner Line still applicable to Arunachal, Mizoram and Nagaland those living behind this frontier have developed a stake in defending this colonial institution: it becomes a legitimate way of limiting the rights of the interloper, or even grounds for expelling him or her.'

37. While Manje la Singpho is running the Eco Lodge at Inthong, the one in the Tai Phake Phaneng basti is defunct and the third, which was supposed to have been established in some Tangsa village, never materialized.

38. Most of the Tangsa leaders, writers, and politicians belong to one of these communities. Mr Kenglang Kengsang, one of the most respected members of the Tangsa community, and who has written extensively about the Tangsa in Assamese, belongs to the Longchang community. The Secretary General, Mr Latsam Khimhun, of the Rangfraa movement is a Moklum, while there are at least a couple of frontline Mossang and Juglei politicians active in the district.

39. So much so that most Arunachalis living in Changlang go down to Margherita and beyond if they are sick, to attend college and university, and also increasingly for their normal needs of food and clothing.

40. In 2012, the district of Longding was carved out of Tirap. However, in this work, the district of Tirap will refer to the undivided Tirap District.

41. Moreover, the number of persons from these districts who have cleared the Arunachal Pradesh Public Service Commission (APPSC) Examinations is relatively low.

42. This replicates at the state-level, the central model of having a separate ministry in New Delhi (called Ministry for Development of North-Eastern Region) specifically to look after affairs of the 'troubled' and 'backward' northeast India.

43. A senior scholar told me on condition of anonymity that a meeting was held in Miao some years back when the NSCN forced all the tribes living in Tirap and Changlang to add Naga behind their names in order to strengthen the Naga claims that the Greater Nagalim area included both the Arunachali districts.

44. Villagers are normally asked for money and food; sometimes young men of the village are made to act as couriers to carry things from one place to another.

Till a few years ago, the civilian population often faced harassment from the army searching for NSCN cadres who would often hide in the villages.

45. According to eye witnesses, armed NSCN cadres surround a village one evening and leave before the next dawn, after having forced everyone in the village (except the very old and the very young) to get baptized by the evangelist they normally also bring along.

    The Buddhist Tikhak villages in the Nampong area had also been threatened with dire consequences by the NSCN if they did not convert within a specified date.

46. Nine families in a Tutsa basti in Tirap later converted back to Rangfraism as a result of which the NSCN created a lot of trouble; they kidnapped the secretary of the local Rangfraa temple, demanded a ransom, and closed down the temple. The Rangfraa leaders had to negotiate long and hard with the NSCN top-brass before the temple was allowed to open again.

47. This fact is also mentioned in Dai (2013: 43). Illegal trade in timber and coal has brought in a lot of money to Changlang, but has subsequently also brought in the extortion slips from various insurgents groups active in the area.

8 Closing the Circle
Festivals and Ethnic Identity

'Tangsa society is in a state of some decay.'
>—Elwin is supposed to have commented in 1960,
>see Roy Burman (1970: 97)

'Either you assimilate, or you learn the tricks of the plains people so well that you can hold out on your own in their midst, or you go back to the hills.'
>—Rajesh Singpho, Margherita

One final event: The date was 7 April 2013, the venue was the nicely laid out Margherita Coal Park in the heart of Margherita town. The occasion was the release of a revised second edition of a book titled Tribes of Indo-Burma Border *by nonagenarian Assamese writer Mr Suren Barua, and laying the foundation stone of the Margherita Ethnological Museum.*[1] *Both projects had been initiated and funded by the local MLA who was also a minister in the Assam Government.*[2] *The meeting was being organized by the Sub-Divisional Officer (SDO), Margherita, at the behest of the minister. The Tangsa minister from Arunachal, who we have met in the last chapter and who was a personal friend of his Assamese counterpart, had been invited to be the Chief Guest of the meeting and to release the book, while the Assamese minister would lay the foundation stone of the museum. Coal India was sponsoring the expenses for the meeting and hosting most of the out-station guests in their guest house in Margherita.*

The park was very well-maintained. In the midst of the profusion of flowers and plants, a many-hued water fountain added to the beauty of the setting.

A neat and sturdy pavilion had been set up at the far end of the park, with a beautifully decorated stage at one end. Another smaller pavilion had been set up on the side for serving refreshments after the event. A small thatched hut in between advertised the book that was to be released—copies of the new edition would be sold there at half price after its release. In between was a marked area where the foundation stone for the museum would be laid. But the actual location for the museum was elsewhere; therefore, although the formal ceremony would be held in the park that afternoon, the 'foundation stone' would have to be transported to the actual site later.

The meeting was scheduled to start at 3:30 p.m. Since I had helped with getting the revised edition ready for publication, I had also been invited. When my husband and I arrived there shortly after 3 p.m., not many guests had arrived. Slowly it started to fill up; first the hosts—the SDO as well as some top Coal India officials—came to do the final check on the arrangements. Then Mr Manje la Singpho arrived, bringing with him two colourfully and traditionally dressed groups of dancers—one from the Singpho and the other from the Tai Phake community. A representative from the publishing house in Guwahati, local leaders from Margherita, as well as journalists and media persons were present. The leaders of many communities living in that area had been invited and were present in large numbers; they included Aphu Tyanglam, Gaonbura Hakhun, the Singpho chieftain Bisa nong Singpho, and some Nepali leaders.

It was well past 4 p.m. when the VIPs started to arrive. The two ministers arrived together. The Arunachali minister was accompanied by his wife and a few other Tangsa leaders. The Tinsukia District Administration was in full attendance led by the Deputy Commissioner (DC). It was not clear till the last moment whether the aged author, Mr Suren Barua, who had not been keeping too well, would be able to attend. But the re-publication of his book meant a lot to him, and he came, accompanied by his whole family, dressed in his traditional best.

Soon the meeting got under way. On either side of Mr Barua on the dais were the two ministers. The DC, the SDO, the representatives from Coal India, and the publishing house and I were also invited to the dais. After the usual extended and time-consuming welcome ceremony, where even my unsuspecting husband was not spared, the meeting got going with a dance by the Tai Phake and a song by the Singpho contingents. After brief speeches by the DC and the publisher, the two ministers took turns at the microphone. They spoke about the various projects they had undertaken for their people, and how, despite the inter-state boundary separating them, the peoples of the two states still remain united. The Tangsa minister offered to buy hundred copies of the book for distribution in libraries in Arunachal.[3] The two of them held forth till well past 6 p.m. when the meeting came to an end.

When Mr Barua realized that the meeting had ended, he protested about not having been given a chance to speak; he was then allowed to speak but by then the audience had started to disperse and had gone off to get their tea and snacks. All the copies of the book the publisher had brought along were sold within minutes. We left soon after since we had a train to catch, and did not stay for the lavish 'ethnic' Singpho dinner hosted by the minister later in the evening.

The next morning, Manje La rang me up. He had been in charge of organizing the song and dance numbers and the dinner for the event. He told me that he was unhappy that although both the book as well as the museum had to do with tribal people, not one tribal leader had been invited to sit on the dais, not one had been invited to say a few words. He claimed that the tribal leaders were not too happy about that. I did not know what to say. I tried to relativize his outrage by reminding him that even the venerable Mr Barua, the star of the meeting, was not given a chance. But it was true: no one seated on the dais that day, except for the Tangsa minister from Arunachal, was tribal.

In the preceding chapters, I have described in some detail the situation for the Tangsa in three villages in Assam and also given a rough idea of the major differences with the situation in Arunachal. I have also discussed Tangsa festivals in different forms and at different places, and given an account of my personal journey and development while working with the Tangsa. In this final chapter I wish to pull all these different strands together, in order to verify some of the claims I made in Chapter 1 and explore some of the questions with which I started out—what does it mean to be Tangsa, what do festivals mean for the Tangsa, what do they tell us about Tangsa identity and culture, and finally, where do we, and also the Tangsa, go from here?

Negotiating Marginalization

The last few chapters have given a glimpse of the ground realities for the Tangsa in Assam, and a sense of why some Tangsa are today being forced into making the choices they are making. The facts of their being marginal and continuing to be further marginalized appear between the lines in much I have described in the preceding chapters. And we have seen this happen over and over again—the state has contributed to their marginalization by continuing to ignore their demand for enforcing the rights of tribal people in the Tribal Belt; it has done so every time it has resorted to short-term appeasement, rather than on negotiation and resolution, as a policy to contain protest; it has done so every time it has set up schools where Tangsa children are taught in Asamiya or has organized festivals to showcase tribal diversity but has put non-tribals in charge of the organization.[4] Moreover, since the demographic situation in the Tirap area where the Tangsa live is so diverse and complex, the bigger and more robust communities have also contributed to the marginalization of their numerically weaker neighbours by competing for and depriving them of scarce resources and employment opportunities. Furthermore, the Tangsa have also themselves contributed, in some measure, to their own marginalization, by falling in line, by playing the role of the exotic tribal expected of them, by allowing others to slot them as the 'other'. What Farrelly (2009b: 85) observes for the Tai case, is also true for the Tangsa: 'Constructions of community can contribute to marginalisation, disempowerment and silencing'.

So much for economic and political marginalization. What about cultural dilution and assimilation? According to one of my Tangsa interlocutors from Kharangkong: 'Tangsa culture will not survive anywhere in India—in Assam it will be overtaken by the Assamese or the pan-Indian culture, in Arunachal by the Christian or the Western tradition' (Kharangkong, 29 October 2009). By Tangsa here, he probably meant only the Pangwa groups. But equally pessimistic comments have been made also for non-Pangwa groups (see Simai 2011). Differences in religion and language are the main factors impeding communal mobilization of the Tangsa. In Assam there are the additional problems of their numerical weakness and the fact that they live in mixed villages that are scattered widely apart. Moreover, the quality and competence of the emerging Tangsa elite is much better in Arunachal, and they wield political power in Changlang. Hence, Bhagabati (1992: 500) is right in his observation that the chances for the Tangsa to survive as a cultural and political unit in Arunachal are higher.

Some Tangsa in Assam have attempted to strategically use their connections with the Naga, with Myanmar, with the NSCN, and/or with their Christian brothers to improve their standing within their immediate local area in which they have to survive, even while maintaining their difference from the lowland non-tribal, predominantly Hindu populations. At an even more micro level, one can observe several processes in operation: The last chapters have shown how some Tangsa in Assam try to negotiate some space for themselves by playing the NSCN card when necessary (to keep the ULFA at bay) but then use the Buddhist card at other times (as a buffer from the Baptist NSCN). Like other minorities, my Tangsa interlocutors too have learnt to use the 'victim' card as well as the 'tribal' card, as and when required, depending on the context. They also often use the Congress card in order to maintain their distance from the other political parties and to make demands from the ruling Congress party (sometimes successfully, as the award of the Development Council shows) even while playing the good citizen card (in that they always go to vote, and many Tangsa serve in the army and so forth) to strengthen their case. Some of my Tangsa informants have also figured out how to get the maximum benefit out of state-sponsored schemes.[5] In that sense, they are not non-state people but often prefer to collaborate with the state, just as Tsing's marginalized Meratus Dayak cultivators.[6] As Jonsson (2001: 159) rightly observes, 'these dynamics are in part about ethnic minorities placing themselves within the nation, not in opposition to it'.

Moreover, 'prospects of a tribal trans-nationalism, cutting across the political boundaries of India and Myanmar appears to be a fact' (Sebastian 1999: 131). The Singphos already have a network extending as far as Thailand and ties between the Tangsa on both sides of the Indo-Burmese border seem to be growing, with or without the help of the NSCN.

However, on the ground, the prospects for most of my Tangsa informants in Assam do not look very promising. The discerning Rajesh Singpho hit the nail on the head when he told me (in response to my query about the options small ethnic communities such as the Singpho and the Tangsa had in Assam), 'either you assimilate, or you learn the tricks of the plains people so well that you can hold out on your own in their midst, or you go back to the hills'.[7] It was pure coincidence, but these are roughly the three scenarios that were evident in the three Tangsa villages of Kharangkong, Malugaon, and Phulbari, respectively.

Rajesh's words spoken in 2012 echo (or are perhaps taken from) those of Kunstadter, written almost fifty years ago, about minority communities of Southeast Asia: 'As the hegemony of the central governments expanded, three choices were available to the vanquished: fleeing to the hills, becoming absorbed in the newly dominant group, or establishing, and in some way maintaining, boundaries around themselves so that their identity could be preserved in spite of their loss of political independence' (Kunstadter 1967: 10).

Thus, not much had changed in all these years.

The overall prospects of some other communities living in the Tirap area are not significantly better than that of the Tangsa. The actual number of Singpho living in Assam is decreasing. While this can be attributed to reasons peculiar to the Singpho such as their strict marriage clan rules which lead to inbreeding and consequent degeneration, it is also a fact that many Singpho have deliberately moved back into Arunachal while others have chosen to become members of other communities.

However, Dollfus and Jacquesson's (2013) work on the Sherdukpen community in western Arunachal Pradesh has shown that that small populations in northeast India have continued to thrive, using a number of adaptive techniques or strategies. Hence, it is not true that smaller groups are necessarily weaker. In their work, the authors have shown the central role played by the Khiksaba festival in the continued vitality and the identity formulations of the Sherdukpen. But the Tangsa in India do not have *a* common festival. In any case, the recent efforts made by the Tangsa in Assam to organize festivals and to invite neighbouring communities as well as administrators and politicians to attend them can be considered to be their first attempts at trying out performing their ethnicity as a strategy for survival.[8] Whether this strategy has been or will be successful or not remains to be seen.

Culture and Festivals

Festivals are about preserving culture, I have been told over and over again by my Tangsa interlocutors. But that seems to be almost a tautology with respect to big mega festivals such as the Dihing-Patkai Festival (DPF) and the Pangsau Pass Winter Festival (PPWF), for the culture such festivals preserve is the culture that is specially created for presentation at such mega events—the songs and dances are created or suitably modified to be presented as 'culture' and then preserved as such. In that sense, the 'culture' that is presented to the world and preserved at such modern-day festivals is really the commoditized externalised 'kassa', to borrow Aphu's word, comprising songs, dances, and costumes.

According to my Arunachali Tangsa father, Phanglim Kimsing, 'the big festivals are different from the village or community level festivals because the organizers only want to show their culture without understanding what that means'. Therefore, in order to analyse the link between festivals and the preservation of culture, I should be looking at smaller festivals, he had advised me. But what did Phanglim Kimsing mean by the word culture? Since he believed that culture was more in evidence in the smaller festivals, he probably did not mean 'kassa'. He possibly meant Aphu Tyanglam's Tangsa-ness, or their culture as defined by Mr Khimhun, Secretary General of the Rangfraa Society:

> Culture of a community is like the name of an individual. Some examples of what culture is are how marriages are performed, how one handles death, how a new-born is named, how the rituals in the field to do with sowing and harvesting are done, what the rituals around their festivals are etc. These are different for different communities and constitute their culture. These practices set communities apart and give them their identity. (Roing, 24 February 2012)

This clearly indicates that for some Tangsa at least there is a clear distinction between their tacit culture that defines who they are and what makes them Tangsa and their explicit culture or 'kassa' which can be considered to be a form of commodification and objectification of their culture, as seen at festivals. But then, how could one claim that ethnic festivals help to preserve Tangsa 'traditional' culture? Furthermore, what about the Christian or Buddhist Tangsa? For them, there are at least three distinct sets of related ideas: their 'kassa', their culture (which has to do with their ways of life before they converted), and their newly adopted cultural traditions based on their new religion. What do festivals mean for them?

The answers are not easy, also because these categories are not watertight and we cannot write off festivals as mere displays of 'kassa' because these new festivals are *all* my Tangsa interlocutors have—especially the Christian/Buddhist Tangsa—to project, display, and claim their Tangsa-ness, their ethnic identity, as opposed to their religious identity. On the other hand, their new religions impose restrictions on which of their traditional practices, for example, which of their agricultural rituals, they can still continue to really practise. But there was no objection to some of those rituals being merely enacted, 'just for show', as performances. And the Tangsa festivals in Assam I have described bear witness to precisely this process—the enactment/performance of a few rituals, packaged with large doses of 'kassa', which then together comprise the performance of their ethnicity.

The Importance of Festivals

In the previous chapters I have looked at festivals, both as physical sites as well as performative constructs (cf. Bennet et al. 2014: 2). There has been ample evidence that festivals and rituals are thus not spaces to reveal tradition but also spaces to create it (cf. Vandenhelsken 2011: 112). In that sense, festivals are sites not just for cultural reproduction but also for cultural production (Guss 2000:11). That is precisely why the study of festivals has become so crucial to the understanding of the transformations taking place in the Tangsa cultural traditions and the processes involved in Tangsa identity formation.[9]

At the same time, one must not read too much into and from these festivals. For there is a great deal of contingency and under-determination in most situations (Rabinow and Marcus 2008: 56). Many of the decisions made at festivals are often random (Q: Why was she chosen as the one to lead the dancers? A: Because she was ready first), ad-hoc, contingent (Q: Why did you put up a bigger pavilion this year? A: Because we were worried it would rain), and the reasons are quite often pragmatic and banal (Q: Why are you sacrificing a red chicken this year? A: Because it is the only one I have). In fact, so much of what happens at these festivals is contingent that it almost calls for 'a systematic study of contingency' (Fuchs, personal communication), however oxymoronic the idea might seem.

As I have shown, most of the details of what actually happens at a festival in any given year is decided often at the last minute, and the rituals observed are entirely dependent on the skills of the older members of the family and the elders of the village who are available and willing to participate. However, as pointed out by Ramirez (personal communication), the content of performances is not totally random— one of the minimum requirements is that it should look *specific*, not necessarily traditional but displaying specific features (for instance, specific attires, with a typical colour and pattern, and so on).

It is also a fact that, like everyone else, a large majority of the Tangsa live their lives without consciously worrying about their identity, their culture, and their ethnicity. Modernization of their lifestyles and the resultant changes means that not many have the time or the interest in organizing or spending a lot of time on celebrating festivals. Just like the Naga, as Longkumer (2015: 54) remarks, 'these choices are very much made in the "ethnographic present", and when people are left to choose between "survival" and "preserving culture", it is often the former that takes precedence'.

However, when a festival is organized by someone in their village or in their community, then most participate, partly because festivals are a change from the routine of everyday life; moreover, they are also simply fun (Jonsson 2001). Most Tangsa who come to attend such festivals come because they felt the need to be present at 'their' festival, although not many know much about what they could expect from it. Many others come for some cultural entertainment; the younger lot attend basically because of the popular entertainers and the fashion shows.[10] There are other uses too; for instance, festivals play a social function by bringing people together and renewing bonds of kinship and of friendship. Thus, festivals bind *a* people together.

The reasons Tangsa community leaders gave for community participation, however, were somewhat different. According to them, people came, not only for social reasons, but also because at the back of their minds many Tangsa worry about erasure as a minority community, and they believe organizing and participating in festivals is one way to prevent that. Some of the elder Tangsa, such as Aphu Tyanglam and Junglum Hakhun, celebrate festivals as individuals with a hope that seeing them, others will follow, and that the younger generation will see and imbibe something of what it means to be Tangsa.

But the festivals they helped to celebrate had different accents. At Kharangkong, the Wihu-kuh was used as a site for cultural reinterpretation and rearticulation, for modification and reformulation—linking it with the past but locating it in the present, which also implied the selective reification of certain cultural traditions. In Malugaon, the festival was instrumentalized for very specific individual ends and was focussed on self-preservation and the self-presentation of the Hakhun as a modern and Christian community, yet one with a unique tribal identity. The Shawi-kuh celebrations in Phulbari were aimed at internal consolidation, at standardization and finding common ground, and about projecting and performing a pan-Tangsa ethnic identity which transcends religious divisions; in other words, regrouping in the present under the given circumstances. That process naturally used political mobilization as a strategy, involved some amount of political negotiation, and hence led to politicization of ethnic identity. In other words, the organization of these festivals can be seen as a manifestation of ethnic activism (Gellner 2009: 10).

In sharp contrast, the festivals in the bastis of Changlang were not about presenting or projecting identity, it was about continuing a tradition, doing what they have done every year. However, many of the rituals had been simplified and the scale of festivities has been reduced to cope with modern-day compulsions. The Catholic Tangsa of Tengman basti had also made some necessary modifications to the manner in which they celebrated the festival, so as not to offend their new Christian sensibilities. But there was almost nothing that anybody did 'just for show', simply because there were no onlookers—whatever they did, they did for themselves. The mega trans-community festivals were at the opposite end of the scale with considerations of what the audience might want to see and the visual impact of the performances taking precedence over everything else.

In any case, it is clear that there have been many changes not just in form but also in content, as well as in function, of these festivals. Various considerations—some nostalgic, some contingent, some religious, and some largely pragmatic (and fuelled by the political and economic aspirations of a small, active elite) have led to a shift in function and purpose of these festivals, from a predominantly ritualistic, celebratory, thanksgiving, or victory-in-war meaning of earlier times to a chiefly social and festive meaning of today. They are now aimed at visual and cultural entertainment and at presenting the ethnic as well as the modern credentials of the Tangsa to the world. And with the change of function, the form of the festivals has also undergone a lot of change: for instance, they are now held in an open arena with a stage and they last only for a day (Barkataki-Ruscheweyh 2013: 254).

There is an imitation effect involved as well: 'Everyone has a festival so we must also have ours'. But it is more than mere imitation.

As pointed out by Ramirez (personal communication), in recent times a new pan-Assam or even pan-Indian language/code of identity performance has emerged; and the shape of Tangsa festivals is influenced by the conventions of this new code, in that they try to present their culture in terms which are understandable by others; for example, since divining with chicken claws has no meaning for a north Indian official, it would not be presented to him.

Tangsa festivals also reveal how the Tangsa leaders wish to project and present themselves to the world around them, besides reinforcing their own idea of what it could mean to be Tangsa—albeit an 'imagined community' (Anderson 1983). But in the process, they also reveal how contrived these attempts can be and how the need to conform to the new notion of a cultural festival and the need to display their tribalness have forced these groups to concoct new ways of performing and presenting their 'culture' in order to satisfy these new expectations.

From Ritual Performances to Secular Festivals

An important difference in the Christian Tangsa understanding of their culture is that it does not have much to do with their new religion—in fact, that is part of the argument church leaders use to justify the organization of such village festivals. As Lumren Hakhun in Malugaon explained to me, religion is something personal, but the Tangsa culture is what gives a Tangsa his/her ethnic identity. Therefore, as long as 'performing' his Tangsa-ness did not require him to do something which is forbidden by his new religion, there was no problem. While the non-Christian Tangsa such as Aphu Tyanglam are not so sure about this separation between culture and religion, even Aphu has come to accept this as the only viable compromise in order to ensure that the Christian Tangsa also join his efforts for the preservation and projection of Tangsa cultural identity. Along the way, Tangsa village festivals have been transformed from events comprising just a sequence of rituals (as we saw in Kantang) to secular events where the ritual component has been diluted and the 'kassa' component has been strengthened, and also where elements from larger cultural festivals and secular government events have been incorporated.

This has necessitated changes in the enactment of traditional songs and their dances. Shorn of the context and reasons for their enactment in earlier times, they have been modified and optimized to produce the maximum impact when 'performed'. This staging of traditional songs and dances along with the 'show' of performing their traditional rituals is what a community understands to be and presents to the world as their 'kassa'.

Sara Shneiderman (2011: 208) has argued that both ritual (which she calls practice) and performance are both essential aspects of contemporary cultural production. While that is true, my explorations have shown that in recent times in communities such as the Tangsa the 'performance' aspects have gone up at the expense of the ritual component, mainly due to conversion to Christianity, even during community level festivals, as I discuss in the next section.

The Externalization of Culture

The problems inherent in finding common shared ground at Phulbari restricted the scope of the presentation of ethnic identity to a few shared symbols and a few items of cultural performance. Some traditional objects, such as the ritual altar, were presented but their function had changed—from the altar where animals would be brought for sacrifice to a mere decorative, simply symbolic function; the rim-rim prayer was recited/sang without actually performing the ritual sacrifice; traditional Tangsa dresses and traditional Naga symbols such as Hornbill feathers were also conspicuously displayed as visual symbols. Certain cultural elements such as the Wihu song and the Sahpolo dance were standardized and presented as symbols of pan-Tangsa identity and culture. But the dances are partly new and not many among the younger lot know how to sing the Wihu song, even few understood the meaning.

Traditions are to some extent always both invented and inherited (Otto and Pedersen 2005: 35). Therefore, there is no way to tell the vintage of the traditions that were on show, but at least one had the feeling that there seemed to be some urgency to create a full repertoire. The Wihu song, which was on the verge of dying along with the lot of older Tangsa, is now being resurrected in the form of an easy-to-learn Wihu dance. Enterprising young Tangsa people are beginning to recast their traditional love songs (which were also becoming a thing of the past because they could not be sung in front of siblings or clan relatives) into modern Tangsa songs (Barkataki-Ruscheweyh 2013).

Similar to the Garo case (De Maaker et al. 2011), traditional Tangsa dances and songs have moved from the fields and forest clearings where they were traditionally performed onto the stage. And since some of the leaders believe that dances, performed by large groups wearing colourful costumes, look better on a stage, that is what the ethnic groups are trying hard to 'invent' for themselves; thus, long songs sung by one or two people are no longer in fashion; short colourful dances with quick footwork, group songs, and songs with a chorus are in vogue. Songs are being composed, for example, with one verse in each of the many Tangsa languages.

The fact that such songs did not exist before is not important. They will become part of their new 'culture' (read 'kassa'). All these processes point to modification, reinvention, and standardization on the one hand, but also to homogenization, modernization, conformism, and influence of the bigger world, on the other. This fits in precisely with Stuart Hall's concept of 'articulation' of ethnic identity which is a process 'of becoming as well of being'.

These processes have made the Tangsa dances and songs suitable for presentation at mega trans-community cultural festivals like the Pangsau Pass Winter Festival and the Dihing-Patkai Festival. The exposure and visibility that the tribal groups get during these festivals have led to a growing awareness among them that somehow it is important to have something to call one's own culture, not just for themselves but also to show to others. This has caused an attitudinal change towards culture—culture has become a commodity, subject to the forces of demand and supply, and it has gradually got transformed into 'kassa'.

These mega-festivals have also demanded amalgamation of the cultural practices of the different Tangsa sub-tribes into one 'Tangsa culture'. And this has naturally also led to efforts, as I have shown, not only to recreate and fix what they have retained of their traditional culture based on the little that is common and acceptable, but also to invent new cultural traditions, in an effort to be seen, heard, and given applause. Earlier, each of the sub-tribes sang songs in their own languages, there were variations in their dresses, and their migration songs were distinctly different in content (if not in structure and melody). But now they all answer to the same term 'Tangsa' necessitating a merger of several distinct forms.[11]

While rewriting or reinventing cultural traditions and histories in order to consolidate under a common label might be easier for oral cultures (like the Tangsa), in the process there is the danger that internal differences between the many Tangsa groups will get elided or at least become difficult to keep apart. A senior Tangsa interlocutor echoed this when he told me, 'Nowadays while trying to "reform" and redefine our culture, the Tangsa have become *more similar* than they were before—in their clothes, in their songs and dances. It would be hard to tell the Tangsa tribes apart just from that, if it were not for the difference in languages, since the older distinctive customs have also been given up'.[12]

The biggest influence on these processes comes from the ubiquitous pan-Indian culture as seen on television and in the (Bollywood Hindi) cinema. Television has reached most Tangsa bastis; many in Tangsa homes watch movies using DVD players. All this is coupled with a growing desire of most Tangsa youth to be seen as smart and modern. Many of them go to English medium schools in Arunachal and wish to set themselves apart as westernized and 'cool'. And, as was evident in Malugaon, the Tangsa youth are in the process of composing and choreographing a new genre of modern Tangsa songs and dances similar to the Bollywood style. Moreover, as was demonstrated by the group from Relang at Malugaon, since there is a felt need to be seen as both modern and Christian, yet another genre of modern religious songs is also being composed and presented.

As for the older forms, modern technology has made it possible for the younger Tangsa to learn them from recordings of earlier performances.[13] Recording their songs and dances is one way of preserving them, and also of replicating them. But since there is usually no one close at hand who one could ask for the meaning of the songs and dances, the stage has come when many sing the songs without understanding the meaning. This marks a break in the age-old process of intergenerational handing down of culture that had been the norm so far.

Keeping Culture in Business

As the presentation of Tangsa 'culture' has moved to distant stages erected for mega cultural festivals, it has been thrown out of the everyday lives of people, and has been reincarnated as performance, as spectacle, even sometimes lapsing into pure mimicry. The task of presenting their 'culture' has moved from the hands of all the Tangsa into the hands of just a few 'keepers' of Tangsa culture—the few Tangsa left who still know how to sing and dance, or in some cases, the ones who have taken on the task to keep inventing new cultural items to present as their 'kassa'.[14] The practice of rituals too has moved out from the hands of the *dumsa* or priests into the realm of performance, and hence, into the hands of those who have made it their business to transform them into items of their new 'culture'. The more the Tangsa are being told that preserving their culture is important, either by researchers like us or by their own leaders, both with their own separate agendas, or by the state who sponsors cultural festivals, the more they have tried to find new items for their 'kassa' repertoire.

That ethnic communities playing along with this idea is understandable, but that they play along to the extent of *deliberately* exoticizing their culture to make it look more dramatic on stage is clearly a sign that these communities have begun to perform their ethnicity in order to instrumentalize it for achieving other bigger ends.[15] In all of this, aspects of culture have moved from being something lived, to something that is just extra, external, put on, just performed at certain times, without any real relevance to their everyday life.

Given this, most Tangsa are torn between this perceived need to keep performing their 'tribalness' and their wish to get on with their lives and live like others around them. If we add to all this the views of the Tangsa in different age groups, we have a Tangsa society in which the term 'culture' has different meanings for different people—for some it is a matter of existential importance, for others it is a weak and uneasy link to their past, and for yet others, it has become a way of reaching out to the future.

The Culture of Festivals

The most oft-cited reason for organizing festivals given by Tangsa community leaders was to present and preserve their cultural and ethnic identity. This idea is not new. Anthropologists have been talking about 'the politics of cultural performance' from the time of Gluckman (1940) at least. But even much closer home, this phenomenon is not peculiar to the Tangsa alone—in fact, the Tangsa are doing today exactly what countless other ethnic groups in Assam have done in recent years in their effort to reinvent themselves and to give themselves a new identity in keeping with the modern order of things (cf. Longkumer 2015; Ramirez 2014; Karlsson 2001).

The Singpho also organize a big annual festival called the Shapawng Yawng Manau Poi in mid-February every year.[16] About the role of the Manau festival in identity considerations of the Kachins in different parts of the world Sadan (2013: 420ff) states:

> The manau festival today has become the main symbol not only of Kachin ethnic identity in Burma but also of Singpho Tribal identity in India and Jingpo identity as a National Minority in China. In recent years it has also gained status as a symbol for a new, formally recognised Kachin cultural presence inside Thailand, as well as many Kachin diaspora groups around the world today …. They also provide the setting for the ongoing negotiation of internal ideologies and symbolic social relations.

In fact, the other two 'older' tribal groups in the area—the Tai Phake and the Sema Naga—also have their own annual festivals. The Sema Naga still celebrate a 'traditional' festival called Tuluni on 8 July every year. Very recently, the Tai Phake have also started the practice of coming together on 17 November every year to celebrate the festival called Poi Pi Mau to mark the Tai Phake New Year.[17] They celebrated it centrally for the first time in 2009. Moreover, there is a growing awareness of their ethnic distinctiveness among these communities—many Tai Phake, for example, have changed their names back from Gohain, which is a sort of generic name, to their clan names. Also Manje La Singpho has recently declared that he would sign his name henceforward only as Manje La. Thus, festivals can also be empowering, by raising the level of awareness within community members.

However, the contradictions inherent in ethnic groups organizing and participating in such ethnic festivals are hard to overlook—on the one hand, they hope to use the visibility they gain at such festivals to lever themselves out of their present situation and as a means of overcoming their present marginalization. But on the other hand, by presenting themselves as 'tribals', they are contributing to their own categorization as the 'other' or as 'backward' by the state and the mainstream population; in fact, they are aiding the state to keep them where they were. Either ways, it is a no-win situation for them, and only serves to show the little room these groups have to manoeuvre.

Festivals, Ethnicity, and Tangsa Identity

Festivals are sites for 'the expressive production of ethnicity in action' (Shneiderman 2015: 7), and are powerful sites to project, display, and also 'enact' their ethnic identity, which is determined by what the state wants them to be and as well as by what they want themselves to be. From what I saw in the field, the Tangsa wish to project a multifaceted identity, asserting both their modern Indianness as well as their ethnic distinctiveness. While at Phulbari, a unified and inclusive pan-Tangsa identity was sought to be projected; at Malugaon it was just about the Hakhun. Furthermore, it was clear that this 'new' Tangsa identity has been consciously and deliberately fashioned by a few Tangsa leaders, keeping in view broader as well as personal considerations, and in order to substantiate their claims of difference within sameness. Again, a parallel is to be found in the Naga story, as evident in Von Stockhausen's work in which

> [he] wishes to demonstrate how the possibility of formulating identity continues to be exploited in our times for both political and religious ends .... Identity seems to be consciously 'shaped' and 'calculated' in equal measure .... More than ever, identity seems to be a political expedient among the Nagas—in both the religious as well as the political context. (2008: 58)

The following sections will examine some of these ideas in greater detail.

The Acquisition of Identity and Modernity

'The self ascribed identity precedes the debate over political status', Ramirez claims, and he goes on to explain why that is the case for the Karbi people: 'Karbi are neither those who live in the autonomous district nor those who are governed by a peculiar set of institutions: they are all those who claim to be Karbi' (Ramirez 2007: 104).

The Garo case described below is not much different:

> People construct ethnicity for many reasons: to be like others; to be different from others; to include; to exclude; to assert superiority; to make claims over territory; to forge unity in aggression or defence against their neighbours. One means of asserting common ethnicity is to share a name, and it may be that the label Garo helped to create Garo ethnicity. (Burling 2012: 60)

The process of the formation of a pan-Tangsa identity is best described with the empty vessel metaphor: An assorted group of tribes were given a new name—Tangsa; they needed to fill it with meaning in order to pass the requirements of being a tribal group as laid down by the Indian state, that is, a group with distinctive and essentialized cultural traits. For them it was neither just a question of defining boundaries nor just a question of inclusion and exclusion; it was also a question of selectively choosing elements from their past, however imagined and contested they might be, to become symbols for as well as proof of their common 'culture' in the present, making sure that a subtle differentiation was maintained between their 'culture' and that of their other tribal neighbours as well as of their dominant non-tribal neighbours.

Moreover, the Tangsa today seek to replace their older tribal image with a more modern one, albeit a kind of 'indigenised modernity' (Sahlins 1999b), which serves their new political and social aims better. For the newly converted Christian or Buddhist Tangsa in Assam, their new religion has also become a significant component of their refurbished identity.

Moreover, this whole process of identity formation is itself a modern process. I have remarked elsewhere (Barkataki-Ruscheweyh 2013) that the readiness and ease with which the many diverse tribes have accepted the term 'Tangsa' and have made it their own is itself very surprising.[18] However, this recognition of the need to find a common name for themselves was perhaps the first step towards recognizing the need to have a new identity; earlier, perhaps, their tribal affiliations were enough, but not in a modern democratic state. Hence, the very need to have a shared common identity is itself a 'modern' need imposed by the Indian state.[19]

Instrumentalization of Ethnicity

Moreover, this modern need is felt more acutely only by a small group of Tangsa leaders who usually have other often personal reasons for wishing to project a new and consolidated Tangsa identity.[20] In Chapters 4, 5, and 6, I have shown how the main festival organizers at Kharangkong, Malugaon, and Phulbari respectively, have used the festival as a springboard for their political ambitions and how the successful organization of a festival was then used as proof of their organizational capability and leadership qualities. This in turn gave them greater credibility in the eyes of their own people and of the powers that be, thereby leading to furtherance of their personal political aspirations. Therefore, it was no coincidence that exactly those three Tangsa leaders who organized the festivals in Kharangkong, Malugaon, and Phulbari have become the only Tangsa members of the Development Council.

In this manner, they have become not only the representatives of their community but also mediators between their community and the government. This in a way is also evidence of the beginning of the process of the formation of 'elites' within the community; elites who take the initiative of organizing these festivals and who influence their shape, according to their vision of what their own culture is or of what 'should' be shown to the external audience.[21] This process is much in line with Brass's argument (1991: 8) that

> ethnicity and nationalism [and in our case, identity] are not 'givens', but are social and political constructions. They are creations of elites, who draw upon, distort, and sometimes fabricate materials from the cultures of the groups they wish to represent in order to protect their well-being or existence or to gain political and economic advantage for their groups as well as for themselves.

Gradually, these elites will begin to make other decisions for the community, and in this process, become even more powerful.

While it is clear that ethnic communities like the Tangsa seek to instrumentalize their ethnic identity for obvious ends, the ground reality is more complex than that. It also stems from a need to find oneself and to position oneself in the world.

> The prevalent modern concern with identity and history among people in the margin of states are not only a matter of instrumental manipulation to gain access to land and resources (though of course this is critical), but concerns also what sociologist Stuart Hall [1996a] talks about as grounding one self and rediscovering a place from where to speak. (Karlsson 2013: 327)

Exploring this further, Karlsson (2001: 31–2) describes it as 'a subtle process of community formation. It is a matter of subaltern resistance and of constructing a "sense of self" in opposition to the dominant, encroaching [neighbour]'. This is exactly how I see the position and compulsions of at least some Tangsa leaders in Assam.

Who Still Calls the Shots

It is the nature of the power structure of the state that creates insecurities in minority ethnic groups, which forces them to rise and take action (Brown 1994: 258). Conversely, the character of their responses are determined by state policies, and, as I have shown, performing their ethnicity at festivals is one way for small minority communities such as the Tangsa in Assam to deal with this insecurity. So much so that just as in the case of the Thangmi people that Shneiderman (2011) discusses, at Tangsa festivals, the enactment of ethnicity is not so much for the benefit of tourism or for the preservation of Tangsa culture, as it is for the consumption of the state, who is the 'consumer of otherness'. This is also borne out in the difference in the intention of the festivals in Assam and in Arunachal. Since the power structure plays out differently in Arunachal, the Tangsa are more secure there, and hence do not need to project and perform their identity to the consumer state as much as they have to in Assam.

This brings us back to the important question of the role of the state in the actual form these festivals take. For a moment, let me go back to the event that I have described in the beginning of this chapter. Although this was not a Tangsa festival, it was a meeting which primarily had to do with the ethnic communities of that area. The book that was released was about the tribal communities living in that Indo-Myanmar border region (including the Tangsa and the Singpho) and the museum was also specifically for the same communities.

What happened that afternoon clearly reveals who still calls the shots in the Tirap area even when the focus is on the tribal communities. The host minister, the writer, the publisher, and their assistants (like me) were all Assamese. Therefore, it is the members of the predominantly Assamese majority community who still claim the right to speak for those ethnic communities, write about them, publish books about them, set up museums to display their traditions, and then organize meetings, like the one under discussion, to inform the communities about all that they have done for the welfare of tribals.

At the end of the day, the two politicians made political capital out of the entire event—the resplendent old man sitting in between the two ministers was necessary only as an excuse for the beautifully orchestrated mutually-reinforcing tandem act of the two ministers. As for the ethnic communities, their presence was necessary because they were the 'objects' of discussion, and they played the role set out for them—by adding ethnic flavour to the cultural asides and the gastronomic offerings. But nobody expected them to be able to speak for themselves: after all, they were just 'objects'—dumb museum exhibits.

Small wonder then that the ethnic communities objected to this, which Manje La Singpho's post-meeting tirade bears evidence of. Veteran Karbi leader Teron (2011: 171) expresses the same sentiment in very strong words: 'At the heart of all the violations of our human rights has been the failure to respect our integrity, and the insistence on speaking for us, defining our needs and controlling our lives.'

But how things evolved that day shows clearly the actual reality in the Tirap region today. And there are other examples too, as discussed in Chapter 2; it is the Assamese and the local administration who decide whether or not to hold the Dihing-Patkai Festival, a festival primarily meant for the tribal groups. The tribal communities might have been given a Development Council, many from these communities might well be educated and well-off, but it is still the case that even today, in 2013, the Assamese writers, politicians, and administrators still feel the need to speak 'for' them, to decide 'for' them. The idea of setting up a museum for these communities might have been well intentioned, but were they actually asked for their opinion before the decision to set up the museum for them was taken?

Taking Stock

This section is written in the postscript style of the other chapters because it looks back and assesses the shortcomings and gaps in this study as well as the important lessons learnt.

Shortcomings of My Work

At the end of it all, I have to admit to significant gaps in my knowledge about the Tangsa. The Tangsa in Assam are too few numerically and too marginal to give a real impression of what being Tangsa could mean: the full range of ethnic and linguistic diversity as well as the religious complexity prevalent amongst the Tangsa is not fully reflected in those living in Assam; for that one would need to also work with the Tangsa in Arunachal and with the Tangshang/Heimi in Myanmar. Even the complexity within the Pangwa groups is not fully reflected: the Mossang are numerically the largest Pangwa group in India but are hardly mentioned since they are mostly in Arunachal.[22]

Even in the three villages in Assam where I spent a lot of time, I cannot speak with any degree of confidence about the hopes and aspirations of the younger Tangsa, or about the women. Since our project had to do with the documentation of the older Tangsa traditional culture, and most of the young people in the village were born Christian, they had not much to tell us, even if there were some exceptions. Although I did make special efforts, time and again, to engage with Tangsa women, they were busy with their children, or in the fields or with housework and did not have the time to talk; at other times, their men answered for them. Since there was a general impression that our team was only interested in past times and older practices, the women often told us that we were better off talking to the men, although a few, like Aphu's wife, had a very sharp memory for details like dates and place names.

We worked mostly with middle-aged and older men. But even with them, I did not think it proper to join them in the drinking sessions in the evenings. Moreover, since I was alone most of the time in the field, I had made it a rule not to take any unnecessary chances. That probably meant that I missed out on a lot of more subtle and sensitive data which would have possibly come my way had I been a little more daring. However, since my focus was on festivals and since almost all decisions about the conduct of festivals were made by the Tangsa leaders, who were mostly older men, I did get a lot of detailed information on festivals.

I have also not been able to work in a rough description of the general Tangsa situation in Assam. For example, quite a few of the Tangsa living in Assam belong to the Tikhak/Yongkuk groups and they are mostly Buddhist. But I have said almost nothing about them here, partly because I had decided to work mainly on the Pangwa groups, partly because there is a lot more known about the Tikhaks, thanks to Simai's (2008) book, and also because there were other researchers working with them around the same time; see, for example, Parker (under examination). I did not manage to visit all the villages in Assam where the Tangsa live. Neither have I mentioned all the interesting features that I observed in the field; for instance, we discovered that there were many instances of paired Tangsa villages which were very close to each other but which had very little contact with one another. Moreover, although I have mentioned them in passing, I have not delved into many of the very interesting debates that are especially relevant to the discussion of ethnic communities in northeast India. For instance, how does the Tangsa case contribute to the debate on Scott's (2009) thesis, namely that hill people have deliberately gone back to the hills to evade the state (see Wouters [2012] for more on this topic).

Another serious 'lack' in my data is that although I have spent more than a year in total in the field, I have been there mostly in the winter months. As such I do not have any idea of how the Tangsa live or survive during the hot monsoon months when most of the gravel roads become unusable. Another consequence is that although I have focussed my analysis on festivals, I have only been present at winter festivals and have not seen the Moh/Mol or any other festival that is celebrated in the spring/summer/fall.

On a personal level, since I am by nature very talkative and very impatient, I have often prompted my interlocutors when they have taken too long to give me an answer, but did not realize that till much later when I played the recordings back. And the facts that we had a linguist in our team who was 'doing' the languages and that I could get around and communicate with everyone using Asamiya or Hindi meant that I did not make any effort to pick up even a few words in any of the Tangsa languages that my interlocutors spoke. In retrospect, I regret that because at the end of the day in that respect I am guilty of having been every bit as arrogant and patronizing as the other Assamese with whom I have found fault. I also have to admit that my inability to keep calm and just let things take its normal course have cost me quite a few stories, such as, for instance, at a village gathering in Malugaon once, when the elders were preparing to relax over a smoke of opium, unable to contain my curiosity, I stupidly asked someone to confirm what was going on, and that was enough for the Gaonbura to ask the elders to disperse, bringing that afternoon's festivities to an abrupt end.

As for what is still left to do, this work has certainly not done justice to the Tangsa living in Arunachal. There are two reasons for this—first because I feel I need to spend a lot more time in the field in Arunachal before I get to the stage of being able to write about them, and second, because I believe that that story deserves to be told in all its detail and complexity, separately. Aspects such as the mindboggling range of religious differences amongst the Tangsa in Arunachal: the Buddhists, the Rangfraites, and the Christians (and their many different denominational variations), and how this plays out in their relations with one another and in their understanding of identity and culture would be the natural sequel to this work.

From the combined work of our project team we are led to conjecture that there is a kind of 'cultural and linguistic continuum' spanning from the Tangsa in Changlang to the Tutsa, Nocte, and Wancho communities in the Tirap and Longding Districts extending all the way to the Konyak Naga groups in Nagaland. This would make sense, both in terms of locational contiguity of these groups and the similarities in their cultural practices. Stephen Morey has already started work on the linguistic aspects of this conjecture (with the help of a linguistics student from Gauhati University, Iftikar Rahman). Someday, hopefully soon, there will be enough data about these communities to be able to say more.

Looking Back and Lessons Learnt

If only to state the obvious, this whole exercise has taught me a lot about the Tangsa. But it has also told me at least as much about the Assamese and about myself.

First about the Tangsa, it was a disappointment to realize that there were no big secrets there waiting to be discovered, that nothing dramatic happened in Tangsaland on a daily basis which I had the exclusive rights to report about, that my Tangsa interlocutors were more or less like me, and that in their everyday lives, decisions were made based not on some exclusive inspiration and wisdom reserved only for them as Tangsa but on common sense and pragmatism. As I got to know them better, I told myself that if festivals for most of them were nothing more than simply occasions to come together, to dress in their traditional finery, and to eat, drink, dance, sing, and be merry, then I would have to be happy with that. And if in the end, being honest about what I found in the field implied that my dissertation did not have anything profound to say about the Tangsa or about their festivals, then I would have to live with that. My job was only to faithfully report what I saw and leave it at that.

Next about the Assamese: my time with my Tangsa interlocutors has left me very uneasy about my being Assamese. I had seen a lot of evidence that Assamese hegemonic attitudes were largely responsible for keeping the Tangsa where they were and for magnifying the perceived differences. Perhaps one is more critical of one's own people, and hence I might have overreacted at times whenever there were Assamese involved, but still, it is a fact that the situation could have been different if the civil administrators, politicians, journalists, and others who have some contact with people from such communities would simply learn to treat them, not so much with sympathy and compassion, but simply with respect due as equal individuals.

I have made many friends among my Tangsa interlocutors, have come to be accepted by many as a member of their families, but in the end, this whole exercise has been an experiment of self-discovery—to find out who you are by placing yourself against who you think you are not, and by realizing that the differences are not all that significant after all. And this has changed my own life world.

In writing this book, I am guilty of doing exactly what I have accused many others of having done: namely speaking 'for' the Tangsa. But I have done so as a friend and ally, with their permission, and because many of them have encouraged me to do so. I have tried my best to remain faithful to what I have seen and heard in the field, in trying to display a snapshot of the (ethnographic) present moment, for their future record. By writing this book, I have tried to give voice to what they—subalterns, in a relative sense—had to say and hence contribute to their empowerment, as Philippe Bourgois (1990: 52) would have anthropologists do; and also because I wish the Tangsa community, and many others like them, to speak up for themselves in the future.

I went to work with the Tangsa not as an Assamese, but as an ethnographer and researcher. However, the fact that an Assamese is writing this book is relevant because as the dominant majority community in the state, the Assamese have been taking advantage of the fact that the Tangsa 'cannot speak up for themselves' for too long. This is my way of trying to make good some of the hurt that we, as a community, have inflicted on many smaller communities, over a long period of time. Someday I hope that we shall find a way to live together, in this land we call our own, treating each other with respect, due not because of anything else, but because of our common humanity.

***

Despite all the shortcomings—due to the improvised nature of my fieldwork methodology, my own diffidence as well as all the various limitations listed in the last section—if I have dared to write about the Tangsa at all, it is because I am convinced that the three villages I have studied are in many ways representative, and that the information I have gathered and the understanding I have acquired during my many months in the field and also at many other locations are enough to give a reliable picture of the Pangwa situation in Assam. Of course, my study leaves out the non-Pangwa mainly Buddhist Tangsa groups living in Assam and also the much bigger partly-Christian Tangsa population in Arunachal. But, including them would have taken the edge out of this study, as their situation and their problems are quite different from those addressed here. Nonetheless, discounting finer details, this study can be thought to be illustrative, in a broad sense, of the problems and issues that confront many other such small ethnic communities living not only in the Tirap area of Assam but also in the larger area called Zomia of which it is a part. The Tangsa case is also indicative of the strategies many such small communities seek out to gain agency and to resist marginalization.

The previous chapters have shown that the Tangsa use the platform provided by festivals to convey different and distinct messages. However, given the general situation in each village and the relatively unenviable position of the Tangsa in Assam, most of what they do during festivals and also in the ways they connect and network with other groups and communities can be considered as expressions of their marginality besides being strategies for survival and for acquisition of agency, be it performing their identity at festivals or wanting to move behind the fence—that is how the different strands and themes in this work so far come together to tell one and the same story.

My main underlying claim therefore is that their marginality is central to any analysis of the Tangsa in Assam. It is their marginality that makes them, in the most part, behave the way they do or take the decisions they take. When a community is forced to perform their ethnicity in order to remain in the reckoning, then this performance is not so much a show of increased agency as it is proof of their continued marginalization. In that sense, festivals can be seen as assertions of difference and of self-worth by the Tangsa in the face of existential threats of being subsumed by the Assamese (or more immediately by the Nepali and the Singpho), by Christianity, or of being rejected by the Nagas. Hence, they also betray a sense of insecurity and nervousness.

Tangsa society today, based on what I saw in the field, is in a state of flux—that is not at all surprising because 'social systems are not naturally stable' (Leach 1954: 285). However, unlike a regular predictable oscillation in Leach's Gumsa-Gumlao model, there are no predictions that one can make in the Tangsa case; different segments are pulling in different directions, evolving in different ways, transforming into different and separate entities.

What is more, contrary to normal expectation, I have demonstrated how the valleys- and plains-dwelling Tangsa in Assam are in many senses relatively less 'developed' both economically, in terms of their education, as well as otherwise in comparison to many of their hill-dwelling relatives in Arunachal. I argue that this is mainly because they are also relatively less advantaged in Assam, primarily due to the different ways in which the two states of Assam and Arunachal handle their tribal populations. Therefore the contexts are different, and this makes the Tangsa also perform their identity at festivals differently in Assam than in Arunachal.

The Tangsa case is also a good instance to observe the twin forces of consolidation and fragmentation in action. While, ethnically and politically, the different Tangsa groups try to come together under a common banner, in terms of religion there is an ever-increasing splintering amongst the Christian denominations within the Tangsa. And as I have demonstrated with the Hakhun example, a section of the new leadership is trying to forge a special identity for themselves, even while remaining under the broader Tangsa umbrella. So these processes are neither uniform nor do they have the same effect on different parts of the Tangsa whole.

And while this tendency amongst the Tangsa to splinter and divide might be an impediment towards the formation of a pan-Tangsa identity, their fractious character is in some sense part of their identity, just as it is for the Naga (see, for example, Jacquesson 2008). Moreover, it is this tendency that forces them to be creative with regard to construction of their common identity and permits them to participate in the production of their own image, by being selective about which elements of their traditions to revive, which to abandon, and which to reinvent (Longkumer 2015: 52).

Summing up, festivals are not only shows of self-confidence, they also reveal the inherent diffidence; they are also attempts at conformity rather than just flaunting difference. The professed culture is no longer something simply practised but something also performed. Furthermore, I claim that the surprisingly thin cultural and ritual content, and the casualness with which these festivals are organized, is not accidental; the Tangsa in Assam are just too few in number and too deeply divided and too weakened by various problems—in other words, they are too marginal—to be able to do much better. But they need to perform their identity in whatever way they can in order to make themselves visible and to remain in the reckoning. This also pays off for some individuals to some extent on certain occasions. But these are small gains compared to the bigger problems that afflict Tangsa society.

Most of all, what some Tangsa decide to do at festivals and how they go about doing it reveal the marginality and insecurity that small groups such as the Tangsa have to face on an everyday basis, so much so that a sense of being victims, of being victimized, can become a part of their identity. Festivals can also be understood as platforms where such communities attempt to turn the very facts, of being discriminated against and of being forced to perform their ethnicity, into instruments for securing special privileges and concessions for themselves. But these acts do not only give evidence of their ingenuity or their ability to strategize; they also reveal the helplessness and desperation of such small communities, who are constantly haunted with the fear of being further marginalized or of being completely annihilated altogether. Therefore, the whole Tangsa project of instrumentalizing ethnicity to come out of marginalization boomerangs as they land up contributing to their own marginalization.

And finally, to end where I began, to answer the question of the young Assamese researcher who we met right at the beginning of this work, given what I know so far, there is nothing so very special about the Tangsa. But why do they have to be special for us to want to know more about them? Is it not enough that they are people just like you and me? If I have only been able to convince my Assamese friends that the Tangsa should not be treated as creatures apart—this exercise would have been well worth the effort.

Notes

1. First published in 1991, this book is based on official records and the personal experiences of the author during his long career as an officer in the office of the Political Officer at Margherita from pre-Independence times.

2. The same Assamese Minister had also initiated the Dihing-Patkai Festival.

3. The books were never ordered.

4. Many policies of the Indian state, such as its basic 3-language education policy, are essentially homogenizing—they try to keep the nation together by eliding differences. While that might have good reasons, it implies that a Tangsa toddler will never be taught in his or her mother tongue even at the primary level.

5. They routinely apply for state subsidies to buy farm equipment like tractors and to get loans from banks by forming self-help groups for setting up small businesses, like weaving units or piggeries.

6. See Tsing (1993). In fact, this study has shown that the ground reality is better described by Tangsa relations to others or Tangsa in relation to others around them as proposed by Jonsson in *Mien Relations* (2005), rather than just opposition to the state, as proposed by Scott (2009).

7. Rajesh Singpho also plays a big part in Mandy Sadan's 2013 monograph. This only goes to show that when dealing with small communities, researchers coming from different disciplines and with different questions, often land up interacting to the same set of people—the so-called ethnic elite. Hence, it is often discussions with such individuals, like Rajesh Singpho, that contribute significantly to the researcher's understanding of the field situation.

   The term *assimilation* is used in the sense of incorporation here, in which one group loses its identity by merging into another group which retains its identity (Harowitz 1981). Brass (1991: 34) explains the reasons as follows: 'An alternative situation favourable to assimilation and decline in ethnic identity occurs when differential modernisation so favors a minority ethnic group that it chooses to assimilate to the language and culture of the ruling ethnic group.'

8. Besides performing ethnicity at festivals, the last chapters have shown many other strategies that the Tangsa have employed to survive as a distinct community. Apart from proactively working on language revitalization, script creation, cultural standardization, and history-writing (facilitated by access to and use of modern technology), they have come together with other tribal groups to gain political agency (as with the award of the Development Council) and have learnt to use their links with other groups,

such as the Naga as well as foreign researchers, to gain greater visibility. Nag (2002) considers insurgency to also be a strategy to tackle marginality.

9. About the importance of the Manau festival for the Kachins, Sadan (2013: 454) states: 'The wider importance of the manau ideologically is not inherently bound by the performance itself. Rather, the manau encapsulates an ideological model of indigenous political culture, a non-institution based domain of public interaction'.

10. Festivals are almost the only occasions when the Tangsa living in the villages have the chance to participate in or just enjoy a cultural show.

    During the course of my fieldwork, I did not get meet anyone who had been asked not to attend or had specific reasons for not desiring to participate in such a festival. Of course, I did meet some Tangsa Baptist Christians who told me that they would not attend festivals where animals would be sacrificed.

11. It is a curious but interesting fact that in terms of mutual language comprehension and religion, the Tangsa groups have diverged from one another. Furthermore, linguistic diversity will persist longer amongst the Tangsa (than what one would have expected say ten years ago) mainly because of the efforts of community activists and their access to modern technology (Morey 2014).

12. What is more, in their clothes, the new 'reformed' Tangsa dress is almost indistinguishable from the Singpho dress, he claimed. The *lungi*, shoulder bag, and men's turban that men of both communities wear at present are more or less the same.

13. Our DOBES project has played a major role in making such CDs and DVDs of recordings available, as mentioned earlier.

14. Brubaker (2004: 10) calls them 'ethnic activists' or 'ethnic enterpreneurs' to highlight the capacity of these specialists of ethnicity to produce what they claim to describe.

15. Although the Tangsa have not gone so far as yet to make big business out of their ethnicity as in the cases stated by Comaroff and Comaroff (2009), and ethnic tourism is not yet really a big factor in Tangsaland, it is beginning to happen slowly in the region, for instance, at the Hornbill Festival.

16. *Poi* is a general term used by the Singpho as well as the Tai/Shan groups for festivals. The Singpho have been celebrating this festival in India since 1985, when it was held in the town of Miao. For more on this festival see Farrelly in http://asiapacific.anu.edu.au/newmandala/2008/02/22/manau-in-arunachal-pradesh/ (accessed 7 April 2015). See Sadan (2013: Ch. 9) for another description of a Manau festival.

    Commenting on the benefits of celebrating the annual Shapawng Yawng Manau Poi Festival since 1985, one Singpho writes: 'What was our cultural identity prior to the celebration of this festival? What was the relationship amongst our people living in Assam and Arunachal? We hardly knew each other and there was complete communication gap …. Had there been no Shapawng Yawng festival, such a tremendous cultural revival could not have been brought about' (*Souvenir* 2000: 14).

The revival of the Chapchar Kut festival in Mizoram is another such example; and further afield, the Gau Tao festival amongst the Hmong in Vietnam (Ngo 2009), and even as far away as in Mexico (see Gross 2011). For a recent study of the 'Festivization of Culture' in Europe and Australia, see Bennet et al. (2014).

17. It is curious how this tiny group, numbering not more than 2000 in all in Assam, have managed to retain their distinctive cultural identity even though they are numerically weak and geographically very scattered; the facts that they possess a long written tradition and that they are almost all Buddhist, possibly make the process slightly easier.

18. Even more surprising is the fact, as already mentioned in Chapter 5, that although linguistically and historically the Hakhun are very close to the Nocte group, every Hakhun we asked told us, without a single exception, that now they consider themselves to be Tangsa and not Nocte.

19. In any case, not older than the official recognition of the term 'Tangsa' itself in the 1950s.

Bhagabati confirms this view, 'consolidation of cultural identity and its assertion, even if in ethno-political terms, are always concomitants of the modernization process' (Bhagabati 2004: 178).

20. As I have mentioned earlier, except for that small group who took all the decisions, the rest of the Tangsa people we met at Phulbari and Kharangkong did not have much idea about, nor did they have very strong opinions about how the festival should be conducted.

21. Tonkinson argues for the conceptualization of tradition as a resource, strategically employed (or not employed) by certain (but not all) community members in pursuit of individual or collective goals (Otto and Pedersen 2005b: 18).

22. For a glimpse of the linguistic diversity in Changlang, see Thomas (2009).

Appendix[1]

Note on the Rangpang Nagas (relevant excerpts)

By Mr T.P.M. O'Callaghan, Political Officer, Sadiya Frontier Tract.

Nagas of the Sadiya Frontier Tract: The regular administration of some of these tribes and clans was undertaken from 1923 to 1924. Previous to this, enquiries into thefts by Nagas of iron rails from the collieries in the vicinity of Ledo brought to light the fact that the practice of human sacrifices undoubtedly still obtained among the Rangpang clans south of the Patkoi range. The Rangpang clans living on the northern slopes of the Patkoi, whilst admitting that they had made them in the past, denied that there had been any in the present generation. These latter Rangpangs were forthwith brought under direct administration, assessed to house tax and the survey of the area taken in hand and will be completed in 1926. This has brought the regularly administered area of the District to the crest of the Patkoi Ridge looking down on the area where barbarism still survives and to eradicate which the Governments of Assam and Burma are cooperating.

The detailed information available at present is given herewith:

Habitat: The Nagas occupy the hills in the Eastern portion of the southern area of the Sadiya Frontier Tract between the Plains of Assam and Burma and may be conveniently divided into (*a*) those between the plains area of the district and the Patkoi Ridge, that is Cis-Patkoi, (*b*) those between the Main Patkoi Ridge and the Assam-Burma boundary—Trans-Patkoi. Actually between the Patkoi Ridge, the Upper Chindwin District of Burma, the Hukawng Valley on the East and the Naga Hills District of Assam on the West is practically unexplored area, inhabited by Rangpang and other Nagas. Those living in the Hills adjoining the Hukawng valley are to some extent under the influence of the Sesan Singpho (Chingpaw) Headmen of Shinbwiyang etc. living in the Hukawng valley.

2) Cis-Patkoi: The Cis-Patkoi tribes of the Sadiya Frontier Tract consist of (a) Laju (Laiyu) and Hatut clans, 16 villages, 1,125 houses, 11,200 souls, living in the head waters area of the Tirap river in an area of about one hundred square miles, that is, a density of over 100 to the square mile a fact which will in time become an administrative problem owing to land hunger. These two tribes are not administered.

(b) The Moklum: 6 villages,185 houses, 1,300 souls who may be classed with the Laju and Hatut; the Yogli and Rangrang both Rangpang clans who live in 10 small villages, 800 people, living between the Tirap river and the Namchik-Tirap watershed.

(c) The Longri, Moshang, Lungphi, Ronrang, Tulem—all Rangpang clans—Yungkup, Kamlan, and Tikkak—30 small villages—2,000 people in the Namchik River Basin and eastwards. (b) and (c) are all administered from Sadiya though at present administration consists only in cold-weather tours and the collection of a house tax of Rs 2 per house. Sadiya to them has hitherto been but a name.

The noticeable features of the Laju and Hatut are the comparatively large village communities. Laju, the main village of the clan, consisting of some 400 houses with a population close on 4,000 is, however, exceptional. These two clans with the Moklum seen to have affinities with the Namsang, and other clans of the South-west and West and have probably been forced Northwards along the Western slope of the Patkoi by clans of the Mokochang unadministered area. They deny performing human sacrifices. They are head hunters and the skulls are still preserved in the 'morungs' or meeting houses. Laju has a good collection, Borduria a small village (60 houses) in the Lakhimpur unadministered Naga area is in proud possession of a collection of many generations, several hundreds carefully preserved and arranged in the 'Morung'!

3) The headmen are elected and their influence rest largely on individual character and personality. The men are physically well-developed but slight in build, averaging 5' 3" and the elder men often refined and

slightly aquiline in appearance though the younger men are course [sic] and heavy-looking. They shave the front of the head but allow the rest of the hair to grow wearing it gathered up in a knot at the back of the head. The high pointed narrow hat of closely woven cane decorated with pigs tushes and bristles and toucan (hornbill) feathers is common and with this and pierced ears ornamented with gural horns or flowers or pocelain [sic] beads—the young 'buck' is a pleasing sight. The Laju women clip their hair as close as possible. Both clans are polygamous, and say they are endogamous. The Laju bury their dead while the Hatut burn. Each village as its young mens 'club' or clubs each with its 'canoe' drum twenty feet in length and two feet in diameter. When beaten alternately in unison by ten or twelve men ranged on either side the effect is impressive and the sound travels a great distance and messages broadcasted. There have been no inter-clan raids of recent years. The arms are the broad bladed dao and spear and an occasional flint lock gun and effective shields of bark are used. The Laju, unlike the Hatut and all others, do not come down to work in the plains. The former are the middlemen—astride the trade route—between the Nagas to the West from whom they take salt, and trade opium, daos and spear-heads from the Trans-Patkoi Nagas to the East.

Borduria in Lakhimpur unadministered area has twenty brine wells and supply salt as far away as the Hukawng valley. To the West of the Laju between them and the Sibsagar Naga area live the Nivongs who are said to go naked and are despised accordingly. Even the children of

4) of the Sadiya are people wear clothes. Both men and women tatoo—the men from the shoulders to the solar plexus a V-shaped diagram on chest and back in lines half-an-inch apart as well as serrated lines round the neck when they have taken a head and the women the lower part of the forehead and upper part of the nose. Slaves are not kept. Very many of the men and some of the women smoke opium.

They are prosperous, contented, and healthy—they can more than hold their own in their area and treasure their independence and do not want to be interfered with by administration or otherwise. The Laju people have been credited with supplying, that is selling victims for human sacrifice to the Rangpang clans. They deny it. It is very probably that they did so in their old raiding days.

As regards (c) who live North-East of the Moklum, they are, with exception of the Tikkak, Kamlan and Yungkup, Rangpang clans who have migrated in search of food and land over the Patkoi from the basin of the Dilli (Namphuk) river where their present clans and affinities still live. They are in physique and general virility inferior to the Laju, Hatut and Moklum.

There is but little known at present of these Naga tribes and clans. The Hukawng Valley is a historical route of invasion of India from the South-East and these Nagas are possibly early arrivals, pushed aside by the Ahoms and Kachin tides of movement, having been left behind by some pre-historic conquerors of Assam. It is noteworthy that other peoples of Assam History are believed to have been addicted to human sacrifices, that is Chutuyas, the Ahoms etc.

The Rangpang clans are monogamous and endogamous:

5) some burn and some bury their dead. They are addicted to opium which is grown everywhere in the trans-Patkoi area. They keep to themselves and there is but little interclan trade. Though their language is one there are noticeable differences in dialect between the clans.

All Nagas do 'jhum' cultivation, rice and Kochu (arum tuber) being the staple crops. They keep cattle, buffalo, pigs, and fowls. The monotony of their primitive lives are varied by feasts which are held on the slightest pretext.

Trans-Patkoi Nagas: The main area of the Rangpang clans is the basin of the Dilli (Namphuk Hka) River system which is a tributary of the Chindwin river. To the East is the Kachin settled Hukawng valley, while on the West is the unexplored area of the big raiding Naga villages East of the unadministered area of the Naga Hills District of Assam, that is East of the Assam–Burma boundary. The clans are Moshang, Morang, Langshing, Yogli, Sangke, Shangwa, Mimung, Katsan, Longri, Lonphai, Sograng, Sangtai, Dungai, Motai, Tulim & c. The general description already given of the Rangpang of the administered area, cover them—a people in no way impressive, living in unkempt hamlets.

Human Sacrifice: This custom has been and is a normal practice among all Rangpang clans which they explain as a reaction to felt necessity to appease the spirits. It is primarily a personal or communal votive and intercessionary gift and will be vowed in times of difficulty, that is promised for the future if a victim be not immediately available and it is such promises already made to the spirits, which many clans in the unadministered area have advanced as one of their main reasons for not immediately abandoning the practice, that is, the fear

292 Dancing to the State

of retribution due to the non-fulfilment of such vows. More than one
house-hold may subscribe to purchase a victim: in time of urgency a
slave victim may be borrowed to be replaced later or may

6) be bought on credit and even buffaloes etc. stolen to provide part
of the price. Victims who are generally slaves, captives in war, may be
of either sex and any age and cost from Rs 300 to Rs 500. Doubtless,
useless members of the community are seized and sold and also weak,
helpless debtors in a powerful turbulent village. Rangpangs do not supply any victims themselves and all admit that the source of supply is
way to the South and South West, that is the Dilli (Namphuk) River
Basin and Westwards, that is West of the sandri Bum and Magri Bum
Ridge where Rangpang area may run with the big raiding, headhunting Naga villages in the unexplored area of the Naga Hills District of
Assam. The Rangpang not only sacrifice but also traffic in victims, the
Dilli basin people not only buying from the West and sacrificing, but
buying and reselling, in fact it is probably the custom for a victim to
pass through more than one hand before meeting his or her end. The
slaves are always described of being of an unknown clan, tattooed
on the cheeks and forehead and speaking an unknown tongue. The
Rangpang of the administered area give the Laju clan one as the sources
of supply in the past. The Laju dwell just inside the Sadiya Frontier
Tract unadministered area—it is the most Northerly of the big head
hunting villages and though they deny keeping slaves or trafficking in
them, it is extremely probable that some of them did it in the past. They
number some 7,500 people. When purchased for sacrifice the victim is
kept in the house of the owner, well cared for and fed but kept in stocks
if there is any suspicion that escape may be attempted. The sacrifice is
within a month of purchase unless bought for resale. On the appointed
day, selected, as is the executioner by divination by the 'wise' men, the
victim is drugged with opium or drink or, failing these, even beaten
into insensibility, led to the front

7) of the front verandah of the house and decapitated by a blow or
blows on the neck from behind at the top of the notched tree which
serves as a ladder entrance to the verandah. The skull when clean is
divided in two perpendicularly and the front hung suspended in the
verandah room. As for the body, one account is that the body is divided
up and the bones, flesh and entrails are sold as charms or divided among
clansmen: another account is that the body is buried in the jungle and

when the bones are cleaned they are distributed or sold. Others have stated that the body is buried unmutilated. The executioner, it may be noted, is never of the household of the donor of the victim.

It has often been alleged that runaway coolies from the Assam tea gardens, and Coal Mines, Earthworks etc. have been enticed away by the Rangpang and others, seized and sold as victims but enquiries have hitherto failed to elicit any evidence whatsoever to support these allegations.

The march of time and progress has brought Government to the question of eradication of this horrible custom. The preliminary enquiries have disclosed a problem of real magnitude: the area concerned inhabited by those who sacrifice and those who are the source consists of tumbled masses of mountains inaccessible and practically all unexplored, totalling in area at least 10,000 square miles. The intimate administration of this area is at present beyond practicability. The obvious action for immediate suspension is the cutting off of the source of supply of victims. Even were Government in an easy position to enforce my arms immediate orders to abandon the practice—which it is not, something more than a force is required. At first s… (sight?) it is easy to assert that with people who have not emerged from barbarism the only law until such time

8) as they can be educated to a higher state of reasoning and conduct is force. Here are children of nature, isolated, hitherto working out their own destinies with social customs, primarily the result of physical environment. Analysis of the principles of human section, which explains particular events in this matter as in everything else must be made and the results studied. Government has started to make it clear beyond all possible doubt and compromise that the practice is opposed to all humanity and these ideas becoming widely prevalent are a substantial coercion to right-thinking according to civilization. Travelling back in thought to the background of our own history in which Sun-worship and the Druidical rites are a dim memory, one can approach the question with understanding and a spirit of patience and of hope and this spirit will give vision and initiate a reasoned onward movement from barbarism. There will be advances and relapses but progress will continue. A good number of villages[2] have already publicly undertaken to give up the practice so there is in existence a right-thinking section to show the way to their fellows. As little interference as possible and full

liberty to arrange the personal details of their lives compatible with our ideas must be the policy. Enthusiasm with patience is necessary if pressure and success is to result, looking beyond the immediate effect of what actual action is taken. So much for theory and generalization, there remains the details of immediate effort indicated. These peoples must be systematically visited by sympathetic understanding officers from Burma and Assam from the South and West and from the North and East respectively and regular campaign undertaken on the lines indicated. Where reasonably possible main routes and intervillage tracks must be improved to become Belloc's channels, not only of trade but of ideas and of progress, to move and

9) control them intellectually as well as physically.

These notes are the results of hurried tours on the fringe of the Rangpang country and it is hoped that they will serve as a basis for the preparation of detailed reliable information of these peoples.

Signed O'Callaghan, Political Officer, Sadiya; dated: 27.4.26

Notes

1. Part of *Annual Administrative Report* for the year 1925–6 of the Sadiya Frontier Tract [*Report* 1926] Political B Sept. 26 No. 801, *Assam State Archives*.
2. Elsewhere it is mentioned that 34 villages have done so.

Glossary

Assamese, Hindi and Singpho are marked as Ass., Hin., Sin., respectively. Words marked as Tan. will mean it is from one or some of the many Tangsa languages. The specific Tangsa language will be written in full, if known.

ang (Hakhun)	king.
ajanti (Ass.)	people who are untouched by civilization; people from a land not well known.
Aphu (Cholim)	elder brother.
Baba (Ass./Hin.)	father.
bandh (Hin.)	strike, blockade
basti (Ass./Hin.)	settlement; part of a village.
bigha (Ass.)	unit of land measurement; 1 acre is roughly 3.025 bighas.
biri-chhung (Cholim)	ritual altar for animal sacrifice .
chai (Cholim)/ *chol* (Juglei)/*kham* (Hakhun)	rice-beer.
cham-thop (Cholim)/ *topola-bhat* (Ass.)	rice-balls wrapped with *nyap-shak/koupat* leaves.
chang (Ass.)	raised platform.
chang-ghar (Ass.)/ *rang-jim* (Cholim)	house on a raised bamboo platform (Photograph 3.2)

chum-ki (*xo xo pyo*, in spoken Cholim)	a kind of flower (as seen in Photograph 4.1).
crore (Indian English)	Ten million, 100 lakhs.
dah-tang (Mossang)/ *dawan* (Ronrang)/ *di-ta* (Kimsing)/ *kha-tang* (Juglei)	human sacrifice.
deka-chang/*morung* (Ass.)	bachelors' dormitories.
dumsa (Sin.)	priest.
gam (Sin.)	suffix to name to mean first son.
gaon (Hin./Ass.)	village.
Gaonbura/GB (Ass.)	village headman.
Gaon Panchayat (Ass./Hin.)	village council.
hara lim (Cholim)	a stone post at the *hara*, the edge of the village.
hija-chung (Cholim)	notched wooden ladder.
janajati(ya) (Ass./ Hin.)	tribe/tribal.
jang (Cholim)	hacking knife *(dao*, Ass.).
jawan (Hin.)	foot soldier.
jhum (Ass./Hin.)	swidden/slash/burn/shifting cultivation is a system whereby fields are cleared by cutting, drying, and burning the vegetation and are cultivated only for a short period before allowing the fields to return to fallow.
kan (Tan.)	mountain.
kani (Ass.)	opium.
'kassa'	a derivative from the word culture, meaning, explicit culture.
khaak shaang (Moklum)	typical Tangsa red shoulder bag.
kham-khit (Hakhun)	ritual altar for performing sacrifices (Photograph 5.6)
khap (Tan.) or *sunga* (Ass.)	a mug or vessel made from a section of a bamboo stem (also *tinko* in Cholim).

khepoh-khesang	new modified ankle-length Tangsa wrapper (usually purple with white stripes and square patches) (see Photograph 7.2).
khepop (Tan.)	purple and green checked scarf usually used as turban by Tangsa men.
khesi/khesang (Tan.)	traditional Tangsa (knee-length) wrapper for women with stripes (see Photograph 7.2).
kot-sam-tung (Cholim)	Naga jacket.
kotoky (Ass.)	mediator/interpreter.
kuh/kuk/kouk (Tan.)	to gather or to assemble; a general term for festivals.
lakh (Indian English)	100,000.
lam (Tan.)	road/song in Hakhun.
lam-roeh (Mossang)	village crossroads.
lengti (Ass.)	short loin cloth; a narrow strip of cloth tied around the waist, passing between the legs from behind and up to the waist in front, whence it falls down again in a square flap (as seen in Photograph 5.3).
lowang/lungwang (Tan.)	chieftain
lungi (Ass.)	ankle-length cotton stitched wrapper for men.
mekhela (Ass.)/*khya-se* (Tan.)/*ningwat* (Tai Phake)	ankle-length stitched wrapper generally worn by women (usually of cotton).
men ryo chhung (Cholim)/*sa-man-thong* (Kimsing)	ritual post (Photograph 4.1).
mongnu khepa (Tan.)	the special cloth Tangsa women wear over their blouses at festival time (see Photograph 4.3).
mouza (Ass.)	the smallest revenue collection unit in the country; the revenue collectors are called *mouzadars*.
nga/noi-tang (Tan.)	Great Buffalo sacrifice (Photograph 3.1).

nyap-shak (Tan.)/ *koupat* (Ass.)	a type of leaf used for various purposes by the Tangsa, for example, to wrap rice in to make rice balls.
'Older' tribal groups of the Tirap area	Tangsa, Singpho, Sema Naga, and Tai Phake
Pangwa	a sub-family of Tangsa, see Chapter 3 for more.
phelap (Cholim.)/ *phalap* (Sin.)	tea.
poi (Sin./Tai(Shaan)/ Burmese)	public meeting; a general term for festivals.
pooja (Ass./Hin.)	religious rituals.
pura (Ass.)	unit of land measurement, in colloquial use in Assam; 1 pura = 0.77 acres.
ra-chuk (Mossang)	conical ritual structure erected at the *lam-roeh* (village crossroads) during Wihu-kuh festival (Photograph 7.1).
raipang/*raitu* (Juglei)	vertically/horizontally striped wrappers used by Tangsa women (Photograph 7.2).
Rang-pang	An earlier name for some Tangsa groups, see Note 41 of Chapter 3
rasta (Hin.)	path.
reiben (Cholim)	wild jute plant.
rhii (Tan.)	traditional violet and green *lungi* worn by Tangsa men.
rhi-khya (Cholim)	basket.
rim-rim (Cholim)	ritual prayer.
rimwa (Juglei)	village priest.
sador (Ass.)	long strip of cloth normally used by Assamese women to cover the upper part of their body; worn over a *mekhela*.
sam-tung (Tan.)	blouse worn by women.
sang-yi (Mossang)/ *ding-du-khya* (Cholim)	special bamboo-cane basket woven in a special manner and kept aside for ritual purposes (as seen in Photograph 4.1).
shamma (Tan.)	diviner, healer (*khamme* in Cholim).
shamsa (Tan.)	people from the plains, in song language.

tang-sa (Tan.)	literally, hill-child or 'children of the hills'; alternatively, cutting-child or 'people who do sacrifice'.
'Tangsaland'	the hypothetical area in India where the Tangsa live today.
Tangwa	a term used for some Tangsa groups, see Chapter 3 for more.
'Tirap'	the area where the Tangsa live in Assam; most of it lies between the Buridihing and Tirap rivers.

Bibliography

Books and articles in Asamiya are underlined. Administrative Reports and Tour Diaries of British officers have been accessed at the State Archives in Itanagar and Guwahati.

ABSU. 1987. *Why Separate State?* Pamphlet. Kokrajhar: All Bodo Students Union (ABSU).

Abu-Lughod, Lila. 1991. 'Writing against Culture'. In *Recapturing Anthropology*, edited by Richard Fox. Santa Fe, NM: School of American Research Press, pp. 137–62.

Ahmed, Abu Nasar Said, ed. 2006. *Nationality Question in Assam: The EPW-Debate 1980-81*. New Delhi: OKISCD and Akansha Publishing House.

Aier, Anungla. 2004. 'Cultural Change among the Nagas: Festivals and Dress'. In *Naga Society: Continuity and Change*, edited by Neivetso Venuh. Delhi: Shipra Publications, pp. 49–59.

Ananthanarayanan, Sriram. 2010. 'Scheduled Tribe Status for Adivasis in Assam'. *South Asia: Journal of South Asian Studies* 33(2): 290–303.

Anderson, Benedict. 1983. *Imagined Communities: Reflections on the Origins and Spread of Nationalism*. London: Verso.

Ao, Temsula. 2006. 'Identity and Globalization: A Naga Perspective'. *Indian Folklife*. 22. Chennai: NFSC. pp. 6–7.

———. 2013 [2010]. 'Benevolent Subordination'. In *The Peripheral Centre: Voices from India's Northeast*, edited by Preeti Gill. New Delhi: Zubaan, pp. 123–32.

Assam Tribune (newspaper). P.G. Barua (ed.). Guwahati.

Austin, John. 1975 [1962]. *How to Do Things with Words*. Oxford: Oxford University Press.

Azara, Iride, and David Crouch. 2006. 'La Cavalcada Sarda: Performing Identities in a Contemporary Sardinian Festival'. In *Festivals, Tourism and Social Change*, edited by David Picard and Mike Robinson. Clevedon: Channel View Publications, pp. 123–32.

Babadzan, Alain. 2000. 'Anthropology, Nationalism and "The Invention of Tradition"'. *Anthropological Forum* 10(2): 131–55.

Bakhtin, Mikhail. 1984 [1968]. *Rabelais and His World*, translated by H. Iswolsky. Bloomington, IN: Indiana University Press.

Bal, Ellen. 2007a. *"They Ask if We Eat Frogs": Garo Ethnicity in Bangladesh*. Singapore/Leiden: ISEAS/IIAS.

———. 2007b. 'Becoming the Garos of Bangladesh: Policies of Exclusion and the Ethnicisation of a "Tribal" Minority'. *South Asia: Journal of South East Asian Studies* Special Issue, New Series XXX(3)Dec: 439–55.

———. 2010. 'Taking Root in Bangladesh: States, Minorities and Discourses of Citizenship'. *IIAS Newsletter* 53(Spring): 24–5.

Bal, Ellen and Timour Claquin Chambugong. 2014. 'The Borders that Divide, the Borders that Unite: (Re)interpreting Garo Processes of Identification in India and Bangladesh'. *Journal of Borderlands Studies* 29(1): 95–109.

Banks, Marcus. 1996. *Ethnicity: Anthropological Constructions*. London and New York: Routledge.

———. 2013. 'Post-Authenticity: Dilemmas of Identity in the 20th and 21st Centuries'. *Anthropological Quarterly* 86(2): 481–500.

Barkataki-Ruscheweyh, Meenaxi. 2013. 'Performing Identity: The Transformation of a Tangsa Festival in Assam, North-East India'. *Barkataki-Ruscheweyh & Lauser*. 241–58.

———. 2015. 'Best of all Worlds: Rangfraism—The New Institutionalized Religion of the Tangsa community in Northeast India'. Special issue, *International Quarterly for Asian Studies*/formerly *Asienforum*. titled *Contemporary Indigeneity and Religion in India*. G. Alles, Lidia Guzy, Uwe Skoda, and Ülo Valk (eds). 46(1–2): 149–67.

———. 2016. 'I[t] will never be the same again.' In *Doing Autoethnography*, edited by Q. Marak. New-Delhi: Serials, pp. 324–47.

———. In process. 'Fractured Christianity amongst the Tangsa in Northeast India—Bible Language Politics and the Charm of Ecstatic Experiences'.

Barkataki-Ruscheweyh, Meenaxi and Andrea Lauser, eds. 2013. *Performing Identity: Politics and Culture in Northeast India and Beyond*. Special Volume of *Asian Ethnology* 72(2).

Barkataki-Ruscheweyh, Meenaxi and S.D. Morey. 2013. 'Wihu Song of the Pangwa Tangsa: Poetry and Linguistic Forms, Meaning and the Transformation to a Symbol of Identity'. In *North East Indian Linguistics*, edited by G. Hyslop, S. Morey, and M. Post, Vol. 5. Delhi: Cambridge University Press, pp. 280–303.

Barpujari, S.K. 1984. 'Christianity and its Impact on the Nagas'. In *The Tribes of Northeast India*, edited by S. Karotemprel. Shillong: Vendrame Missiological Institute, Shillong, pp. 106–13.

Barth, Fredrik. 1998 [1969]. 'Introduction'. In *Ethnic Groups and Boundaries: The Social Organisation of Cultural Difference*, edited by Fredrik Barth. Long Grove, IL: Waveland Press, pp. 9–38.

Barua, Surendranath. 2013 [1991]. *Tribes of the Indo-Burma Border*. Guwahati: Bhabani.

Baruah, Sanjib. 2001 [1999]. *India Against Itself: Assam and the Politics of Nationality*. New Delhi: Oxford University Press.

———. 2004. 'Citizens and Denizens: Ethnicity, Homelands and the Crisis of Displacement in Northeast India'. *Social Change and Development* 2(1) (March): 105–30.

———. 2005. *Durable Disorder: Understanding the Politics of Northeast India*. New Delhi: Oxford University Press.

———. ed. 2009. *Beyond Counterinsurgency: Breaking the Impasse in Northeast India*. New Delhi: Oxford University Press.

———. 2010. "Indigenes and Interlopers." *Himal,* July 2010. http://old.himal-mag.com/component/content/article/213-indigenes-and-interlopers.html (accessed 28 December 2016).

———. 2012. 'The Rise and Decline of a Separatist Insurgency: Contentious Politics in Assam, India'. In *Autonomy and Ethnic Conflict in South and South-East Asia*, edited by Rajat Ganguly. London and New York: Routledge, pp. 27–45.

———. 2013. 'Politics of Territoriality: Indigeneity, Itinerancy and Rights in North-East India'. In *Territorial Changes and Territorial Restructurings in the Himalayas*, edited by Joelle Smajda. Delhi: Centre for Himalayan Studies, CNRS, France and Adroit Publishers, pp. 69–83.

Baumann, Gerd. 1999. *The Multicultural Riddle: Rethinking National, Ethnic and Religious Identities (Zones of Religion)*. New York and London: Routledge.

Behal, Rana P. 2014. *One Hundred Years of Servitude: Political Economy of Tea Plantations in Colonial Assam*. Delhi: Tulika Books.

Bennet, Andy, Jodie Taylor, and Ian Woodward, eds. 2014. *The Festivalization of Culture*. Farnham & Burlington: Ashgate.

Bennison, J.J. 1933. 'Report on the Census of Burma, 1931'. *Census of India, 1931*, Vol XI. Burma: Part I: Report. Rangoon: Office of the Supdt., Govt. Printing and Stationery, Burma.

Bentley, G. Carter. 1987. 'Ethnicity and Practice'. *Comparative Studies in Society and History* 29(1): 24–55.

Berger, Peter and Frank Heidemann, eds. 2013. *The Modern Anthropology of India: Ethnography, Themes and Theory*. London: Routledge.

Béteille, André. 1977. 'The Definition of Tribe'. In *Tribe, Caste and Religion in India*, edited by Romesh Thapar. Delhi: Macmillan, pp. 7–14.

Béteille, André. 1986. 'The Concept of Tribe with Special Reference to India'. *European Journal of Sociology* 27(2): 296–318.

———. 1998. 'The Idea of Indigenous People'. *Current Anthropology* 39(2) (April): 187–91.

Bhagabati, A.C. 1992. 'Tribal Transformation in Assam and North-east India: An Appraisal of Emerging Ideological Dimensions'. In *Tribal Transformation in India*, Vol. 3, edited by B. Chaudhuri. New Delhi: Inter-India Publications, pp. 487–509.

———. 2004. 'The Tribe as a Social Formation: The Case of the Tangsa in Arunachal Pradesh'. *Anthropology for North-east India: A Reader*, edited by A. Basu, B.K. Dasgupta, and J. Sarkar. Kolkata: INCAA, pp. 177–86.

Bhagabati, A.C. and S.K. Chaudhuri. 2008. 'Social Transformation Process in Arunachal Pradesh'. *Bulletin of the Department of Anthropology, Gauhati University* (Special Issue) 10: 15–24.

Bhattacharjee, Meenaxi. 2008. 'Problematising Identity in Assam'. Unpublished M.A. Thesis. University of Würzburg, Germany.

Bhattacharjee, T.K. 1987. *Alluring Frontiers*. New Delhi: Omson.

Bhattacharya, Rajeev. 2014. *Rendezvous with Rebels: Journey to meet India's most wanted men*. New York: HarperCollins.

Bhaumik, S. 2007. *Insurgencies in India's Northeast: Conflict, Co-option and Change*. Washington: East-West Center.

Bhuyan, Suryya Kumar, ed. 1932. *Tungkhungia Buranji; or, a History of Assam, 1681–1826 A.D.* Guwahati: Directorate of Historical and Antiquarian Studies.

Biswas, Prasenjit and Chandan Suklabaidya. 2008. *Ethnic Life Worlds in North-east India*. New Delhi: Sage Publications.

Blackburn, Stuart. 2010. *The Sun Rises: A Shaman's Chant, Ritual Exchange and Fertility in the Apatani valley*. Leiden/Boston: Brill.

Boal, Barbara M. 1982. *The Konds: Human Sacrifice and Religious Change.* Warminster: Aris and Phillips.

Bora, Borun, ed. 2012. *Patkair kase kase, Dihingor pare pare*. Ledo: Ledo Sahitya Sabha.

Borah, Tapan Kr. 1991. *The Tangsas*. Directorate of Research, Govt. of Arunachal Pradesh.

Borgohain, B.K. 1952. 'Tour Diary of the Political Officer, Tirap Frontier Tract'. (Files P 59/51 and P 22/52, Assam State Archives).

Borgohain, H. 1992. 'The Village Council and the Village Authorities of the Tangsas in Tradition and Transition'. *Resarun* xviii(1 and 2): 29–37.

Borneman, John and Abdellah Hammoudi. 2009. 'The Fieldwork Encounter, Experience, and the Making of Truth: An Introduction'. In *Being There: The Fieldwork Encounter and the Making of Truth*, edited by J. Borneman and A. Hammoudi. London: California University Press, pp. 1–24.

Borthakur, Raju. 2006. 'Winds of Change: *Arunachalee* in Tradition and Transition'. *Indian Folklife*, 22. Chennai: NFSC, pp. 8–9.

Bouchery, Pascal. 2007. 'Naga Ethnography and Leach's Oscillatory Model of *Gumsa* and *Gumlao*'. In *Social Dynamics in the Highlands of Southeast Asia: Reconsidering Political Systems of Highland Burma by E.R. Leach*, edited by François Robinne and Mandy Sadan. Leiden and Boston: Brill, pp.109–25.

Bourdieu, P. 1977. *Outline of a Theory of Practice*. Cambridge: Cambridge University Press.

Bourgois, Philippe. 1990. 'Confronting Anthropological Ethics: Ethnographic lessons from Central America'. *Journal of Peace Research* 27(1): 43–54.

Bradley, John. 2012. *Singing Saltwater Country: Journey to the Songlines of Carpentaria*. ReadHowYouWant.

Brass, Paul. 1991. *Ethnicity and Nationalism: Theory and Comparison*. New Delhi: Sage Publications.

Bräuchler, Birgit, and Thomas Widlok. 2007. 'The Revitalisation of Tradition'. *Zeitschrift fuer Ethnologie* 132: 5–14.

Brosius, Christiane and Ute Hüsken, eds. 2010. *Ritual Matters: Dynamic Dimensions in Practice*. New Delhi: Routledge.

Brosius, Christiane and Karin M. Polit, eds. 2011. *Ritual, Heritage and Identity: The Politics of Culture and Performance in a Globalised world*. New Delhi: Routledge.

Brown, David. 1994. *The State and Ethnic Politics in Southeast Asia*. London and New York: Routledge.

Brubaker, Rogers. 2004. *Ethnicity without Groups*. Cambridge: Harvard University Press.

Brubaker, Rogers and Frederick Cooper. 2000. 'Beyond "Identity"'. *Theory and Society* 29(1)2: 1–47.

Burling, Robbins. 1963. *Rengsanggri: Family and Kinship in a Garo Village*. Philadelphia: University of Pennsylvania Press.

———. 1967. 'Tribesmen and Lowlanders of Assam'. In *Southeast Asian Tribes, Minorities and Nations*, edited by Peter Kunstadter. Princeton: Princeton University Press, pp. 215–29.

———. 1982. 'The Sal Languages'. *Linguistics of the Tibeto-Burman Area* 7(2): 1–31.

———. 2003. 'The Tibeto-Burman Languages of Northeastern India'. *The Sino-Tibetan Languages*, edited by G. Thurgood and R. LaPolla. London: Routledge, pp. 169–91.

———. 2012. 'Where did the Question "Where Did My Tribe Come From?" Come From?'. In *Origins and Migrations in the Extended Eastern Himalayas*, edited by Toni Huber and Stuart Blackburn. Leiden and Boston: Brill, pp. 49–62.

Burma Report. 1942. *Brief Notes on the Naga Hills District (Burma) with Details of Routes*. Compiled in the Defence Dept., Govt. of Burma. Simla: Govt. of India Press.

Butler, Harcourt. 1925. 'Report on My Visit to the Hukawng Valley and the Arrangements Made and Proposed to Abolish Slavery and End Human Sacrifice'. No. 366B-22. India Office files P&J 2463 /1925 and P&J 3066/1925. Rangoon, 12 February 1925.

Cantile, Audrey. 1984. *The Assamese: Religion, Caste and Sect in an Indian Village*. London: Curzon.

Cannell, Fenella. 2006. 'Introduction'. In *The Anthropology of Christianity*, edited by Fenella Cannell. Durham and London: Duke University Press. pp. 1–50.

Census of India (various years). New Delhi: Government of India, Office of the Registrar General and Census Commissioner, India.

Chakravorty, B.C. 1981 [1964]. *British Relations with the Hill Tribes of Assam since 1858*. Calcutta: Firma KLM Pvt. Ltd.

Changmai, Jagat. 2003. *Singpho Jati aru Bisa rojar Itibritta*. np: Muingdam Gam.

———. 2012. *Patkair premot bondi tinita jonogsothi aru kaitaman sketch*. Ledo: Ledo Sahitya Sabha.

Chatterjee, Suniti Kumar. 1955. *The Place of Assam in the History and Civilization of India*. Gauhati: Gauhati University.

Chaudhuri, Sarit Kr. 2013. 'The Institutionalization of Tribal Religion: Recasting the Donyi-Polo Movement in Arunachal Pradesh'. *Barkataki-Ruscheweyh & Lauser*, pp. 259–77.

Chit Hlaing (F.K. Lehman). 2007. 'Introduction: Notes on Edmund Leach's Analysis of Kachin Society and Its Further Applications'. In *Social Dynamics in the Highlands of Southeast Asia: Reconsidering Political Systems of Highland Burma by E.R. Leach*, edited by François Robinne and Mandy Sadan. Leiden and Boston: Brill, pp. xxi–lii.

———. 2012. 'Oral Histories and the "Origins" of Current Peoples: Dynamic Ethnogenesis, with Remarks upon the Limitations of Language-Family Subgrouping'. In *Origins and Migrations in the Extended Eastern Himalayas*, edited by Toni Huber and Stuart Blackburn. Leiden and Boston: Brill, pp. 239–52.

Chowdhury, Urmi. 1987. 'A Study of the Traditional Religion of the Tangsas in Two Villages in Tirap District, Arunachal Pradesh'. PhD Diss. Gauhati University.

Chua, Glen. Unpublished. 'Evangelizing in the Borderland: Christian Tribals and Migrant Others in Meghalaya'. Working Paper, presented at the *Negotiating Ethnicity* Conference, Vienna, June 2013.

Clifford, James. 1986. 'Introduction: Partial Truths'. In *Writing Culture: The Poetics and Politics of Ethnography*, edited by James Clifford and Goerge E. Marcus. Berkeley and London: University of California Press, pp. 1–26.

———. 1988. *The Predicament of Culture: Twentieth Century Ethnography, Literature and Art*. Cambridge: Harvard University Press.

Cobo, José R. Martínez. 1986. *The Study of the Problem of Discrimination against Indigenous Populations (Conclusions)*. New York: United Nations. [UN Document E/CN.4/Sub.2/1986/7/Add.4.]

Cohen, Abner. 1969. 'Political Anthropology: the Analysis of the Symbolism of Power Relations'. *Man* 4(2): 215–35.

———. 1981. *The Politics of Elite Culture: Explorations in the Dramaturgy of Power in a Modern African Society*. Berkeley: University of California Press.

Cohen, Anthony P. 2003. *The Symbolic Construction of Community*. London: Routledge.

Cohen, Erik. 1988. Authenticity and Commoditization of Tourism. *Annals of Tourism Research*. 15: 371–86.

Cohn, Bernard S. 1987. *An Anthropologist among the Historians and Other Essays*. New Delhi: Oxford University Press.

Colson, Elisabeth. 1996. 'The Bantu Botatwe: Changing Political Definitions in Southern Zambia'. In *The Politics of Cultural Performance*, edited by David Parkin, Lionel Caplan, and Humphrey Fischer. Oxford: Berghahn Books, pp. 61–80.

Comaroff, J. and J. Comaroff. 1991. *Of Revelation and Revolution Volume 1: Christianity, Colonialism, and Consciousness in South Africa*. Illinois, Chicago: University of Chicago Press.

———. 1997. *Of Revelation and Revolution Volume II: The Dialectics of Modernity on a South African Frontier*. Chicago: University of Chicago Press.

———. 2009. *Ethnicity Inc*. Illinois, Chicago: University of Chicago Press.

Das, Debojyoti. 2014. 'The Construction and Institutionalisation of Ethnicity: Anthropology, Photography and the Nagas'. *The South Asianist* 3(1): 28–49.

Das, Murlidhar. 2011. 'Etiya Rhan-rhing-kanot malou paharor Tangsa.' *Pratidin Enajori*. 28 May.

Das, N.K. 2011. 'Naga Peace Parleys: Sociological Reflections and a Plea for Pragmatism'. *Economic and Political Weekly* xlvi(25) (18 June): 70–7.

Dasgupta, J. 1997. 'Community, Authenticity and Autonomy: Insurgency and Institutional Development in India's Northeast'. *Journal of Asia Studies* 56(2): 345–70.

Das Gupta, K. 1978. "A Note on the Tangsa language." *Resarun*, IV (2). Journal of the Research Department. Shillong: Directorate of Research, Govt. of Arunachal Pradesh. 6–16.

———. 1980. *The Tangsa Language (a Synopsis)*. Shillong:

Dasgupta, Pranab Kr. 1991. 'Ethnicity and Boundary Maintenance in a Poly-ethnic Situation'. In *Stratification, Hierarchy and Ethnicity in north-east India*, edited by R.K. Bhadra and S.K. Mondal. New Delhi: Daya Publishing House, pp.177–88.

Dai, Mamang. 2013 [2010]. 'Arunachal Pradesh—The Insurgency Scene'. In *The Peripheral Centre: Voices from India's Northeast*, edited by Preeti Gill. New Delhi: Zubaan, pp. 80–94.

De Maaker, Erik. 2012. 'Have the *Mitdes* Gone Silent? Conversion, Rhetoric, and the Continuing Importance of the lower deities in Northeast India'. In *Conversion to Christianity in Modern Asia*, edited by Richard Fox Young, and Jonathan Seitz. Leiden: Brill, pp. 135–59.

———. 2013. 'Performing the Garo Nation? Garo Wangala Dancing between Faith and Folklore'. *Barkataki-Ruscheweyh & Lauser*, pp. 221–39.

De Maaker, Erik, F. Dubois, K. Polit, and M. Riphagen. 2011. 'From Rituals Ground to Stage'. In *Ritual, Media and Conflict*, edited by R.L. Grimes, U. Hüsken, U. Simon, and E. Venbrux. Oxford and New York: Oxford University Press, pp. 35–61.

De Maaker, Erik and Vibha Joshi. 2007. 'Introduction: The Northeast and Beyond: Region and Culture'. Special Issue, *South Asia: Journal of South East Asian Studies*, n.s. XXX(3)(December): 381–90.

De Maaker, Erik and Marcus Schleiter. 2010. 'Indigeneity as a Cultural Practice: "Tribe" and the State in India'. *IIAS Newsletter* 53(Spring): 16–17.

Deka, Kaustubh. 2014. 'The Politics of Student Movements: Limits and Possibilities with Special Reference to Assam, 1985–2010'. PhD Diss., Jawaharlal Nehru University, New Delhi.

———. Under review. 'Epochs of "ethnic massacre": The State and the framing of the "ethnic other" in Assam'. In *Geographies of Difference: Explorations in Northeast Indian Studies*, edited by Mélanie Vandenhelsken, Meenaxi Barkataki-Ruscheweyh, and B.G. Karlsson.

Dewar, T. P. 1927. *Report on the Naga Hills (Burma) Expedition for the Abolition of Human Sacrifice. Season 1926–27*. Rangoon: Office of the Superintendent Govt. Printing and Stationery, Burma.

———. 1931. 'Naga Tribes and their Customs. A General Description of the Naga Tribes Inhabiting the Burma Side of the Patkoi Range'. *Census 1931. XI. Report, App.*

Dollfus, Pascale and Jacquesson François. 2013. *Khiksaba. A Festival in Sherdukpen Country (Arunachal Pradesh, North-East India)*. Guwahati and Delhi: Spectrum Publications.

Douglas, Gavin. 2013. 'Performing Ethnicity in Southern Shan State, Burma/ Myanmar: The *Ozi* and Gong Tradition of the *Myelat*'. *Ethnomusicology* 57(2): 185–206.

Downs, F.S. 1976. *Christianity in North east India*. Delhi: Ispeck.

Duncan, Christopher R. 2004. 'Legislating Modernity among the Marginalised'. *Civilizing the Margins: Southeast Asian Government Policies for the Development of Minorities*, edited by Christopher R. Duncan, London and Ithaca: Cornell University Press, pp. 1–23.

Durkheim, Émile. 1995 [1912]. *The Elementary Forms of the Religious Life*. Translated by Karen E. Fields. New York: The Free Press.

Dutta, Dibyalata, ed. 2011. *Ronrang sokolor itihaax aru xadhokotha*. Jorhat: Barkataki and Co.

Dutta, Parul. 1969. *The Tangsas of the Namchik and Tirap Valleys*. Shillong: NEFA.

Dutta, Uddipan. 2009. *Creating Robin Hoods: The Insurgency of ULFA in Its Early Period, Its Parallel Administration and the Role of Assamese Vernacular Press (1985–1990)*. New Delhi: WISCOMP.

Eaton, R.M. 1997. 'Comparative History as World History: Religious Conversion in Modern India'. *Journal of World History* 8(2): 243–71.

Ebron, Paulla. 2002. *Performing Africa*. Princeton: Princeton University Press.

Elwin, Verrier. 1964 [1957]. *A Philosophy for NEFA*. Shillong: NEFA.

———. 1965. *Democracy in NEFA*. Shillong: NEFA.

Endle, Sidney. 1911. *The Kacharis*. London: Macmillan and Co.

Eriksen, Thomas Hylland. 2010 [1994]. *Ethnicity and Nationalism: Anthropological Perspectives*. London: Pluto Press.

Evans, Nicholas. 2009. *Dying Words: Endangered Languages and What They Have to Tell Us*. Oxford: John Wiley and Sons.

Falassi, A. 1987. 'Festival definition and morphology'. In *Time out of Time: Essays on the Festival*, edited by A. Falassi. Albuquerque, NM: University of New Mexico Press, pp. 1–10.

Farrelly, Nicholas. 2009a. '"Ak47/M16 Rifle – Rs. 15,000 Each": What Price Peace on the Indo-Burmese Frontier?' *Contemporary South Asia* 18(3): 283–97.

———. 2009b. 'Tai Community and Thai Border Subversions'. In *Tai Lands and Thailand: Community and State in Southeast Asia*, edited by Andrew Walker. Singapore: National University of Singapore Press, pp. 67–86.

———. 2013. 'Nodes of Control in a South(east) Asian Borderland'. In *Borderland Lives in Northern South Asia*, edited by David Gellner. Durham and London: Duke University Press, pp. 194–213.

Fiske, John. 1996. 'Opening the Hallway: Some Remarks on the Fertility of Stuart Hall's Contribution to Critical Theory'. In *Stuart Hall: Critical Dialogues in Cultural Studies*, edited by David Morley and Kuan-Hsing Chen. London: Routledge, pp. 212–20.

Franke, Marcus. 2009. *War and Nationalism in South Asia*. London and New York: Routledge.

Furniss, Eliszabeth. 1998. 'Cultural Performance as Strategic Essentialism: Negotiating Indianness in a Western Canadian Rodeo Festival'. *Humanities Research* 3: 23–40.

Gait, Edward. 2003 [1905]. *A History of Assam*. New Delhi: Surjeet Publications.

Galanter, M. 1991 [1984]. *Competing Equalities. Law and the Backward Classes in India*. New Delhi: Oxford University Press.

Gazetteer. 1980. *Tirap District Gazetteer*, edited by S. Dutta Chowdhury. Govt. of Arunachal Pradesh.

Gazetteer. 2010. *State Gazetteer of Arunachal Pradesh* (Vol. I), edited by Sokhep Kri. Govt. of Arunachal Pradesh, Gazetteers Dept.

Geertz, Clifford. 2000 [1973]. 'Thick Description: Toward an Interpretative Theory of Culture'. In *The Interpretation of Cultures*, edited by Clifford Geertz. New York: Basic Books, pp. 3–30.

Gellner, David N. 2009. 'Introduction: How Civil are "Communal" and Ethnonationalist Movements?' In *Ethnic Activism and Civil Society in South Asia*, edited by David N.Gellner. New Delhi: Sage Publications, pp. 1–24.

———. ed. 2013. *Borderland Lives in Northern South Asia*. Durham and London: Duke University Press.

Gertz, D. 1991. *Festivals, Special Events and Tourism*. New York: Van Nostrand Reinhold.

———. 1994. 'Event Tourism and the Authenticity Dilemma'. In *Global Tourism*, edited by W.F. Theobald. Oxford: Butterworth–Heinemann, pp. 409–27.

Gluckman, M. 1958 [1940]. 'Analysis of a Social Situation in Modern Zululand'. *Rhodes-Livingstone Papers* No. 28. Manchester: Manchester University Press.

GoA. 1990. *Land Administration in Protected Belts and Blocks*. Dispur: Government of Assam.

Goffman, E. 1974. *Frame Analysis. An Essay on the Organisation of Experience*. Cambridge: Harvard University Press.

Gogoi, Sadhan. 2012. '<u>Rhan-ring-kane ringiyai</u>'. In *Saukan giri-pathar akhe-pakhe*, edited by Latumoni Gogoi. Ledo: Ledo Sahitya Sabha, pp. 120–34.

GoI. 2005. *National Commission for Scheduled Tribes: a Handbook*. New Delhi: Government of India.

Goswami, Namrata. 2011. 'Armed Ethnic Conflicts in Northeast India and the Indian State's Response: Use of Force and the "Notion" of Proportionality'. Working Paper no. 60, Heidelberg Papers in South Asian and Comparative Politics. March 2011. [http://hpsacp.uni-hd.de].

———. 2012a. 'Naga Armed Factionalism Back to Centre-Stage Once Again'. IDSA Publications 29 June 2012. Available at http://idsa.in/idsacomments/NagaArmedFactionalismBacktoCentreStageOnceAgain_NamrataGoswami_290612.

———. 2012b. 'The Naga Armed Conflict: Is a Resolution Finally Here?' IDSA Publication, 8 November 2012. Available at http://www.idsa.in/idsacomments/TheNagaArmedConflictIsaResolutionFinallyHere_ngoswami_081112 (Accessed 1.01.2017).

———. 2014. 'Naga Identity—Ideals, Parallels, and Reality'. The Hindu Centre for Politics and Public Policy, 16 June 2014. Available at http://www.thehinducentre.com/the-arena/current-issues/article6114531.ece (accessed 9 August 2014.

Goswami, Uddipana. 2014. *Conflict and Reconciliation: The Politics of Ethnicity in Assam*. New Delhi: Routledge.

Gravers, Mikael, ed. 2007. *Exploring Ethnic Diversity in Burma*. NIAS Studies in Asian Topics Series, 39. Copenhagen: NIAS Press.

Grierson, George Abraham. 1903. *Linguistic Survey of India*. 11 Vols in 19 Parts. Delhi: Low Price Publ. (2005). Searchable Database at http://www.joao-roiz.jp/LSI/.

Gross, Toomas. 2011. 'Divided over Tourism: Zapotec Responses to Mexico's "Magical Villages" Program'. *Anthropological Notebooks: Slovene Anthropological Society* 17(3): 51–71.

Gupta, Akhil and James Ferguson. 1997. 'Discipline and Practice: "The Field" as Site, Method and Location in Anthropology'. In *Anthropological Locations: Boundaries and Grounds of a Field Science*, edited by A. Gupta and James Ferguson. Berkeley, Los Angeles, and London: University of California Press, pp. 1–46.

Gurdon, P.R.T. 1904. 'The Morans'. *Journal of the Asiatic Society of Bengal* 73: 36–48.

Guss, David. 2000. *The Festive State: Race, Ethnicity, and Nationalism as Cultural Performance*. London: University of California Press.

Haksar, Nandita. 2013. *Across the Chicken Neck: Travels in Northeast India*. Delhi: Rainlight Rupa.

Hale, Charles. 2006. 'Activist Research vs. Cultural Critique: Indigenous Land Rights and the Contradictions of Politically Engaged Anthropology'. *Cultural Anthropology* 21(1): 96–120.

Hall, D.G.E. 1955. *A History of South East Asia*. New York: St. Martin's Press.

Hall, Stuart. 1986. 'On Postmodernism and Articulation. An Interview with Stuart Hall', edited by Lawrence Grossberg. *Journal of Communication Inquiry* 10(2): 45–60.

———. 1991 'Old and New Identities, and New Ethnicities'. *Culture, Globalization and the World-System*, edited by Anthony D. King. London: Macmillan, pp. 41–68.

———. 1996a. 'Introduction: Who Needs "Identity"?' In *Questions of Cultural Identity*, edited by Stuart Hall and Paul du Gay. London: Sage Publications, pp. 1–17.

———. 1996b. 'The Question of Cultural Identity'. In *Modernity: An Introduction to Modern Societies*, edited by Stuart Hall, David Held, Don Hubert, and Kenneth Thompson. Cambridge, MA: Blackwell, pp. 595–634.

Handelman, Don. 1990. *Models and Mirrors: Towards an Anthropology of Public Events*. Cambridge: Cambridge University Press.

Handler, Richard. 1994. 'Is "Identity" a Useful Cross-Cultural Concept?'. In *Commemorations. The Politics of Nation and Identity*, edited by J. Gillis. Princeton: Princeton University Press, pp. 27–40.

Handler, Richard. 2011. 'The "Ritualisation of Ritual" in the Construction of Heritage'. In *Ritual, Heritage and Identity: The Politics of Culture and Performance in a Globalised world*, edited by Christiane Brosius and Karin M. Polit. New Delhi: Routledge, pp. 39–54.

Hanson, O. 1906. *A Dictionary of the Kachin Language*. Rangoon: Baptist Board of Publications.

Harnish, David. 2005. 'New Lines, Shifting Identities: Interpreting Change at the Lingsar Festival in Lombok, Indonesia'. *Ethnomusicology* 49(1) (Winter): 1–24.

Harowitz, Donald. 1981. 'Ethnic Identity'. *Ethnicity: Theory and Experience*. Nathan Glazer and Daniel Patrick Moynihan (eds). Cambridge and London: Harvard University Press, pp. 111–40.

Harth, Dietrich. 2006. 'Rituals and other Forms of Social Action'. In *Theorising Rituals: Issues, Topics, Approaches, Concepts*, edited by Jens Kreinath, Jan Snoek, and Michael Stausberg. Leiden and Boston: Brill, pp. 15–36.

Hayes, Ben. 2012. *The Other Burma? Conflict, Counter-insurgency and Human Rights in Northeast India*. Amsterdam: Transnational Institute.

Hazarika, Sanjoy. 1995. *Strangers in the Mist: Tales of War and Peace from India's Northeast*. New Delhi: Penguin.

———. 2000. *Rites of Passage: Border Crossings, Imagined Homelands, India's East and Bangladesh*. New Delhi: Penguin.

Hobsbawm, Eric. 1983. 'Introduction: Inventing Traditions'. In *The Invention of Tradition*, edited by Eric Hobsbawm and Terence Ranger. Cambridge: Cambridge University Press, pp. 1–14.

Hobsbawm, Eric and Terence Ranger, eds. 1983. *The Invention of Tradition*. Cambridge: Cambridge University Press.

Huber, Toni. 2012. 'Micro-migrations of Hill Peoples in Northern Arunachal Pradesh: Rethinking Methodologies and Claims of Origins in Tibet'. In *Origins and Migrations in the Extended Eastern Himalayas*, edited by Toni Huber and Stuart Blackburn. Leiden and Boston: Brill, pp. 83–106.

Huber, Toni and Stuart Blackburn, eds. 2012. *Origins and Migrations in the Extended Eastern Himalayas*. Leiden and Boston: Brill.

Hussain, Monirul, ed. 2005. *Coming out of Violence: Essays on Ethnicity, Conflict Resolution and Peace Processes in North-east India*. New Delhi: Regency Publications.

Hutton, J.H. 1921. *The Sema Nagas*. London: Macmillan and Co.

———. 1928. The Significance of Head-Hunting in Assam. *Journal of the Royal Anthropological Institute* 58 (July–December): 399–408.

Iralu, Kaka D. 2005. 'The Fifty-four year old Indo-Naga Conflict'. In *Coming out of Violence: Essays on Ethnicity, Conflict Resolution and Peace Processes in North-east India*, edited by Monirul Hussain. New Delhi: Regency Publications, pp. 170–96.

Jaarsma, Sjoerd, ed. 2002. *Handle with Care: Ownership and Control of Ethnographic Materials*. Pittsburgh: University of Pittsburgh Press.

Jackson, Michael. 1989. *Paths towards a Clearing: Radical Empiricism and Ethnographic Enquiry*. Bloomington: Indiana University Press.

Jacob, J.F.R. 1997. 'India's troubled North-east: Countering Insurgency and Winning Hearts and Minds'. *Peace Initiatives*, Vol. III, No. III May–June. New Delhi: International Centre for Peace Initiatives.

Jacquesson, François. 2008. 'The Speed of Language Change, Typology and History: Languages, Speakers and Demography in North-Eastern India'. In *Past Human Migrations in East Asia: Matching Archaeology, Linguistics and Genetics*, edited by A. Sanchez-Mazas, R. Blench, M.D. Ross, I. Peiros, and M. Lin. London: Routledge, pp. 287–309.

Jenkins, Richard. 1994. 'Rethinking Ethnicity: Identity, Categorization and Power'. *Ethnic and Racial Studies* 17(2): 197–223.

Jones, Delmos J. 1970. 'Towards a Native Anthropology'. *Human Organisation* 29(4) (Winter): 251–9.

Jonsson, Hjorleifur. 2001. 'Serious Fun: Minority Cultural Dynamics and National Integration in Thailand'. *American Ethnologist* 28(1): 151–78.

———. 2005. *Mien Relations: Mountain People and State Control in Thailand*. Cornell: Cornell University Press.

———. 2010. 'Mimetic Minorities: National Identity and Desire on Thailand's Fringe'. *Identities* 17(2): 108–30.

Joram, Rina. 2001. 'Conversion in Arunachal Pradesh—A Study with Reference to Crisis'. *Resarun* 27: 180–4.

Joshi, Vibha. 2007. 'The Birth of Christian Enthusiasm among the Angami of Nagaland'. *South Asia: Journal of South Asian Studies* xxx(3) (December): 541–57.

———. 2012. *A Matter of Belief: Christian Conversion and Healing in North-East India*. Oxford: Berghahn Books.

———. 2013. 'The Micropolitics of Borders: The Issue of Greater Nagaland (Nagalim)'. In *Borderland Lives in Northern South Asia*, edited by David Gellner. Durham and London: Duke University Press, pp. 163–93.

Karlsson, Bengt G. 2000. *Contested Belonging: Indigenous People's Struggle for Forest and Identity in Sub-Himalayan Bengal*. London: Routledge Curzon.

———. 2001. 'Indigenous Politics: Community Formation and Indigenous People's Struggle for Self-determination in Northeast India'. *Identities* 8(1): 7–45.

———. 2003. '"Anthropology and the Indigenous Slot": Claims to Debates about Indigenous Peoples' Status in India'. *Critique of Anthropology* 23(4): 403–23.

———. 2011. *Unruly Hills: Nature and Nation in India's Northeast*. New Delhi: Orient Blackswan and Social Science Press.

———. 2013. 'Evading the State: Ethnicity in Northeast India through the Lens of James Scott'. *Barkataki-Ruscheweyh & Lauser*, pp. 321–31.

Keesing, Roger M. 1989. 'Creating the Past: Custom and Identity in the Contemporary Pacific'. *The Contemporary Pacific* 1(1 and 2): 19–42.

Kenglang, Maipa. 2002. 'A Study of Social Relations among Three Subgroups of Tangsa'. M.Phil. Diss., Rajiv Gandhi University, Itanagar.

Kertzer, David. 1988. *Ritual, Politics and Power*. New York: Yale University.

Khilnani, Sunil. 1999. *The Idea of India*. New York: Farrar, Straus and Giroux.

Khimhun, L. 2006. *The Second Coming of Rangfraa*. Changlang: RFPS.

Kimura, Makiko. 2013. *The Nellie Massacre of 1983: Agency of Rioteers*. New Delhi: Sage Publications.

Kingdon-Ward, F. 1955. 'Aftermath of the Great Assam Earthquake of 1950'. *The Geographical Journal* 121(3) (September): 290–303.

Kotwal, Dinesh. 2000. 'The Naga Insurgency: the Past and the Future'. *Strategic Analysis* 24(4): 751–72.

Kumar, B.B. 2005. *Naga Identity*. New Delhi: Concept Publishers.

Kunstadter, Peter, ed. 1967. *Southeast Asian Tribes, Minorities and Nations*. Princeton: Princeton University Press.

Lassiter, Luke Eric. 2005. *The Chicago Guide to Collaborative Ethnography*. Chicago and London: University of Chicago Press.

Leach, E.R. 1954. *Political Systems of Highland Burma: a Study of Kachin Social Structure*. London: G. Bell and Sons.

Linnekin, Jocelyn. 1992. 'On the Theory and Politics of Cultural Construction in the Pacific'. In *The Politics of Tradition in the Pacific*, edited by Margaret Jolly and Nicholas Thomas. Special Issue *Oceania* 62(4): 249–63.

Lintner, Bertil. 1996. *Land of Jade: A Journey from India through Northern Burma to China*. Thailand: Orchid Press.

Litzinger, Ralph A. 2000. *Other Chinas: The Yao and the Politics of National Belonging*. Durham and London: Duke University Press.

Longchar, A. Wati, ed. 1985. *Encounter between Gospel and Tribal Culture*. Jorhat: Tribal Study Centre.

Longkumer, Arkotong. 2010. *Reform, Identity and Narratives of Belonging: The Heraka Movement of Northeast India*. London and New York: Continuum.

———. 2015. '"As Our Ancestors Once Lived": Representation, Performance and Constructing a National Culture amongst the Nagas of India'. *Himalaya*, the Journal of the Association for Nepal and Himalayan Studies 35(1): 51–64. Available at http://digitalcommons.macalester.edu/himalaya/vol35/iss1/10.

Lotha, Abraham. 2008. 'Naga Identity: Enduring Heritage'. In *Naga Identities: Changing Local Cultures in the Northeast of India*, edited by Michael Oppitz, Thomas Kaiser, Alban von Stockhausen, Rebekka Sutter, and Marion Wettstein. Gent: Snoeck Publishers, pp. 57–96.

Lyngdoh, Margaret. 2016. 'Transformation, Tradition, and lived Realities: Vernacular Belief Worlds of the Khasis of Northeastern India.' Unpublished PhD. Dissertation. University of Tartu.

Lyndoh, Mary Priscilla Rina. 1991. *The Festivals in the History and Culture of the Khasi*. New Delhi: Har Anand Publications and Vikas Publishing House.

MacCannell, Dean. 1976. *The Tourist: A New Theory of the Leisure Class*. London: Macmillan.

Mackenzie, Alexander. 2012 [1884]. *History of Relations of the Government with the Hill tribes of Northeast Frontier of Bengal*. Delhi: Mittal Publications.

Magliocco, S. 2001. 'Coordinates of Power and Performance. Festivals as Sites of (Re)presentation and Reclamation in Sardinia'. *Ethnologies* 23(1): 167–88.

Mahanta, Juri. 2011. *Singphos of North-east India*. Guwahati: DVS Publishers.

Mahanta-Kalita, Inoo. 2012. 'Buridihing Upotyokar Bikhipta Itihas.' *Ledo*, Souvenir of the Ledo Sahitya Sabha, Ledo, pp. 184–5.

Malinowski, Bronislaw. 1922. *Argonauts of the Western Pacific*. London: George Routledge and Sons; New York: E.P. Dutton and Company.

Marcus, George E. 1995. 'Ethnography in/of the World System: The Emergence of Multi-sited Ethnography'. *Annual Review of Anthropology* 24: 95–117.

Mauss, Marcel. 1990 [1925]. *The Gift* [Original title *Essai sur le don. Forme et raison de l'échange dans les sociétés archaïques* ('An Essay on the Gift: The Form and Reason of Exchange in Archaic Societies') Originally published in *L'Année Sociologique* in 1925. Republished in French in 1950 and translated into English in 1954, first, by Ian Cunnison and in 1990 by W.D. Halls.

Means, Gordon P. 2000. 'Human Sacrifice and Slavery in the 'Unadministered' Areas of Upper Burma during the Colonial Era'. *Sojourn: Journal of Social Issues in Southeast Asia* 15(2) (October): 184–221.

Memorandum. 2004. Submitted by Tirap Autonomous District Council Demand Committee, HQ. Bisa.

Mepfhü-o, Ketholenuo. 2016. 'Conversion: perception of the Christian "self" and the "other"'. In *Fluid Attachments in Northeast India*, edited by Mélanie Vandenhelsken, B.G. Karlsson, and Jürgen Schöpf. Special Issue of *Asian Ethnicity* 17(3): 370–83. [DOI: 10.1080/14631369.2015.1091652, http://dx.doi.org/10.1080/14631369.2015.1091652]

Mibang, T. 1989. 'The origin and role of the Kotokis'. *Resarun* XV(1 and 2): 45–9.

Michaud, Jean. 2010. 'Editorial—Zomia and Beyond'. *Journal of Global History* 5(2): 187–214.

Middleton, T. 2013. 'States of Difference: Refiguring Ethnicity and its "Crisis" at India's Borders. ' *Political Geography* 35 (July) (Special Issue: Geographies at the Margins: Interrogating Borders in South Asia): 14–24.

Mills, J.P. 1995. *The Pangsha Letters: An Expedition to Rescue Slaves in the Naga Hills*. Oxford: Pitt Rivers Museum.

Misra, Udayon. 2000. *The Periphery Strikes Back: Challenges to the Nation-state in Assam and Nagaland*. Shimla: Indian Institute of Advanced Study.

Mitchell, H.J. 1929. 'Report on the Naga Hills (Upper Chindwin) Expedition for the Release of Slaves and the Suppression of Human Sacrifice (15th December 1928 to 14th April 1929)'. India Office file P&J 2966/1929. Maymyo: Government Branch Press, 1929.

Moerman, Michael. 1993. 'Ariadne's Thread and Indra's Net: Reflections on Ethnography, Ethnicity, Identity, Culture and Interaction'. *Research on Language and Social Interaction* 26(1): 85–98.

Morang, H.K. (translated by Luit Pathak). 2008. *Tangsas—The Children of Masui Singrapum*, edited by D. Dutta. Guwahati: Aank-baak.

Morey, S.D. 2011. 'Tangsa Agreement Markers'. *North East Indian Linguistics*, 3, edited by G. Hyslop, S. Morey, and M. Post. New Delhi: Cambridge University Press India, pp. 76–101.

———. 2012. Workshop presentation. 'Can a "Common Language" Work for the Tangsa? The Problems of Language Standardisation in Linguistically Diverse Communities'. Paper presented at a workshop titled 'Linguistic diversity in a globalised world: Perspectives on language use and standardisation for marginalised, transnational and diasporic languages' held at Centre for Research on Language Diversity, La Trobe University, 17–18 December 2012.

———. 2014. 'Ahom and Tangsa: Case Studies of Language Maintenance and Loss in North East India'. Language Documentation and Conservation Special Publication No. 7 (January 2014) *Language Endangerment and Preservation in South Asia*, edited by Hugo C. Cardoso. pp. 46–77. Honolulu: University of Hawai'i Press.

Morey, S.D. and Jürgen Schöpf. under review. 'The Language of Ritual in Tangsa—The Wihu Song'. *Ritual Speech in the Himalayas: Oral Texts and their Contexts*, edited by Martin Gaenszle et al.

Mossang, Komoli. 1983. 'Review of "The Tangsas" by Parul Dutta'. *Arunachal News* (April–May 1983).

Nag, Sajal. 2002. *Contesting Marginality: Ethnicity, Insurgency and Subnationalism in North-east India*. New Delhi: Manohar.

Nag, Sajal. 2016. *The Uprising: Colonial state, Christian Missionaries and Anti-Slavery Movement in North-East India (1908–1954)*. New Delhi: Oxford University Press.

Nair, P.T. 1985. *Tribes of Arunachal Pradesh*. Guwhati: Spectrum Publications.

Narayan, Kirin. 1993. 'How Native is a "Native" Anthropologist?' *American Anthropologist* 95(3) (n.s.): 671–86.

Nath, Lopita. 2006. 'Migration, Insecurity and Identity: The Nepali Dairymen in India's Northeast'. *Asian Ethnicity* 7(2): 129–48.

Nath, Palash. 2013. 'A Multilingual Education Programme for the Singpho Language in Northeast India'. PhD Diss., Gauhati University.

Nayak, Prasanta Kumar. 2011. 'The Dialectics of Globalisation in Arunachal Pradesh'. *Economic and Political Weekly* xlvi(26 and 27) (25 June): 263–7.

Neog, A.K. 1999. 'Constitutional Safeguards to Scheduled Tribes and Scheduled Castes'. *Bulletin of the Assam Institute of Research for Tribals and Scheduled Castes* I(xii): 18–23.

Ngo, Tam T.T. 2009. 'The Short-Waved Faith: Christian Broadcastings and the Transformation of the Spiritual Landscape of the Hmong in Northern Vietnam'. In *Mediated Piety: Technology and Religion in Contemporary Asia*, edited by K.G. Francis and Lim. Leiden: Brill, pp. 139–58.

Ningkhi, Rajib. 2009. 'Tirap Simanta: Jibon, Sahitya aru Sangram'. In *Janajati Saurav*, edited by Paim Thi Gohain. Dibrugarh: Tribal Research Dept. Sonowal Kachari Autonomous Council, pp. 345–50.

Nongkynrih, A.K. 2010. 'Scheduled Tribes and the Census: a Sociological Enquiry'. *Economic and Political Weekly* XLV(19) (8 May): 43–7.

Nutini, Hugo G. 2004. *The Mexican Aristocracy: An Expressive Ethnography 1910–2000*. Austin: University of Texas Press.

O' Callaghan, T.P.M. 1923. 'Tour Diaries of the Political Officer, Sadiya Frontier Tract for 1923'. (Pol 312/1923, Pol 46/1922, Assam State Archives).

———. 1926. 'Notes on the Rangpang Naga'. Part of *Annual Administrative Report* for the year 1925–26 of the Sadiya Frontier Tract (*Report* 1926). [Included as Appendix.]

Oppitz, Michael, Thomas Kaiser, Alban von Stockhausen, Rebekka Sutter, and Marion Wettstein, eds. 2008. *Naga Identities: Changing Local Cultures in the Northeast of India*. Gent: Snoeck Publishers.

Oppitz, Michael, Thomas Kaiser, Alban von Stockhausen, Rebekka Sutter, and Marion Wettstein. 2008. 'The Nagas: An Introduction'. In *Naga Identities: Changing Local Cultures in the Northeast of India*, edited by Michael Oppitz, Thomas Kaiser, Alban von Stockhausen, Rebekka Sutter, and Marion Wettstein. Gent: Snoeck Publishers, pp. 11–28.

Otto, Ton and Poul Pedersen. 2005. 'Disentangling Traditions: Culture, Agency and Power'. In *Tradition and Agency. Tracing Cultural Continuity and Invention*, edited by Ton Otto and Poul Pedersen. Aarhus: Aarhus University Press, pp. 11–49.

Pachuau, Joy L.K. 2014. *Being Mizo: Identity and Belonging in Northeast India*. New Delhi: Oxford University Press.

Pachuau, L. 1997. 'In Search of a Context for a Contextual Theology: the Socio-political Realities of "Tribal" Christians in Northeast India'. *National Council of Churches in India Review* 117 (December): 760–72.

Parker, K. (under examination). 'A Grammar of Tikhak Tangsa: A language of North East India'. PhD Diss. under examination, La Trobe University, Melbourne, Australia.

Parkin, David, Lionel Caplan, and Humphrey Fischer, eds. 1996. *The Politics of Cultural Performance*. Oxford: Berghahn Books.

Pathak, Suryasikha. 2010. 'Tribal Politics in Assam: 1933-1947'. *Economic and Political Weekly* xlv(10)(6 March): 61–9.

Pelto, Pertti J. 1970. *Anthropological Research: The Structure of Inquiry*. New York: Harper & Row.

Phadnis, Urmila and Rajat Ganguly. 2012 [1989]. *Ethnicity and Nation-Building in South Asia*. New Delhi: Sage Publications.

Phukan, Supriti. 2005. *The Phakes*. Guwahati: Students Stores.

Picard, David and Mike Robinson, eds. 2006. *Festivals, Tourism and Social Change: Remaking Worlds*. Clevedon, Buffalo, and Toronto: Channel View Publications.

Prabhakara, M.S. 2012. *Looking Back into the Future: Indentity and Insurgency in Northeast India*. New Delhi: Routledge.

Prasad, Chunnu. 2008. 'Chakma refugees in Arunachal Pradesh: Questions of Identity and Citizenship'. *Eastern Anthropologist* 61(1): 95–104.

Pruett, Gordon. 1974. 'Christianity, History, and Culture in Nagaland'. *Contributions to Indian Sociology* 8(1): 51–65.

Rabinow, Paul and George E. Marcus. 2008. *Designs for an Anthropology of the Contemporary*. Durham, NC: Duke University Press.

Ramirez, Philippe. 2007. 'Politico-ritual Variations on the Assamese Fringes: Do Social Systems Exist?' In *Social Dynamics in the Highlands of Southeast Asia: Reconsidering Political Systems of Highland Burma by E.R. Leach*, edited by François Robinne and Mandy Sadan. Leiden and Boston: Brill, pp. 91–108.

———. 2013. 'Ethnic Conversions and Transethnic Descent Groups in the Assam-Meghalaya Borderlands'. *Barkataki-Ruscheweyh & Lauser*. 279–97.

———. 2014. *People of the Margins: Across Ethnic Boundaries in North-east India*. Guwahati: Spectrum Publications.

Rao, Narayan Singh. 2003. 'Origin and Migration of the Mossang (Hewa) Tangsas of East Arunachal Pradesh'. *Proc. North East India History Association*. XXIV session Gauhati.

———. 2006. *Tribal Culture, Faith, History and Literature—Tangsas of Arunachal Pradesh*. New Delhi: Mittal Publications.

Report. 1921–2. *Report on the Administration of North-east India* (1921–22). New Delhi [Reprinted Mittal Publications, 1984.]

———. 1924. *Report of the Assam Opium Enquiry Committee, 1924*. [Reprinted in *Documents of Northeast India, Volume 3. Assam (1664–1935)*. 2006. Compiled by S.K. Sharma and Usha Sharma. New Delhi: Mittal Publications, pp. 155–88.]

———. 1926. Extract from the *Annual Administrative Report 1925–26* of the Sadiya Frontier Tract. Political B. Nos. 800-01. September. Assam State Archives.

Report. 1929. Extract from the *Annual Administrative Report 1925–6* of the Sadiya Frontier Tract. Political A. Nos. 159–236. December. Assam State Archives.

———. 1936. *Annual Report of the Frontier Tribes of Assam for the year 1935–36.* Shillong: Assam Govt. Press.

———. 1939. *Annual Report of the Frontier Tribes of Assam for the year 1938–39.* Shillong: Assam Govt. Press.

———. 1996. Report on the Women's Independent Enquiry Committee on the New Kamlow Religious Immolation Case, August 1996. [Reprinted in *Documents of Northeast India, Volume 2. Arunachal Pradesh.* 2006. Compiled by S.K. Sharma and Usha Sharma. New-Delhi: Mittal Publications, pp. 243–48.]

Robbins, Joel. 2004. "The Globalization of Pentecostal and Charismatic Christianity." *Annual Review of Anthropology* 33: 117–43.

Robinne, François and Mandy Sadan, eds. 2007. *Social Dynamics in the Highlands of Southeast Asia: Reconsidering Political Systems of Highland Burma by E.R. Leach.* Leiden and Boston: Brill.

Ronrang, Molem. 1997. *Emergence and Growth of Baptist Churches among the Tangsas of Arunachal Pradesh.* Guwahati: Saraighat Printers.

Roosens, Eugeen E. 1989. *Creating Ethnicity: the Process of Ethnogenesis.* Frontiers of Anthropology. Vol. 5. Newbury Park, London: Sage Publications.

Roy, Ramashray, Sujata Miri, and Sandhya Goswami. 2007. *Northeast India: Development, Communalism and Insurgency.* Delhi: Anshah Publishing House.

Roy Burman, B.K. 1970. *Demographic and Socio-economic Profiles of the Hill Areas of North East India.* Delhi: Controller of Publications. Census of India, 1961.

———. 2008. 'Preface'. In *Human Ecology and Statutory Status of ethnic entities in Sikkim. Report of the commission for review of environmental and social sector policies, plans and programmes.* Gangtok: DIPR, Government of Sikkim, pp. i–xiii.

Ruotsala, Helena. 2001. 'Fieldwork at Home: Possibilities and Limitations of Native Research'. In *Rethinking Ethnology and Folkloristics,* edited by Pille Runnel. Tartu: NEFA RÜHM Tartu, pp. 111–31.

Rustomji, Nari. 1985. *Imperilled Frontiers: India's North-eastern Borderlands.* New Delhi: Oxford University Press.

Sadan, Mandy. 2012. 'Cords and Connections: Ritual and Spatial Integration in the Jingphaw Cultural Zone'. In *Origins and Migrations in the Extended Eastern Himalayas,* edited by Toni Huber and Stuart Blackburn. Leiden and Boston: Brill, pp. 253–74.

———. 2013. *Being and Becoming Kachin: Histories beyond the state in the borderworlds of Burma.* Oxford and London: Oxford University Press and the British Academy.

Sahlins, Marshall. 1999a. 'Two or three things I know about culture'. *Journal of the Royal Anthropological Institute* 5(3) (n.s.): 399–421.

Sahlins, Marshall. 1999b. 'What is Anthropological Enlightenment? Some Lessons of the Twentieth Century'. *Annual Review of Anthropology* 28: i–xxiii.

Saikia, A. 2011. 'Imperialism, Geology and Petroleum: History of Oil in Colonial Assam'. *Economic and Political Weekly* 46(12): 48–55.

Saikia, Yasmin. 2004. *Fragmented Memories: Struggling to be Tai-Ahom in India*. Durham and London: Duke University Press.

Saul, Jamie. 2005. *The Naga of Burma: Their Festivals, Customs, and Way of Life*. Bangkok: Orchid Press.

Schechner, Richard. 1988. *Performance Theory*. New York and London: Routledge.

Schein, Louisa. 2000. *Minority Rules: The Miao and the Feminine in China's Cultural Politics*. Durham and London: Duke University Press.

Schlemmer, Grégoire. 2003/2004. 'New Past for the Sake of a Better Future: Re-inventing the History of the Kirant in East Nepal'. *European Bulletin of Himalayan Research* 25/26: 119–44.

Scott, J.C. 2009. *The Art of Not Being Governed: An Anarchist History of Upland Southeast Asia*. New Haven and London: Yale University Press.

Sebastian, K.O. 1999. 'The Tangsas of Arunachal Pradesh and the Socio-economic Changes since 1947'. PhD Diss., Arunachal University, Itanagar.

Sharma, Chandan Kr. 2007. 'A Suitable Script: The Politics of Script and Identity in Assam'. In *Tribes of India: Identity, Culture and Lore*, edited by P.C. Pattanaik. Guwahati: Angkik Publishers, pp. 205–17.

Sharma, Jayeeta. 2012. *Empire's Garden: Assam and the Making of India*. Ranikhet: Permanent Black.

Shekhawat, V.S. 2007. *Assam: From Accord to ULFA*. New Delhi: Anamika Publishers.

Shneiderman, Sara. 2011. 'Synthesising Practice and Performance, Securing Recognition: Thangmi Cultural Heritage in Nepal and India'. In *Ritual, Heritage and Identity: The Politics of Culture and Performance in a Globalised World*, edited by Christiane Brosius and Karin M. Polit. New Delhi: Routledge, pp. 202–45.

———. 2014. 'Reframing Ethnicity: Academic Tropes, Recognition beyond Politics, and Ritualized Action between Nepal and India.' *American Anthropologist* 116(2): 279–95.

———. 2015. *Rituals of Ethnicity: Thangmi Identities Between Nepal and India*. Philadelphia: University of Pennsylvania Press.

Shneiderman, S. and T. Middleton. 2008. 'Reservations, Federalism and the Politics of Recognition in Nepal'. *Economic and Political Weekly* 43(19) (10–16 May): 39–45.

Simai, Chimoi. 2008. *A Profile of the Tikhak Tangsa tribe of Arunachal Pradesh*. New Delhi: Authors press.

———. 2011 'An urgent call of Tangsa'. *Namdapha: Souvenir*. 6th NEC Festival at Miao, Changlang.

Singer, M., ed. 1959. *Traditional India: Structure and Change*. Publications of the American Folklore Society. Bibliographical Series, Vol. X. Philadelphia: American Folklore Society.

Singh, K.S., ed. 2003. *People of India. Assam*. Volume XV (Part One) Anthropological Survey of India. Calcutta: Seagull Books.

Singpho, Rajesh. 2000. 'The Singphos'. *Souvenir*: 26–9.

Sökefeld, Martin. 2001. 'Reconsidering Identity'. *Anthropos* 96: 527–44.

Souvenir. 1997. *Souvenir, Silver Jubilee Celebration Tangsa Baptist Churches Association 1972–1997*. Molem Ronrang, Yongtu Lungphi and Wanglong Simai (eds). Lakla: TBCA.

———. 2000. *Souvenir of the 16th Annual Shapawng Yawng Manau Poi (Festival) 2000*. Margherita, Assam.

———. 2011. *Dehing Patkai, towards Integrity, Harmony … Peace*. Souvenir, Dehing Patkai Festival 2011. Lekhapani, Tinsukia.

Spiro, Melford. 1967. *Burmese Supernaturalism: A Study in the Explanation and Reduction of Suffering*. Englewood Cliff: Prentice-Hall.

Srikanth, H. 2014. 'Who in North-east India are Indigenous?' *Economic and Political Weekly* xlix(20) (17 May): 41–6.

Srivastava, Vinay. 2000. 'Teaching Anthropology'. *Seminar* (495): 33–40.

Statezni, Nathan. (unpublished). 'Names for the Tangshang of Myanmar'.

Stoeltje, Beverly J. 1992. 'Festival'. *Folklore, Cultural Performances and Popular Entertainments*, edited by Richard Baumann. Oxford and New York: Oxford University Press, pp. 261–71.

Subba, Tanka. 1988. 'Interethnic Relationship in Northeast India and the "Negative Solidarity" Thesis'. *Human Science* 37: 369–77.

Subba, T.B., A.C. Sinha, and B.G. Tandon. 2000. *The Nepalis in Northeast India: A Community in Search of Indian Identity*. Delhi: Indus Publishing Company.

Subba, T.B. and G.C. Ghosh. 2003. *The Anthropology of Northeast India*. New Delhi: Orient Blackswan.

Subba, T.B. and Jelle J.P. Wouters. 2013. 'Ethnography of North-East India: The Politics of Identity'. In *The Modern Anthropology of India: Ethnography, Themes and Theory*, edited by Peter Berger and Frank Heidemann. London: Routledge, pp. 193–207.

Surita, Pearson. 1981. *Story of the Assam Railways and Trading Company Limited 1881–1981*. Calcutta: Pearson Surita for the Assam Railways and Trading Company Limited.

Tandy, E.A. (Surveyor General of India). 1927. 'ASSAM & BURMA. Lakhimpur District, Sadiya Frontier Tract & Tribal Area. Seasons 1912–15, 1917–18, 1925–26' Reg. No. 2354 D.26 (E.C.S.F.D.), Map Record & Issue Office, Calcutta. [Survey of India. 1934. Map: Assam and Burma, Sadiya Frontier Tract and Tribal Area. No. 83 N/N.E. Calcutta: Survey of India Office.]

Tangshang Naga Migration History. (as told by Shumaung at the Naga Knowledge Sharing Program, NCRC, Yangon to Nathan Statezni) shared via e-mail on 8 September 2012.

Teron, Dharamsing. 2011. *Reclaiming the Ancestors' Voices*: Karbi Studies. Vol. 2. Guwahati: Book Hive.

Terwiel, Barend J. 1980. *The Tai of Assam and Ancient Tai Ritual*. Vols I and II. Gaya: Centre of South East Asian Studies.

Thamphang, Ongtang. 1999. 'Social Structure of the Tangsas in Arunachal Pradesh: A Case Study of Chaglang District'. M.Phil. Diss., AITS, Rajiv Gandhi University, Itanagar.

Theodossopoulos, Dimitrios. 2013. 'Introduction: Laying Claim to Authenticity: Five Anthropological Dilemmas'. Special Collection, *Anthropological Quarterly* 86(2): 337–6.

Thomas, John. 2015. *Evangelising the Nation: Religion and the Formation of the Naga Political Identity*. New Delhi, London, and New York: Routledge.

Thomas, Mathew. 2009. 'A Sociolinguistic Study of Linguistic Varieties in Changlang District of Arunachal Pradesh'. PhD Diss., Annamalai University, Tamil Nadu.

Traditional Systems. 2005. *Traditional Systems of the Tangsa and the Tutsa*. Guwahati: Vivekanada Kendra Institute of Culture.

Tsing, Anna Lowenhaupt. 1993. *In the Realm of the Diamond Queen: Marginality in an Out-of-the-Way Place*. Princeton: Princeton University Press.

Tucker, Shelby. 2000. *Among Insurgents, Walking Through Burma*. Delhi: Penguin.

Turner, Victor W. 1982. *Celebration: Studies in Festivity and Ritual*. Washington, DC: Smithsonian Institute Press.

———. 1986. *The Anthropology of Performance*. New York: PAJ Publications.

Upadhyaya, Khilanath. 2012. 'Jagun, Tirap, Lekhapani Anchalor atit aru bartaman'. *Ledo*, Souvenir of the Ledo Sahitya Sabha, Ledo, pp. 172–5.

Vandenhelsken, Mélanie. 2011. 'The Enactment of Tribal Unity at the Periphery of India: The Political Role of a New Form of the Panglhabsol Buddhist Ritual in Sikkim'. *European Bulletin of Himalayan Research* 38: 81–118.

Vandenhelsken, Mélanie, B.G. Karlsson, and Jürgen Schöpf, eds. 2016. *Fluid Attachments in Northeast India*. Special Issue of *Asian Ethnicity* 17(3).

Van der Veer, Peter, ed. 1996. *Conversion to Modernities. The Globalization of Christianity (Zones of Religion)*. New York and London: Routledge.

Van Driem, George. 2008. 'The Naga language groups within the Tibeto-Burman language family'. In *Naga Identities: Changing Local Cultures in the Northeast of India*, edited by Michael Oppitz, Thomas Kaiser, Alban von Stockhausen, Rebekka Sutter, and Marion Wettstein. Gent: Snoeck Publishers, pp. 311–21.

Van Ginkel, Rob. 1995. 'Texelian at Hart. The Articulation of Identity in a Dutch Island Society'. *Ethnos* 60(3–4): 3–4.

Van Ham, Peter and Jamie Saul. 2008. *Expedition Naga: Diaries from the Hills in Northeast India, 1921–1937 & 2002–2006*. New Delhi: Timeless Books.

Van Schendel, W. 1992. 'The Invention of the "Jummas": State Formation and Ethnicity in Southeastern Bangladesh'. *Modern Asian Studies* 26(1): 95–128.

———. 2002. 'Geographies of Knowing, Geographies of Ignorance: Jumping Scale in Southeast Asia'. *Environment and Planning, D: Society and Space* 20(6): 647–68.

———. 2005. *The Bengal Borderland: Beyond State and Nation in South Asia*. London: Anthem.

———. 2011. 'The Dangers of Belonging: Tribes, Indigenous Peoples and Homelands in South Asia'. In *The Politics of Belonging in India: Becoming Adivasi*, edited by Daniel J. Rycroft and Sangeeta Dasgupta. London: Routledge, pp. 19–43.

Van Schendel, W. and Ellen Bal. 2002. 'Beyond the "Tribal" Mindset: Studying Non-Bengali peoples in Bangladesh and India'. In *Contemporary Society: Tribal Studies, Volume Five: Concept of Tribal Society*, edited by Georg Pfeffer and Deepak Kumar Behera. New Delhi: Concept Publishing Company, pp. 121–38.

Von Fürer-Haimendorf, C. 1962 [1939]. *Naked Nagas*. Calcutta: Thacker Spink and Company.

Von Stockhausen, Alban. 2008. 'Creating Naga: Identity between Colonial Construction, Political Calculation, and Religious Instrumentalization'. In *Naga Identities: Changing Local Cultures in the Northeast of India*, edited by Michael Oppitz, Thomas Kaiser, Alban von Stockhausen, Rebekka Sutter, and Marion Wettstein. Gent: Snoeck Publishers, pp. 57–96.

———. 2014. *Imag(in)ing the Nagas: The Pictorial Ethnography of Hans-Eberhard Kauffmann and Christoph von Fürer-Haimendorf*. Stuttgart: Arnoldsche.

Waddell, L.A. 2000 [1901]. *The Tribes of the Brahmaputra Valley*. New Delhi: Logos Press.

Weiner, Myron. 1988. *Sons of the Soil: Migration and Ethnic Conflict in India*. New Delhi: Oxford University Press.

Wellens, Koen. 2012. 'Migrating Brothers and Party-State Discourses on Ethnic Origin in Southwest China'. In *Origins and Migrations in the Extended Eastern Himalayas*, edited by Toni Huber and Stuart Blackburn. Leiden and Boston: Brill, pp. 299–319.

Wimmer, Andreas. 1993. 'Ethnischer Radikalismus als Gegennationalismus: Indianische Bewegungen im sechsten Jahrhundert nach Kolumbus'. In *500 Jahr danach: Zur heutigen Lage der indigenen Voelker Amerika*, edited by Peter Gerber. Chur: Rueegger.

Wouters, Jelle J.P. 2012. 'Keeping the Hill Tribes at Bay: A Critique from India's Northeast of James C. Scott's Paradigm of State Evasion'. *European Bulletin of Himalayan Research* 39: 41–65.

Xaxa, Virginius. 1999. 'Transformation of Tribes: Terms of Discourse'. *Economic and Political Weekly* 34(24): 1519–24.

———. 2010. '"Tribes", Tradition and State'. *IIAS Newsletter* 53(Spring): 18.

Zama, Margaret Ch. 2006. 'Globalization and the Mizo story'. *Indian Folklife* 22 July. Chennai: NFSC, pp. 10–11.

Principal Internet Resources (accessed at various times):

Arunachal Pradesh official website <http://arunachalpradesh.gov.in/>

Assam State Gazetteer <http://online.assam.gov.in/web/guest/assamgazetter?webContentId=172302>

The Assam Tribune <http://www.assamtribune.com/>

Burma Link <http://www.burmalink.org/>

The Census of India <http://censusindia.gov.in/>

Centre for Research in Computational Linguistics, Bangkok which hosts on-line dictionaries and word lists of several of the Tangsa and other languages <http://sealang.net/>

DOBES: Documentation of Endangered Languages <http://dobes.mpi.nl/>

Don Bosco Centre for Indigenous Cultures, DBCIC, Mawlai, Shillong <http://www.dbcic.org/>

Economic and Political Weekly <http://www.epw.in/>

Ethnologue: Languages of the World <http://www.ethnologue.com/>

Himal Southasian <http://www.himalmag.com>

The Hindu Centre for Politics and Public Policy <http://www.thehinducentre.com>

Linguistic Survey of India <http://www.joao-roiz.jp/LSI/>

Moussons: Social Science Research on Southeast Asia <http://moussons.revues.org/>

The People of India Project <http://www.ansi.gov.in/people_india.htm>

Wikipedia <http://en.wikipedia.org/>

Index*

* All Tangsa groups that appear in the index as main entries are further classified as Pangwa or non-Pangwa.

About the Author

Meenaxi Barkataki-Ruscheweyh is Research Fellow at the Department of Social and Cultural Anthropology at the Vrije Universiteit (VU), Amsterdam. She has been working with the Tangsa groups living in Assam and Arunachal Pradesh in northeast India since 2008, initially as part of a VW-Foundation funded DOBES (Documentation of Endangered Languages) Project. She was awarded a PhD from the VU in November 2015 for her thesis titled 'Performing Ethnicity to Resist Marginalisation: The Tangsa in Assam'.

She is interested in questions of survival and marginalization of small ethnic communities in multi-ethnic milieus, and the complex dynamics of disempowerment and disenchantment that can and have resulted in (sometimes militant) sub-nationalistic movements in northeast India. Besides continuing to work with the Tangsa she has also started working with the Moran-Matak communities in upper Assam. Recently she has also co-edited the second (enlarged and revised) edition of the *Historical Dictionary of the Peoples of the Southeast Asian Massif* (Rowman and Littlefield, 2016) together with Jean Michaud and Margaret Swain.

Assamese by birth, Meenaxi now lives in Germany. She began her professional career as a mathematician (with a D.Phil. from Oxford University in 1992), and taught at the Indian Institute of Technology (IIT), Guwahati, for several years before moving to the social sciences. She is intimately involved in the literary scene in Assam and is an active blogger (http://luit-pariya.blogspot.de/) and an occasional writer and translator.